INKY *F*INGERS

INKY FINGERS

The Making of Books in
Early Modern Europe

ANTHONY GRAFTON

THE BELKNAP PRESS OF
HARVARD UNIVERSITY PRESS

Cambridge, Massachusetts
London, England

First Harvard University Press paperback edition, 2022
First printing

Library of Congress Cataloging-in-Publication Data
Names: Grafton, Anthony, author.
Title: Inky fingers : the making of books in early modern
Europe / Anthony Grafton.
Description: Cambridge, Massachusetts : The Belknap Press of Harvard
University Press, 2020. | Includes bibliographical references and index.
Identifiers: LCCN 2019051295 | ISBN 9780674237179 (cloth) |
ISBN 9780674271210 (pbk.)
Subjects: LCSH: Early printed books. | Books—History. |
Humanists—Europe—History. | Printers—Europe—History.
Classification: LCC Z124 .G688 2020 | DDC 094/.2—dc23
LC record available at https://lccn.loc.gov/2019051295

For Lindsay Waters, Maker of Books

CONTENTS

INKY *F*INGERS

Making Book

THE WAY OF THE HUMANISTS

SCISSORS, PASTE, AND BEST-SELLING ETHNOGRAPHY

IN 1517, a German humanist named Joannes Boemus set out to make a book: a comprehensive ethnography of Africa, Asia, and Europe. A scholar of modest attainments, he knew neither Greek nor Hebrew. No great traveler, he lived in the free imperial city of Ulm, deep in the center of the Holy Roman Empire, where he served as chaplain to the Teutonic Knights.[1] He gave his book an ambitious title: *Omnium gentium mores, leges et ritus* (*The Customs, Laws and Rituals of All Peoples*).[2] But it was far from comprehensive. Boemus's treatise did not mention the American societies that European guns and microorganisms were destroying as he wrote. Boemus discussed only the three continents that the ancient Greeks and Romans had known. Nonetheless, his work found eager readers everywhere. In 1525, the prominent Nuremberg scholar Willibald Pirckheimer copied descriptions of England, Ireland, Spain, France, Ethiopia, and many other lands from *Omnium gentium mores*. He attached them, lightly edited and abridged, to the new maps of Europe, Africa, and Asia that he added to his massive, splendidly printed edition of Ptolemy's *Geography*.[3] Both Protestants and Catholics reprinted the Latin text again and again for a century to come. It was also translated into an impressive range of languages—English, French, German, Italian, and Spanish—and became a classic work in the burgeoning literature of ethnography, sometimes in expanded forms.[4] Why did this brief compendium, obsolete on its publication day, become a best seller?

Modern scholars have pointed to Boemus's method. By his own account, it was as traditional as the organization of his book. For three years, Boemus told his publisher, Siegmund Grimm, he had gathered material systematically "from many outstanding writers."[5] This was, in fact, his work's chief claim to fame. It deserved credence because it rested on the best sources. Boemus expanded on this point in his preface, in which he described his work as an exercise in the deft use of scissors and paste:

> In my leisure hours, O most serious connoisseur of histories, I have gathered, and then written out in this register, the more remarkable customs, rites, and laws of the peoples, and the places they inhabit. These were commemorated in passing and, as it were, in pieces by Herodotus, the father of history; Diodorus Siculus, Berosus, Strabo, Solinus, Pompeius Trogus, Ptolemy, Pliny, Cornelius Tacitus, Dionysius Afer, Pomponius Mela, Caesar, Josephus, and, from the more moderns, Vincent, Aeneas Silvius who later took the name Pius II, Antonius Sabellicus, Iohannes Nauclerus, Ambrosius Calepinus, Niccolò Perotti in his *Cornucopiae* and many other famous writers. This will allow you to have them recorded in a single book, and it will be easy for you to find them when you need them.[6]

Writing with confidence and pride, Boemus characterized his work as a patchwork of passages taken from earlier writers. He treated the bookish origins of the knowledge he offered readers as a major selling point. And the proud author was not alone: his friends agreed that a collage of texts, selected from established authorities and systematically organized, made a fine book. Short Latin poems by Boemus's friends preceded his preface. They highlighted the "great care" with which he had copied his material "from the books of the authors."[7] An accompanying letter from another scholar, Andreas Althamer, appeared at the very end of the book. He described the work as "copied out by my friend Boemus from a vast number of classical writers."[8] Most modern readers have adopted these terms in describing Boemus's book.

Boemus declared that he preferred this traditional, bookish method to the newer one, supposedly founded on eyewitnessing, that recent travel writers had adopted. In his prefatory letter to Grimm, Boemus remarked that his publisher had specialized in literature on "foreign nations." In the preceding year alone Grimm had printed Maciej Mieochwita's treatise *On the Two Sarmatias* and Ludvico di Varthema's work *On the Southern Peoples:* recent works that described parts of the world previously little known to Latin Christians.[9] Printing solid travel literature, Boemus argued, was a vital service, especially for those engaged in government. Those who never left their family estates were not taken seriously by the good and the great. Those who knew the world, by contrast, became known as inspired authorities: "everything that they attempt or do is embraced by all as the instruction of a divine oracle, and everyone loves it."[10] One could attain such knowledge by travel, but one could also gain it by systematic reading.

And there was the rub. Grimm's readers needed him to publish reliable texts, "not the work of fly-by-night tricksters, nor that of wandering beggars, who make it their practice to lie criminally and without shame to make themselves popular and admired with the crowd."[11] Their lies had made prudent readers distrust all writers who dealt with foreign parts. But they had also created a readership for what Boemus could offer: a panorama of the lands and cultures of the world, based on sources so old that they deserved credence—so much, apparently, for Varthema's vivid, challenging account of the Middle East and South Asia (based for the most part on first-hand experience), which Boemus did not excerpt. Like Boemus, his readers deliberately turned away from the potential challenges of new knowledge about the world outside Europe.

Boemus's practices as an author, as he and his associates described them, strikingly resemble those of Ordralphabétix, the fishmonger in the imaginary village of Astérix the Gaul. Obdurately refusing to deal in fish freshly caught in the nearby ocean, Ordralphabétix sold only what the wholesale dealers in Paris shipped to him. But there was one salient difference between them. The Gaul's old fish stank, and their stench caused fights. Boemus's extracts from old texts, by contrast, attracted readers as flowers attract bees. One way to make a salable book in the sixteenth century, apparently, was not only to construct it using scissors and paste, but also to take care that potential buyers knew that the author had done so—in a few years, during his spare time.

In fact, Boemus, like many authors, misdescribed his own work. It was far more than a straight collection of excerpts from texts, and its conclusions were often as far from traditional as its methods. And that is why he claims our attention here. This book collects nine studies in the forms of scholarly authorship in Western Europe between the fifteenth and the eighteenth century. They re-create lost ways of writing and publishing, tracing the ways in which the material worlds of reading, writing, and printing affected texts and their reception. Watching Boemus handle his sources as he reads them, copies them, and transmutes them will help us frame and follow the larger set of inquiries that follow his story.

"I'm writing a book" is a very suggestive phrase. Images immediately spring to mind: images of solitary creativity, pursued in a comfortable study, cozy café, or bleak garret. None of them, as we will see, fit the world of the Renaissance humanists who are the protagonists of this book. Their life of scholarship could cramp the hands and buckle the back. Reading and writing were as closely connected in the age of the quill pen as they are in that of the laptop. Readers often worked, just as writers did, pen in hand, actively responding to the texts they read in their margins or eagerly chopping them into extracts for storage and reuse. Writers were as often copyists as composers, seeking, not to make it new, but rather to refashion what they had read in subtle but powerful ways, so that ancient writers could teach modern lessons. Making a book—or even mastering someone else's book—required hours of physical labor, carried out with strenuous attention, tongue in teeth. Often the most ingenious ideas and practices that they devised came into being less in silent study than in the course of what looks, in the age of the computer, like exhausting, unremitting work.

Much of this work, moreover, was anything but solitary. Humanists engaged in discussion, imaginatively, with their ancient and modern sources, from which they learned vital lessons but with which they also disagreed. They also collaborated, practically, with the correctors and compositors who turned handwritten texts into printed books. Even the most detached of early modern intellectuals practiced the necessary crafts of reading and writing. And some of the most char-

acteristic intellectual innovations of the Renaissance—formal methods
for textual criticism and paleography, for example—took shape in the
hard-pressed worlds of scribes' and printers' workshops, as deadlines
pressed and artisans demanded to be allowed to go to work. The world
of the writer and reader, in other words, was often more social than we
are likely to think nowadays, and more closely connected to artisanal
skills. The case of Boemus introduces these themes, which later chapters will pursue over many borders, chronological, geographical, and
intellectual.

HOW TO EMPTY A NOTEBOOK: WRITING AS READING

Excerpting of the sort Boemus described was a standard way to make
a book in the early sixteenth century. As Ann Blair, Martin Mulsow,
Helmut Zedelmaier, and others have shown, many humanists saw the
notebook as their central tool.[12] They educated themselves by copying
passages from classical authors, which they filed for reuse under topical headings: Erasmus advised anyone who hoped to be fully cultured
to make systematic excerpts, at least once, from all of ancient literature. But excerpting was also a research practice. Antiquarians like
Ciriaco of Ancona and Felice Feliciano filled their notebooks with
copies of ancient inscriptions and images of ancient buildings.[13] Philologists like Marsilio Ficino and Angelo Poliziano filled theirs with transcripts of newly discovered texts.[14] Specialists like Johann Buxtorf—who
dedicated himself, a century after Erasmus and Boemus, to the study
of Jewish literature—made their copybooks into rich banks of specialized information. Buxtorf scrutinized every Hebrew text he could
find, from best sellers to esoteric rarities. In most cases, he copied out
only passages that seemed to be directed against Christianity, as part
of his single-minded campaign to reveal the evil character of the
Jews.[15] Collecting excerpts from authoritative texts was a natural way,
not only to survey, but also to define, a field—such as Jewish hatred
of Christianity and Christians, or the customs, laws, and rituals of
the world.

Collection, as Buxtorf's case suggests, was never a simple, mindless
activity. The stones that Boemus used to make his mosaic often clashed
with one another. Clues in his text enable us to reconstruct parts of

his long-lost notebooks and to understand what it took to make and use them as he did. In the second chapter of his book, Boemus laid out what he called "The true opinion of the theologians about the origins of mankind."[16] By this account, God created humanity with a propensity to violence. As the population increased, so did evil conduct. God solved this problem with the Flood, which left only Noah, a just man, and his family alive. But some of Noah's descendants, as they moved from Armenia, where the ark came to rest, left behind the "rituals and customs" of their ancestors and lost their knowledge of the truth. Laws, customs, and religions became increasingly diverse—and, in many cases, increasingly divorced from the truths that Noah had known. Knowledge and piety degenerated over time.

In the third chapter, Boemus described "The false opinion of the pagans about the origin of mankind."[17] By this account, the world had originally been a damp, chaotic mass of matter. As the sun dried it out, humans emerged by spontaneous generation. Necessity was their teacher. To create communities, protect themselves against cold, and feed themselves, they devised language, built fires, sewed clothing, and developed other new tools and practices. In different parts of the world, these practices took different forms. The ensuing cultural diversity was the work of humans faced with different challenges. So, more strikingly, was civilization itself—which, as Boemus had emphasized in his preface, had developed over time. His book, he told readers, "will enable you to know with what elegance and happiness we live now, and in how crude and simple a way the first mortals lived." Knowledge and skills, if not piety, had grown with time. Boemus's book, in other words, offered a challenge to an assumption that dozens of early modern readers shared: that all forms of knowledge, theoretical and practical alike, had been revealed in full to Adam but lost over time as humanity sinned.

In a subtle essay, Philipp Nothaft has used these linked chapters to begin reconstructing Boemus's method as a compiler. They reveal both some of the clashing contents of his now lost notebooks and how he managed their disagreements. Boemus drew his contrasting views of early human history from the sources he excerpted: the Book of Genesis and chronicles based on it, for the "true" history of humanity; the *Historical Library* of Diodorus Siculus and the *De rerum natura* of

Lucretius for the "false" one; and the recent world histories of the Dominican forger Annius of Viterbo and the Venetian humanist Marcantonio Coccio, known as Sabellico, for particular accents. Biblical history taught the traditional story of the patriarchs and their families, beginning with their expulsion from the happy life in Eden and the curse of labor that Adam and Eve brought upon the human race. Diodorus and Lucretius offered something completely different: a bold conjectural history that eliminated divine minds and hands and treated human energy and labor as the creative forces that had brought humanity from its impoverished, primitive way of life to its current wealth and power.[18]

We do not know what form Boemus's working notes took. But many humanists organized their collections of extracts topically. The fifteenth-century Venetian patrician Bernardo Bembo, for example, drew up an immense notebook, now in the British Library, which was stuffed with passages from texts as classical as Cicero's speeches and as up-to-date as Leon Battista Alberti's treatise on architecture, which he read in manuscript before it was printed. He organized his excerpts by topics, which he then listed and indexed—as if he saw himself assembling a set body of knowledge.[19] If Boemus worked in a similar way, the physical process of copying and compilation could have made him see that his authorities contradicted one another. In any event, he dealt with their disagreements by setting them side by side in his text: in effect, underlining and highlighting their discord. True, as Nothaft suggests, some readers might have reconciled these apparently contradictory accounts by taking the "false" one as only a summary of history after Noah's Flood. But Boemus himself discouraged such efforts. He made clear, by his choice of chapter titles, that the traditions he drew on included radically diverse ways of tracing humanity's origins. His book revealed that taking extracts from the best sources gave no assurance that the resulting account would be unified, or even coherent. A well-made notebook could yield a very disturbing book.

Boemus was not the first to make this point in a prominent way. More than a generation earlier, Hartmann Schedel had begun his immense, magnificently illustrated Nuremberg Chronicle—also the product of massive excerpting—with a biblical account of the Creation, labeled as true, and Diodorus's version of the origin of the world, labeled as false—as well as a Ptolemaic world map populated by the three sons of Noah and an illustrated list of the monstrous races that lived at the edges of the world.[20] In this case, Schedel's hard-pressed content provider, the medical man and humanist Hieronymus Münzer, had assembled the sources and noted their conflict. Evidently, Boemus was one in a series of writers who approached the problems of narrating world history and describing ethnic diversity by compiling bits from the best sources: in the full knowledge that these authorities sometimes disagreed sharply, and that labeling one version as "false" would hardly prevent it from stimulating the imaginations of readers. In such cases, the compiler's ink and scissors were no guarantee of a unified, orthodox, and calming narrative.

This was not the only instance in which Boemus juxtaposed divergent accounts of great events in sacred history. In his account of Judaea, for example, Boemus cited the Bible and Josephus as his authorities. He characterized Palestine as a promised land of milk and honey, described its conquest by Joshua, and gave an extended account of the written laws of the Jews, as composed by "that outstanding theologian," Moses.[21] Boemus's account of Jewish observances ended with the sacrifices prescribed for the holiday of Shavuot. At that point, however, his chapter took an unexpected twist. "On the Jews and their leader Moses," he wrote, "the pagan writers disagree with the ecclesiastical ones."[22] A long passage from Tacitus's *Histories* followed.[23] In line with older writers, whose ideas he may have known through Josephus's refutations of them, Tacitus explained that the Jews had caused a plague in Egypt, which led to their expulsion (so much for the Exodus and its divine protector).[24] More strikingly still, Tacitus ridiculed Jewish customs and observances. They were nothing more than rational Roman ways of life and worship, turned on their heads: "there everything that we consider sacred is profane, and they allow everything that we forbid."[25]

Instead of refuting these views, Boemus found another Roman writer, Pompeius Trogus, who confirmed them.[26] He then segued into a description of the "three Jewish sects," Pharisees, Sadducees, and Essenes, drawn at second hand from Josephus's history of the Jewish war, and wound up—without explaining what happened to the Jews during that war—with a short treatment of the forms of Syrian Christianity.[27] Who, exactly, was the authority here? Who deserved belief? Which history of the Jews was true? Readers wanted to know. Henry Haule, a Sussex antiquarian who annotated his copy of Boemus's work from end to end in the later sixteenth century, was chiefly interested in the term that Boemus applied to the Pharisees' phylacteries: "pittacium a band or clothe to lay to ones forehead."[28] But he also used marginal signs and a trefoil to make clear that he had taken Boemus's most radical point: Tacitus and the Bible gave irreconcilable accounts of the Exodus and the Jewish law.[29]

ELEGANT VARIATION: THE LIMITS OF SCISSORS AND PASTE

Since the sources themselves disagreed, systematic excerpting could produce something less like a seamless narrative than like critical mass, where contact caused explosions. Filing, moreover, often involves much more than copying. Compilers interpreted, translated, corrected, and rewrote the passages they recorded. In the words of Rocco di Dio, "Through a process of reduction and reworking, formulae, images, ideas, patterns of argument and models employed by the earlier tradition acquired a new meaning as they were selected and displayed in the textual repertoire and then integrated into a new work."[30] The notebook could preserve texts against the possibility of loss, which always haunted the humanists, and make them accessible for obedient exercises in Latin prose composition on set themes. But the passages it contained could also suffer a sea change into something rich and strange.

Though Boemus's notebooks are lost, his finished book reveals much about his methods as a compiler. He did not always allow conflicts between his sources to emerge in his text. In reading about ancient Egypt in two Greek historians, Herodotus and Diodorus Siculus, Boemus found himself confronted again by radically different views. Herodotus described Egypt as a land of marvels, "which has more wonders than any other place" (2.35.1). Diodorus admired Egypt, but he rejected "the stories invented by Herodotus and certain writers on Egyptian matters," which he dismissed as fables made up to entertain readers (1.69.7). Boemus, encountering this dispute, sided, silently, with the earlier writer. When describing Greek and non-Greek customs, Herodotus loved to compile lists of opposites. He had supported his assertion that Egypt was marvelous by describing a whole series of customs in which Egyptians practices were the reverse of normal ones.[31] Boemus reproduced parts of Herodotus's list:

> Their women made a custom of going to market, engaging in trade and making sales: the men wove within the walls of their houses. The men carried burdens on their heads, women on their shoulders. The women urinated standing, the men sitting. They commonly relieved themselves in their houses, and ate in the streets.[32]

Yet even this passage was not a simple quotation. Boemus omitted the introductory sentence, in which Herodotus made clear that these upside-down customs made a larger point: "they have established a great many customs and laws that differ from those of other people" (3.35.2). He also made running editorial changes, as he copied text into notebook or notebook into book. Boemus's description of Egyptian ways read, in Latin:

> Eorum foeminae olim negotiari/cauponari/institoriaque obire munera consueverunt. Viri intra murorum parietes texere: hi onera capitibus gestare, mulieris humeris: illae stantes micturire, hi sedentes: domi vulgo ventrem exonerare: in vijs comessari.

The original passage that he adapted, in Lorenzo Valla's Latin translation of Herodotus, was quite different:

> Apud quos foeminae quidem negociantur cauponanturque: & institoris operis vacant. Viri autem intra domos texunt. Alii villum subtegminis desuper tramant: aegyptii subter. Onera viri capitibus: Foeminae humeris baiulant. Foeminae stantes mingunt: viri sedentes. Domi ventrem exonerant: exterius in viis comedunt. (Among them women, to be sure, engage in trade and bargain, and practice the merchant's art. But the men weave inside their houses. Others push the weft from above: the Egyptians from below. Men carry burdens on their heads, women on their shoulders. Women urinate standing up: men sitting. They relieve themselves at home: they eat outside in the streets.)

Reworking this short passage, Boemus omitted a sentence about methods of weaving, which highlighted the topsy-turvy order of Egyptian society; replaced several words and phrases with synonyms; and changed the forms and tenses of the verbs that he retained. At the end, as at the beginning, he omitted one of Herodotus's general points: that the Egyptians preferred to do things that were "shameful but necessary" in private and those that were "not shameful" in public (2.35.3). Clearly, the set phrase "scissors and paste" does not describe Boemus's method of composition, even when he was making excerpts. At some point, in his notebooks or in the drafts he composed from them, he freely rewrote his texts, omitting much and reshaping what he retained. Excerpting, as Boemus practiced it, was laborious: it required close attention to detail and multiple copyings of every sentence.

EMBRACING THE PAIN: HOW BOEMUS DEALT
WITH TRAVEL LITERATURE

Readers of Boemus have often emphasized the stodgy, conservative tone of his book. Some have assumed, reasonably enough, that his negative remarks about travel writers applied to the very books Grimm had already published, the works of Mieochwita and Varthema.[33]

But it seems unlikely that Boemus actually meant to criticize the texts his own publisher had brought out. Moreover, those two texts differed sharply in method. Mieochwita's vivid description of Poland and Russia rested, not on experience, but rather on reading: he never saw the territories he wrote about.[34] Varthema, by contrast, wrote for the most part about what he saw and built his own position as a curious outside observer into his account, as early readers appreciated.[35] Boemus can hardly have meant to condemn them both on the same grounds—especially since he himself drew heavily on Mieochwita's book for ethnographic details about the Muscovites.[36]

Travel literature, after all, did not come into being only after Columbus's voyages. As Boemus himself made clear, Mieochwita's and Varthema's books were not isolated phenomena. The fifteenth century had witnessed cultural contacts of many kinds. Europeans traveled to Africa and India and wrote about what they saw, from Egyptian antiquities to Ethiopian Christianity. The general councils of the fifteenth century—especially those of Basel and Ferrara-Florence—brought Christians from many lands into direct, if not always productive, conversation. New forms of narrative, from the vivid, wide-ranging travel writing of Pius II to tightly focused monographs on particular lands, took shape, reached print, and found readers. Boemus, as we will see, drew both material and inspiration from this recent literature as well as from ancient and medieval texts.

FROM PATCHWORK TO TAILORING: THE AUTHOR'S CRAFT

More important, as Boemus insisted, his work did not rest on copying alone. Writing to Althamer as his book was going through the press, he made clear that Althamer's accompanying letter was a second draft. The first draft had annoyed him, precisely because it treated his book as derivative. "You dared," he scolded his friend, "to pronounce, in my face, that all the contents of my work were contained in other texts. But I took such pains, I added so much of my own devising, that if our friendship, from which I thought you were speaking, had not prevented it, I would not have taken this kindly."[37] Boemus clearly knew that he had done more than rearrange sentences and paragraphs.

Althamer's second letter, which Boemus preferred to the first and used, still described his friend as making excerpts. But Althamer also energetically praised the distinctive qualities that Boemus had brought to his task:

> all the more remarkable customs and rituals of humans can be seen, laid out with a care and artistry that no one before him ever showed in their treatment: he has made his vintage by gathering the grapes with great diligence, he has made his harvest by gleaning where others had missed—a book no less juicy than it is pleasant, and no less pleasant than it is useful and necessary.[38]

Boemus himself, moreover, made clear in his preface that he offered novelties: for example, his account of the contrast between the primitive life of the first humans and the "beautiful and fortunate" life of his contemporaries.[39] For all his insistence on the quality of his sources, Boemus also made clear that his book represented something more than a careful, competent synthesis.

True, some segments of the book might well lead a reader to think that it was, as Althamer first suggested, a mass of second-hand materials, loosely connected. Boemus sometimes followed his source with a pertinacity worthy of a better cause, never making clear whether it

described antiquity, modernity, or points in between. His first substantive chapter, on Ethiopia, drew heavily on the universal history of
the Venetian humanist Marco Antonio Sabellico, as Boemus himself
acknowledged. He noted, as Sabellico had, that the framework of Ethiopian politics had changed in recent times.[40] But when Boemus returned to his own continent, Europe, in part 3 of his book, he followed
ancient sources.

In Boemus's discussion of Greek customs for burying the war dead,
for example, he described how both men and women conveyed the
bodies of male family members outside the city of Athens, where they
were buried after a carefully chosen individual had given a funeral oration. He used the present tense throughout—exactly as he did when
describing the Russian customs of his own day.[41] But he drew all of his
information, as he himself pointed out, from a very venerable source:
Thucydides's account (2.34, 2.46) of the funeral oration of Pericles, held
in 430 BCE, as translated into Latin by the fifteenth-century humanist
Lorenzo Valla.[42] Boemus repeated word for word Valla's statement that
the Athenians carried out these rituals "iuxta monumentum Callisti,
apud Suburbia" (next to the monument of Callistus in the suburbs).[43]
Thucydides had actually written that they did this at the sepulcher "ἐπὶ
τοῦ καλλίστου προαστείου τῆς πόλεως" (at the most beautiful suburb of
the city); though the word "καλλίστος" could be used as a male proper
name, in this case it was an adjective modifying "suburb." Boemus, as
this case reveals, sometimes presented his materials without showing
much concern for their date of origin. As his timeline zigged and
zagged, without announcement, from the ancient past to the day after
next week, the reader could reasonably gain the impression that he
slotted whatever excerpts he had into the appropriate chapters, without
worrying much about their original context and bearing, and that he
usually wrote within the terms that his sources had established.

In other cases, though, Boemus self-consciously reshaped the passages that he worked up as he incorporated them into his text. In order
to describe the forms of pagan worship that had survived into the fifteenth century in Lithuania, Boemus drew on a wide-ranging book by
Pius II. Pius had not visited Lithuania himself, but he made a short
book on the life and times of the Holy Roman Emperor Frederic III into
a wide-ranging survey, more political than ethnographic, of European
lands. At the Council of Basel, Pius had met a Bohemian priest named

Jerome John, who had done his best to convert the Lithuanians to Christianity. Drawing on Jerome's remarks, he described what his acquaintance had encountered:

> The first Lithuanians whom I encountered worshipped snakes. Each head of the household kept his own snake, lying on hay in a corner of the house, to which he gave food and offered sacrifice. Jerome ordered all these to be killed, brought to the market place, and burned in public. Among them was found one larger than the others, which the fire wholly failed to consume despite many attempts.[44]

Others worshipped a sacred fire, which Jerome exposed as a fraud.[45] Still others, further inland, "worshipped the sun and venerated, with remarkable devotion, an iron hammer of extraordinary size" that a giant had supposedly used to free the sun after a powerful king imprisoned it in a tower.[46] Boemus repeated the first story word for word.[47] He collapsed the second one into a single clause: "others worship fire, and draw auguries from it."[48] And he summarized the third one so briefly that it became unintelligible: "Some worship the sun, in the form of an iron hammer of great size."[49] Always alert to questions of credibility, Pius remarked that Jerome had told these tales "with a straight face and no hesitation." He and his companions were convinced, "when we left his presence," that Jerome had told the truth.[50] Boemus omitted these reflections from his discussion of Lithuania: presumably, though he did not say so, because he took this material not from conversation, as Pius had, but from an authoritative written source. In other words, he not only copied passages from his sources, but also selected and compressed his materials.

REWRITING AND ITS RATIONALES

Boemus's cuts and changes can be suggestive. The last "Asian" people that he discussed, before he turned to something like an ethnography of Europe, were those of Ottoman Turkey. His account was strikingly favorable. Boemus described the modest habits of Turkish women and their chaste relations with men with evident admiration:

> On their heads they use miters with veils overlaying them, in such a way that while they are decently and properly wrapped, a part of

the veil remains hanging down right or left of their face. If a woman has to leave their house or encounter men in the house, she can immediately pull it across to cover her entire face, except for her eyes. A woman never dares to make an appearance where men are meeting, and to go into the public square. It is entirely forbidden for a woman among them to sell or buy anything. In the larger churches they have a place very distant from that of the men, and so concealed that no one can look into it or enter it in any way. . . . A conversation between a man and a woman in public is so uncommon that if you spent a year among them you would hardly encounter it once.[51]

Here Boemus transcribed what the fifteenth-century Dominican George of Hungary, who had spent a long period as a slave in Turkey, had written. He often changed what he copied. George emphasized that these rules applied to all Turkish women, poor as well as rich, but that it was especially heinous for the wife of a rich man to leave her house without a veil. Boemus skipped these points. In other cases he made arbitrary changes. George described women's veils as positioned to the right of their faces, Boemus as to the left or the right. Yet even Boemus's apparent appeal to personal experience—"if you spent a year among them"—came word for word from George's account.[52] Boemus, in short, used this written source not only to provide vital information for his readers, but also to give his work something of the immediacy of an eyewitness report.

Yet Boemus omitted much of the concrete detail that lent George's book its distinction. In a rich passage, George retold a story about Mehmet II that he had heard from fellow Dominicans in Galata, formerly the Genoese district of Constantinople:

I omit much that I heard about him: how he was approachable in conversation, ripe and generous in judgement, bountiful in his charities and benevolent in his other actions. Hence the friars in Pera said that he entered their church and sat down in the choir to see their ceremonies and the form of their liturgy. They celebrated the mass before him, since he desired it, and showed an unconsecrated host at the elevation, since they wished to satisfy his curiosity and not to put pearls before swine. After he had held a long discussion with them about the law and ritual of the Christians and had learned that bishops presided over churches, he wanted them to appoint a bishop to console the Christians. He promised him everything needful for his estate and that he would show favor and aid without fail.[53]

George interpreted this complex tale of Ottoman curiosity and tolerance and a mixed Christian response to it as evidence of Mehmet's personal "simplicity," his goodness. Boemus did not retell the story. But he drew its moral without hesitation, and included it in his account:

> Sarracens force no one to deny his religion or sect, and do not try to persuade anyone to do that, though the Coran teaches that they should destroy their enemies and their prophets, and persecute them in every way. Accordingly, people of every sect live in Turkey, and each worships God by his own custom.[54]

It was a striking remark. "In Turkey," Haule wrote at this point in his copy of Boemus, "every people cultivates its own religion."[55]

In this case, Boemus changed the text he borrowed from in two complementary ways. He pruned away most of the local details that appeal most strongly to a modern reader. George's story about Mehmet, like other stories about his personal dealings with Ottomans, failed to make a transition, either from the base text to Boemus's notebook or from the notebook to the final text. Boemus also simplified the meaning of the material that he did include. In chapter 14 of his treatise, for example, George provided a long and varied account of Ottoman religious practices. He described the version of Islam practiced in Turkey as austere and simple, in ways that contrasted sharply with Christianity. He also vividly evoked the varieties of Ottoman religious experience, from the unremitting asceticism of "those who go through the most extreme cold of winter with their whole bodies naked, and do not feel it, and do the same in the heat of summer," to the supernatural visions or revelations received by inspired visionaries.[56] George wrote with what seems particular admiration of the dervishes, who danced to the rhythm of a special musical instrument, "with decent and very appropriate motions of all their members." They arrived at last at a circular motion so rapid that "those watching them could not tell whether it was a man or a statue, and they show an almost supernatural bodily agility" that no one outside their order could possibly imitate.[57]

Boemus used only a very small amount of George's material on Ottoman religious life. He emphasized the charitable activities of the religious, who sounded, in his account, like members of the more pious and ascetic Christian religious orders:

> That sect includes many different religious men. Some of them, leading their lives in groves and empty places in the country, avoid contact with other men. Some of them, providing hospitality in the cities, admit poor foreigners to their hostels, even if they have no food to offer them, for they too live by begging. Others, wandering through the cities, carry good, fresh water in certain skins, and they freely offer it to anyone who asks to drink. If they are offered something, they accept it. They want nothing.[58]

Boemus derived this respectful description from George—but he did so by carving away all George's material about whirling dances and ecstatic revelations.

The conclusions the two men drew from their material were also sharply different. George commented on the air of holiness that surrounded the Ottoman religious, who "are of such model conduct in all their sayings and actions, and display such deep piety in all their customs and movements, that they seem to be not men but angels."[59] But he tempered, and ultimately denied, his apparent admiration for their practices by subjecting them, immediately after, to profound criticism. All the apparent good qualities of the Turks' religion, he claimed, were actually deliberate inventions of the devil, designed to win converts for Islam. The Turks were not models of true piety but rather Tartuffes, puffed up with poisonous pride.[60] George's book, which was full of material but ambivalent in attitude, did not offer its contemporary readers—or its later ones—any clear lessons. Boemus took over the most enthusiastic sentence in George's account, changing its phrasing but not its content. The Ottoman priests, he claimed, showed so much piety "in their words and actions, that they could be believed to be not men but angels": a remark that Haule underlined.[61] He did not mention the devil, much less look for the diabolical motivations of apparently pious actions. All the ambivalence was filtered out of George's text as Boemus cut it up and reorganized his words.

These practices stuffed Boemus's book with food for thought. By reducing his sources' rich accounts of foreign customs into short summaries, largely free of first-hand detail, he made them easy to compare. As Haule worked his way through the book, he repeatedly noted parallels and differences in the margin. The Ottoman law that required citizens to marry reminded him of Solon's similar Athenian law.[62] A reference to the extreme incontinence of the Tartars, who took as many wives as they wished, recalled the more disciplined Turks, who limited themselves to four.[63] And the rudeness and contempt that Franconians showed for foreign peoples brought back to mind the similar attitude and conduct of the Tartars.[64] Jean Bodin's *Method for the Easy Comprehension of History* was designed to teach readers how to compare historians and the constitutions they described. He did not think much of Boemus.[65] Yet Haule, who read Bodin, still found it worth his while to work through Boemus's book as well, weaving a web of cross-references that revealed similarities—and, perhaps, historical connections.

THE ETHNOGRAPHIC EYE: ESTRANGING THE FAMILIAR

Boemus's willingness to entertain thoughts that went against conventional wisdom—to praise non-Christian peoples and to summarize non-Christian accounts of sacred history—also made his work stimulating. And as he moved toward completing his survey, both the way in which he deployed his materials and the content of his chapters became increasingly original. The last chapter of section 2 dealt, not with an Asian people, but rather with a religion that had been founded there: Christianity. From early on in his book, Boemus made clear that Christianity, like the non-Christian religions he discussed, had a history. In describing ancient Egypt, Boemus listed, as many others had before him, the Greeks who had crossed the Mediterranean to seek an older wisdom. Seeking the origins of Christianity, he found them in the same ancient culture: "Most of the devices that we use in our Christian religion were borrowed from the customs of the Egyptians: for example, the surplice and rochet, and similar linen garments; tonsures; turning at the altar; the solemnities of our Mass, our organs, our kneeling, crouching, prayers and other things of that kind."[66] In this case, as Boemus made clear, he borrowed his claim from a massive work of fifteenth-century erudition. The Bolognese humanist Filippo Beroaldo, whose massive commentary on the *Golden Ass* of Apuleius

appeared in 1500, had argued at length that the core of Christian observances derived from Egyptian and Roman ritual.[67] But what had
been only a suggestive observation in Beroaldo's work became the core
of a new history in Boemus's book.

In his chapter on Christianity, Boemus worked with distinctive care
and precision to lay out the implications of this early suggestion. He
drew up, not a survey of Christianity in his own time—or even of Latin
Christianity—but rather a history of the church. Starting with the arrival of the Messiah and the creation of the first diocese in Antioch,
Boemus showed how the church had adapted existing prototypes to
new purposes in order to create its institutions, offices, and practices.
Transformed in meaning, the vestments of the Temple priests became
the ecclesiastical vestments of their Christian successors. Transformed
in essence, the hierarchy of ranks that had underpinned the power of
the Roman Empire became the ecclesiastical hierarchy of the new
church.[68] Every aspect of Christian organization and practice, Boemus
showed, had developed over time, and many of them were based on the
imitation of older, non-Christian models.

Earlier writers on liturgy and related subjects had traced some of
the same developments. The thirteenth-century canon lawyer Guillaume Durand collected rich material in his treatise on church architecture and liturgy, the *Rationale divinorum officiorum*. Every prelate
and every would-be reformer knew this indispensable book. When
Thomas Cranmer wanted to know how the old church that he rebelled
against had developed its forms and usages, he traced them in the
margin of his copy of the *Rationale*.[69] Durand explained, for example,
how the Mass had taken shape over the centuries, sometimes in response to challenges:

> In the church, in general, nothing is to be sung or read which has not
> been formally canonized and approved or allowed in practice by the
> Holy Roman Church. In the primitive church, however, everyone sang
> different things as he preferred, so long as what he sang had to do with
> the praise of God. Certain prayers were observed from the beginning,
> as established by Christ, in the Lord's Prayer, or by the Apostles, in the
> Creed. Later, because the church of God was split by heresies, the Em-
> peror Theodosius, the extirpator of heretics, asked Pope Damasus to
> have the liturgy put in order by some prudent and Catholic cleric.[70]

Damasus turned to Jerome for help. Later, Gelasius and Gregory made further additions, which Hadrian turned into standard practices that were binding on the whole church.[71] Cranmer followed this exposition with pen in hand, and his scribes later transferred some of it into his Great Commonplace Books.[72] Boemus, however, offered a full-fledged history of the Mass, attributing every component from the offertory to the final "Ite, missa est" to its proper author and doing the same for church architecture, music, and more. A year before Polydore Vergil laid out the first detailed, material history of Christianity in topical form in books 4 through 8 of *De inventoribus rerum*, Boemus stole some of the Italian scholar's thunder as he showed that Christianity itself had a history.[73]

Boemus's study of Christianity, moreover, shows how well he knew that customs, laws, and rituals, his chief subjects, changed over time—even if his accounts of African and Asian peoples sometimes suggested the contrary. By the time that he reached Muscovy, he used the present tense to show that he was describing a new society, recently founded: "Girls show a bit of hair from the back, but once they have been placed in marriage they carefully avoid that. Men have their hair cut above the ears: any visible concern for the hair earns their sex criticism. The whole people is given over to love and extremely fond of its dram."[74] Boemus's descriptions of Muscovite cities—which seemed oddly empty, with many open spaces—were equally derivative and clearly cast, like his passage on the Russians' hair, in the present tense. When he came to Lithuania, as we have seen, he took time out to describe the pre-Christian customs and beliefs and their destruction in the fifteenth century.

When Boemus reached his own German *Land*, Franconia, his style changed again. Now he described contemporary religious life and practices, not in the clipped, abbreviated manner of his own first two books, but rather in the discursive, vividly detailed style adopted by Pius II and George of Hungary. Like them, he painted a marvelous pointillist portrait of a people. Franconians, like other Germans, worked hard but remained poor: "the Franconian nation does not differ at all from other Germans in its body or its condition. It can stand any amount of work. Men as well as women are employed in cultivating the vineyards. No one has any leisure. For the most part they sell the wine that they derive from this, because of their native poverty, and drink water. They loath beer and are most unwilling to have it served to them."[75] Equally sharp passages revealed the Franconian propensity to despise other nations, to worship God, and—unfortunately—to blaspheme and steal, "since they think the one practice is proper and the other honorable, and permitted to them by long custom."[76] Unlike Boemus's Greeks or Turks, his Franconians were every bit as complex and contradictory as the non-Christians described by his sources.

When it came to religion, no detail was too insignificant for Boemus to relate. He gave the recipe for the Christmas pancakes, made of wheat, honey, ginger, and pepper, into which the mother of each house inserted coins. Some were given to the poor. But the family member who found a coin in his portion "is greeted by all as the king, placed in a high seat, and raised in the air three times to the sound of cheers. He himself holds a piece of chalk in his hand, with which he draws the sign of the Cross three times above him on the paneled ceiling of the dining room. Since these crosses are believed to have the power to fend off many illnesses, they are greatly esteemed."[77] Boemus eagerly revealed the details of the Franconian festivals of inversion, in which men dressed as women and women as men and all wore masks, which were staged every year between Christmas and Epiphany, and told of the scented candles that were burned in every house to keep demons and witches away.[78] A spellbinding passage portrayed the wooden wheels that were covered with straw, carried up to mountain tops, and, at dusk, set afire and allowed to roll down into the valley below: "a stupendous spectacle, so that those who have not seen it before think the sun or moon is falling from heaven."[79] He paid special attention to youth groups and popular practices. And he made it clear that he saw some of these practices as "superstitions"—additions to the proper stock of Christian practices.[80]

In some cases, Boemus traced these rituals back to origins in Roman antiquity. In the twelve days between Christmas and Epiphany, he remarked, "some run about naked, playing the Luperci [the celebrants of the Roman Lupercalia], from whom, I think, that annual custom of running mad passed down to us."[81] The "ancestral custom" of giving gifts on New Year's Day reminded him of the Roman rituals for that day, including the giving of gifts.[82] Similarities could have documentary

status. They could link apparently modern peoples of barbarian origins, like the Franconians or the Ottomans, to the most civilized nations of the ancient world—or show that Christian life had been infil-
trated by pagan survivals. In other cases, though, Boemus felt unable
to identify the reason for, or source of, a Franconian custom. On Ash
Wednesday, young women who had gone to dances during the year
were "brought together by young men and yoked to a plow, in place of
horses." As a flutist played, sitting on the plow, they pulled him into
a lake or river. Sounding rather like Tevye in *Fiddler on the Roof,* Boemus confessed that "I do not see clearly why this is done"—and could
only suggest that the women had danced on the feast days of the church,
and might be expiating this sin.[83] At times—as when he had laid out
conflicting sources and left the reader to decide—he willingly ended a
discussion on a faltering note.

One point was clear: ethnography had a solid epistemic status of
its own. Boemus stated that he wished to record the "remarkable rituals" of his own people "lest the accounts of foreign peoples be taken
as empty fables."[84] Far from despising eyewitness knowledge, he learned
from reading George of Hungary and others how to look at customs
with an ethnographer's inquisitive eye. More remarkable, he turned
this eye on his own home, and saw the strangeness of his own society, which practiced rituals and held beliefs as odd as any turned up
by his reading about the peoples of Asia and Africa.[85] Boemus continued to deploy new sources and pose new questions as he passed
from one province of Germany to another. Discussing the ancient
Bavarians and Carinthians, he quoted their laws at length to reveal
"the customs and way of life of the people."[86] Describing the ancient
Swabians, he quoted Tacitus's book on Germany to evoke the austere
life they had led in their ancient forests, without trade or agriculture.
In modern Swabia, however, he noted that "customs have changed,
and, as is very regrettable, for the most part for the worse."[87] In particular, Swabian men and women alike had dedicated themselves to
making cloth: both the mixed cotton and linen fabric known as
Barchent and the pure linen known as Kölsch. The inhabitants of
Ulm alone, Boemus had established, made 100,000 cloths of both
kinds every year, which they sold, via the trade fairs at Frankfurt, "to
the most remote nations."[88]

Yet the rapid expansion of the cash nexus had had tragic results for the Swabians themselves. Modern Swabians all engaged in trade, forming partnerships to buy everything from exotic spices to spoons and needles and forcing others to buy necessities from them:

> This is harmful, not only to artisans and farmers, who sell their products in advance to those merchants—or should I call them Harpies?—and then are forced to buy them back at twice the price, but also to the whole province. They must obtain whatever they need not from nearby peoples, from whom they could buy them more cheaply, but from those merchants in Stuttgart, or wherever else they have markets.[89]

To Boemus's all-seeing eye, the vast manufacturing economy of the late medieval imperial cities was a new development, historically contingent and socially harmful: a development as strange, and as characteristic of the contemporary German world, as the successful armies of their Ottoman neighbors. This was not his only critical reflection on the mores of his own time and nation. German women, he noted, had abandoned the extravagant clothing and jewelry that had once been fashionable and returned to the ancient tradition of frugality. But German men had become fashion plates, eagerly adopting new styles of clothing from France and Italy.[90] Meanwhile, the peasants led a "hard and wretched life," housed in thatched huts made of wood and mud and eating bread, oats, and boiled legumes.[91] Germany boasted rich and sophisticated cities and well-endowed mendicant study houses. But the rise of material culture, which Boemus had evoked so eloquently at the beginning of his book, was not a simple good.[92]

As he completed his book, Boemus became a cosmopolitan and critical observer. He not only freed himself from dependence on older written sources but also supplemented them with his own keen observations. Instead, his methods of collecting and deploying information changed as he worked, in ways that he himself may not have expected when he began and that were considerably more varied than he himself suggested when he described them. The richness of Boemus's book suggests something of the complexity of compilation itself. Many of the Renaissance notebooks that look like products of busy fingers were also—like Boemus's book and the notebooks that fed into it—the work of busy minds. The collection of written materials could stimulate observation, and observation could illuminate the stock of excerpts.

Like Boemus, Bernardo Bembo continually juxtaposed authoritative texts with personal experiences in his commonplace book. At one point, he cited a description of Heliogabalus's fondness for "disarmed lions and leopards" from the *Scriptores historiae Augustae*, a fourth-century compilation of imperial lives. The often fanciful text explained that the emperor had trainers bring these beasts to his dinner table, "in order to terrify and mock those who did not know that they were disarmed."[93] Beside this passage he recalled his own experience of close and personal contact with large cats: "Much the same thing happened to me, Ambassador Bernardo Bembo, the first time that I dined with His Serene Highness Charles, Duke of Burgundy. With no warning he brought out a disarmed lioness to meet me. I shuddered violently and turned pale, which gave the courtiers who were standing around a good laugh. August 1471, in Abbeville, Picardy."[94] Alongside a passage from the same ancient source praising Hadrian's villa at Tivoli, Bembo inscribed an account of his own delight at seeing the villa's ruins.[95] Boemus's book rested, not only on at least three years of patient copying of extracts, but also on the sorts of comparative operations that Bembo carried out in his Zibaldone (commonplace book) as observations were recorded next to quotations. Publication and study—writing and reading—look like separate practices now. But it is hard to distinguish them from one another in the world of humanists who made books. Both were carried out pen in hand, neither involved blind subservience to textual knowledge—and both could lead to radical conclusions.

THE CRAFTS OF THE BOOK

Boemus's experience of making a book differed in one vital way from Bembo's. Boemus aimed his book at the press. And though he had published only one short work, he had learned enough about the ways of printers to take care that it appeared in a form of which he approved. In his letter to Andreas Althamer, for example, he noted that "I confessed quite frankly in the title of my book that it was a collection of material." The full title of the book actually reads *Omnium gentium mores leges et ritus ex multis clarissimis rerum scriptoribus, a Ioanne*

Boemo Aubano sacerdote Teutonicae Militiae devoto nuper collectos,
& in libros tris distinctos, Aphricam, Asiam, Europam, Optime lector
lege (*The Customs, Laws and Rituals of All Peoples, Recently Col-*
lected from Many Excellent Historians by Ioannes Boemus, Faithful
Priest of the German Order, and Arranged into Three Books, Africa,
Asia, Europe. Read Them, Gentle Reader). As we have seen, this title
did not accurately reflect either Boemus's method or his results. But
he clearly chose it himself, perhaps as an effort to avert criticism by a
profession of modesty.

Boemus evidently went further, specifying at least some of the details of the book's mise-en-page and typography. We do not know if he
played any part in choosing the format of the first edition, a handsome
small folio. In his preface to Grimm, Boemus noted that he and his publisher had agreed on one aspect of the book's presentation. He thanked
Grimm for having printed the book "very accurately and with images
set before each of the chapters, as you promised." The first edition was
not illustrated. But the preface and the three main sections of the book
each began with a magnificent initial, composed of multiple smaller
forms, wreathed in vine-like lines and sometimes adorned with small
faces. These must be the "images" that Grimm promised to provide.
It seems possible that Boemus also requested the marvelous woodcut
border that surrounds the separate title page of the index, a riotous fan-
tasia of cherubs and trophies of arms and armor. And it is not surprising that Boemus's book—a near contemporary of such innovative
reference works as Erasmus's *Adages*—arrived on the market with a
clear set of chapter divisions and a separate, detailed topical index, designed to make the book accessible for consultation as well as continued reading. Though not a prolific author, Boemus was well
informed—well enough to thank his printer in the preface, the last part
of the book to be written and printed, for doing such a handsome job.
It is no wonder that his book appeared in the best period form. *Om-*
nium gentium mores was much more than the product of leisure-time
cutting and pasting. Its evolution, as reconstructed from internal evidence, shows how routine procedures could result in recursive, self-
critical arguments; how traditional forms of knowledge-making could
yield challenges to commonly accepted tenets about life, the universe,
and everything; and, above all, how much material work was involved

in creating the texts that we now discuss as though they were disembodied entities.

The nine chapters in this volume trace further connections between what have too often been seen as separate spheres in the larger world of humanist scholarship. Chapters 1 through 3 examine the work of printers and scribes and their impact on the ways in which scholars made knowledge. The first chapter examines textual criticism, the humanist art of arts. It emphasizes that this apparently immaterial, almost mystical, scholarly art was shaped in important ways by the fact that it was practiced in printing houses, as editions went through the press. Scholars corrected texts in inky workplaces as well as quiet studies, and the pressures of time and practicality that they encountered there shaped their methods in vital ways. The second chapter argues that textual criticism had unexpected connections to a very different kind of intellectual work, the illicit divination supposedly practiced by witches and necromancers. Again, the material conditions of book production help to explain how divinatory criticism lost its associations with necromancy and came to seem like a primary product of scholarly genius. The third chapter follows the forgotten historical connection between new forms of scribal work—a brand of labor that actually expanded after the invention of printing—and one of the most original forms of early modern scholarship, paleography. In each case, one of the most technical, demanding, and apparently esoteric forms of scholarship turns out to be organically connected to pursuits that seem utterly distant from them.

Chapters 4 through 6 offer further case studies in the practices of compilation—and of the tight connections between scholarly reading and writing—that Ann Blair surveyed so brilliantly in *Too Much to Know*.[96] Choosing, storing, and deploying excerpts from documents, as Boemus's case shows, was a "complex and concrete" form of intellectual work.[97] It often involved the use of older collections of material, themselves the products of earlier forms of close reading, excerpting, and storage.[98] As we follow the multiple ways in which scholars collected and organized texts and excerpts from them, we learn that compilations, archives, and notebooks were more than receptacles for nuggets of information. When organized in the proper way, they could become tools of knowledge in their own right, epistemic machines that imposed interpretations and meanings on the apparently dull and indistinguishable extracts that were stored in them—or that mobilized them in support of novel, far-reaching arguments.[99] Chapter 4 shows how the systematic compilation—and the reuse of older compilations—could inspire a radically new understanding of the history of Christianity. Chapter 5 follows one of the great collectors of the early modern period, Matthew Parker, and investigates what he thought it meant to create an archive. And Chapter 6 suggests that humanistic traditions of commonplacing showed unexpected resilience and proved remarkably useful in the Atlantic world of the seventeenth and seventeenth centuries.

The last three chapters examine the ways in which collections of material were reused and transformed for polemical purposes. Some of the most novel historical arguments put forward in early modern Europe, it turns out, rested on existing compilations that creaked with age or drew on studies carried out by harassed correctors of the press who had served as content providers, and were poorly paid and poorly regarded. Paradoxes abound. Chapter 7 argues that the imaginary histories of the most proficient forger of the Renaissance, Annius of Viterbo, began life as an act of opposition to the contemporary humanists' revival of ancient Greek historiography. Annius drew vital materials from Dominican compilations that had been available for centuries to historicize Jewish law, in ways that in their turn shaped late humanists' approaches to the subject. Chapter 8 shows how John Caius elaborated one of the most richly documented historical arguments put forward in the sixteenth or seventeenth century—and wound up spinning a fantasy that he himself, had someone else created it, could easily have detected. And Chapter 9 suggests that Baruch Spinoza's approach to the history of the biblical text owed more than has been realized to the work of earlier scholars. Even Spinoza did some compiling—though he also missed earlier work that could have enriched his arguments.

These studies were written at different times and for different occasions. But they all are in the service of a single cause. Textual and empirical, scholarly and artisanal approaches to the study of the past or the investigation of the contemporary world were not the programs of opposed parties but rather available combinations of practice and habitus, method and attitude. Scholars toggled back and forth among these combinations, choosing terms and practices as projects drove or inspiration took them. And a great deal of what they achieved rested on unremitting, physically taxing work. The complex choreography of their efforts remains to be traced in the fragments of their collections of documents and images and the margins of their books.

None of the projects of early modern scholarship could have been realized without labor, and none of the scholars whose portraits glare down from the walls of universities and Gymnasien or out from the pages of celebratory collections of biographies spent their lives with clean hands. Cosimo de' Medici and a writer of advice to merchants after him advised anyone who hoped to succeed in that fiercely competitive trade to have inky fingers.[100] Historians have attended to his advice, tracing the vital role of accounting in economic and political history.[101] This book tries to put the inky fingers back into the story of learning.

CHAPTER I

Humanists with Inky Fingers

THE CORRECTOR IN THE
PRINTING HOUSE

SPECTERS HAUNT THE history of publishing and of humanistic scholarship in early modern Europe: lean, shabby ghosts. Correctors, as they were usually called, prepared manuscripts for the press, read proofs, and often added original material of their own. They were everywhere in the world of print, and many early modern humanists—including those whose names remain familiar—either praised or denigrated them and their work. The Basel scholar Theodor Zwinger makes an ideal Vergil to guide a descent into the literary underworld in which they lived and suffered. Zwinger was the sixteenth century's master theorist of learned travel. In his *Methodus apodemica,* which appeared in 1577, he offered readers a set of neatly diagrammed questionnaires or templates that they could take with them when they set out on their grand tours.[1] Firmly clutching their copies of Zwinger's book, they would read, interview natives, and look around themselves alertly every time they visited a new city. Zwinger made clear that his method could apply equally to the present—he offered accounts of model tours to Paris, Basel, and Padua—or the past—his last model tour took the reader to ancient Athens. Looking at Basel, he offered a schematic introduction to one of the city's special institutions: its printing houses.

A skilled ethnographer, Zwinger used branching-tree diagrams to help his readers make sense of the complex scene that they would encounter in a printing house.[2] A single chart offers both a table of organization and an inventory of equipment, materials, and operations to be performed with them (Plate 1). At the top right, Zwinger notes that printers have employees of two sorts: theoretical and mechanical. The theoretical employees, the correctors, compare the text printed in the shop with the "example," or copy, that it reproduces. The mechanical employees come in two categories: compositors, who set the type, and pressmen, who ink the forms and print the pages. Both theoretical and mechanical employees have servants to help them. Readers work with the correctors, in an inferior capacity, while menials help the workmen.

Zwinger's second diagram is a crisp flowchart that shows how a printed text takes shape (Plate 2). Correctors and readers, he explains, examine the proofs produced by the pressmen and correct the errors in them, in a formal sense; then the compositors make material corrections, replacing type that was incorrectly set. Evidently they correct the first and second proofs in the same way: presumably, by collating them with the original copy. The third proofs, by contrast, they compare with the corrected second proofs. This description neatly matches what other, less abstract sources report about practices in the great Basel printing houses. On July 1, 1534, for example, the Frisian jurist and statesman Viglius Zuichemus described the routines of Hieronymus Froben's celebrated printing house to a compatriot, Dooitzen Wiaarda. He explained that a shop like Froben's normally employed a scholarly corrector, "who reads over the composed formes with understanding and checks whether all types and letters are correctly joined together, and all words and paragraphs properly separated," and who benefits from the help of a lector or reader.[3] He also noted that "in well-regulated shops it is customary for THREE PROOFS to be produced, and duly to be READ individually, by which faults and errors may be expurgated throughout."[4] Zuichemus confirms that Zwinger's diagrams were generally accurate—at least for the larger houses, which actually employed correctors.

Yet Zwinger's neat diagram might deceive us if we take it too literally, for the people and operations that he describes on the neat lines of his Ramist diagram were not neatly separated in day-to-day work.

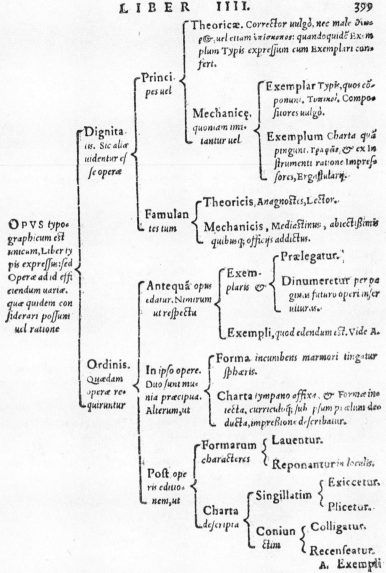

PLATE I Theodor Zwinger, *Methodus Apodemica* (1577): divisions of the workforce in a printing house. Department of Rare Books and Special Collections, Princeton University Library.

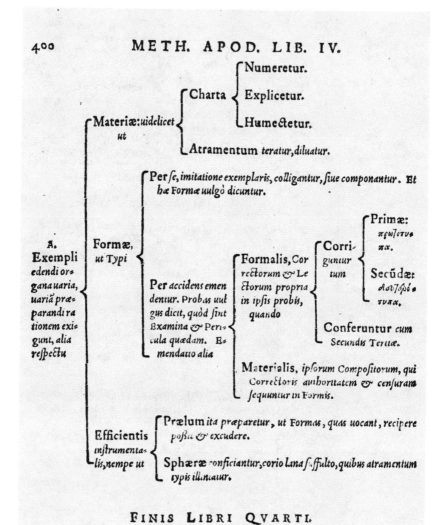

A.
Exempli *edendi or-*
gana uaria,
uariá præ-
parandi ra-
tionem exi-
gunt, alia
respectu

Materiæ: *uidelicet* *ut*
— **Charta**
—— Numeretur.
—— Explicetur.
—— Humectetur.
— **Atramentum** *teratur, diluatur.*

Formæ, *ut Typi*
— Per *se, imitatione exemplaris, colligantur, siue componantur. Et hæ Formæ uulgò dicuntur.*
— Per *accidens emen-dentur. Probas uul gus dicit, quòd sint Examina & Peri-cula quædam. E-mendatio alia*
—— **Formalis,** *Cor rectorum & Le ctorum propria in ipsis probis, quando*
——— **Corri-** *guntur tum*
———— **Primæ:** *πρω]οτυ-πα.*
———— **Secûdæ:** *δευ]όρι-τυπα.*
——— **Conferuntur** *cum Secundis Tertiæ.*
—— **Materialis,** *ipsorum Compositorum, qui Correctoris authoritatem & censuram sequuntur in Formis.*

Efficientis *instrumenta-lis, nempe ut*
— **Prælum** *ita præparetur, ut Formas, quas uocant, recipere possit & excudere.*
— **Sphæræ** *conficiantur, corio lana suffulto, quibus atramentum typis illiniatur.*

FINIS LIBRI QVARTI.

PLATE 2 Theodor Zwinger, *Methodus Apodemica* (1577): flowchart of typesetting in a printing house. Department of Rare Books and Special Collections, Princeton University Library.

The first handbook of correction, Jeremiah Hornschuch's *Orthotypographia,* included a wood engraving that shows a printer's shop in action.[5] In this version, the theoretical and the mechanical members of the printer's team work intensively together, in close quarters. Workmen dressed in simple clothing moisten paper so that it will hold ink, then pull the sheets and raise them to dry on a rack just below the ceiling. Men of higher standing dressed in doublets and ruffs argue, perhaps about a text to be printed. Another man in a ruff sets type. A woman enters the room, bearing a mug of beer for the workman. And the master printer, in a lavish robe, presides over the whole scene. Different kinds of clothing, whose styles were laid down by sumptuary laws, set craftsmen apart from members of the privileged orders.[6] Yet they all occupied and labored in the same noisy, dirty space. Learned men who worked in a shop like this could not escape without inky fingers.

In the early modern period, this situation was unusual. The society of the Ancien Régime distinguished sharply—as Zwinger's diagram shows—between those who worked with their hands and those who worked with their brains: in his terms, between "theoretical" and "mechanical" workers. In the printing house, however, the work of craft required, at every point, the presence of intellectual supervisors. And the supervisors, in turn, could not avoid touching metal type and forms that were wet with ink. Aldus Manutius was a Roman scholar, the author of his own Latin grammar. But Martin Sicherl, a pioneering student of the Aldine press, used the inky fingerprints still present in manuscripts of the Greek texts Aldus printed as vital clues by which to identify the *Vorlagen,* or base texts, from which Aldus and his correctors worked.[7] Aldus himself inserted a missing line of Greek, by hand, in dozens of copies of the Psalter that he printed between 1496 and 1498.[8] One way or another, the scholar who worked in a printing house was likely to wind up with ink on his fingers: mute evidence that the preparation and correction of texts were not a purely cerebral matter. Authors, for their part, underlined the drudgery involved in correction by their own complaints when made—or allowed—to correct their own proofs.[9] As scholars investigate the rich remaining documents from early modern printing shops, they find increasing numbers of visual and tactile clues to the working world of the corrector.

There is thus every reason to take the wood engraving as an accurate representation of a social world where abstract knowledge and oily black ink merged in a single product.

THE CORRECTOR'S TASKS

What, then, did correctors and readers do? The account books of some of the great firms survive, and they provide first-hand evidence. The surviving ledger of the Froben and Episcopius firms, for example, records the wages paid to employees from 1557 to 1564.[10] Each list of employees begins with a corrector or castigator: clear evidence that these learned employees, whose names appeared before those of the compositors and pressmen, enjoyed a certain status, which was higher than that of those who worked with their hands. Each list also includes a lector, whose pay is usually half that of the corrector or less. To that extent, the account books confirm Zwinger's diagrams. But they also supplement them. Sometimes the document states that a given corrector or reader received payment for other activities as well. In March 1560, for example, the lector Leodegarius Grymaldus received payment both for reading and for two other named tasks: making an index and correcting a French translation of Agricola's work on metals.[11] In March 1563, Bartholomaeus Varolle was paid for correcting but also for preparing the exemplar, or copy, of a thirteenth-century legal text, Guillaume Durand's *Speculum iuris,* and for drawing up an index for the work.[12]

Percy Simpson described the correctors' tasks comprehensively in a massive book, *Proof-Reading in the Sixteenth, Seventeenth and Eighteenth Centuries.* Unfortunately, he also sowed confusion, since the title of his vast collection of material indicated that it would deal with proofreading alone.[13] Historians of printing from Rudolf Wackernagel to Barbara Halporn and Edward Malone have emphasized that the term "corrector" can best be translated, in modern terms, not by its English or other derivatives, but rather by a much more general term like "print professional."[14] Once we move from general descriptions to other forms of evidence, it will become clear at once that they are right. True, a corrector was paid, in the first instance, for correcting or castigating the proof. But this was an activity that others—above all, authors—

carried out as well. Viglius Zuichemus, for example, informed his friend Wiaarda that he was staying in Basel for two months while his commentaries on Justinian's *Institutes* went through the press so that he could correct the proofs himself.

But correctors did many other things as well. They corrected authors' copy as well as proofs. They identified and mended typographical and other errors, to the best of their ability. They divided texts into sections and drew up aids to readers: title pages, tables of contents, chapter headings, and indexes. This pattern of activities recurs in many careers. The Franciscan Conrad Pellikan, an expert corrector who worked for the Amerbachs and the Frobens, got his start as a print professional when Johann Amerbach lost the services of another member of his order, Franciscus Wyler, who had been preparing the copy for Amerbach's edition of Augustine but was transferred away from Basel. "He came to me," Pellikan recalled, "for young as I was, I also worked very hard, and he asked me to take the place of the man who had been transferred. I was to take the rest of Augustine's works, which had not been divided into chapters, to divide them up and to add a brief summary for each chapter."[15] He claimed that he took on the task unwillingly, but eventually took such pride in his work that he recorded, in the copy of the edition that Amerbach gave him, exactly which texts he had laid out for the compositor.[16]

Pellikan, in other words, began his distinguished career as a professional corrector by editing copy rather than correcting proofs. Later he became a specialist in making indexes. Eventually he transferred his skill at making information accessible from the printing house to the Zurich library, which he catalogued.[17] But he also worked for Amerbach and others as a corrector in the strict sense. Looking back, Pellikan made clear that he had mastered the best practices of the craft by watching a master at work and learning both his methods and his standards: "Amerbach was a man of great learning and of extraordinary diligence. He expended both money and effort in large quantities on the correction of his books, always with the help of two or three readers, with as many copies, so that his negligence would not be at fault for any defect in the work. Anyone who carefully examines one of his editions will see that if a single word was misprinted, he preferred to repeat the day's work, with all its costs."[18]

Some correctors composed texts as well as paratexts, serving as what might now be called content providers. In 1512, Henri Estienne set out to print an edition of one of those ancient books that were as popular in the Renaissance as they are now forgotten: the world chronicle of Eusebius of Caesarea, in the Latin translation by Jerome. This rich and fascinating work laid out the history of nineteen ancient civilizations in parallel columns, from the time of Abraham to that of Eusebius himself, around 300 CE. Lists of rulers defined and bounded the course of history, showing how ancient states rose and fell, until only Rome and Israel were left, and then only Rome, as the world was unified in time for the Savior's message to reach all its inhabitants. Between the long columns of names, short notes located in time the lives of famous men and the invention of everything from triremes to tragedy. The book offered vital information, not only about states and cities, but also about the history of culture, wrapped in an attractive if complicated passage. Jerome translated it into Latin and brought it up to date a century after Eusebius, integrating Roman literature into the story and extending the story, which Eusebius had brought to a climax with the accession and conversion of Constantine, into his own more troubled times.[19] Augustine crafted his polemical arguments about the shape of the past and the priority of Jewish to pagan writings on the new last that Eusebius and Jerome had crafted.[20] Almost a millennium later, it was still both useful and popular. Petrarch covered his copy, now lost, with annotations.[21] Through the Middle Ages and after, writer after writer brought the work up to his own time, writing supplements that followed the history of emperors and bishops over the centuries.[22]

Estienne wanted to add value to his edition. One of his correctors, Jehan de Mouveaux, drew up a detailed index—which he adapted, without saying so, from an earlier edition. By doing so, he transformed the book. A linear timeline designed, in the age of manuscripts, to be consulted by readers who hoped to follow the movement of history from year to year and epoch to epoch, it became a sort of database that readers could cross and recross in many different ways. Mouveaux also brought the book up to date. Drawing his information mostly from a recent edition of the most popular fifteenth-century world chronicle, the *Fasciculus temporum* of Werner Rolewinck, he compiled a supplement. His holograph survives, and as Peter Way has shown, it served as the basis for the last pages of Estienne's edition.[23]

A scrupulous printer, Estienne employed ten correctors and, according to tradition, he hung copies of the proofs of his editions of Greek texts outside his shop, offering a reward to anyone who could find an error. For all the care that printer and corrector lavished on the edition of the *Chronicle*, there were still glitches. Mouveaux copied one passage that described miraculous signs that fell from the heavens onto peoples' garments as "instar dominicae crucis," like the Cross of Jesus. Working too quickly, Mouveaux transcribed "instar" as "instas," a non-word. Either the typesetter who read his supplement or another corrector, under pressure to provide a text that made sense from end to end, tried to improve it. He turned "instas" into something even further from the original: the words "iustas dominicae crucis" were all real, but in that order they were also meaningless. The errors, however, matter less than what the documents reveal about the production process. An edition like this involved the work of more than one corrector. If Mouveaux provided copy, someone else evidently corrected the proofs, for a great many of Mouveaux's single vowels metamorphosed into diphthongs in the course of printing—evidence that a corrector with a more classical formation also took part in the work, and did so, like Mouveaux, before the compositors began setting type.

At times, finally, correctors acted as expert intermediaries between an author and his publisher. Theodor Poelman, for example, was not one of the staff correctors whom Christophe Plantin carried on his books, the men whose seventeenth-century successors worked in what is still called the "correctors' room" of the Plantin house. He earned his basic income as a fuller, finishing cloth for Antwerp's chief industry. But Poelman corrected many classical texts for Plantin, with a crisp and unusual precision that suggests that he had learned from his legendarily well-organized publisher. In the critical apparatus for his 1589 edition of Lucan, he referred to the manuscripts whose readings he cited in the way that has become standard since the nineteenth century, by sigla (letters) rather than by the names of their owners.[24]

Poelman's own contemporaries clearly saw him as one of Plantin's correctors. They took their cue from the blurbs praising his work that appeared in some of Plantin's books. Surviving documents in the

Plantin archive make clear that they were right to do so. In a letter to a poet whose work Plantin had agreed to publish, Poelman says "there are some passages that I have marked in the margins, which I cannot understand; I would be grateful if you could explain them to me." He also proposed a set of standards for spelling, which he described as based "on the authority of the best scholars," and explained that he had eliminated the poet's marginal notes, both "because the margins of the printed book would be narrow and so that everyone would be free to write anything there."[25] These remarks adumbrate in style, if not in substance, the communications that copyeditors still provide. When Andrea Schottus, far away in Spain, discovered that three superfluous letters, left by the compositor when entering Schottus's corrections, remained in his edition of Sextus Aurelius Victor, he turned to Poelman for help. The error, which disfigured the preface, was very prominent, even jolting. Schottus compared his own encounter with it to a shipwreck: a rapid, violent interruption to what should have been a smooth glide through the text. Surely, he wrote, Poelman could persuade Plantin that the printers were at fault and that he should correct their error.[26] Sadly, either the letter came too late or Plantin turned a deaf ear to these entreaties: the correction was never made. Anne Goldgar showed long ago that the correctors of the late seventeenth and early eighteenth centuries carried out many of the tasks of a modern desk editor or literary agent.[27] Printing-house evidence makes clear that these practices began far earlier: began, indeed, not long after printing itself.

The corrector seems to represent a new social type: a phenomenon brought into the world by printing, and a native-born son of the new city of books that printing created. It seems obvious that the new art created new tasks. The printer confronted many rivals in the marketplace. He or she had to show that a particular product was superior to those of rivals. One way to do so—as printers rapidly decided—was to emphasize, in the colophon or, later, on the title page, that learned men had corrected the text. In Italy and Germany alike, books printed in the fifteenth century promised their readers, not just texts, but texts "diligently emended," "vigilantly emended and revised," or "most diligently and accurately revised" by particular scholars.[28] Hiring someone to correct a text—or claiming to have done so, as many printers did even though they had not—represented a rational and effective way to claim a larger market share.

CORRECTION BEFORE PRINT

In fact, the correctors' tasks did not all come into being with Gutenberg. The commercial stationers of the fourteenth and fifteenth centuries created some of the networks and developed some of the practices that enabled the rapid spread of printing.[29] Jehan de Mouveaux was not the first Renaissance content provider to bring the chronicle of Eusebius and Jerome up to date. The fifteenth-century Florentine scholar Matteo Palmieri drew up a historical work entitled *De temporibus:* a redaction and continuation of the ancient *Chronicle*, simplified in layout, which covered history from the incarnation to the mid-fifteenth century. Palmieri added useful materials for the period that Eusebius and Jerome had covered as well as for more recent times. He told beloved stories that Eusebius left out, such as that of King Lucius, who converted England to Christianity at the end of the second century CE, with the help of Pope Eleutherius. And he also provided a brief but continuous history of the church, from late antiquity to the Conciliar Movement and its aftermath.[30] "His work was and is greatly esteemed," the Florentine bookseller Vespasiano da Bisticci remarked, adding, "countless copies were made, so that they went to all parts of the world."[31] Vespasiano and his rivals marketed sumptuous manuscripts of Palmieri's Christian chronicle to connoisseurs.[32] Printed editions of the *Chronicle* engorged the later part of Palmieri's work, which brought the text up to his time. Jehan de Mouveaux's supplement to the text began where Palmieri's had left off.[33] The print corrector took up a baton handed over by a colleague whose race had been run in a world of scribal publication.

Correction had regularly taken place in the manuscript world, in monastic scriptoria and then in urban ateliers. But the rise of the printer's corrector certainly had its novel side. As printing transformed itself from an innovative and largely improvisatory enterprise to a more organized and stratified one, the way into the corrector's craft became normalized. One started off as a lector, a reader. Readers, like correctors, prepared copy, corrected proofs, and drew up indexes: facts that have led some modern scholars to define the task of reader in these terms. Contemporaries saw things differently. Just as the corrector, in the first instance, corrected, so the reader, in the first instance, read: read aloud from the copy, that is, while the corrector examined, and when necessary emended, the proofs. A set of rules for the correctors in the Plantin firm, drawn up by Balthasar Moretus when his most experienced corrector retired, makes this clear: "The corrector should make a habit of staying one word ahead of the reader. And the reader should read rather slowly, and in fact should stop short if he notes that the corrector has been overwhelmed and held up by a large number of errors."[34]

In this case, the practices of printers' correctors grew from very deep roots. In late antique Rome, as in early modern Antwerp, correction was normally collaborative and oral. The junior partner, who served as reader, read the original aloud. The senior partner, who served as corrector, entered corrections in the new manuscript.[35] In the Palestinian city of Caesarea, in the years around 300 CE, the wealthy priest Pamphilus collected, and corrected, manuscripts of the Greek Bible. Like Origen, whom he esteemed and defended against Christian critics, he occupied himself intensively with the text of the Bible. Subscriptions in later manuscripts describe how he worked. One of these, which is hard to read yet moving when deciphered, describes how Pamphilus and a friend corrected a text of the Bible while in prison, awaiting execution during the Great Persecution of Christians by the Roman state. It portrays the act of correction as oral and collaborative: "Antoninus, the confessor, collated; I, Pamphilus, corrected."[36] The subscriptions in Latin manuscripts, the originals of which were entered in the years around 400 CE, show that pagan practices were identical to Christian ones.[37] The new practices of the printing house reproduced the ancient ones of the scriptorium—very likely transmitted not in third-person accounts but rather by immemorial scribal routine.

CORRECTION: A JOB FOR WOMEN AND CHILDREN?

Yet the world of the printer, nested in its owner's household, was different from the ecclesiastical world of Eusebius and Pamphilus. In 1576 Johannes Elstius wrote to ask Poelman about the rumors that Plantin's daughters really knew how "to read and write not only Latin but also Greek and Hebrew."[38] Poelman replied that he knew women—notably the wife and daughter of the Englishman John Clement and the daughters of the Antwerp merchant Joannes Hovius—who had mastered Greek and Latin. Plantin's daughter Magdalena, by contrast, "could read [legebat] Hebrew, Greek and Latin quite fluently, but she did not understand them."[39] In this context, "legebat" can only bear one meaning: "read" in the sense of "read aloud." Magdalena, evidently, worked as a "reader," reading the original copy aloud while the corrector checked the proofs. Plantin himself noted in a letter that his four oldest daughters had learned to read while very young. From the ages of four or five to twelve—when he thought it became indecent for them to work with men—they had helped correct books in many languages. Material evidence shows that Poelman and Plantin told the truth. A copy of a late proof of the Antwerp Polyglot Bible of 1572, Plantin's most ambitious project, survives in the Plantin house. Its margins bear both ink stains that attest to its presence in the composing room and notes in which the editor, Benito Arias Montano, and the corrector, Franciscus Raphelengius, discussed questions that ranged from format and font size to technical points of textual criticism. A single note written in Hebrew by Montano, which was discovered by Theodor Dunkelgrün, contains a telling complaint: "tell the girl who is coming that she should hurry to come every day, because she takes too long, and I haven't been able to follow her."[40] No doubt Montano wrote in Hebrew so that Plantin, if he happened to see this critical remark about his daughter, would not understand it.

Unlike Plantin's daughter, young men hoped to rise from lector to corrector. Like any other complex occupation, correction developed its own culture. Its practitioners soon developed their own technical languages and practices. For example, they devised a set of standardized correction marks that are still recognizable in the German and English worlds.[41] More important, correction came to be seen as requiring a particular sort of person. Plantin's letter of recommendation for his own son-in-law, Franciscus Raphelengius, etches the frightening portrait of an ideal corrector: "He has never been passionately interested in anything so much as the study of the Latin, Greek, Hebrew, Chaldean, Syriac and Arabic tongues (in which those who confer with him familiarly affirm that he is no mean scholar) and of the humanities; also he will correct loyally, carefully and faithfully whatever is entrusted to him, without ever seeking to parade his learning or show off before others, for he is very retiring and most assiduous at the tasks assigned to him."[42] In theory, at least, the corrector's job called for meticulous attention to detail, expert knowledge of languages, and a complete absence of thought: paradise for Stakhanovites.

In practice, correctors often made mistakes. Like early chymists' assistants, correctors were mentioned most prominently by the good and the great when they did something catastrophic. Beatus Rhenanus, an erudite man in his own right and a supreme craftsman of proofs and formes, oversaw the production of Erasmus's 1515 edition of Seneca. The title page made great promises of critical attention: Erasmus, it said, had emended every error—or at least a great many. The book, in its new form, would in turn emend its reader, who would receive rich moral lessons for a modest price. But the contents disastrously included a late antique confection, the Latin letters of Seneca to Saint Paul: only one of the many forged works by Seneca that found more readers, in the Renaissance, than the ones now classed as authentic, which helps to explain why editors tended to include them even if they had their doubts.[43] Erasmus insisted that he had been away from Basel when the offending edition was being prepared. No one, he insisted, could imagine that he had accepted as genuine a text in which Seneca offered to send Saint Paul a treatise that would help build up his Latin vocabulary. Ever cooperative, Beatus admitted that it was all his fault. Yet Erasmus had to wait until 1529 to see a new edition appear. And even this still included the forged works of Seneca, though it relegated them to a separate section.[44]

Many questions still surround the social and cultural origins of the corrector. What intellectual and technical tools, what formal practices, what sense of his task did a corrector bring with him as he went to work? And where did these intellectual resources come from? One of the most striking facts about correctors was, and is, depressing: for all the utility of what they did, they usually found themselves the objects less of gratitude than of anger, pity, or derision. As early as 1534, when Zuichemus described Froben's shop, he mentioned the chief corrector there, Sigismund Gelenius, only to say how much he regretted seeing him employed in this capacity. Gelenius, he explained, was "an extraordinarily learned man, and worthy of far better things."[45] Pretty much everyone agreed. Hornschuch, the proud corrector and author of a textbook on the craft of correcting, admitted that he himself had taken up the trade to avoid the worse one of a tutor, and that most of his colleagues, if they could, "would be off like a shot from this sweatshop, to earn their living by their intelligence and learning, not their hands"—a clear admission that the corrector was not the "theoretical" worker envisioned by Zwinger.[46] Even Johann Conrad Zeltner, who published in 1716 what remains by far the fullest study of the lives and practices of learned correctors, recognized that their status posed a problem. In the controversies that swirled through the Republic of Letters in the years around 1700, for example, many polemicists used the ad hominem argument that an opponent—even a very prominent one like Jean Le Clerc—had worked as a corrector when young and poor. Zeltner protested that such views were misguided, but his very effort to dispel the prejudice shows that it existed.[47] Sadly, many of the correctors whose lives he passed in review were evidently condemned by poverty or temperament to spend their lives bent over proofs, grumbling about the incompetence of some more prominent author or editor: Friedrich Sylburg, for example, who worked every hour of the day except the one before dinner, which he spent walking, or Stephan Bergler, who lived, by choice, completely isolated, in the highest attic of the house of the learned Fritsche family in Leipzig. It was no wonder that even the name of their calling carried the threat of social discomfiture.[48]

Correctors had every reason to feel ill used. True, their names came first, as we have seen, in the Froben and Episcopius payrolls. But their actual pay was modest: lower than that of the best-paid compositors and pressmen. The rich archives of the Plantin house record the long years that Raphelengius and Cornelis Kiliaan put in working faithfully for their master, evidently contented with their lot. But they also preserve the memory of one Sterck, who left because he did not want to board at Plantin's house, as correctors normally did, and could not afford to live elsewhere in Antwerp on two florins a week. "I had predicted this to him," wrote Plantin, and noted that they parted as friends.[49] Even sadder is the case of Olivier a Fine. The ledger records the payments made to him, week by week, for thirteen years. Suddenly, in 1593, "he became discontented and left without saying goodbye."[50] "The toad beneath the harrow knows / Exactly where each tooth-point goes." Plantin's correctors knew exactly how poor they were and exactly whom to blame. The *Concordia*, an archival document that records the correctors' agreement, in 1664, to hold a yearly feast, also records the whispers, if not the cries, that passed among the correctors when they met to exchange gossip: "I, Philip Jac. Noyens often heard from others, and the venerable De Kleyn heard from Master Vanderweyden, and Hieronymus de Bravio heard from Vanderweyden as well that the correctors used to receive a rise in salary when they had been here for two years. Noyens and the aforesaid De Kleyn also heard this often."[51] Other notes recalled the names of colleagues wrongfully dismissed—and of still others who had managed to leave for a benefice rather than spend thirty or forty years correcting. The learned corrector, in other words, suffered what sometimes seems to be the quintessential fate of humanists: his classical education endowed him with discriminating tastes but qualified him only to be a poor devil of letters, neither better paid nor more secure in his employment than the inky-handed men of toil who sweated beside him.

Even more grating, probably, was the fact that the corrector's cultural and social status was as shaky as his financial standing. Many correctors were educated men who lacked the means, the health, or the temperament to get ahead in a profession. But some were artisans. Poelman worked, apparently, in what he liked to call the "combined study and fuller's shop" (musognapheum) from which he signed one of his prefaces, as he said farewell to his reader ("Farewell, then, fuller," wrote Joseph Scaliger in the margin of his copy).[52] Bartholomaeus Varolle, who in 1563 prepared copy, corrected proofs, and drew up indexes for Froben, was a compositor by training and went back to that better-paid trade when he had the chance.[53] Some of Plantin's compositors also corrected proofs for pay. This was a natural extension of their work. Compositors regularly corrected the first or "foul" proof of the texts that they themselves had set. Ordinarily, these swarmed with literal and technical errors and were not meant for the eye of the author or anyone else outside the printing house. Moving to correction in the fuller sense required only an extension of skills that the compositors had already begun to develop. To the corrector, however, such a move was obviously threatening: it meant that the culture in which he took a frail but vital pride no longer set him off, as a "theoretical" worker, from the rude mechanicals.

CORRECTION IN RENAISSANCE ROME: A CASE STUDY

Correctors, in other words, were men of low income. Measured by their own sense of worth, they were also men of low standing. These problems intersected with the very nature of the calling they practiced in ways that caused constant trouble—trouble to correctors, to authors, and to publishers—but were also unavoidable. One well-known episode—the history of correction at Rome in the first years of printing—is especially illuminating. Between 1467, when the German printers Conrad Sweynheym and Arnold Pannartz moved from Subiaco to Rome, and the early 1470s, when the mass of grand classical texts produced by them and their competitors sent the book market into a tailspin, problems emerged that would recur over and over again.[54] Sweynheym and Pannartz produced beautiful books—books so handsome that owners had their opening pages illuminated, as if they were fine humanistic manuscripts. But the scale of what they achieved is even more astonishing than the quality of their work. In five years Sweynheym and Pannartz produced between 11,000 and 12,000 copies of texts, virtually all of them classical. By doing so they cut the prices of these books by half or more. Roman scribes charged a ducat a gathering for a nice manuscript in folio. A big book like Pliny's *Natural History* could cost thirty ducats or more to commission. Then as now, "scholar" did not rhyme with "dollar": many humanists envied the Vatican librarian, Platina, who earned ten ducats a month. Handmade books were simply too expensive for ordinary library mice who lived on their modest incomes. A printed Pliny, on the other hand, cost a mere eight ducats: a discount of more than two thirds from the price for a manuscript.[55]

Contemporaries realized that Sweynheym and Pannartz had transformed this economy of literary scarcity into a land of Cockaigne: their shop, one observer wrote, was "stuffed with books" that could be had for very little. It is easy to recapture the excitement their work created. In November 1467, the papal secretary Leonardo Dati bought a copy of Augustine's *City of God* from "those Germans who do not write, but form, innumerable books of this kind."[56] Not long after, Leon Battista Alberti wrote an innovative manual, *On Ciphers*, in which he described his own device for reproducing texts mechanically: a pair of metal wheels, one belonging to the sender and one to the receiver, which could automatically encrypt a text in a random form no enemy could break. Noting the similarity between this way of transforming messages and that of the printers, Alberti cast the work as a dialogue with Dati, which he set in the Vatican Gardens. The two men effusively praise the device, which enables "no more than three men to turn out more than 200 copies of a book, from a given exemplar, in a hundred days."[57] One can practically follow the news from the Campo de' Fiori, where Dati must have bought his book, across the Ponte Adriano to the Vatican. Unfortunately, overproduction saturated the market. Within five years, the printers complained to the pope that their house was full of printed gatherings but empty of food. Intellectually ambitious printers like Aldus Manutius and Henri Estienne would encounter similar disasters in the decades to come. Only in the later sixteenth century did canny businessmen like Jean Wechel work out how to devise lists of learned books for which "no risk was taken unless there was a good chance of uptake by the market."[58]

CORRECTION IN ROME: A CASE STUDY

Rome in this fertile moment became a *locus classicus* for prominent correctors: notably Giovanni Andrea Bussi, bishop of Aleria and Vatican librarian. They not only prepared texts for the press but also set their stamp on them with prefatory letters in which they described, far too briefly, how they had improved the texts they edited. These correctors went about their task using methods that had been devised over the last century, in a very different context. In the fourteenth and fifteenth centuries, Italy developed a lively book trade, both secular and commercial, in Latin. In this period humanist authors could reach a substantial number of readers: some works by Leonardo Bruni and Pius II survive in as many as two to three hundred manuscripts. In the brilliant Latin prolegomena to his *Supplementum Ficinianum,* published in 1937, Paul Oskar Kristeller laid out the rules of the publishing game that humanists played.[59] To make a text accessible, the humanist prepared a fair copy for the copyist or the typesetter: a so-called archetypus. Doing this exposed the author to grave risk. Making a mistake in Latin at school could lead to physical punishment. Making a mistake in Latin in a published text, given out in definitive form, could lead to much worse humiliation: as Poggio found when his enemy Lorenzo Valla dedicated a whole dialogue to his mistakes. In it the cook and stable boy of another great Latinist, Guarino of Verona—who were Germans, and therefore barbarians—read Poggio's text aloud and castigated it, solecism by solecism.[60] As Doctor Johnson observed, the prospect of being hanged concentrates the mind: the chances of public exposure not only made humanists think, but also spurred them to find ways of avoiding punishment—attitudes that became, if anything, even more intense in the age of print, when Thomas Nashe had a woodcut made that depicted the object of one of his polemics, Gabriel Harvey, about to urinate in terror at the prospect of Nashe's book appearing.[61]

Humanists who wished to publish in Latin and to escape whipping generally submitted them to the judgment of a friend—someone capable of assessing and correcting both substance and content. Ideally, the author would not send presentation copies of his work to patrons and colleagues, or allow a *cartolaio* (stationer) to make and sell further copies, until it had undergone this process of purgation (in practice, of course, copies of uncorrected texts also entered circulation). Individual humanists, like Niccolò Niccoli and Antonio Panormita, became famous for their skill at identifying others' errors and correcting them. When Poggio wrote his dialogues on avarice, for example, he sent them to Niccoli for comment. The experience that followed remains a familiar one to anyone who has written a dissertation and sent chapters to a supervisor or written a book and sent chapters to an editor. For two months Poggio heard nothing. He sent off a follow-up letter in which he asked, mildly, if Niccoli had received his book. By return he received a blast. Niccoli made clear that there was nothing wrong with Poggio's work except the style and the content, and he suggested multiple corrections for both. Clearly hurt, Poggio replied that friends in Rome had liked the book. Still, he made the changes Niccoli proposed.

The work eventually circulated in this improved form, as well as in the original one.[62]

The humanists who edited others' works were, and called themselves, correctors and castigators. They referred to the stylistic and substantive changes they suggested as "emendations," and described their activities as "emendation"—just as Bussi did when he corrected an ancient text.[63] The work they did on modern texts closely resembled—in both its relatively banal character and its sometimes radical proposals to violate authorial intention—the work that printers' correctors later did to classical texts. If anything, their pursuit of readers was even more unscrupulous—and imaginative—when they were selling the works of the ancients. Francesco Rolandello, who prepared Marsilio Ficino's Latin version of the works of Hermes Trismegistus for the first edition in these same years, though not at Rome, also drew up the marvelous blurb that greeted any reader on the first page:

> You, whoever you are, who are reading this, whether you are a grammarian or an orator or a philosopher or a theologian, know that I am Mercurius Trismegistus, whose remarkable learning and theology amazed first the Egyptians and barbarians, and then the ancient theologians among the Christians, and won me their admiration. Accordingly, if you buy and read me, you will gain by doing so. For I will cost you little and yet I will provide my readers with both pleasure and profit.[64]

No modern Latin text received a blurb in Latin of a more purple hue—or had its corrector speak more volubly for its author.

The case of one of Bussi's rivals—the corrector Giannantonio Campano—is especially revealing. He edited Livy and other ancient texts for a Viennese printer in Rome, Ulrich Han. In the years just before printing arrived in Rome, Campano distinguished himself as a corrector of manuscripts in the manner of Niccoli. Michele Ferno, his biographer, records that "everyone brought him whatever they had created, as if to a common censor and supreme oracle. No scholar would have dared at that time to publish anything before he had investigated his critical judgment. Anyone who obtained his commendation thought that it brought his work immense glory."[65]

One of the most brilliant and authoritative humanist writers of Latin, Pope Pius II, gave Campano permission to edit his *Commen-*

taries. This magnificent book, which is rich with vignettes of Pius's matchless ability to best his enemies in argument and preserve his chastity from the assaults of eager young women, came together, not as one man's work, inspired throughout by a single vision and couched in a single style, but through a collaborative effort: a normal way for humanist secretaries to produce their texts. Sometimes, Pius dictated in his "cubiculum" and one of his secretaries—usually Agostino Patrizi—wrote down what he had to say. Sometimes Pius himself wrote. Some of his most pungent additions to the text came in the form of marginal corrections and additions to what his secretary had taken down. The secretaries also made corrections or suggestions. Eventually, a first draft took shape, in what is now a Vatican manuscript, known as Reginensis lat. 1955.

Pius handed this, and perhaps later drafts as well, on to Campano.[66] He went so far as to prohibit their circulation until they had been "emended."[67] And Campano in turn supervised the creation of a second version of books 1–12 which is now in the Biblioteca Corsiniana (MS 147). At the end of this text, Campano wrote a long assessment of the *Commentaries,* in which he claimed that Pius had given him "the power to delete anything superfluous, correct anything that seemed false, and explain anything that was stated obscurely." It seems certain that what he says is true, for Pius was very much alive when Campano prepared this manuscript of his work. Diplomatically, Campano claimed that he had found Pius's work so elegant that it needed no "second hand to enhance its qualities."[68] In fact, however, as Concetta Bianca has emphasized, he made changes and additions. Five times in the course of the *Commentaries,* Pius II remarks that Campano had written an elegant poem to celebrate an event: for example, the discovery of the papal alum mines at Tolfa. A note in the original manuscript, the Reginensis—to which Campano added what he thought were his most important corrections—shows that he not only composed this poem, but inserted it into the text himself—apparently in the full assurance that Pius, the author, would accept such additions as part of an "emended" text of his own book. The same is true of the other four poems.[69]

Evidently, the terms "emendation" and "correction," in the years just before printing came to Rome, embraced not just radical rewriting, but also the insertion of full-scale supplements. Evidently, too, their use implied something like a collaborative vision of authorship, even when the author in question was someone of high authority.[70] According to Ferno, Campano's skill as a corrector of modern Latin texts that circulated in manuscript won him his employment in the printing house: "that was why no printer in Italy in those days apparently wanted to undertake a publication which did not have one of his prefatory letters to illuminate its path."[71] No wonder that Bussi felt he could print a text of Pliny or Aulus Gellius that he had improved, in a fair number of places, without further indication of details: he was only "correcting" it—as Campano himself was when he passed for printing an immense, influential, and wildly careless edition of the Latin translations of Plutarch's *Lives*.[72]

Bussi prepared texts to circulate in the humanist book market by doing their toilette. But he had no intention of making his printed texts records—as his manuscripts were—of the thought and research that had gone into creating them. Doing so would have made his products ugly and unreadable or added niggling annotations to their margins. Bussi's and Campano's assumptions and practices were perfectly understandable in context—and they survived for centuries at the inky crossroads where publishing and scholarship intersected. The great Thomas Ruddiman, master humanist of eighteenth-century Edinburgh, a publisher in his own right, and librarian of the Edinburgh Faculty of Advocates, corrected not only the proofs of important works by Gavin Douglas and Drummond of Hawthornden, but also the Latin texts of theses submitted to the faculty, without clearly indicating that he had done so. Dr. Johnson, shaking his head in disapproval at the faults of Latinity in James Boswell's thesis, murmured, "Ruddiman is dead."[73]

The daring of the correctors was outrageous. Even a man of standing like Bussi provoked sharp, bitter criticism from George of Trebizond and other contemporaries. George denounced him and all his works. Bussi's audacity infuriated George. He had tried to set his own stamp on the ancients. He had distorted their texts. Even worse, he had added prefaces—something basically unheard of in the manuscript world except for in translations from the Greek—to the words of the mighty Roman dead. George called for papal censorship of the press to prevent a repetition of the massacre that Bussi had perpetrated on Pliny's

Natural History.[74] Practices for the correction of classical texts changed, slowly. Commentaries flourished, in which editors explained, if not how the texts they accompanied had been created, at least how they might be emended.

CORRECTION AS EDITING

Yet where the writings of the moderns were concerned, the correctors happily went on doing what they had always done. In 1627, Scaliger's favorite younger colleague, Daniel Heinsius, edited an edition of his late friend's Latin correspondence for Elzevir in Leiden.[75] Isaac Casaubon had already printed some of Scaliger's letters in 1610. Across Europe, citizens of the Republic of Letters gathered their unpublished letters from Scaliger and sent them to Leiden. Given the clarity of Scaliger's handwriting, one might think that Heinsius only had to set the texts in order and give them to the printer. In fact, however, when Paul Botley and Dirk van Miert produced their splendid critical edition of Scaliger's correspondence, they showed that Heinsius had found plenty of work for his nimble pen. The edition was meant as a memorial to a great man. But Scaliger's Latin, though fluent and forceful, was imperfect. Scaliger did not worry about maintaining the sequence of tenses or putting verbs at the ends of sentences. Heinsius made him do both.[76] Scaliger was famously indiscreet, as Franciscus Raphelengius Jr. noted in a letter to Lipsius: "those he calls scoundrels, asses, beasts and ignoramuses today will be gentlemen, scholars and savants another day."[77] His letters swarmed with unkind remarks about friends and colleagues—not to mention enemies like Martin Delrio, S.J., whom he termed "the devil's shit"—"stercus Diaboli" (Delrio's reply was simple but devastating: the devil does not shit).[78]

Heinsius did his best to make the letters grammatical and decorous, as befitted the personal testimony of a great man. Sometimes he did the work so seamlessly that no reader could have noticed it. In a letter of 1599 to the Pensionary of Holland, Jan van Oldenbarnevelt, Scaliger—the best-paid member of the Leiden faculty—complained that he had to pay an especially high tax assessment. He described this as "not a decree of the Estates but a conspiracy of the professors, who would like to ease their burdens and enlarge mine."[79] Heinsius neatly snipped out the one word "professors," leaving a grammatical if slightly confusing sentence that would irritate no one.[80] Elsewhere Scaliger complained, in ways more difficult to soften, of the injuries that individual dunces had inflicted on him. In 1590, Franciscus Junius had defiled Scaliger's edition of Manilius by reprinting it and adding his own comments, in which he presumed to criticize the great man. Scaliger took revenge by defacing his own copy of the book with irritable remarks like "cacas" ("you're full of shit").[81] He also said unkind things about Junius in more than one letter. In this and many other cases, Heinsius replaced the names of those who served as Scaliger's targets with asterisks. But context made many of these references transparent. Owners of the published letters enjoyed the game of filling in the missing names, especially after Paul Colomiès published a key to them in 1669. Richard Bentley, for example, entered the names in his copy of Scaliger's letters, now in the British Library.[82] Many readers—especially those who felt the stab of Scaliger's bent nib— were not amused. Gerardus Joannes Vossius, Junius's son-in-law, complained to Scaliger's literary executor, Franciscus Gomarus, that Scaliger and Heinsius had slandered a worthy man. The editors— namely, Heinsius—had failed to carry out their full duty when presenting such incendiary materials to the public: "They did right, and deserve praise when they put an asterisk in place of Junius's name at every point. . . . But I would have preferred for them to omit the entire sentences. For as it is a fair number of readers will understand what is being said from what precedes and follows these passages. In particular, those who lived in the time of Junius and Scaliger will be quite clever enough."[83] To a modern reader, trained to believe that an author's every word matters, these changes seem wrong-headed. In the early modern period, as Botley and van Miert showed, they were normal practice. When the first collection of Isaac Casaubon's letters was published a few years after Scaliger's, the editor took care to remove potentially offensive passages and leave no trace.[84] And in fact there were many earlier precedents for subtle scholarly bowdlerism. Aldus Manutius deliberately redacted the letters of Angelo Poliziano when he printed them in 1498.[85] The corrector who printed the letters of Joannes Trithemius at Haguenau in 1536 edited the salutations found in the original manuscript, which indicated that Trithemius had received mail from "the gymnosophist of the University of Cologne" (and which suggest that his correspondence, like some of his other writings, was partly, if not wholly, fraudulent).[86] Even some of those who printed their own letters did the same. When Erasmus published his correspondence in 1521, for example, he admitted that when he had come across letters that were intemperate in tone, he had either omitted or softened them, and he asked Beatus Rhenanus, the master corrector who oversaw the edition, to ensure that the publication did his reputation as little harm as possible.[87]

In theory—as Erasmus himself argued—letters should directly and transparently represent the writer's self. The rise of letter writing in the Renaissance, as Kathy Eden has argued, both documented and made possible a new kind of intimacy.[88] But the self that letters represented was supposed to be decorous: the self that the writer wanted the public to know. Like the girls who attended school with Jane Eyre, the humanist letter-writer was to be the child, not of Nature, but of Grace. All humanists looked back to such models as Cicero, who filled his correspondence with formulas of politeness; Pliny, who insisted that he would never have collected and circulated his letters on his own; and Jerome, who sometimes wrote under the names of his female friends and companions. Apparently the ancients had not simply collected their letters, but had also altered them to achieve certain rhetorical ends. Many no doubt suspected that Petrarch, the first of the modern letter-writers, had done the same when he edited and reshuffled his letters in the collections that he entitled *Familiares* and *Seniles*. If so, they were right.[89] It seems likely that most of the humanists whose letters were edited after their deaths would have preferred to reach the public more or less as Scaliger did, rather than to be the object of a scrupulous philology that exposed them, warts and all. Correctors took liberties with modern authors that they would—theoretically at least—no longer have dared to take with the classics.

CORRECTING COPERNICUS

Considering the practices of correction—like reading all the letters of a great scholar—can yield a new narrative. In 1543 the cunning Nuremberg printer Joannes Petreius brought out Copernicus's *De revolutionibus*. The author, far away and ill, could not see the book through the press. Instead, copy was prepared and proofs were read by men experienced with publishers and printing: Georg Joachim Rheticus, who, like many correctors, acted as an agent for Petreius, hunting new authors and manuscripts, and Andreas Osiander. They did not leave the work unchanged. After the holograph of Copernicus's work came to light in the nineteenth century, philologists noticed that the Petreius edition deviated from it in hundreds of details. Naturally, they restored the text to what Copernicus himself had written. What they failed to notice was that not only the changes in the text proper, but a large number of further ones, some proposed in an errata sheet that accompanies some copies of the work and some made in pen in Petreius's shop, were actually improvements: a point that is relatively easy to establish in the case of a technical work. Copernicus himself must have made many of these changes in an intermediate text that served as printer's copy and that no longer survives. Others were the result of— as should by now be obvious—correction.

Osiander made one especially radical change: one that has long been infamous. Copernicus believed that he had discovered the truth about the universe, and presented his work as an account of the real world. That claim made his book a direct and radical challenge to the entire structure of natural philosophy, as well as astronomy. Osiander, accordingly, added an anonymous preface to the work, which was addressed to the reader. Here he dialed down the book's radicalism by claiming that Copernicus had presented his theory, not as the truth, but only as a hypothesis meant to stimulate discussion. From 1543 to the present, Osiander's maneuver has infuriated admirers of Copernicus. Rheticus threatened to assault him—and did take him and Petreius to court, unsuccessfully. At the end of the sixteenth and the beginning of the seventeenth centuries, Johann Kepler, Willebrord Snell, and others sorted out the story of how the preface was added: notes in their copies of the text record their indignation. They were right to argue that Osiander had gone against Copernicus's manifest intentions.[90]

Yet Osiander's decision also helped to keep Copernicus's book in circulation. *De revolutionibus* began attracting sharp criticism as soon as it appeared, and some censors tried to suppress it, or at least to slow its circulation. But it never became the object of a serious campaign of repression, except to some extent in Iberia. As Owen Gingerich has shown by the simple but vital expedient of examining the dozens of preserved copies, the book not only circulated, but also attracted readers, who filled the margins with marginalia and made Copernicus's work a standard text. By the end of the sixteenth century, accordingly, the Copernican genie was out of the box, and no imaginable act of repression—even the attack on Galileo—could put it back.[91]

Seen on its own, Osiander's act looks outrageous. Even seen in the context of Renaissance methods of correction, it still seems problematic—the act of a little man imposing his own caution on a greater one. But it also seems a prudent and ingenious effort to practice the corrector's trade—and one that had many counterparts in the sixteenth- and seventeenth-century worlds of erudition. The correctors were figures in a landscape that is now disappearing: one in which authors expected their printers—or their scribes—to improve the work they handed in. In this world many writers envisioned their work as collaborative rather than individual. For centuries, correctors served as the intermediary between writers and readers. They were the distant forefathers, not only of the modern philologist, but also of the modern editor, who has done so much to shape the work of important writers. In the twentieth-century United States, T. S. Eliot, Thomas Wolfe, F. Scott Fitzgerald, Richard Wright, and Raymond Carver had their work reshaped by erudite friends, most of them literary professionals, and every one of them saw his work succeed in part because of the changes that their correctors proposed. Many powerful threads of continuity run through the millennial history of authorship and editing. The consequences of these facts for the history of scholarship—the history of scholarly editing—still await full investigation. But one point is clear. Every time authors become enraged at copyeditors, professors, editors, or agents—and every time editors complain that authors do not appreciate their work—they are replaying a scene that is deeply embedded in the classical tradition.

CHAPTER 2

Philologists Wave Divining Rods

ISAAC CASAUBON AND THE GROUNDS OF BELIEF

CORRECTION WAS NOT always a strict and technical pursuit. Humanist editors confronted texts marred by passages that scribes had made incomprehensible and binders had put in the wrong places, as well as simple gaps. At times, they had to find ways of imagining what the original author had written—and of deciding whether their own and others' conjectures deserved belief. The philological imagination was disciplined by scholars' mastery of grammar and usage, genre rules, and historical context. But it also depended on the scholar's ability to divine, by means he could not always explain, what had been lost. The humanist's toolbox included techniques apparently related to those used by magicians, as well as those used by correctors. How did scholars who had thought hard about the nature of argument and the grounds of belief assess scholarly efforts to restore what seemed irrevocably lost words and passages?

Isaac Casaubon was a careful man when it came to believing what he read and heard. When Lancelot Andrewes told him ghost stories, Casaubon listened hard for details about their chain of transmission and scrutinized his friend's demeanor for signs that he was telling the truth. While they were on an excursion in 1613, for example, Andrewes recited a tale about an apparently pious man who had died of the plague on Lombard Street in 1563. The gentleman shocked his wife by speaking to her when she came to lay out his corpse. He asked for food but refused to wait for meat or fowl to be cooked and ate the bread and cheese that she gave him. When the minister came, the former corpse explained that he had been sent back from the afterlife, to confess that he had murdered his first wife with his own hands cleverly enough to escape detection. Then he died again. Casaubon believed what he heard. After all, he explained, Andrewes had had the story directly from an eyewitness who was personally involved, who was a minister and "was a man of the highest credibility and of known piety" (fuit presbyter homo summae fidei et notae pietatis).[1] On the same trip, Andrewes told the story of the crosses that had fallen from the sky on the inhabitants of Wells—including the bishop and his wife. Again Casaubon accepted his account, partly because his friend had received it "from many people, but in particular from the late bishop," and partly because he delivered it "in such a way as to forbid anyone to doubt the truth of the narrative."[2] Yet Casaubon offered no gloss of his own on either story. He seems to have felt that he did not have enough information to explain the phenomena.

As Mark Pattison pointed out in his biography of Casaubon, the supremely erudite Hellenist was, by the standards of his time—the age of Aldrovandi and Bodin, among other retailers of marvels—a critical listener and reader.[3] At the end of Casaubon's life, James Martin wrote to him of miraculous doings in Gamlinga, in Cambridgeshire, some twelve years before. Though the letter does not survive, another one to William Camden does, in which Martin summarized the vivid tale of the supernatural that he had told Casaubon:

> A little child, being left in the Cradle, was very strangely conueyed out of the house, being all in a flame, into the midst of the street; the linnen-apron being all powdered with Crosses; an unknown boy telling the maid, that wept and thought the child was burnt, to this effect, viz. I have thought on the child, and have delivered it; but go and look for it.[4]

Even before the fire, a shining cross had appeared in the air above the house. More recently, crosses had fallen on the linen of the child's mother and sisters, only to fade—or be washed—away. "Some of these my self have seen: they are of a brownish colour, and of this form [a cross]."[5] Casaubon had neither direct visual evidence nor a full account of his witness, and the sources of his account, to go on, and Martin seems to have directly asked for his interpretation of the events. Casaubon's reply was clear: he accepted Martin's account of the facts, but he lacked both the evidence and the gifts that would have made it possible to provide their causes:

> I received lately two letters from you: The first transform'd me wholy into Wonder: without doubt the thing you write of, is miraculous: But WHENCE, I cannot affirme [whether from God or the Devil]. They may best coniecture, that were Eye-witnesses, or of their neerest acquaintance, & they that haue the Spirit of Discerning, &c. In which regard I leaue the discerning thereof to the Most Excellent Diuines of your Illustrious Vniversity. The *Knowledge* of it [τὸ ὅτι] was pleasing to me; the *Cause* [τὸ διότι] I referre to them, whose Iudgements on such an Admirable Euent, I should be very glad to haue.[6]

Casaubon was an Aristotelian, not a skeptic, as his use of Aristotle's distinction between "the fact" and "the reasoned fact" (or simply "the reason why") suggests.[7] Yet he seems to have taken Aristotle's distinction as setting the limit of what he himself could offer in cases like these. He could judge if an account of facts that seemingly violated the order of nature deserved belief, but he had no second premise with which to construct a synthetic syllogism, and hence he could not explain the facts. His consistency in applying this self-denying ordinance is impressive.

CASAUBON ON DIVINATION

Yet when Casaubon assessed the quality of the foundations on which he and his fellow scholars based their hypotheses about the business of their lives, ancient books and their correction and interpretation, the analysis he applied and the terminology in which he couched it were strikingly loose—so loose, indeed, that he sometimes seems to have used the same word in opposite senses. Take the term *divinatio*—a term whose English equivalent now serves as a laudatory description of unexpected and convincing conjectural emendations that transmute the scrambled letters of transmitted texts into plausible passages of Latin and Greek, not to mention English.[8] A classic example of successful divination was inspired by the famous crux in Shakespeare's *Henry V*. The hostess describes the dying Falstaff: "his nose was as sharpe as a Pen, and a Table of greene fields." Critics and scholars did their best to correct the passage. Pope, for example, ingeniously argued that a stage direction that referred to the property master, or Greenfield, had somehow entered the text. But the eighteenth-century editor Lewis Theobald—aided by an annotated book in his possession—divined what the passage must read, in a way still generally accepted. He transformed "a Table of green fields" into "a'babled of green Fields"—presumably, though he did not say so explicitly, a garbled reference to the Twenty-Third Psalm. This became a classic case of conjectural reasoning—so much so that Cardinal Newman used it as an exemplary case in chapter 8 of his *Grammar of Assent*. This kind of jaw-dropping, transformative conjecture is what Frank Kermode referred to when he spoke of A. E. Housman's "exquisite divinatory intelligence," and what we still, admiringly, refer to as divination.

Casaubon already used the word in exactly this sense. He worked his way, pen in hand and page by page, through one of the masterpieces of sixteenth-century textual divination—the edition of the Latin lexicon by the Augustan scholar Festus that Joseph Scaliger had issued in 1575. This was a masterpiece of conjectural criticism. Almost two decades before, the Spanish philologist and jurist Antonio Agustín had transformed the condition of this fragmentarily preserved text. He worked directly from the eleventh-century Naples manuscript, which preserved part of the original text, but which had been partly lost, partly damaged by fire, its outer margin burned away: "a soldier whose comrades have been defeated and massacred, and who creeps along at random with his legs broken, his nose mutilated, one eye gouged out, and one arm broken," in his words.[9] From it he produced a very rough type facsimile, which broke the lexicon up into individual articles but also indicated physical gaps in the text, and gave their approximate length.[10]

Scaliger learned from Agustín's commentary, as well as from his friends in the lively world of French legal and historical scholarship, how to dig in the later, derivative lexicon of Paul the Lombard and in a wide range of other texts for materials from which he could carve out supplements and fit them into place in the facsimile. Again and again he filled the spaces Agustín had left with dazzling, unexpected reconstructions of quotations and rituals. As Casaubon encountered these, he wrote enthusiastic notes. Eventually he reached Scaliger's restoration of the proverb, "Sabinos solitos quod volunt somniare" (the Sabines dream of that they desire)—a correction that became famous, as did the proverb itself.[11] "Foelix divinatio, et plane divina" (a splendid divination, and clearly divine), wrote Casaubon in the margin of his copy.[12] A bold conjecture that went well beyond the transmitted evidence, in this case, evoked his enthusiasm. Evidently Casaubon was sometimes willing to see τὸ ὅτι (the facts), filled in by the sort of imaginative leap that he had refused to apply to explaining the supernatural. In his edition of the *Apologia* of Apuleius, which appeared in 1594, he admitted that he had disagreed with Scaliger on certain points. Nonetheless, he felt certain that the "most noble" Scaliger would not insist that his views be taken as κύριαι δόξαι (authoritative doctrines) "in this realm of letters, which—as Celsus says of medicine—is in large part a matter of conjecture."[13] For his part, Casaubon did insist that he was right to follow the custom of the Greek orators and insert titles whenever Apuleius quoted a document, "even without the authority of the manuscripts."[14]

Yet divination, in Casaubon's philological vocabulary, was not always a positive term. In 1603, he brought out his edition of the *Scriptores Historiae Augustae,* the strange set of narratives of Roman imperial history that purported to be the work of six separate writers. Unlike many twentieth-century scholars, Casaubon did not reject the work as a deliberate forgery. But like his friend Joseph Scaliger, he knew the whole range of late antique apocrypha and pseudepigrapha—not just the Hermetic Corpus—very well.[15] This series of texts, too, seemed to have something wrong with it. Supposedly four of the writers had each written lives of all the emperors, but gaps and contradictions within some of the texts suggested that none of these texts had reached completion: an odd coincidence to say the least. Casaubon decided that the lives had been assembled, badly, from excerpts, rather as the works of the Roman jurists had been assembled, badly, in the *Digest,* one segment of the Roman *Corpus iuris:* "I don't doubt that when this Tribonian did this job, he thought he was a goodly man, though in fact he was a stinking fish."[16]

Even without the sting in its tail, Casaubon's reference to Tribonian, the sixth-century jurist who headed the committee that created the *Digest*, would have revealed his opinion of the way the *Scriptores* had been put together. The French jurists who created the *mos Gallicus* specialized in collecting the fragments of early jurists scattered through the *Digest* and using them to reconstruct what they saw as the true history of Roman law, and they often had little good to say about their chief source. François Hotman cast his polemic on the subject in the form of a pamphlet with the memorable title *Anti-Tribonian*.[17] Unable to frame a hypothesis that would explain what he had found in the *Scriptores Historiae Augustae*, Casaubon threw up his hands and contented himself with offering suggestions about how the text might have taken shape. "As to the plan that this author was following when he put the collection together in this form," he commented, "I leave it to prophets to divine."[18] In this instance, "divination" referred not to a brilliant restoration of "the facts," but rather to the sort of explanatory hypothesis a scholar might devise for them in the absence of hard evidence: the sort of premise Casaubon might have framed, had he been willing, to explain the return of dead men and the fall of crosses.

PHILOLOGISTS ON DIVINATION:
A CHORUS OF DISAPPROVALS

The latter, disapproving usage was much more deeply established than the former in the language of humanistic philology, as Silvia Rizzo showed long ago in her classic *Il lessico filologico degli umanisti*. As early as the fourteenth century, Boccaccio had excused himself to the readers of his work on geographical terms for being unable either to correct all the texts he used or to identify all the ancient terms he had compiled with their modern counterparts. "True," he noted, "I was able to make some further progress by using conjecture: for example, I conjecture that what we now call the Lake of Perugia was 'Trasimene' in ancient times. . . . For the rest, it was necessary to resort to divination, rather than to follow the traces of any of the ancients, and I never learned how to do this."[19] Poggio, similarly, noted in a famous letter to Francesco Barbaro that the scribe who had copied the *Silvae* of Statius and Manilius for him was "the most ignorant of all living men." In reading and correcting part of the manuscript, he complained, "one must divine, not read."[20] As Rizzo pointed out, Poggio regularly used the term *divinare* when describing the efforts required to use a very inaccurate and illegible codex. His comment on the ninth-century manuscript of Cicero's *Philippics*, now known as Vat. Bas. S. Petri H 25 (V), was typical: "I corrected Cicero's *Philippics* with this old manuscript. It is written in such a childish way, with so many errors, that when I copied from it I needed divination rather than conjecture. There is no little woman so ignorant and tasteless that she couldn't have done a better job."[21] An avid reader of Cicero, Poggio very likely used the term *divino* as he did partly because Cicero had often applied it to what he saw as weak and methodologically problematic ways of attaining knowledge. The problems of evidence and logic that afflicted standard forms of divination formed part of the subject of one of Cicero's major dialogues, *De divinatione*. He used terms for divining and conjecture in his political correspondence as well when indicating to friends the level of security with which he felt he could predict the likely course of events in the immediate future.[22] Renaissance scholars knew these passages well. In a letter to Lentulus, Cicero praised his own political astuteness and his correspondent's grasp of affairs: he would tell Lentulus, not the ordinary news, but rather "the things that are in the realm of conjecture."[23] In his commentary, the sixteenth-century Ciceronian scholar Paolo Manuzio took this opportunity to explain the difference between conjecture and divination and to show the superior rigor of the former, smaller category: "Conjecture and divination are not the same. For conjecture is drawn from signs, but divination often does not follow signs. Accordingly, while all conjectures are divination, the contrary does not follow."[24] Manuzio followed Cicero, who had made his own character in *De divinatione* use the arguments of the Academic skeptic Carneades to attack the diviners because they could not explain how they reached their conclusions or what the phenomena they observed had to do with their pronouncements.[25]

DIVINATION AS A BLACK ART

Cicero's own attitude toward divination is hard, perhaps impossible, to establish, and his contemporaries could have read his work in many ways. In his dialogue, after all, he had his brother Quintus make a strong case, in Roman terms, on behalf of divination, and he may well have composed the whole text as an exercise in argument *in utramque partem* (on both sides of a question).[26] But the term *divinatio*, in the fifteenth and sixteenth centuries, would have called to the minds of most readers stranger texts than the *De divinatione* and Cicero's letters, and other practices as well as the ones that Quintus Cicero described and defended in his brother's dialogue. These early modern texts and practices, together with orthodox views of them, formed a screen through which some humanists read Cicero, and which helps to explain why they took him as accepting the skeptical critique of divination. In the fifteenth century and thereafter, Europeans practiced many forms of divination. Among the many witnesses who offered taxonomies of these practices was Johannes Hartlieb, a well-traveled man and serious book collector who lived from around 1400 to 1468, studied at German and Italian universities, and later worked for the rulers of Bavaria, serving as a counselor and physician to Albrecht III. He wrote his *Book of the Forbidden Arts* late in life, around 1460, at the request of Markgrave Johannes of Brandenburg. In it he defined and classified what he called the seven forbidden arts, all of which he treated as forms of divination: necromancy, or diabolic magic; geomancy, or prediction by throwing dice; hydromancy, or prediction by examining water; aeromancy, or the examination of wind direction and sneezes; pyromancy, or seeing visions in fires made from wood cut on a special day; chiromancy, or palm-reading; and scapulomancy, or the use of shoulder-blades and other bones for divination.[27] Hartlieb repeatedly made clear in his work that he drew his material, not only from legal and theological texts that denounced magic, but also from the practitioners whom he himself had interviewed and whom he referred to as "masters in the art."

Hartlieb studied these black arts with eager fascination. All forms of divination, he argued, ultimately involved the same mortal sin. They all relied, not on the supposed words of power and rituals that their practitioners carried out, but rather on the devil. Sometimes divinatory practice wrongly treated natural phenomena as supernatural. When a diviner threw molten lead into water and used its new color and shape to predict the future, he was only reading things into the changes that were caused naturally by the degree of heat to which the metal was subjected and the altitude from which it was dropped. The devil, of course, could make such predictions come true—when he wanted to do so—but otherwise remained aloof. In other cases, diabolic influence was more evidently at work.[28] Only the devil could make visions appear in a small boy's fingernail—a form of divination that Hartlieb described in particularly vivid detail. And the same devil who enabled this technique to work, when he wished, could also disable it. In either case, those who practiced divination, like the diviners Cicero had criticized, could not show how their conclusions followed from their method of inquiry. Hartlieb, like many others, saw astrology as something different from divination, a rigorous system of prediction that used the ever-changing influences of the planets to predict the future. But others, like Pico della Mirandola, swept astrology too into the vast basket of condemned practices labeled as divination because they did not rest on clear inferences from solid evidence.[29]

As Richard Kieckhefer, Claire Fanger, and many others have taught us, the divinatory practices that Hartlieb described were not, unlike those ascribed to witches who worshipped the devil, the products of his imagination. Across Europe, members of what Kieckhefer describes as a "clerical underground" devoted themselves to the *ars notoria*, subjecting themselves to ascetic regimens and scrutinizing complex diagrams in the hope of gaining knowledge of the future. From royal courts and the papal curia to the streets of Europe's cities and villages, divination belonged to the practices of everyday life.[30]

While some scholars condemned all of these forms of divination, others showed themselves to be highly ambivalent about them. Consider the testimony of the learned humanist Gaspare of Verona, who taught groups of young men in Rome how to read and interpret Latin poetry.[31] A committed classicist who valued his connections to such Roman power centers as the Curia of Nicholas V and the palace of Cardinal Capranica, Gaspare wrote with disdain of the ways of predicting the future mentioned by Juvenal in his sixth satire: "The divine law says much about the different kinds of divination. They are prohibited, as are several forms of divination, such as necromancy, chiromancy, auguries, divination from entrails, divination by fire, auspices. And that is how it rightly dealt with the individual forms."[32] He underlined these words by citing an impressive example of the right way to deal with those who engaged in such filthy practices: "The exemplary

Cardinal Capranica ordered that a certain woman, a witch and necromancer, who practiced that vile art in the region of Perugia, should be burned. He could have done nothing better or more just, and indeed from the top of his head to the soles of his feet, he is at once a most just and most prudent, most learned and profoundly wise prince."[33] Gaspare also dismissed the medieval prophetic tradition that associated the Virgin Birth with the collapse of the Temple of Peace. As he and his erudite friends knew, it violated the chronological framework for Roman history that they were busily constructing from written sources and material evidence: "For the immaculate Virgin Mary bore her child before Vespasian or Titus existed, and before the Temple of Peace of which we are speaking." With impressive phlegm, Gaspare assured his listeners—and his chosen reader, Nicholas V—that "I don't care much whether you believe this or not. For it is not an article of faith. That great scholar Leonardo Bruni, who was no mean historian, agreed with me. So did my fellow-countryman Guarino, and Carlo Marsuppini, Leonardo's compatriot. So did Giovanni Tortelli, my close friend, and the most erudite scholar I have ever known."[34] In passages like these, humanist philology seemingly allied itself with late scholasticism in a sharp critique of the magical tradition and the forms of divination that it included. Philology, evidently, relied on evidence, not on predictions and other unfathomable efforts to go beyond human powers of reason.

Yet Gaspare also claimed a certain expertise in magical practices, even when he refused to discuss them: as when he remarked that he would leave any discussion of "how poison is cooked up" to poisoners.[35] He dedicated a long excursus to illiterate diviners in his native countryside, whose methods he praised unreservedly for their effectiveness:

I have seen certain old men in my countryside outside Verona, peasants, who, if someone lost an ass or a horse, could predict and immediately see where the lost possession was. After they recited their words and carried out certain rituals, a sort of star seemed to fall in the place in which the thing in question was being sought, and finally it was found. Once, when there were very violent storms, with thunder, lightning, and rain, one of these men predicted that there would suddenly be a thunderbolt, and it would strike the top of a certain mountain, and it happened just as he predicted. This illiterate and ignorant man was then in his eightieth year.[36]

Gaspare's approval of this traditional form of divination—the sort that had been practiced by cunning men and women across Europe for centuries—evidently did not extend to more learned practices. In his will, he forbade his son to engage in standard forms of magic: "and Francesco, the son of the testator, must not venture to do any alchemy or to hunt for treasures or to follow any part of necromancy," on pain of losing his inheritance and receiving his father's curse.[37] Yet he recorded that he himself dug "a great cave, where he found marvelous minerals," in the time of Pope Paul II.[38]

FICINO AND ERASMUS ON PHILOLOGY AND DIVINATION

The term and practice of divination thus had associations that were both exciting and frightening. Philologists divined—or refused to divine—as their larger assumptions about the proper ways to gain knowledge and the practical tasks that confronted them dictated. Marsilio Ficino did not read Plato historically, but he was nonetheless a skillful philologist.[39] To produce Latin translations of Plato and later Neo-Platonists, he often found himself required to emend the original Greek texts. Like Plato and Plotinus, Ficino believed that knowledge could be obtained by direct revelation, with the help of higher beings. The planet Saturn, which had presided over his birth, had endowed him with prophetic powers. As Denis Robichaud has shown in a subtle article, when Ficino emended Plotinus, he took care to make clear both that he had mastered the tools and terminology of the philologists and that he combined with them, at least in some instances, a higher level of insight:

> It is useful to note that many sentences seem to have been transposed in the Greek manuscript, and words often to have been interchanged. For my part, I emended these things diligently, in keeping with my power, relying on my vocation as a prophet [vates], so to speak, rather than as an interpreter [interpres].[40]

Ficino labored hard at his scholarship, gathering excerpts from his favorite Neo-Platonists and gradually building his interpretations of them. When he pretended to work only from inspiration, he exaggerated greatly.[41] In the case of Plotinus, though, his self-description was accurate. With only one Greek manuscript, Laur. 87, 3, at his disposal, he had to produce a coherent translation. To do so he proposed more than 120 emendations that editors of the *Enneads* still regard as worthy of consideration.[42] A hundred years later, the Jesuit Martin Delrio, another skillful philologist, made his career in two fields: as an expert on magic, including all forms of divination, which he condemned, and as a textual critic of Seneca and other Latin writers. As Jan Machielsen has shown, Delrio condemned divination in philology as energetically as Ficino practiced it.[43]

It seems easy, and natural, to connect textual criticism with the rationalist side of Renaissance thought.[44] Yet Delrio was no rationalist—and Ficino, who was also anything but a rationalist, was a splendid textual critic. Another case will make clear how hard it is to fit the history of philology into these well-worn categories. One renowned philologist above all returned to the problem of divination as faithfully and regularly, as the Biblicists of the sixteenth century liked to say, as the dog to its vomit. Desiderius Erasmus made clear more than once that he rejected all forms of magical divination. In the *Adagia*, for example, he commented on the phrase *Mortuos videns* (seeing the dead): "Your business will fail if you dream of the dead. This is recorded by Suidas as something commonly uttered from divination based on dreams, the most vain by far of all superstitions."[45] He also devoted one of his colloquies, "Ars notoria," to ridiculing that popular form of attaining knowledge of divinity and the future. Yet Erasmus also recognized that ancient references to divination were not wholly negative. In his comment on Adage I.x.8, *Cribro divinare* (divining by the sieve), he quoted classical references to the practice of spinning a sieve and remarked that "certain superstitious persons still use this practice of hanging a sieve on a string to divine nowadays"—an observation fully confirmed by Keith Thomas's great panorama of magic and divination in early modern England.[46] At the start of his discussion, though, he reflected, "this means to grasp something by a shrewd conjecture, or to divine hidden things in a foolish way"—thus leaving some space at least for intelligent guesswork.[47]

Like Poggio, when discussing philological questions, Erasmus sometimes applied the term "divination" as a pejorative. In the *Adagia*, for example, he discussed the expression *Vapula Papyria*, which he had come across in "the fragments of Festus." According to Festus, the grammarian Sinnius Capito had explained it as a proverb used when rejecting threats. Erasmus's own efforts to frame an explanation were hesitant. Perhaps, he thought, the expression might refer to Papyrius Praetexatus, who refused to reveal the secrets of the Senate to his mother, but in that case it needed emendation. Perhaps it had to do with Papyria, the first wife of Paulus Aemilius, who never revealed his reasons for divorcing her. "What can you do?" he asked plaintively. "When the authors are of no help at all, you must divine."[48]

A second case makes Erasmus's view clearer. He drew from Terence's *Phormio* the adage, "Ita fugias ne praeter casam" (When you're running away, don't pass your own house). Erasmus himself took this proverb in a moral sense, as an admonition not to flee from committing one evil and wind up involved in a worse one.[49] But he also noted that the commentary on Terence ascribed to Donatus offered no fewer than three explanations of the same line:

> Donatus, if indeed the commentary is by Donatus, interprets the figure of speech in the proverb thus: In flight do not pass by your own dwelling, which is your safest refuge. Or, Do not flee past your dwelling, where the thief can best be seized and guarded and flogged. Or, he says, the word is spoken by a man driving away a thief and taking care that the thief does not pass his dwelling, lest even in passing he should snatch something.[50]

In the same terms that Erasmus had used to characterize his own hemming and hawing, he said what he thought of the ancient authority's stumbling efforts at explication: "No one could tolerate this sort of divination, the result of wild and fanciful guesswork, if we did not see that interpreters of Greek proverbs and legalistic niceties had exactly the same custom."[51] Donatus, as his pupil Jerome had explained in a famous passage in *Contra Rufinum*, had believed that a commentator should not offer definitive explications of a passage, but accumulate multiple ones. The reader, like a good moneychanger, would identify the one that rang true.[52] Like Poliziano before him, Erasmus rejected this vision of hermeneutics. He made clear that when a commentator offered multiple weak hypotheses that were not supported by clear evidence, he did so not because he wanted to be inclusive but rather because he knew that he had no solid explanation to offer. It is no wonder, then, that in a highly polemical reply to the criticism of Edward Lee, he remarked that he was not just "carrying out divination by the sieve."[53] In such cases, Erasmus used "divination" more or less as Casaubon had, though without his Aristotelian terminology: as a term for invalid explanations.

Yet Erasmus was even less consistent than Gaspare of Verona. He referred more than once, in prominent places, to his own "powers of divination." A particularly notable example appears on the title page of his second edition of Seneca, which was published at Basel by Froben in 1529. This advertises the contents of the book as the product of skillful conjecture. As emended by Erasmus, the works of Seneca will now emend their reader:

> The works of Seneca, which are most useful both for eloquence and for living well. These have been corrected to such effect by Erasmus, on the basis of the authority of old manuscripts, also of the best authors, and finally of divination which can sometimes be shrewd, that he rightly rejects the previous edition, which was printed in his absence. Compare the two and you will see that this is true.[54]

This blurb—which was prepared at the end of Erasmus's longest period of residence in Basel—connects "divinatio" with the positive adjective "sagax," which he had applied to it in the *Adagia*. There is every reason to suspect that he drafted it himself.

DIVINATION IN THE PRINTING HOUSE

What lay between the conservative Erasmus of the *Adagia* and the aggressive editor of Seneca was his first experience of being in charge of a massive edition: that of the correspondence of Saint Jerome, which Erasmus edited for Froben in Basel from 1514 to 1516. In this edition, Erasmus himself took charge of Jerome's letters. He established the text, which he then swathed with a detailed commentary. As he worked, the need for conjecture made itself clear. His scholia record many of his divinations. In Jerome's letter to Laeta, for example, Erasmus found one passage puzzling: "A man is a candidate for the faith when he is surrounded by a believing crowd of sons and grandsons. I think that Jove himself [etiam ipsum Iovem], if he had had this sort of

extended kin, could have believed in Christ."[55] In his note he suggested
that he could find the solution by conjecture: "*Etiam ipsum Iouem)*
This passage seems to have an error. Why would he bring Jove in here?
But I can divine what should be written here. Perhaps, in place of
Iouem, one should read *proauum* [great grandfather, ancestor]."[56]

In fact, the passage made sense as it stood. Still, encouraged by this
and other equivocal successes or discouraged by their infrequency,
Erasmus wrote to Gregor Reisch, whom Froben had previously entrusted with the project, and who remained engaged with it: "I have
divined many things, but I can't do them all." He asked Reisch's advice on some specific cruxes.[57]

Erasmus's letter identified a number of passages in which he was
looking for help. In the same letter to Laeta, for example, he confessed
that "a passage bothers me: 'Quibus corax, niphus, miles' [ep. 107.2]."[58]
Apparently still uncertain, he commented in the edition: "This passage is so corrupt that we need an oracle of Delos to restore it. But I
will indicate as much as I could attain by conjecture. *Corax)* This is a
people between Callipolis and Naupactus."[59] In the same letter, he told
Reisch, "'Cibus eius olusculum sit et simila, caroque et pisciuli,'
should, I divine, read: 'Cibus eius olusculum <sit> et e simila garoque
pisciuli.'"[60] Erasmus both stated the problem that he detected here and
offered a solution in his note:

> [Let] her food be herbs) It is clear that this passage is corrupt. For in
> many texts it reads: *Cibus eius olusculum sit et simila, caroque et
> pisciuli* [Let her food be herbs and wheaten bread, and meat and
> small fish]. Since Jerome is here advising against luxuries, if he al-
> lows meat and fish, I would like to know what he leaves out except
> cake. I think the reading should be: *Cibus eius olusculum sit, & e
> simila, garoque pisciuli* [herbs and small fish with *garum* and wheat]
> so that you understand that herbs and fish are allowed, but not any
> and all fish, or those richly prepared, but small and ordinary ones
> spiced with *garum* and wheat.[61]

The second conjecture made the passage clearer than it had been by
replacing *caro* (meat) with *garo* (fish sauce). Modern texts replace *garo*,
in its turn, with *raro* (rarely): "olusculum . . . et e simila, raroque pisciculi" (herbs and wheaten bread, and very occasionally some little

fish). In the first case, by contrast, Erasmus groped in the dark. Jerome's letter listed titles assigned to new worshippers of Mithras: "Those I mean by which the worshippers were initiated as raven, bridegroom, soldier." Erasmus was right to call for help from an oracle.

What matters, in this context, is not the correctness or even the quality of Erasmus's conjectures but the fact that he made them, and labeled them as the results of divination. Erasmus had a unique position in Froben's printing house—an environment often connected, by cultural historians, with the rise of modernity and such modern disciplines as textual criticism. But he had to approve the text of Jerome's letters, sheet by sheet—even though he knew that the text from which his compositors worked was filled with puzzles and contradictions. Erasmus acknowledged the need for divination not only in individual scholia, but also in his preface to the edition. Illiterate scribes, he explained, had left Jerome's works "not corrupt, but completely crushed and obliterated."[62] He still held that divination was risky: "It is extraordinarily difficult either to conjecture from varied corruptions what the author originally wrote, or to divine the original reading from fragments and traces of figures."[63] In the end, though, no other approach could make the text usable, and Erasmus fiercely defended his right to correct the text even where the evidence ran out.[64] When revising the edition a decade later, Erasmus noted again that he had resorted to divination even as he confessed that it had not always succeeded: "Some passages remain, but only a very few, in which I was not entirely happy in my own mind with my divination."[65] Under the pressure exerted by the need to produce a usable edition, both Erasmus's practices and his attitude changed. He accepted the need to divine "the facts"—or the original reading—where obvious problems loomed and no manuscript or parallel source offered an obviously convincing solution.

Evidently, then, by the early sixteenth century, "divination" had taken on a richer variety of senses than it had had in the world of the Italian humanists: as a pejorative term, it applied to unfounded efforts both to rebuild a text and to explain its meaning. But it could also apply, as a guardedly laudatory adjective, to emendations in the bold style later captured by Moritz Haupt: "If the sense requires it, I am prepared to write *Constantinopolitanus* where the MSS have the monosyllabic interjection *o*."[66]

THE USES OF DIVINATION IN EARLY MODERN SCHOLARSHIP

The later history of the term remains to be traced in the detail it deserves. Many sixteenth-century scholars argued that too much boldness in conjectural emendation should be discouraged. When Francesco Robortello set out to make textual criticism into an art, as he had already done for history and rhetoric, he took the side of Pier Vettori, the greatest of conservative critics. Robortello insisted on the primary need to consult the manuscripts, ideally ancient ones, and did his best to supply rules for making conjectures that reflected the actual habits of scribes.[67] Justus Lipsius and many others who commented on what they described as a crisis in the condition of ancient texts agreed: bold efforts to emend the classics could harm them, especially when practiced by young editors.[68]

The term never entirely lost its pejorative sense, or the slipperiness that let it do more than one sort of duty. Casaubon, for example, found one word out of place in Aelius Lampridius's striking description of the temper of the young Commodus Antoninus:

> For even from his earliest years he was base and dishonorable, and cruel and lewd, defiled of mouth, moreover, and debauched. Even then he was an adept in certain arts which are not becoming in an emperor, for he could mold goblets [ut calices fingeret] and dance and sing and whistle, and he could play the buffoon and the gladiator to perfection.[69]

Fingeret, Casaubon insisted, must be wrong, and he emended it to *frangeret:* the young emperor did not make goblets, he smashed them: "molding goblets is more appropriate for a craftsman at a vineyard than for someone who is raised to the imperial station. But the rest of the passage refutes that reading."[70] It is not easy to see why Casaubon thought that the context made the term *fingeret* impossible, as Janus Gruter respectfully pointed out. Both manuscripts of the text in the Palatine library in Heidelberg read *fingeret,* and Gruter explained that "somehow I prefer their reading to those others' divination, *calices frangeret,* though I don't consider that ludicrous." Moreover, Commodus was not the only emperor whom historians represented as enjoying the practice of various crafts.[71] One man's artful conjecture, in other words, was another's baseless divination, which flew in the face of the evidence. Scaliger himself complained that an Italian critic had rejected his edition of Festus as an example of divination at its worst: "one of the most distinguished men of letters in Italy said that I was clearly engaging in divination and soothsaying."[72] Yet in the same years, as we have seen, Casaubon praised him for exactly the same ability to call up plausible readings from the vasty deep of which Carlo Sigonio and other Italian scholars sharply disapproved.

The term *divination*—and the operation it denoted—did not figure only in textual criticism. By the sixteenth century, scholars realized that the historian and student of history, as well as the critic, often had to divine. In the first decades of the sixteenth century, scholars turned their attention to the early history of Christianity. It soon became clear to them that neither the New Testament nor Eusebius, the only surviving historian of Christian origins, answered basic questions. Polydore Vergil, who traced the history of Christian institutions and observances, one by one, in books 4 to 8 of his *De rerum inventoribus*, which first appeared in 1521, made the difficulty painfully clear: "I would not dare to state for certain in what place the first temple was dedicated to our Saviour, after the teaching of the Gospels was published among the peoples, lest I seem to divine rather than to stick to the truth."[73] Apparently, though, historical conjectures did not seem so irresponsible as textual ones. Vergil went on to do exactly what he had condemned: "when something is unknown, conjecture is permitted."[74] He suggested, in a very gingerly way, that the first churches might have been created in remote places, perhaps underground, and that James might have dedicated a tiny church to Jesus at Jerusalem.[75] A generation later, Flacius Illyricus used both the term and the process in a more positive way. When editing medieval Latin poems that he prized for their exposure of clerical ignorance and empty ceremonies, he fixed their date, as he confessed, by divination—but reasonable divination, based on tangible evidence:

> These songs, Christian reader, as we may divine from signs that are not at all obscure, were composed no less than three hundred years ago. For first of all the manuscript from which I copied them has such an air of age about it that it seems to have been written two hundred or more years ago. Quite a bit of its content, moreover, is written in

correct Latin, so that it seems that it was copied from other, older manuscripts. Finally, the music, to which these songs are to be sung, can provide a very strong testimony of antiquity. For it was in use three hundred years ago, but now is understood by no one, and for that reason I have omitted it, though the form of the text also has an air of uncommon age about it.[76]

In this case, the conjecture rested on a series of pieces of evidence, which Flacius classified as *minime obscuris signis:* a strong form of divination, whose relation to the evidence was transparent.

Like Flacius, Casaubon sometimes used divination in this positive sense. In an unpublished treatise, one of a pair on the rise and fall of Rome, he set out to "examine the destruction of that great edifice." Once again τὸ ὅτι and τὸ διότι made their appearance. Casaubon explained that before he laid out the facts—about which no one could be in doubt—at length, he planned to discuss the "causes of the destruction of so great an empire."[77] Once again, establishing τὸ διότι proved hard. Reflection showed, Casaubon argued, that the task was difficult: "as nature does nothing in vain, so in events nothing happens, without preceding causes to bring it about—but these often remain concealed from men . . . for things often turn out very differently from the way that everyone thinks, as Synesius says."[78] Accordingly, Casaubon found himself forced to use what he described as "the form of divination practiced by prudent men, and mentioned by authors in many places. They hold that this prudence is a sort of foreknowledge, and the foreknowledge of prudence."[79] As Casaubon described the impiety and greed, military failures and loss of prudence, which in his view explained the fall of Rome, he too was practicing a form of divination—even though he insisted that careful excerpting of the sources, both pagan and Christian, would sustain his arguments.[80] Casaubon sharply criticized the most fashionable readers of history in his time, Justus Lipsius and Jean Bodin, in his preface to Polybius.[81] But he agreed with them that the political and military value of history depended on its interpreters' willingness to engage in a form of divinatory interpretation, a search for "the reason why," which could not, in the nature of things, be supported fully by clear evidence.

DIVINATION MODERN AND ANCIENT

The humanists' juxtaposition of divination with textual criticism was both justified and insightful: more so, perhaps, than their own analyses may suggest. After all the manuscripts have been collated and all the variants assembled, there comes a moment when a text has to be created. At that point, in the words of E. J. Kenney, the answer "comes in a flash, or not at all"[82]—and despite the fact that the answer must, in complex ways, rest on the critic's mastery of language and style, antiquities and cultural history, it is anything but easy to make explicit, as Robortello tried to, the ways in which these and other considerations interact before being fused into a new reading in the critic's hot alembic. Attentive observers from Carlo Ginzburg to Michael Fishbane have called attention to the resemblances between the procedures of conjectural emendation and those of divination.[83] Kari Kraus draws a parallel between the procedures of textual criticism, as applied to Shakespeare, and the wordplay of historical characters: "The ludic language of Shakespeare's fools, soothsayers, and madmen seemed to me to uncannily resemble the language of Shakespeare's editors as they juggled and transposed letters in the margins of the page, trying to discover proximate words that shadow those that have actually descended to us in the hopes of recovering an authorial text."[84]

It seems quite likely that, as Ginzburg and Kraus have both argued, following Michael Fishbane and others, ancient divinatory procedures are actually the source from which conjectural emendation emerged. In two respects, moreover, the situation seems to have been even more complex than they suggest. In the first place, it seems that even in antiquity—and long before Cicero—the connection between divination and exegesis was visible, and that divination was hedged about with enough doubts that it added uncertainty, not certainty, to the procedures in question. The earliest surviving study of variant readings, after all, is the famous passage in which Thucydides made fun of his contemporaries' way of choosing which of the two forms of an oracle to believe. During the plague that struck Athens early in the Peloponnesian War, he wrote, the Athenians "called to mind this verse said also of the elder sort to have been uttered of old":

A Doric war shall fall,
And a great plague withal.

"Now were men at variance about the word, some saying it was not *loimos* [plague], that was by the ancients mentioned in that verse, but *limos* [famine]. But upon the present occasion the word *loimos* deservedly obtained. For as men suffered, so they made the verse to say. And I think if after this there shall ever come another Doric war and with it a famine, they are like to recite the verse accordingly"[85]

The modern story also has its contradictions. Ginzburg argues powerfully that textual criticism could become a scientific discipline even though it ultimately rested on divinatory practices, because "its objects were defined in the course of a drastic curtailing of what was seen to be relevant." Critics ceased taking an interest in the intonations of voice and gestures that had once accompanied the reading of texts, and then in the characteristics of script. Textual criticism in its scientific form dealt with a text that had essentially dematerialized.[86]

But the genealogy of scientific philology is not straightforward. Some early modern critics tried to make their discipline an art by insisting on the need to examine manuscripts, identify the best ones on the basis of their form and script, and work from their evidence. In Robortello's words,

> How reliable, O Gods, was Poliziano! Even today anyone can examine the manuscripts he used, in the libraries of the Medici and San Marco at Florence, where they are publicly preserved. Equally reliable is that most reverend and erudite old gentleman, Pierio Valeriano, a man who deserves the affection of all, and who used the Roman codex to emend Virgil. My friend Pier Vettori did the same. When he engaged in this business of emendation, he sought to earn a reputation less for great learning then for great goodness and reliability. He always made clear which manuscripts he used, where they are, and whether they were written in Lombardic or Roman script.[87]

When a scholar deliberately ignored the evidence of manuscripts—as Scaliger claimed to in his first edition of Manilius—he made a powerful and contentious claim about the power of his "divinatory intelligence." It was not easy to reconcile with the claim—one Scaliger himself had made in his edition of Catullus, Tibullus, and Propertius—that textual criticism could become a rule-bound art when it based itself on close study of the material evidence.[88]

The language of divination—both classical and contemporary—corresponded to something that scholars experienced when working with ancient texts. It also seems plausible that as scholars moved from redoing individual manuscripts created by incompetent scribes to creating new texts for print, this terminology captured something of the ambivalences that editors necessarily felt: especially when they found themselves forced, while correcting proofs in the printing house, to devise conjectures, not only to remedy problems in the transmitted text but also to correct the brand-new errors that the compositors introduced in the course of setting type.[89] "Every cold empirick, when his heart is expanded by a successful experiment, swells into a theorist, and the laborious collator some unlucky moment frolicks in conjecture"—so Dr Johnson reflected on one of the earlier editors whose demerits he ruthlessly revealed in his preface to Shakespeare. Yet he also went back to Erasmus, another reluctant diviner, to find the language in which he admitted that he too had had to frolic in the same dangerous meadows: "That many passages have passed in a state of depravation through all the editions is indubitably certain; of these the restoration is only to be attempted by collation of copies or sagacity of conjecture. The collator's province is safe and easy, the conjecturer's perilous and difficult. Yet as the greater part of the plays are extant only in one copy, the peril must not be avoided, nor the difficulty refused."[90] Sooner or later, every textual critic found himself examining obviously corrupt passages as if they were the diagrams of the *ars notoria*. To realize that was to take a first step toward framing a rational skepticism about what philology could achieve—while leaving a space for the dubious but essential art of philological divination.

CHAPTER 3

Jean Mabillon Invents Paleography

ON SEPTEMBER 16, 1685, Jean Mabillon looked at a manuscript in the Vatican Library, in the company of the librarian, Emanuel Schelstrate, and a painter, Giovanni Pietro Bellori. The Vatican Virgil (Vat. lat. 3225), written and illustrated in Rome in the first decades of the fifth century, is one of the most impressive manuscripts to survive from antiquity, a masterpiece of late antique calligraphy and art.[1] The three men examined it with microscopic attention. As Schelstrate explained, they noted every detail, starting with format and the general appearance of the script: "It is a quarto, square in shape, written in capital letters, with no word divisions except at points of punctuation." They decomposed words into letters and letters into strokes of the pen: "The letter A is written without a crossbar; the letter P is not completely closed; the letter U is always round; the letter I has a very short upper line."[2]

In the end, as Ingo Herklotz has shown, the gorgeous miniatures of pagan gods and rituals in the manuscript misled them. They dated it to the third century, before Constantine made Christianity the official religion of the Roman Empire and suppressed pagan sacrifices. But the nature of the examination they mounted is still telling. For centuries, humanists had met in libraries to talk about manuscripts and examine them, doing their best to date them and assess their value. Poliziano, for example, collated Pietro Bembo's ancient manuscript of Terence with the young Bembo as his assistant, as he recorded in a famous note:

> I, Angelo Poliziano, collated this [printed] codex of Terence with a codex of venerable antiquity, written in capital letters, which Pietro Bembo lent me. . . . I followed my custom, and copied even the obvious errors. The book is laid out in verse form, in a script almost identical to those in which the Florentine Pandects and the Palatine codex of Virgil ware written. Pietro himself helped me.[3]

But Mabillon and his friends worked in a new way: a way that has a clear period flavor. The natural philosophers of the seventeenth century paid close attention to microscopic beings and craft processes, which their learned predecessors would have dismissed as insignificant. These scholars were doing the same thing. They found meaningful patterns in the movements of a long-dead scribe's pen. Trendy specialists no longer speak of a scientific revolution. Yet the way in which Mabillon and his colleagues addressed their ancient codex has the look of a philological revolution.[4]

Mabillon was usually the kindest of men, the soul of modesty: it seems only appropriate that the first school he attended was the Collège des Bons Enfants in Reims. When it came to radical philology, however, he played the role of Robespierre. In 1681, Mabillon published his *De re diplomatica:* the book that transformed the study of documents and manuscripts. An engraved frontispiece used the traditional visual language of mythology to highlight the importance of his accomplishment. By laying out the rules for dating and authenticating documents and manuscripts, the image showed, the book served two ancient divinities at once: Justice and Clio, the Muse of history. As a writer, however, Mabillon adopted a much more up-to-date idiom: that of the late seventeenth century—an age of prestigious scientific societies and dramatically staged experiments in which many thought novelty a prime virtue. He began his book by staking a claim to innovation: "I am creating a new branch of the antiquarian's art, which deals with the methods, formulas and authority of old documents."[5]

The bold tone of this remark is not hard to account for. Mabillon's book responded to an equally bold provocation. In 1675, Daniel van

Papenbroeck, a Jesuit and member of the hagiographical task force known as the Bollandists, added what he called an "antiquarian preface" to the second April volume of the *Acta Sanctorum.* Taking off from a debate about a document dated August 26, 646 CE, which granted villages to the cloister of Oeren, near Trier, he argued that most of the early charters of the Merovingian kings—the documents that recorded their gifts of land and privileges to the Benedictines—were fakes.[6] Mabillon set out to prove both that the Benedictines' properties and privileges rested on genuine titles—an argument about privileges and jurisdictions—and that he was a better antiquary than Papenbroeck— an argument about the proper way to study historical documents.

In the *De re diplomatica* Mabillon assembled virtually everything known in his time about the history of books and documents in the Latin world since antiquity. Working with colleagues—especially Michel Germain—he described papyrus and vellum, pens and ink, scrolls and codices, the palatial and monastic scriptoria where documents had been written and the libraries where they had been stored.[7] Above all, he used engraving, the central, and powerful, illustrative technology of his time, to present the evidence to the reader (see Plate 3). Vivid facsimiles made it possible to inspect the early documents that Jesuit scholars had impugned, as well as many others that provided a new context for their study.[8] The book expanded as Mabillon moved from diplomatics into the wider field of paleography. He reproduced specimens of every kind of Latin writing, literary as well as documentary. And he analyzed many of the scripts used in his samples, showing letter by letter how to write them, as well as how to transliterate them into modern Roman characters. Full alphabets supported further study. In the words of Alfred Hiatt, Mabillon's specimens "provided a kind of visual history of documentary form. Above all, they were designed to provide vital reference points for contemporary and future historians attempting to determine the veracity of particular documents."[9] When Mabillon examined the Vatican Virgil letter by letter, stroke by stroke, he was playing—as scholars often do—his own best reader.

Mabillon made any number of mistakes. Sometimes the Jesuits and others, who took a more critical view of documents than he did, were correct.[10] His history of scripts was oversimplified, as Scipione Maffei and others would show in the eighteenth century.[11] Still, his display

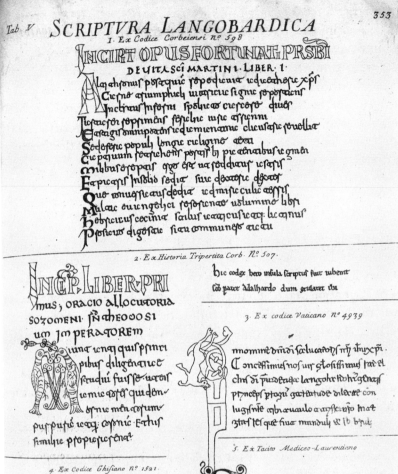

PLATE 3 Jean Mabillon, *De re diplomatica* (1681): examples of Lombardic script with analyses of the alphabets. Department of Rare Books and Special Collections, Princeton University Library.

of primary sources overwhelmed opposition. His book refuted his opponents with lucid arguments and crushed any survivors under the weight of accumulated evidence. In the age of Pascal and Locke, this seemed a rigorously empirical form of scholarship. Papenbroeck said as much in the famous letter in which he withdrew his claims. He admitted defeat, but insisted that he was proud to have provoked so brilliant and erudite a refutation: "I like nothing in my own little essay, eight leaves long, on this subject—except that it provided the occasion for this outstanding, truly perfect work."[12]

THE IMPACT OF *DE RE DIPLOMATICA*

To gain a sharper sense of the impact of Mabillon's weighty book, we may turn to England. The study of manuscripts and documents had flourished there, as scholars strove to lay solid foundations for histories of the nation and its church. But progress in establishing criteria for dating scripts and other material features of documents had been moderate. During early August 1625, while the Useless Parliament dragged out its last days at Oxford, the local antiquarian Brian Twyne showed a charter from the archives of the priory of St. Frideswide to two of England's most expert students of historical documents and manuscripts, Robert Cotton and Henry Spelman. Dated to 1201, it referred to Oxford as a university.[13] "Sr Robert Cotton," Twyne recalled,

> hauinge well viewed ye sayde Recorde, answerd and replied, that by ye character of ye letters, and forme of hande writing vsed in ye sayde chriographe, it should seeme (and he constantly avouched so much) that ye saide chirographe was not written before ye time of kinge Henry ye sixt as beinge written in an hand not vsuall before his time, and consequently, that this my Recorde was corrupt and falsified and not so antient as ye date promised.[14]

When Twyne continued to defend the document, he encountered still more resistance, though of a paradoxical kind: "But as Sr Robert Cotton excepted against ye hande that it was to newe so Sr Henry Spellman beinge there present excepted against ye sculpture of ye seale, as beinge to old, for those times, and therefore also counterfeyte and forged."[15] No conclusion was reached: "These matters were argued to and fro amongst vs at that present; but nothinge stated or determined, because they were called away to ye committee." Twyne had seen and copied hundreds of documents. But he denied, in general terms, that material evidence could settle the discussion: "we must not perdere substantiam propter accidens." And he rejected Cotton's effort to date the charter's script, arguing that "antient handes were not allwayes every where alike at ye same time, which appeareth by MS bookes written in diverse Landes in ye selfe same age and time, and yet they are not to be reiected for this difference."[16]

Ten years after *De re diplomatica* appeared, an English friend of Mabillon's, the Oxford Arabist, astronomer and manuscript hunter Edward Bernard, printed a visual history of the world's alphabets.[17] This began from that of Adam (which Bernard identified as Samaritan). His enterprise was hardly new: many polyhistors drew up histories of languages and writing.[18] But Bernard executed it in a novel way. When he examined Latin script, for example, he laid out abstract alphabets and tied them, as Mabillon had, to dates.[19] Bernard created a chronology, as well as a genealogy, of scripts. Mabillon's efforts to compose a precisely dated history of writing both inspired and underpinned his project.

If Mabillon shaped Bernard's project, he gave Humfrey Wanley a vocation. A draper's son, Wanley began compiling historical alphabets at the age of fifteen, drawing them from "an old Latine Grammar" and the English translation of Henry Cornelius Agrippa's *De occulta philosophia*.[20] Two years later he was copying documents and manuscripts. His collection began with an alphabet like one of Mabillon's, though more elaborate, drawn from a Latin Bible that he thought "very ancient, for it was written before the Bible was divided into Chapters by Stephen Langton Archbishop of Canterbury who was consecrated 1207."[21] Conversation with William Elstob and others clarified his intentions. By the late 1690s, he was engaged in a massive effort to trace the history of writing from coins, inscriptions, and manuscripts, its alphabets to be "engraven by either Mr Sturt or Mr Burghers who are the two only men in England capable of engraving Plates of this Nature to any tolerable degree of Perfection."[22] Though Wanley's "Book of Specimens" never reached print, his elegant redrawings of historic scripts were used with pleasure and profit by George Hickes and many others.[23] Wanley

knew and learned from Bernard's table. In 1695, when he visited the
Cottonian Library, he wrote to Thomas Tanner that he could read the
sixth-century Cotton Genesis "after my fashion" because he "remembered the Letters of Dr Bernards Greek Alphabets."[24] But when he
began seriously to copy the scripts of ancient manuscripts, he "durst
not presume at first to begin with the MSS. themselves, but chose
rather to take the 4 specimens from Mabillon."[25] As Kenneth Sisam
wrote, Wanley "learnt more than pencraft from Mabillon's book: he
saw that handwriting had a historical development; that the study not
merely of documents in the narrow sense but of all kinds of manuscripts, their dates and provenance, was a science."[26]

Mabillon's impact was no less weighty on the Continent. When
Francesco Bianchini supplied a facsimile of a leaf from a Farnese manuscript, now lost, in his edition of the *Liber pontificalis* and described
in detail how it had been made, he went beyond Mabillon, as Carmela
Vircillo Franklin has shown.[27] But he also made clear that Mabillon's
work had inspired him, by citing the French scholar as a master in the
field of manuscript studies, employing his method for ordering scripts
taxonomically, and reproducing a facsimile of another manuscript from
Mabillon's book for comparison.[28]

THE STUDY OF SCRIPTS BEFORE MOMMSEN

Many traditions flowed into Mabillon's project. The Benedictines
themselves had been expert scribes for centuries. Their scriptoria restored old manuscripts and forged old documents with equal skill. Humanists had studied the manuscripts assembled in the new, secular
libraries of fifteenth-century Italy and torn from monastic collections
by the religious wars of sixteenth-century France. By the fifteenth
century they began to classify Latin scripts, using category terms like
"Lombardic," which designated an unfamiliar and difficult minuscule
hand.[29] Classification did not always lead to clarity, however. In or before 1492–1493, Annius of Viterbo, the bad boy of Renaissance philology, announced that he had discovered marble slabs with inscriptions. One of them, which was circular in form, recorded a decree of
Desiderius, King of the Lombards, from the late eighth century. It was
cut, Annius noted, "in ancient and decayed Lombard letters."[30] Only
after a long search did the Viterbese find someone who could read the

ancient script, a local lawyer named Bernardino Cerrosi. In this case, sadly, a little knowledge proved dangerous. Annius knew that Lombardic script flourished in early medieval Italy. But he did not know that it had been used exclusively for manuscripts, not for inscriptions. Fortunately, his contemporaries knew no more. Even Poliziano fell for Annius's imaginative fake and quoted it.

Still, from the fifteenth century on, scholars and collectors tried, in an increasingly systematic manner, to assess and specify the age, quality, and scripts of the manuscripts they owned and used. Johannes Hinderbach is now remembered as the prince-bishop of Trento who presided over the executions of Jews falsely accused of murdering a Christian boy named Simonino. As Daniela Rando has shown in a classic study of Hinderbach's rich and informative marginalia, he was also a serious collector of manuscripts, who had made himself an expert at evaluating their age and script.[31] Over time, these scholars' and collectors' tools were sharpened. The sixteenth-century Roman scholar Gabriele Faerno notoriously judged the age of codices from their script as easily and precisely as grooms inferred a horse's age from its teeth.[32] Fine-meshed work as a textual critic taught some scholars the value of studying and identifying scripts. Joseph Scaliger was inspired by Poliziano and Vettori, whose scrutiny of manuscripts had enabled them to draw up genealogies and identify, in a few cases, the extant manuscript from which all others were descended. He spent time as a student of law with Jacques Cujas, who assembled an immense collection of manuscripts, and borrowed from like-minded friends among the jurists, including Jacques Bongars, Pierre Daniel, Claude Dupuy, and others. In the early 1570s he had the chance to work with a particularly impressive manuscript: the ninth-century codex of Ausonius in Visigothic script now known as Leiden University Library Voss. Lat. fol. 111. Scaliger realized that similar letter-forms—*a* and *u*, for example, and *c* and *g*—could easily have confused later scribes and caused errors. In his 1577 edition of Catullus, Tibullus, and Propertius he ingeniously reverse-engineered this insight. Working backward from a fifteenth-century manuscript, now British Library MS 3027, and his own conjectures, not all of them equally solid, Scaliger argued that all manuscripts of Catullus must be derived from a lost original, written in a script like that of the Ausonius.[33]

Others simply found the peculiarities of past scribes worth recording, as much for aesthetic as for philological reasons, or else from simple curiosity. The Tübingen Greek scholar Martin Crusius remains a figure in academic memory because he taught Johann Kepler Greek and dreamed strange dreams, which he recorded in his immense diary.[34] But he deserves better. A passionate student of the contemporary Greek world, he preserved the material details of the letters he received from Greek scholars. Crusius noted the shapes and qualities of the paper they used, reproduced their seals, and even attended to their complex, ornamental signatures. Often these were ambitious works of monocondylic art, magnificent series of curlicues written without lifting the pen from the page. Crusius reproduced and deciphered many of them.[35]

Mabillon did not discuss Crusius's work, which dealt exclusively with Greek writing. But thanks to his friend, the historian and jurist Jean Bouhier, he knew Bernardo de Aldrete's study of the origins and nature of the Castilian language. Aldrete provided a striking facsimile made of a page in what he called "la letra Gotica" and transliterated its text into standard letters to help his readers.[36] Mabillon included tiny sample facsimiles of this and another manuscript in the *De re diplomatica,* complaining all the while that Spanish scholars should not leave such treasures unpublished while some of their compatriots spent their time "shaming themselves by stuffing the world of letters with fake chronicles" (the chronicle he had in mind was the account of the rise of Christianity in Spain by one Dexter, a skillful forgery by the Jesuit Jerónimo Román de la Higuera).[37]

Other humanists envisioned projects close in scale to Mabillon's enterprise. Late in the sixteenth century, Juan Bautista Cardona, bishop of Tortosa, proposed that a colleague undertake a paleographical project in the new library of the Escorial. Antonio Agustín, bishop of Tarragona and a renowned philologist, was one of the most expert philologists and epigraphers of the sixteenth century. In his dialogues on medals and inscriptions, he showed an unmatched mastery of the letter-forms carved and stamped by ancient Romans—as well as the efforts of modern forgers to reproduce them.[38] Cardona suggested that Agustín—or, better, a group—should create "a book in which those letters are set out by distinct periods, and which assigns each period its letters. Once comparison is made easier in this way, it will be easy to work out the age of each manuscript in the library with more certainty."[39] Though this project did not come to fruition, later Spanish scholars—notably Benito Arias Montano—displayed similar skills when asked to authenticate the strange inscriptions, supposedly made by early Spanish Christians, on plates found on the Sacromonte in Granada.[40]

Others preceded Mabillon in using this sort of evidence to assess the historicity of documents. In 1672 the erudite historian and lawyer Hermann Conring set out to deconstruct a charter ascribed to a Carolingian emperor named Louis, which a convent had used to claim independence from the jurisdiction of the city of Lindau.[41] Conring subjected the document to a savage public anatomy, which revealed historical as well as genealogical, juridical, and linguistic errors. In a letter to Claude Sarrau, the philologist Claude Saumaise had argued that manuscripts in which the two letters of the diphthong æ were written separately "are particularly old and accurately written." Manuscripts in which the letters were fused were also fairly old. But those in which a cedillated *e* (e caudata) represented the diphthong "must be confined to a recent period."[42] Though Conring had only a partial facsimile of the source to work with, he cited Saumaise's expert testimony as evidence that it was spurious.[43]

Still, the connection between Mabillon and these apparent precedents for his enterprise in the world of humanistic scholarship remains too loose to be comfortable. Two cases will give a sense of what Mabillon knew, and when. The Florentine state possessed an ancient manuscript known to scholars across Europe: the sixth-century codex of the Pandects or Digest of the Roman law, which had been discovered in the twelfth century and, four hundred years later, was shown even to distinguished visitors through a grill and by the dim light of torches. Through the late fifteenth and sixteenth centuries, a few scholars gained permission to see and handle it. In 1489, Angelo Poliziano argued that corrections in the introductory constitution proved that it was the official original, the *archetypus* from which all others were descended. In the 1540s, the great Spanish jurist Antonio Agustín contradicted him, arguing that the corrections were scribal and that the manuscript must have been a little later than Justinian's own time. In 1553, finally, Lelio Torelli published an edition of the Pandects based on the Florentine manuscript. He included the Greek sections, traditionally omitted, which he printed in capitals to reflect the practice of the original scribes.[44] Mabillon printed a specimen of the script of the Florentine Pandects, which the Florentine scholar-librarian Antonio Magliabechi provided. And in his caption he laid out the humanistic discussion of the nature and date of the manuscript, with full references to, and quotations from, the sources.[45]

Yet Mabillon came by his knowledge of these discussions of the Florentine Pandects only in the later stages of his work on *De re diplomatica*. His massive book took shape very quickly.[46] A close ally, Emery Bigot, described the formation of Mabillon's project in a letter of 1679—just two years before publication, and one year before the text reached completion—to his friend Nicolaus Heinsius, a Dutch specialist in Latin textual criticism. Mabillon had already had the beginnings of several early charters engraved, he explained, and was now looking for dated manuscripts of great age. "I called his attention to the Florentine Pandects, which Antonio Agustín thought were written in the time of Justinian (I know that Cujas and others doubt this, but they had not seen the MSS. Inspection of the script will make it possible to judge)."[47] Evidently, Mabillon recognized Bigot's superior expertise and better connections with Italian librarians—and learned from him, rather than from his own research, about the accomplishments of humanist textual criticism.

When Mabillon relied on earlier humanists' efforts, moreover, he did not always use the richest and most precise ones. In the text of *De re diplomatica*, Mabillon discussed the earliest Roman book scripts at length. He argued that the script normally used for literary works had consisted of slightly informal, "round" capitals. In making this argument, as he indirectly suggested, he drew directly the work of an earlier expert humanist. In 1636, a young nobleman from Viterbo, Curzio Inghirami, had gone fishing with his sister. When he broke open what looked like an oddly shaped stone or clod, he found paper inside it, with what he identified as Etruscan writing. Further discoveries followed, and soon Inghirami had unfolded, copied, and translated more than a hundred Etruscan and Latin documents.[48] In an example of what Amos Funkenstein called "counter-history," these documents told the story of the defeat of Catiline by Cicero, from the standpoint of Catiline's Italian allies.[49] They also gave Etruscan rules for thunder divination and much else. These documents were printed in Florence, with no small splendor and a fake Frankfurt imprint to evade censorship.

Ingrid Rowland and Luc Deitz have told the story of Inghirami with wit and erudition.[50] What matters about it for our purposes, and what mattered for Mabillon's, is the response of the prefect of the Vatican Library, Leone Allacci. In a polemical pamphlet, Allacci denounced the new texts as fakes. The writing in the Etruscan texts went in the wrong direction, from left to right. More important—and more telling—was the fact that the Latin texts were written in minuscule. Drawing on earlier humanists, many of whom had discussed the subject briefly or in passing, Allacci insisted that the Romans had always cast their literary texts in majuscules.[51] He used the Vatican and Roman Virgils, as well as the Florentine Pandects, to make this point. Allacci's sketch for a history of early Latin writing, starting with different forms of capital letters, provided the model for Mabillon, who cited it. Like Allacci, he distinguished between the most formal writing and what he called the "minute and round letters, formed with less artistry" now known as rustic capitals.[52]

Mabillon, however, combined Crusius's attention to minute detail with Agustín's comprehensive project and Allacci's vision of a history of scripts, and by doing so he transformed the character of arguments about Latin scripts beyond recognition.[53] No one had examined and illustrated so wide a range of manuscripts as Mabillon did. Inaccurate though his plates often were in detail, their impact was explosive.[54] Early modern philologists and antiquarians, as Francis Haskell and others have shown, rarely used their eyes to good effect.[55] Even when they dug an actual site, as Simon Ditchfield has argued, the text came before the trowel. Fragments of what they had read and sermons they had heard hung before their eyes, forcing them to see scenes of martyrdom on the walls of the Catacombs, though none existed there.[56]

Even when visual evidence about script played a vital role in an argument, scholars might make little effort to capture and display it for their readers. Maffeo Vegio, a papal datary and canon of St Peter's Basilica, explored the old church assiduously. In his treatise on it, he gathered evidence to prove that Constantine had actually founded the basilica, copying out two verses that appeared "on the great triumphal arch" in the nave. The characters used to write them, he claimed, "are very old indeed, and I might almost say senile. They seem to point very clearly to the time of Constantine, when they were written there."[57] Despite his emphasis on the period style of the letters, however, Vegio apparently made no effort to have them reproduced realistically when he quoted the verses, even in a presentation copy of his treatise.

Even in later periods, humanists and antiquarians who took a serious interest in the material qualities of the manuscripts they used often made little or no effort to reproduce their scripts. Agustín examined the Florentine Pandects with great care, and substantially revised the conclusions that Poliziano had drawn from it. Yet he cast his description of the manuscript in general terms: "that most ancient monument of the civil law is written with few or no spaces between words and clauses, and the form of the letters seems to come very close to ancient Roman and Greek writing—except that we seemed to notice certain things drawn from the Goths, who were connected to the Latins and Greeks from the times of Theodosius onwards."[58] Even Torelli's edition of the *Pandects*, produced with his help, was not an attempt to provide a facsimile. Agustín based his edition of Festus on an eleventh-century manuscript (Naples, Biblioteca Nazionale, MS IV.A.3). Its earliest portion was lost and the outer columns were largely burned away. Italic type distinguished the work of Festus from the later epitome of it by Paul the Deacon, which Agustín also printed. His edition, as we have seen, was a very rough facsimile of the entries as they appeared in the manuscript. But he did not have type cut on the model of the script of the Neapolitan manuscript.[59]

The erudite archbishop of Canterbury, Matthew Parker, and his secretaries built up a splendid library of medieval manuscripts, many of them in Anglo-Saxon. As they read these and prepared some of them for publication, they became intimately familiar with Anglo-Saxon scripts. The fonts that they had made for their editions of these texts followed manuscript conventions closely.[60] They also collected and examined manuscripts of Latin texts written in what they called "Saxon" script: a flat-topped script closely connected to Anglo-Saxon writing.[61] But in 1574, when Parker edited the Latin life of Alfred the Great that was traditionally ascribed to Asser, he had it printed, not in a facsimile of Saxon script, but in Anglo-Saxon type.[62] This edition, though he described it as a facsimile of the now lost original, misrepresented it systematically.[63]

Even scholars who had exceptional experience in the study of manuscripts cited brief and vague passages from earlier scholars' work, as if these could somehow give their arguments more authority. In 1606 the antiquarian Henry Spelman drew up a list of Latin abbreviations and their resolutions for the use of his sons.[64] This work, on which beginning students still relied in the nineteenth century, reflected his considerable direct knowledge of manuscripts.[65] A copy in the British Library includes somewhat later "Notes on Manuscript Books."[66] The notes begin with a very broad statement: "Other things being equal, the older books are, the better they are said to be."[67] A more detailed observation comes next, with a reference to back it up: "Books accurately written in uncials, or capitals as they are called, are of high quality and reliability. Aubert le Mire at the end of the Chronicle of Jerome, Antwerp 1608, in the margin."[68] The reference is precise, but it does nothing but repeat a brief and general statement. In his edition of the *Chronicle* of Eusebius and Jerome and related works, the Flemish ecclesiastical historian Le Mire reproduced the colophon of his "very ancient manuscript" of the *Chronicle,* in capitals. Next to that, his marginal note stated: "For it is accurately written in uncials or capitals, as they are called: manuscripts of this kind are of the highest quality and reliability."[69] Citations like this one give the impression that in the seventeenth and eighteenth centuries, even experienced manuscript users felt themselves to be poorly supplied with detailed, expert guidance in print. Using the processing techniques that Ann Blair and Helmut Zedelmaier have reconstructed, they excerpted texts of very different value and recycled what they found in their own work.[70]

LEARNING FROM THE WRITING MASTERS

Mabillon, by contrast, insisted in the second edition of his book that only rigorous practice and direct experience—only the viewing of dozens of documents—could equip a scholar to practice his new art, by training and focusing his senses: "All you need in this matter is eyes: but I want expert eyes."[71] The friends with whom he had compiled his book had had eyes of this sort, not blinded by prejudice. The judge of manuscripts, he explained, needed the kind of discriminating visual skills possessed by master artisans. At its sharpest, the trained sensibility of such a master yielded immediate insight into the nature of an object: a process that resembled an instinctual recognition of the aura of genuineness.

> Genuine documents have a sort of stamp of truthfulness about them, which often ravishes the eyes of experts at first sight. In the same way, expert goldsmiths sometimes distinguish real gold from fake by touch alone; painters distinguish original examples of panels from copies; and numismatists, finally, always distinguish genuine coins from spurious ones by their appearance alone.[72]

Mabillon's own visual acuity comes through in what Peter Rück called his *"graphische Regesten"*—compressed graphical records—of documents, which sometimes abbreviated the actual texts, but found room to reproduce the visual signs of their genuineness: seals, monograms of rulers, and designs.[73] When it came to the study of literary scripts, Mabillon hinted—though he never stated—that a particular group of expert artisans had given him essential help in framing his new form of scholarship. These artisans had sharpened their sensitivity to what they saw by undertaking systematic and rather prosaic exercises. Mabillon, we will see, did much the same.

For a first clue as to the identity of these artisans we can turn to Daniel van Papenbroeck, Mabillon's adversary. An expert antiquarian, he was experienced in the study of buildings and monuments as well as documents and manuscripts.[74] He had hunted and copied historical and hagiographical manuscripts in libraries across Italy. And he insisted that the whole debate between the Jesuits and the Benedictines revolved around one minute but vital point: "the form of the letters." Though he worked from facsimiles, he insisted that these had been made with exquisite care. One fellow Jesuit, whom Papenbroeck quoted, recalled his working method: "I tried first to render the details very accurately at the glass window, so that the letters were visible through the sheet placed on the membrane; then, once I had taken the paper off the parchment, I went over each letter, one by one, with a sharper pen."[75] Antiquarians had always confronted the problem of how to transport the immovable across space: how to make massive stones and precious coins accessible, in accurate copies, to colleagues across Europe. They showed endless ingenuity in devising techniques for reproducing antiquities.[76] Students of documents and manuscripts also worked on material objects that could not be moved. Accordingly, they faced another version of the same problem. Papenbroeck's facsimiles were made by tracing: this became the palaeographer's counterpart to the epigraphist's squeezes and the numismatist's molds.

To collect the images for his book, Mabillon and his friends asked scholars and librarians across Europe to provide precise specimens from early manuscripts in their custody, working exactly as Papenbroeck had described, tracing the original letter by letter, tongue in teeth. In July 1679 Bigot asked for help from Magliabechi. His letter reveals both how Mabillon's facsimiles were made and how carefully his associates were taught to work:

> By your love of letters, I beg you to have the first two lines of the [Medici] *Aeneid* copied for me. To that end I am sending you a piece of transparent paper to put on top of the writing. After the paper is put on top of the writing, you have to sketch the writing, as it is in the manuscript, with pen and ink. I think it's a lovely device. You will take care to stretch the paper that you put on top of the writing so that when the paper expands, the writing does not become larger with it, and so fails to portray the writing of the manuscript.[77]

Bigot went on to ask for a transcript from the Florentine Pandects. Even when manuscripts lacked a firm date, he pointed out, "the comparison of the scripts will make it possible to conjecture the time in which they were written."[78]

Tracing was not a novelty in seventeenth-century Europe. The manuscript collection of artists' practices compiled by the erudite physician Turquet de Mayerne in the early seventeenth century includes detailed instructions on how to make what might now be called tracing paper. Recommended materials included the allantois (amniotic membrane) of a cow's embryo, the pericardium of an ox, or paper from Lyon or Venice. Preparations were elaborate. The paper had to be rubbed with linseed oil, turpentine, or pork fat and then dried. The allantois could easily attract worms, and a marginal note recommended keeping it "in a portfolio and in urine." The utility of some of these materials was disputed. Where the text recommends beef pericardium, an interlinear note replies: "completely useless." Apparently, though, these materials actually could be used, with an English lead pencil, to transfer a portrait sketch.[79] We must imagine that across Europe, librarians and scholars laid sheets of oiled paper or scraped animal membrane on the most precious manuscripts in their collections, filled their pens, and traced their letters. Bianchini followed Mabillon's example when he sent "Chinese paper" to be used in tracing the script of the Farnese codex of the *Liber pontificalis*—though in the event, the "expert scribe" who did the work copied the page in question on ordinary paper.[80] Others were more successful: Scipione Maffei, for example, made extensive use of oiled paper for tracing manuscripts. He remarked enthusiastically that "this favor is granted in all the royal libraries."[81]

Opposites coincided: Papenbroeck and Mabillon adopted the same technique. And that provides a second, vital clue. Papenbroeck recalled that when he and Gotfrid Henschen worked in Florentine libraries in fall and winter 1661–1662, they could not hire a scribe who was "skilled in the ancient characters, and especially the Greek ones," and had to do their copying themselves.[82] Tracing had long formed part of scribal practice. In a digression in Erasmus's book on the correct pronunciation of Latin and Greek, his two protagonists, Lion and Bear, discuss the best way to teach a young boy to write well. Bear treats script as a serious art form: "Calligraphy, like painting, has a pleasure of its own, and not only does the writer linger over its execution, but also the reader over its appreciation."[83] After a long discussion of the best way to form Greek and Latin letters, Bear makes a practical suggestion: "Ingenuity can suggest many ways of helping a boy to learn. One possibility is to put the model under transparent parchment so that the boy can draw his nib over the lines that are showing through."[84] Evidently, both the Jesuits and the Benedictines used an established scribal practice to make their facsimiles. Could the old art of the scribe have a substantive connection to the new science of Mabillon?

In his preface, even as he asserted the novelty of his art, Mabillon mentioned predecessors: the Italian writing master Giovanni Battista Palatino and the French writing master Pierre Hamon, who had served as one of the secretaries of King Charles IX. Both men were the sort of

professional scribes whose workloads and numbers expanded dizzyingly in the sixteenth century.[85] The prophets of *Wired* magazine once
told the world that the computer would eliminate paperwork from offices. Instead, it has generated more paper than ever before. The creation of printing did the same. Scribes were more necessary than ever,
and not only because their scripts metamorphized into many of the
fonts that printers needed.[86] Only they could provide genuine—that is,
not printed—documents. Only they could service the needs of govern-
ments and churches for legible paperwork, the demand for which ex-
ploded as bureaucracies grew, in the new age of sale of offices and titles, worldwide shipping networks and blue-water navies, political and
episcopal visitations: the age of Philip II, the "paper king."[87] Printing—
which enabled particularly skillful scribes to reproduce and sell multiple examples of their writing—made some scribes famous and prosperous. Their craft lived on for centuries, its long decay commemorated
by Melville and Dickens.

Writing masters not only taught the scribe's craft, but also provided
model books from which anyone could learn the basics of this deeply
embodied craft, as well as the details of the new italic chancery hand
and the older Gothic forms of official script.[88] Mastering an alphabet
meant learning how to form each letter. From the start, accordingly,
the writing masters helped their readers by breaking scripts down into
alphabets and describing the characteristics of each letter or group of
letters. Ludovico Vicentino degli Arrighi, a scribe in the papal chancery, published the first manual of chancery cursive in 1522. He showed
his readers, for example, how to form all the letters that used the same
"flat and bold stroke," making "the top slightly thicker than the stem,
which is easily done if the first stroke is reversed and then turned on
itself."[89] The exacting nature of his scribal work and the sharpness of
his eye for the sizes and shapes of letters are both attested by a manuscript of Paolo Giovio's history of his time, now in the Morgan Library.
Arrighi copied a draft of one book of Giovio's work. He left a spare leaf
in it, on which he inscribed a number of trial openings for the text. In
them Arrighi can be seen experimenting with different sizes for the
initial A with which the book began.[90] These iterations give a sense of
the passionate attention with which Arrighi made and examined
slanting and vertical lines and curves.

Arrighi's successors offered equally detailed instructions. Giovanno Antonio Tagliente analyzed every letter in chancery cursive, comparing their forms and showing how to maintain uniformity of scale: "The letter *h* is created as if it were the letter *b*, except that its body is not closed on the bottom . . . know that all the bodies of the letters in an alphabet, which are ten in number, that is *a b c d e f g h o p q*, should be of the same size, quality, roundness and dependence."[91] Palatino and Pierre Hamon both laid out multiple script samples, treated exactly as Mabillon would treat his: above or below each specimen appeared its alphabet. Like Mabillon, the writing masters analyzed examples of both documentary and literary scripts.

True, Mabillon emphasized one essential difference between his work and that of the writing masters: "on the whole they showed only examples of recent scripts."[92] But this was the sort of exaggeration to which innovators were and are prone. Palatino, for example, included two examples of "Lombardic" script in his manual. The first, which he printed in 1540, was genuinely Lombardic (see Plate 4).

The second example of "Lombardic" script, which Palatino added in the 1545 edition, was an early medieval minuscule that he reproduced in a looser, more approximate way.[93] Like the esoteric Latin and Oriental scripts that also adorned Palatino's collection, these examples reveal that he cultivated a historical, as well as a practical, interest in writing.

Hamon went much farther than Palatino in this direction. "He had the idea," Mabillon himself conceded, "of publishing examples of all sorts of writing."[94] Unlike his colleagues, moreover,

> Hamon was also interested in collecting ancient examples. He obtained letters from Charles IX, and the privilege of borrowing books from the Royal Library in Fontainebleau, and of consulting the archives of the monasteries of S. Denis and S. Germain. He carried out this project, making some specimens very skillfully, though they were not printed, in the years 1566 and following.[95]

Mabillon's publisher, Louis Billaine, provided him with Hamon's notebook. Mabillon admitted that he had drawn some specimens from it, though he also noted, a little defensively, that his work "was already far along" when he gained access to Hamon's work.[96]

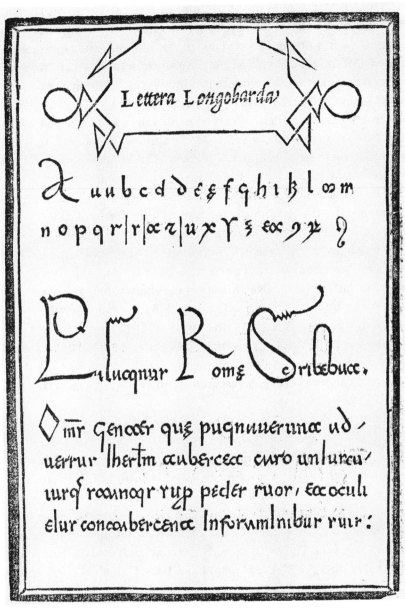

PLATE 4 Giovanni Palatino, *Libro . . . nel qual s'insegna à scriuere ogni sorte lettera* (1556): text in Lombardic script with an analysis of the alphabet. Department of Rare Books and Special Collections, Princeton University Library.

Though Mabillon made no attempt to conceal his use of Hamon, his account of what he learned from the scribe is as incomplete as it is crisp. Hamon's notebook survives, in the Bibliothèque Nationale de France (MS fr. 19166).[97] It contains the sources from which Mabillon learned that Hamon had mounted an impressive research campaign: a letter from Charles IX to Jean Gosselin, garde of the Royal Library, which authorized Hamon to borrow manuscripts; a letter from Charles to the abbot and monks of Saint-Denys, authorizing Hamon to do research in their archive; and a note from Hamon acknowledging that he had borrowed two books from the royal collection.[98]

The manuscript itself contains a rich collection of script samples, interspersed with Hamon's comments. These date and describe his work and show that he took full advantage of the king's support. Hamon copied a full page of Tironian notes—the shorthand devised by Cicero's secretary—from a codex in Saint-Germain-des-Prés, now BNF MS lat. 13160. Above this specimen he wrote: "These Ciceronian notes are more than 1,200 years old. By P. Hamon, scribe to the king and secretary of his Chamber, 1566."[99] Other notes specify that Hamon worked in Saint-Germain-des-Prés in August and September 1566 and in the Royal Library in late September of the same year, and carried on further research in other libraries in March and April 1577.[100]

Hamon had a sharp eye for the most striking forms of script preserved in these collections. In the later sixteenth century, the Royal Library owned one of the fragments of the Urbino Table: an inscription on bronze, dating from the late second century BCE, twelve fragments of which were discovered near Urbino in the late fifteenth century.[101] The Roman legal texts these preserved, which dealt with abuses by magistrates and land distribution, fascinated sixteenth-century scholars. The jurist Barnabé Brisson published the text of the Paris tablet in 1583.[102] A few years later, Isaac Casaubon noted in his copy of Brisson that "this bronze tablet is in the Royal Library now. I saw it at Fontainebleau" (est hodie regia biblio[the]ca haec ta[bu]la aenea: eam nos [vi]dimus Fonti[sbell]aquei).[103] Apparently the tablet was one of the library's treasures. Yet neither Brisson nor Casaubon showed any special interest in the form of its very ancient letters. When Hamon copied extracts from them, he carefully reproduced the epi-

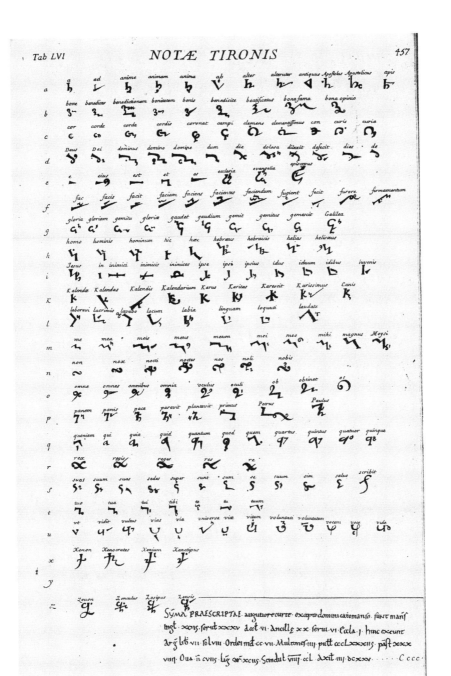

PLATE 5   Jean Mabillon, *De re diplomatica* (1681): Tyronian notes, from Pierre Hamon. Department of Rare Books and Special Collections, Princeton University Library.

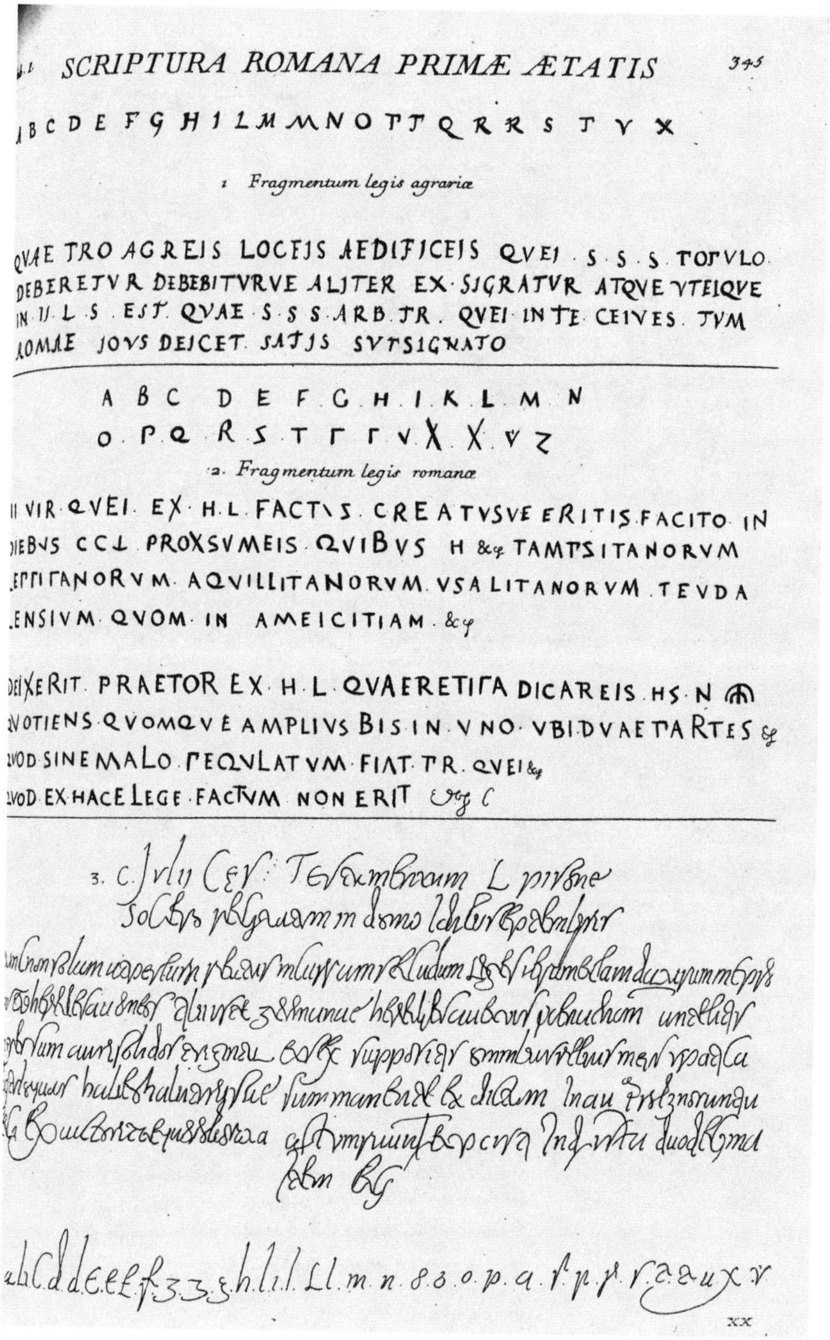
SCRIPTURA ROMANA PRIMÆ ÆTATIS 345

1 *Fragmentum legis agrariæ*

QVAE TRO AGREIS LOCEIS AEDIFICEIS QVEI . S . S . S . TOPVLO
DEBERETVR DEBEBITVRVE ALITER EX SIGRATVR ATQVE VTEIQVE
IN . V . L . S . EST. QVAE . S . S . S . ARB . TR . QVEI . IN TE CEIVES . TVM
ROMAE IOVS DEICET SATIS SVTSIGNATO

A B C D E F G H I K L M N
O P Q R S T T T V X X V Z

2. *Fragmentum legis romanæ*

II VIR QVEI EX H . L . FACTVS CREATVSVE ERITIS FACITO IN
DIEBVS CCL PROXSVMEIS QVIBVS H &c. TAMTSITANORVM
EPTITANORVM AQVILLITANORVM VSALITANORVM TEVDA
ENSIVM QVOM IN AMEICITIAM &c.

DEIXERIT PRAETOR EX H L QVAERETITA DICAREIS HS N
QVOTIENS QVOMQVE AMPLIVS BIS IN VNO VBI DVAE TARTES &c.
QVOD SINE MALO TEQVLATVM FIAT TR . QVEI &c.
QVOD EX HACE LEGE FACTVM NON ERIT &c. C

3.

XX

PLATE 6 Jean Mabillon, *De re diplomatica* (1681): examples of Roman characters, including the supposed will of Julius Caesar, from Pierre Hamon. Department of Rare Books and Special Collections, Princeton University Library.

graphic capitals in which they were written and reconstructed the underlying alphabet.[104] He also examined another item that had caught Brisson's eye: the *Charta plenariae securitatis*, a Ravenna legal papyrus in late Roman cursive.[105] In this case too, Hamon copied a passage and laid out the alphabet in which it was written.[106]

Mabillon took these specimens directly from Hamon: he simply reproduced the latter's treatment of Tironian notes (see Plate 5). In one respect at least, he got more than he bargained for. Hamon, who was as ingenious as he was curious, added two lines to his transcript of the Ravenna papyrus, which identified it as the will of Julius Caesar, and copied this too into his notebook.[107] Mabillon reproduced Hamon's transcript in his book, accepted his identification of the text, and cited it as Caesar's will in his text (see Plate 6).[108] By the time the printers had reached book V of the *De re diplomatica*, Mabillon had reread Brisson, recalled the true date and nature of the late antique document in question, and realized his mistake. He duly corrected it, showing considerable embarrassment—especially as he could not change the sheets on which it appeared, since they had already been printed.[109]

MABILLON MAKES KNOWLEDGE

It seems likely that Mabillon himself did substantial scribal work while the *De re diplomatica* took shape. The plates for the book were engraved by Pierre Giffart (c. 1643–1723). His son, Pierre-François Giffart, prepared the plates for Montfaucon's *Palaeographia graeca* (1709). The contract between Mabillon and Pierre Giffart does not survive, but that for Montfaucon and Giffart jeune was discovered by Henri Omont and has been published twice. It states that Giffart will base his copper plates "sur les desseins donnez par ledit Révérend Père, lesquels dessins luy seront livrez parfaits et achevez & prets à graver" (on the designs provided by the Reverend Father, which will be presented to him in complete form, ready to engrave).[110] They were to contain "old letters, except three or four at most, which will consist of figures."[111] Evidently, Montfaucon designed the facsimiles for his book. It seems probable that Mabillon had done exactly the same.

What matters more than the specific materials Mabillon took from Hamon is the style of analysis and presentation that he derived from the writing masters. The *De re diplomatica* resembles other early modern intellectual projects in which illustration transformed a field of study: for example, the botany of Leonhard Fuchs and the anatomy of Andreas Vesalius. True, Mabillon's book does not have quite the look or feel of a contemporary work on natural philosophy. One early reader, Jean Leclerc, was particularly committed to making philology in all its forms into a systematic discipline. He remarked that "there is a particular art for establishing the age of manuscripts and judging their scripts: a proper treatment of this topic would provide the subject for a substantial volume. Yet no one has treated it until now in a sufficiently systematic way."[112] In a footnote, he clarified his malign statement: "Jean Mabillon has something about this in book 1 of *De re diplomatica:* but it would be profitable for scholars to have this treated more fully."[113] Leclerc was terminally ungracious here. As Ludwig Traube pointed out, "Aber freilich Clericus hat wie gewöhnlich nur kritisiert."[114]

Yet Leclerc had a point. Mabillon did his best to formulate rules: but his passion for what he thought to be true and his refusal to ignore exceptions made his work far from neat or easy to follow.[115] As a diarist, traveling in Italy and elsewhere, he exhibited a Cartesian clarity of mind. As the author of a polemic, writing against Papenbroeck and exploring large, unknown territories, he did not.[116] Montfaucon, by contrast, writing a generation later, revealed that he had employed a kind of experimental method. Working from dated manuscripts to undated ones, he developed not only an effective way to date manuscripts at sight, but also an elegant public demonstration of his powers:

> In the year 1693, I began to make trials. I excerpted samples from any manuscripts in the royal library and hat of Colbert that had a record of the year and the scribe. Then I moved to others without any records, and by making frequent comparisons with the previous ones, that were marked, I attained some skill in this affair. After this, when I went to Italy, I never gave up this effort at research. Going over a range of Greek manuscripts in the libraries, I found that the age I assigned them at a first look agreed very well with the records of the scribes that indicated the year and, where they existed, were placed at the end. And I often did this in the presence of other scholars. There are many witnesses to this, especially at Venice, where I stayed for two months. In Italy, as in France, I excerpted samples as accurately as I could from the best manuscripts of every period.[117]

By staging these demonstrations and then describing them in print, Montfaucon represented himself as in sovereign command both of his materials and of rules for assessing them. Leclerc appreciated what he must have seen as a more philosophical approach to the problem of dating manuscripts. In the 1712 edition of the *Ars critica*, he praised Montfaucon's "outstanding work" and noted its superiority to Mabillon's.[118] It is not easy to draw straight lines from the new philosophy to Mabillon's new antiquarianism.

Still, Mabillon's book too had something in common with innovative forms of natural philosophy and antiquarianism. In each case, artisanal skills and forms of knowledge played a special role, as the authors acknowledged. Fuchs celebrated the artisans who illustrated his work by including portraits of them in his book. Vesalius, who worked intimately and intensively with artists, himself mastered the artisanal skills of the surgeon.[119] Nearer to Mabillon's time, Robert Hooke trained his microscope on human hairs and worm-eaten books. He revealed that every dust mote was a new world inhabited by amazing creatures. Hooke normally did not need to rely on artisans. He belonged to a new, hybrid breed: he was an expert technician as well as an erudite scholar.[120] Closest of all to Mabillon, in style and spirit, were the illustrations made by other contemporary antiquarians. As Stephanie Moser has shown, by the middle of the seventeenth century, Cassiano dal Pozzo and others were using illustrations systematically. By grouping objects of the same type in a single image and by portraying them in a flattened, schematic way that emphasized their shape and function, antiquarians turned illustrations into tools for making new knowledge about the past. Mabillon did much the same—and did so, like his fellow antiquarians, with visual means that were effective but clumsy.[121]

Few early modern natural philosophers emulated Fuchs and named their helpers. Technicians, as Steven Shapin has taught us, usually remained anonymous.[122] So, as Ann Blair has shown, did the amanuenses on whose work Erasmus and many other scholars depended.[123] Mabillon was less generous than Fuchs—but more forthcoming than many other erudite men—when he managed at least to name the artisans of writing from whom he had learned a new way to assess the evidence of scripts. Two hundred, or even a hundred, years before Mabillon, scribes had enjoyed great prestige. Often it was hard to tell scribes and scholars apart.[124] By Mabillon's time, the pursuit of scholarship and the art and craft of writing were clearly separate.[125] And how much did it matter, in the end, who created which forms of scholarship? As a good Benedictine, Mabillon insisted that writing mattered less than other things. At the end of his treatise *On Monastic Studies*, this lover of the written word quoted Jerome: "Whatever time I spend in dictation, in rereading, in correcting, is so much taken from my life. Each dot that my secretary makes is so much taken from my life."[126] Whatever his reasons, Mabillon made it hard for us to see that the road to the history of ancient writing had led through the manuals created by the makers of modern scripts. Perhaps he himself did not realize how far his scholarship depended on the creative art of humanistic scribes.

Still, in one crucial passage he suggested the extent of his debt. Mabillon, as we saw, claimed that he had invented "a new branch of the antiquarian's art." Historians have assumed that he was referring to the antiquarians of his day, with their interest—which he shared—in the material remains of the past. But another meaning of "antiquarius," in ancient and humanist Latin, was "scribe." A number of the most proficient antiquarians of the Renaissance, such as Felice Feliciano and Gerardus Mercator, were also inventive and influential scribes, who combined their deeply embodied craft with more abstract pursuits. What Mabillon created—as he knew better than anyone, but we have forgotten—was a new, richly historicized form of the ancient graphic art of the scribe. Critical paleography began, not in humanistic philology, but in creative calligraphy.

CHAPTER 4

Polydore Vergil Uncovers the Jewish Origins of Christianity

RABBI JESUS

In 1742, J. C. Schöttgen did his best to shock the world of learning. He argued that Jesus, when he came as the Messiah, had done so as a Jew. The circumstantial evidence, he insisted, was clear. Those who heard Jesus preach called him "rabbi" (John 1:38, 1:50). He dressed as the rabbis did. The "coat without seams" (John 19:23) that the soldiers divided after they crucified Jesus was identical to the seamless garment that the Jewish masters had worn: at least as described by the Danish scholar Georg Ursinus in his *Antiquitates Hebraeorum Scholastico-Academicae.*[1] Comparison of practices yielded a vision of Jesus radically different from that of the synoptic Gospels: not an opponent of the Jewish leaders, but one of them.

True, Schöttgen admitted, Jesus was not merely a rabbi: he was the greatest and most learned rabbi of them all. In the quality and character of his learning—for example, the speed with which he mastered the sources and the methods for interpreting them—he left the others "parasangs behind him." He became a teacher on his own authority, without the ceremonies and laying on of hands that humans needed to give them legitimacy.[2]

Comparisons revealed more: Jesus's mastery was founded on the very codes he came to suspend. The many points at which he corrected the Mishnah made clear that he knew it, even as the phrase he used to do so—ἐγὼ δὲ λέγω ὑμῖν (Matt. 5:34: but I say to you), which translated the Hebrew v'ani omer lachem—was "a phrase that the rabbis regularly used."[3] The fact that he drew on existing Jewish prayers also showed his mastery of Jewish codes and practices. Jesus did not use the eighteen blessings traditionally ascribed to the men of the Great Synagogue because they had some independent value, as even more enthusiastic Christian scholars had claimed. Rather, he did so because his Jewish followers knew them and he had to speak in a language familiar to them.[4] Like the other rabbis, Jesus "taught in public places, in the temple, school, synagogue and elsewhere." Like them, he spoke through parables, even if he did not use their set phrase "what is the thing like?"[5] Like them, he had a court that followed him. Like them, he learned a craft. Like them, he disputed—though he did so with a skill and power they could not match. In the Talmud, Schöttgen wrote, "there is almost no page that does not propose disputations about matters of no importance." Jesus, by contrast, "had such great powers in disputing that he easily defeated all opponents."[6]

Rabbis were given a key to symbolize their right to interpret sacred scripture in public. Jesus, too, possessed a key: the "keys to the kingdom of heaven" that he gave Peter (Matt. 16:19). Disciples called their rabbis by their title, not by their name. The disciples of Jesus did the same. The cumulative evidence of these comparisons yielded a definitive conclusion: "The whole world knows how Christ trained his disciples, and how much they profited from his learning. Even the Jews know this, as they mention them, and the miracles they did in the name of their master, in the Talmud. Hence they teach us beyond a doubt that Jesus, their master, was the supreme Rabbi."[7]

It would be easy—and anachronistic—to argue that Schöttgen's comparisons were prescient. Parallels to them crop up everywhere in the most respectable of modern secondary literature on the Jesus movement and the Jews, though they are used very differently. In fact, though, they belonged to the ordinary scholarship of the seventeenth and eighteenth centuries, not the twenty-first. True, Schöttgen earned his living, not as a professor of Oriental languages, but as a librarian and then as the headmaster of Gymnasien in Leipzig, Stargard, and Dresden—a job, according to Christian Gottlob Heyne, whose holders begged to be hanged because of the sheer poverty it involved. Yet he was a known expert on Jewish letters—especially the earliest forms of rabbinical writing, such as the Mishnah. He evaluated some of these as virtually Christian, and did so not only in his Latin *Horae hebraicae et talmudicae,* which was aimed at a small and learned readership, but also in his German periodical, *Der Rabbiner.*[8] When Schöttgen picked out parallels between Jesus and the rabbis—and indeed, when he insisted that no human rabbi, however great a prodigy, could compete with the Messiah who had transcended rabbinical law and learning—he worked on the basis of expert knowledge of the most relevant sources then known. If his argument was a paradox, it was also fiercely and fully established—even if, as critics of the comparative method might point out, Schöttgen took full advantage of the comparatist's traditional liberty to use both parallels and their absence as evidence of a historical connection.

THE JEWISH ORIGINS OF CHRISTIANITY:
AN EARLY MODERN HYPOTHESIS

Schöttgen's views exemplify, in a strong form, one version of the comparative study of early Christianity and Second Temple Judaism that flourished, in various quarters, from the fifteenth to the eighteenth centuries—and that has been mostly forgotten by modern specialists. Even some contemporary experts on the New Testament who are steeped in the history of their discipline may find this notion a surprise. No historian of religion has devoted more thought to comparison, as a method, a metaphor, and much else, than the late Jonathan Smith. In *Drudgery Divine,* his crackling study of comparative approaches to early Christianity, he revealed the massive harm that comparison had wrought to his subject. From Isaac Casaubon writing in the 1610s to our own period, scholars have found in comparison, not the rich and stimulating hermeneutical method that they should have found—"a playful enterprise of reconstruction and reconstitution" that allows the scholar to negotiate relations between theory and data in creative ways—but something more like a knife with one edge, Smith argued, and that one quite dull. Comparison has enabled Protestants to argue for the historical uniqueness of the earliest Christianity. They have connected such developments as rituals of initiation with pagan parallels that serve as evidence of accommodation, and by doing so, they have extracted Jesus and his movement from their original Jewish world. The end of comparison, in this sense, is to establish the incomparability, known in advance, of the movement Jesus led with any previous form of religious life.[9]

The case of Schöttgen suffices, on its own, to suggest that comparisons played a wider range of roles than are dreamed of in Smith's historical theology. They could reveal, as well as conceal, the Jewish matrix in which Christianity first took shape. It is only fair to note that decades have passed since Smith wrote: decades during which Schöttgen and his many colleagues have emerged from oblivion, in early modern and Jewish history, if not so much in New Testament studies. Aaron Katchen, Carsten Wilke, Eric Nelson, and others have revealed that something like a methodological revolution took place early in the seventeenth century. Biblical scholars from Hugo Grotius and Petrus Cunaeus to John Lightfoot used evidence from the Mishnah and many other texts to explicate the New Testament.[10] Sometimes they did more than explicate texts. Gerald Toomer's rich intellectual biography of John Selden states without equivocation that Selden treated the earliest Christianity as a "Jewish sect."[11]

More important still, when Selden attended the early sessions of the Westminster Assembly, which was convened to design a new church for England, he insisted that comparison must provide the foundation for any truly Christian ecclesiology. As the eighteenth-century ecclesiastical historian John Strype made clear, several of the participants in the Westminster Assembly—especially Selden and John Lightfoot—took what they called the Jewish Church as the model for the Christian Church and drew on a vast range of sources to reconstruct its ways of praying and its position in the Jewish state:

> For these Divines in their Enquiries into the Primitive Constitution of the Christian Church and Government thereof in the Apostles Days, built much upon the Scheme of the Jewish Church; which the first Christians being Jews, and bred up in that Church, no question conformed themselves much to: And therefore those leveled at settling the Like Government in the English Church.[12]

It did not take the ministers long to tire of Selden's lectures about the esoteric contents of his library, though the interpretation of the Jewish law and commonwealth in which he did pioneeer work had a lasting impact on political theory.[13] The nature of the scholar's agenda, and his ambitions for it are clear.

Relative celebrities like these men, of course, were not the only ones to draw on rabbinical learning. The interest in comparing early Christianity with rabbinical sources leaped over national and denominational lines. No early Enlightenment figures differed more in training, assumptions, or larger cultural ambitions than Campegius Vitringa, a professor of theology at Franeker, far up in the Dutch North, and Benedetto Bacchini, a Jansenist, Benedictine of Monte Cassino, editor of a lively journal that commented on all the scientific advances of his time, and ally of Ludovico Antonio Muratori. Yet they converged in researching and writing elaborate analyses of the early Christian Church. Vitringa insisted that every structure and office of the early church, from the diaconate to the diocese, had been transferred, as if by messenger RNA, not from the Temple—which had often been identified as the source of Christian practices in earlier scholarship—but from the exactly similar ecclesiastical DNA of the existing Jewish synagogue. Bacchini agreed—so far as the synagogues of the East, with their largely Jewish membership, were concerned. In the western parts of the Roman Empire, however, he argued that the Christian Church had not grown from Jewish roots but rather crystallized in a brand-new form, without inheriting older institutions or practices.[14] Within the larger consensus, in other words, plenty of room remained for arguments: arguments many of which had to be drawn from the rabbinical sources that were as familiar as the New Testament itself to such men. Then as now, in other words, the scholar could choose from a broad palette of full, and partial, comparative approaches—and then as now, it was certain that no new discovery was likely to prove a thesis absolutely right or wrong.

Many questions remain. When did Christian scholars begin to make systematic comparisons between early Christianity and Judaism as it was in the centuries around the beginning of the Common Era? When did they begin to look systematically at the earliest Jewish sources available to them? When, to put it more sharply, did the ancient contrast between Synagoga and Ecclesia mutate into something

more like an inquiry? This chapter is a first look at some of these questions. As will become clear, the direction from which the winds of
intellectual change blew can be surprising.

COMPARATISTS AND ANTIQUARIANS

The comparison between Christianity and other religions was deeply
rooted in the world of antiquarian scholarship: and many scholars, very
reasonably, have argued that the origins of comparison in the early
modern study of early Christianity lie in that tradition. Consider, for
a start, the work of Guillaume Du Choul, a mid-sixteenth-century antiquarian from Lyons whose expertise in the study of ancient coins
won recognition across Europe. Du Choul took a special interest in
Roman religion, to which he devoted a heavily illustrated book. Careful
illustrations drawn from coins and reliefs portrayed intact Roman
temples and the rituals that took place in them. Du Choul's Roman
priests carried sacred implements, fed sacred chickens, and slaughtered
animals and caught their blood. Nothing could seem more alien from
Christianity.[15] Du Choul's interests sometimes seem to hark back to
the scholarship and art of the fifteenth century, when antiquarians and
artists collaborated to evoke the full, blood-spattered sexual energy of
the fantastic rituals of the ancients. On April 19, 1485, the well-
preserved body of a Roman girl was discovered in a sarcophagus on
the Appian Way. The whole city came to admire her and push her still-
flexible nose to left and right, until at last the pope, fearing a revival of
paganism, had her body secretly removed and buried.[16] Antiquarian im-
agery often served to mark the radical break between classical culture
and Christianity. By placing the birth of Jesus or the rebirth of Lazarus
in a splendid scene of ruins, artists could emphasize the distance between pagan death and darkness and the new light of Christianity.[17]

Yet Du Choul did not simply show readers how the Romans worshipped. He emphasized the dignity of the Roman priests and their
garb, such as the Alba Longa of pure white linen. In passing, he mentioned many analogies between Roman and Christian practice: Vestal
Virgins had their hair shaved, like Christian nuns; pagan priests prayed
facing east, "as we still do"; pagans worshipped the thunder bolt of
Zeus, according this symbol the real power to protect them from light-

ning, as Christians worshipped the lamb that symbolized Jesus and the dove that stood for the holy spirit.[18]

Such similarities had what Margaret Hodgen long ago called "documentary properties."[19] They could identify the pagan shrines that had become churches and reveal the forgotten origins of Christian rituals. Du Choul noted repeatedly that Roman temples—from the Pantheon in Rome to much smaller, ruinous shrines in his own France—had been converted for Christian use. The same applied to the vestments that Christian priests wore, the postures they assumed, and the liturgies they performed: "If we look with care, we will learn that several of the institutions of our religion were taken and translated from the ceremonies of the Egyptians and the pagans: for example, the tunics and surplices, their crowns, their bowing of the head around the altar, the ceremonies of sacrifice, the music of the temples, their adorations, prayers and supplications, processions and litanies, and many other things that our priests use in our mysteries."[20] True, he went on to argue that Christians were superior to pagans; they, unlike the pagans, understood the true purpose of these ceremonies.[21] But the warp and weft of Christian religious life, so Du Choul argued, came from ancient paganism. To examine the reliefs and coins that depicted ancient Roman priests at prayer was to see the Christian priests who had replaced them.

Du Choul was hardly the first scholar to make such comparisons or to draw such conclusions from them. For more than a century, antiquarians had been scrutinizing the components of Christian churches in order to establish which of them were transformed pagan temples. Poggio Bracciolini surveyed the ruins of Rome in his *De varietate fortunae*, which he wrote in the 1430s and 1440s. In the Forum, he noted, a splendid ancient wall made of squared stones, originally part of the temple of Romulus, "is today consecrated to Cosmas and Damian."[22] "Next to this," he continued, "was the temple of Antoninus and Faustina, now dedicated to Saint Lawrence. In its portico, many marble columns have escaped ruin."[23] The Temple of Castor and Pollux had metamorphosed into Santa Maria Nova.[24] At the foot of the Aventine Hill, near the Tiber, the Temple of Vesta had become the Church of Santo Stefano alle Carrozze.[25] Poggio was often wrong about the details: Santa Maria Nova actually stood on the ruins of the Temple of

Venus and Rome, and the Temple of Vesta was really the Temple of Hercules in the Forum Boarium. Still, his reader came away with a clear sense that a close look at any ancient church might reveal the remains of a place of pagan ritual and sacrifice.

Flavio Biondo, who charted the antiquities of Italy as well as those of Rome in the middle decades of the fifteenth century, also kept a sharp eye out for the material remains of pagan worship. In his *Roma triumphans*, he set out to survey Roman institutions as they had been in the time of Augustine: a time, as he and his readers knew, when more than one religion flourished in the Roman Empire.[26] Biondo's statements about ancient religion, in this case and others, were not entirely consistent. At the start of his work, he declared how much he detested pagans and all their works:

> Before I begin I would like to state, however, that in speaking about the Romans' religion and that of other Gentiles, when I impart information about the names of the gods along with the words for their temples, temple buildings [aedes], and holy precincts [fana], I have the intention, [first], of indicating at the same time the places in the city of Rome where they were situated; then, by demonstrating the foulness, impiety and also the utter levity of the rites that the gods of the ancients—demons, as the prophet says—required to be employed in their sacrifices, of making the sanctity of the Christian religion more welcome to men of good will.[27]

Yet when he analyzed precise cases, he argued that Christians had deliberately appropriated pagan buildings and cult objects in order to win over those who had worshipped them. The basilica of Sant'Ambrogio in Milan possessed, as it still does, a short column bearing a bronze statue of a serpent, brought to Milan from Constantinople around 1001. Biondo identified it as an idol, used by an ancient pagan cult, and claimed that Ambrose had deliberately installed it, for religious reasons:

> Marveling at this madness, Ambrose, the holy Doctor of the Church, decided to keep this Ophion, later called Serpent in Latin, in which state it was worshipped by the Italic Gentiles in imitation of the Phoenicians, in his church in Milan—even now it is seen quite intact—in order to make the holy religion of our God Jesus Christ more welcome to Christians.[28]

We will encounter versions of this rationale again.

Appropriating Roman practices, for Biondo, was a reasonable decision. The Romans themselves had been selective as they built up their religion, and "in their adoption of gods avoided many of the follies and superstitions of the Egyptians, Phoenicians and Greeks."[29] Moreover, for all their errors, they had exemplified one quality that Christians also regarded as central to religion:

> The Romans' false religion furnishes much that I must tell of, but it is all to be repudiated and is completely abominable, save for one aspect and this, I think, a Christian ought to embrace and put in the best light. That is, the fact that the Roman people were scrupulously devoted to religious observances [sacra], as of course they called them, and to religion.[30]

Even Augustine had admitted that the Romans were pious. Biondo, accordingly, was not advancing outré arguments when he noted repeatedly that Christian religious practices resembled Roman ones.[31] Roman sacrifices for the dead resembled Christian masses on the seventh day after death or on the dead person's birthday; their public supplications looked like Christian litanies or "public days of prayer": the ancient priests' announcement that "the omens are good" was akin to the moment, in a Christian Mass, when the priest turns from the altar to the congregation and asks in a low voice for all to pray for him. Biondo traced in detail the resemblances between an imperial and a papal funeral (in each, he noted, a wax effigy represented the dead man and served as the object of mourning; and in each, boys waved fans to keep flies off the effigies).[32] And while he insisted that the foolish pagans, unlike Christians, had misunderstood the reasons for their ceremonies, some contemporaries who shared his interest in the details of the ancient world did not—or at least did not consistently—agree.

No Christian student of Roman religion viewed ancient rituals with more optimism than the late fifteenth-century Bolognese scholar Filippo Beroaldo. He drew up a sprawling commentary on one of the great documents of Roman life and religion: the *Metamorphoses* of Apuleius.[33] Like Du Choul, Beroaldo looked for parallels because they revealed sources. The priests of Isis tied their rituals to particular hours: "so," Beroaldo remarked, "our priests consider the first, third, sixth and ninth hours proper for certain sacrifices."[34] The priests of Isis shaved their heads; "this ritual of the followers of Isis," Beroaldo argued, "seems to be the reason why our priests too are forbidden to grow their hair."[35] Romans were forbidden to look down on the gods as they passed by from upper rooms: "hence, when religious processions take place, we too forbid boys and girls to look down from windows, that is, to look on them in the lower place from a higher one."[36] Beroaldo used the narrated procession in Apuleius as Du Choul used the recorded rituals in his coins and reliefs. As he detected resemblance after resemblance, he wrote, "as I read this, I feel that I see and recognize all the glory of our ceremonies."

Beroaldo came to a sweeping conclusion:

> As I keep thinking about these customs of pagan cult I come to the view that almost everything pertaining to the celebration of our rites has been taken over and transferred from them. Undoubtedly from the religion of the pagans are linen vestments, the shaved heads of priests, the turning around at the altar, the sacrificial procession, strains of music. The obeisance, prayers and many other things of that sort that our priests solemnly employ in our mysteries have undoubtedly been taken over from the ceremony of the ancients.[37]

If this sounds familiar, there is a reason. Du Choul's similar declaration, quoted earlier, is translated from it, word for word. Nor was he the only writer to find Beroaldo's sharp, explicit statement attractive. Joannes Boemus, as we saw, summarized it in his compendium of the world's customs and rituals, which first appeared in 1520:

> For (as Philip Beroalde writeth in his commentary vpon Apuleius booke, entituled the Golden Asse) the moste parte of the deuices that we vse in our Christian religion, ware borowed out of the maner of Thegiptians. As surpluis and rochet, and suche linnen garmentes: shauen crownes, tournings at the altare, our masse solempnities, our organes, our knielinges, crouchinges, praiers, and other of that kinde.[38]

Historians often cite Boemus's influential work as evidence that the discovery of previously unknown peoples and religions spurred the development of comparative study of religions.[39] But he evidently learned from the fifteenth-century antiquarians as well. Their comparisons between their own world and antiquity enhanced his ability to compare the rites and customs of many peoples in his own time. As John Howland Rowe wrote in 1965, inspired by the work of Arnaldo Momigliano, "men trained in this [humanist] tradition were better prepared than any of their contemporaries to observe and record contemporary cultural differences."[40]

These men differed in one crucial respect, however. Du Choul, who was writing in a time of censorship and religious war, insisted that the pagans had not understood what they were doing. Beroaldo, who was writing in the last sunlit years of fifteenth-century syncretism, the age of Ficino and Pico, argued that the pagan ceremonies had been taken over because the pagan religion itself had anticipated Christianity. Lucius's prayer to Isis, he wrote, "could be applied most appropriately to the goddess of the Christians, so that whatever is said in this place about the moon or Isis could be said reverently and properly about the blessed Virgin."[41] When Lucius hesitated to accept the ascetic life that came with dedicating himself to Isis, Beroaldo compared him to Augustine, demanding chastity "but not yet."[42] And when Lucius underwent initiation and recognized the priests who carried out the ceremony as his true parents, Beroaldo explained, "a man who is truly consecrated and has been made a pure and holy priest through a kind of death, puts off this irreligious life and is carried away by the prompting of the divine will through the supernal and infernal regions so that he sees and recognizes the things that the apostle Paul saw and recognized."[43] Paganism, in Beroaldo's view, offered its followers not only the same rituals as Christianity, but also the same sort of deep, genuine religious experience. Antiquarian comparison did not, in its origins, come with the assumptions that—as Smith argues—often encrust its later forms. And some writers—for example, Niccolò Machiavelli—rejected any analogy between the religion of the Romans, which had celebrated bloody sacrifices and filled the ancients with manly courage, and that of the Christians, whose rituals are "gentle solemnities rather than magnificent ones, and have nothing of energy or ferocity in them" and whose religion glorified "humble and contemplative men."[44] Antiquarian comparisons could differ strikingly in their implications.

For all their elegance and intricacy, these essays in comparative religion resemble later efforts to root Christianity in Greek and Roman, rather than Jewish, culture. The antiquarians worked on Roman sites and from Latin and, occasionally, Greek, sources. They were warmed by the possibility of endowing Christianity with the cultural prestige and lost grandeur of pagan rituals. After all, even Biondo, who dutifully expressed his horror at ancient devil-worship, admitted that when he came upon an ancient relief of ecstatic women, he could not move until he had examined it thoroughly.[45] Beroaldo, of course, made clear that he felt the same way even when he used his mind's eye to examine an ancient festival. Schöttgen's Renaissance ancestors remain unidentified.

HISTORY, COMPILATION, AND THE JEWS: JOANNES BOEMUS AND POLYDORE VERGIL

Modern readers of Du Choul have rightly emphasized his interest in tracing classical origins for Christian buildings and institutions. Yet Du Choul, like other Renaissance compilers, did not restrict himself to classical texts, or even to humanist antiquarians like himself. Toward the end of his book, he explained that when Egyptians took priestly vows, their friends gave them gifts and a feast, and "the first priest, whom we could call, in our religion, the bishop, taught them, and gave them a book in the form of a scroll, as those of the Hebrews do today."[46] As usual, he found the origins of Christian rules and customs elsewhere:

> The Romans had another way of organizing their priestly ranks: as with the great Pontiff, the lesser Pontiffs, Flamens, Archiflamens, and Protoflamens, just as we have the Pope, the Cardinals, Bishops, Archbishops and Patriarchs, colleges, like those of canons, and satellites, like the Knights of Saint John of Jerusalem. And the ancients obeyed all of them with great reverence and honor, painstakingly observing their religion.[47]

Frances Muecke, in a luminous article on Biondo's studies of ancient religion and their impact, notes that Du Choul was using unclassical terms here. She also makes clear that Biondo, for all his passionate interest in material remains, was also a textual scholar, whose works consisted to a great extent of extracts from earlier writers.[48] In this case, Du Choul followed another, earlier textual scholar. Guillaume

Durand, a thirteenth-century canonist, laid out the forms and sources of high medieval Catholic liturgy in his massive *Rationale divinorum officiorum*. Long before Du Choul, Durand had drawn on earlier writers to list the orders of Roman priests: "according to Isidore the pagan temple rituals included Archiflamines, Protoflamines, Flamines and priests."[49] For Durand, though, unlike Du Choul, the Christian ordering of priestly ranks resembled other systems as well as that of the Romans. The Hebrews had had a similar range of offices. "In the temple were the high priest, as Melchisedech, lesser priests, Levites, Nathinaei, extinguishers of lights."[50]

Boemus came across the same passage in Durand that struck Du Choul, but he emulated the eclecticism of his source. After listing the Roman priesthoods, he continued: "And by like ordre among the Hebrues: an high Bishoppe, and inferiour Priestes, Leuites, Nazareis [Nazirites], candle quenchers, commaunders of Spirites, Churche Wardeines, and syngers, which we call Chantours after the Frenche."[51] The apostles had decided that they would build a Christian hierarchy, modeled on the Roman political hierarchy. Peter, who ruled the universal church, resembled the emperor, who ruled the universal state.[52] In creating the new church, however, the Christians also drew on the law of Moses, which Christ had come, not to destroy, but to fulfill.[53] When a bishop performed the Eucharist, for example, he wore "sanctified garments drawn from the Mosaic law," all fifteen of which Boemus listed.[54] In other cases, Hebrew precedents worked less directly. Preaching "was not really established, but grew up by the example of Nehemiah and Ezra."[55] Boemus agreed that the early church had emulated the pagans, but he revealed that Jewish models and mores had also played a crucial role in creating the new religion. Boemus's chapter on the development of Christianity made clear that rituals had developed and changed over time. Once he had drawn up this account and made it comparable to those of other religions, from ancient paganism to Islam, Boemus took a new direction: he began to record local practices in contemporary Christian life, acknowledging that they were as curious, and sometimes as inexplicable, as those of any other religion.

A year after Boemus's book appeared, an older Italian humanist published a more systematic account of the early development of Christianity. Like Boemus, Polydore Vergil extended the comparative method that he too had learned from Beroaldo and Biondo to include the Jews. In 1499 Polydore had issued a neat little work in three books on the inventors of everything from religion and obelisks to printing: a subject that fascinated his contemporaries, keen to work out whether possessing the compass, gunpowder, and the printing press really made them superior to the ancients.[56] In 1521 he added five new books, in which he followed the history of Christianity, feature by feature. Systematically compiling the evidence, text by text, Vergil traced the development of churches and prayers, the parochial system of organization, the giving of communion, and much more. An iconoclast by temperament, Vergil had made himself unloved in England, where he served as a collector of papal revenues, by informing the English aristocracy that they were not really descended from a noble Trojan named Brutus. In his history of the church, he innovated on a much larger scale, as much in the hope of exposing superstitions as in the hope of elucidating the past.[57]

Polydore set out to provide something that no one else had done before him: an account of the church, external and internal, that would identify the origins and trace the development of every aspect of its organization and life: prayer and sacrifice, priestly vestments and canonical hours, marriage and the kiss of peace. He did not draw on original sources in Hebrew and Aramaic, as Selden and Schöttgen would, or ask Jews what they could tell him about the rituals practiced in the Temple or in synagogues in the time of Jesus or the Fathers. His book looks like an extension of methods he probably mastered as a schoolboy: above all, the practice of taking systematic notes on everything he had read.The most prominent and influential of Renaissance teachers, as we have seen, treated the making of commonplace books as indispensable to anyone who hoped to become a scholar.[58]

Polydore said little about his working methods. By contrast, Boemus—whose work resembled Polydore's in many ways—described his book as a mosaic of excerpts: "In my leisure hours, O most serious connoisseur of histories, I have gathered, and then written out in this register, the more remarkable customs, rites, and laws of the peoples, and the places they inhabit." After listing his ancient and modern sources, he claimed that he had added nothing to them: "This will allow you to have them recorded in a single book, and it will be easy for you to find them when you need them.[59] Boemus, as we have seen, oversimplified his account of his own practices. But he seems to have depicted Polydore's methods with graphic precision. Where Boemus organized his book geographically, Polydore ordered his systematically, by topics—much as Bernardo Bembo organized his Zibaldone in the same period.[60]

Polydore revolutionized the study of early Christianity, not by bringing new sources into play, but rather by turning what had become a standard method of self-education into one of composition. His lists of topics, or *loci*, became the table of contents for his book. And the materials he compiled—which came from standard and nonstandard sources, including compendia of many kinds, but were artfully arranged and regularly revised—developed into something that the Christian world had not seen: an account of Christian history that was, in our terms rather than Polydore's, interdisciplinary in its scope and informed by multiple traditions. His book became a great arcade, in which readers could chase up, find, and learn from every existing interpretation of Christian history.

Polydore studied with Beroaldo, and like Du Choul, he copied large passages from Beroaldo's commentary on Apuleius into his book.[61] Like Beroaldo and Du Choul, too, he read for similarities and translated them into evidence of origins. To read Polydore was to learn lessons that have become familiar: the pure linen tunics, the shaved heads, and even the final words of the Mass, "Ite, missa est," all came from the pagans. Yet Polydore's approach was not identical to theirs.

Comparison, for Polydore, was a research tool, as precise in its application as the collation of manuscripts was for Angelo Poliziano. Like Poliziano's collations, Vergil's comparisons were meant to transform apparent chaos into neat stories of filiation. The earliest history of Christianity, as he complained, was a bitterly obscure topic: the scholar who hoped to reconstruct the first churches and the practices used in them had almost no sources to go on. Some form of guesswork was unavoidable: "I do not dare to state where the first temple was dedicated to our Saviour after the teachings of the Gospels were disseminated among the nations, lest I seem to engage in divination [divinare] rather than to stick to the truth. Still, in matters that are barely known, it is permissible to guess [coniectare]."[62] Hesitantly, Polydore guessed that the first church might have been in some distant corner of the Christian world—or might have been built by James in Jerusalem.

One assumption provided guidance. Early Christian leaders had found it advisable to adopt existing customs in order to win over those who were used to them. From that starting point, which was richly attested by the Fathers and approved by the antiquarians, Polydore leaped to what were sometimes radical conclusions. Some comparisons tied Christian institutions to earlier pagan ones, which were their sources. Thus, he derived Christian nuns from pagan Vestal Virgins: to the astonishment of readers and the horror of censors.[63] Others pointed elsewhere: "But as not a few practices were established by the Jews, so a good many were either established or taken by chance or decision from other peoples, and they came into such common and customary use as to be considered ours."[64]

Unlike the antiquarians, and like Boemus, from the start Polydore looked to Jewish, as well as pagan, rituals and practices for the sources of Christian ones. He explained at length that the orders and the vestments of Catholic priests were drawn, in large part, from those of their Jewish predecessors: "I explained each of these customs in order, as they were established by the Jews, so that the origin of each, as is my special aim, might be revealed in the most appropriate way. As all of these things were only the shadow of future ones, I will now set out what followed."[65]

Detailed comparisons made clear that the material accoutrements of Catholic priesthood retained a heavily Jewish stamp:

> Our priests have the sacred garments in which they are clad from the Jews . . . and this is shown by the fact that both our bishops and priests wear in part the same vestments, such as the bright sash, the belt, the long tunic, which we call the alb; the hyacinth tunic, and the mitre.[66]

In making this argument Polydore remained within the strictest bounds of orthodoxy. Catholic tradition held that the vestments and practices of Catholic priests reproduced those of the Jewish priests of the first century. In this case, Polydore embroidered only a little on the standard account given by Durand. Like Polydore, Durand explained:

> In the Old Testament there were two tunics, the tunic of fine linen, and the blue tunic. And today as well certain bishops use two tunics,

to show that it is their task to have knowledge of both testaments, so that they may know how to bring out of the Lord's treasure things new and old; or that they may show that they are both deacons and priests. . . . The second tunic ought to be blue, as in olden days it was of the colour of the hyacinth, which imitates the sereneness of the sky. Hence it is a figure of the saints with their heavenly thoughts and lives, and of celestial thought and conversation.[67]

Similarly, Polydore followed and developed existing tradition when he argued that the popes had accepted "the practices of the Jews" when they ordained priests by rank, to serve as ostiaries, readers, exorcists, and so on; and that Boniface I had done the same when he decreed "that no one under thirty be made a priest."[68]

Not all of Polydore's comparisons were conventional. Some, the censors decided, went too far. They could not accept his juxtaposition of pagan and Christian sacrifices: "When the priest turns to the people at the altar, saying *Dominus vobiscum*, this too is taken from the ceremonies of the Hebrews. Their priest turned around during the ritual, aspersing the blood of the slaughtered animal."[69] In all cases, what inspired Polydore as he set the early church back into its context was not antiquarianism alone, but a potent combination of new humanist approach and medieval ecclesiastical learning.

Sometimes, following Beroaldo, Polydore traced Jewish practices, in their turn, back to Egyptian or Pythagorean sources.[70] He learned much from the antiquarians, but the upshot of his work was different. He used church traditions that previous historians had ignored to revise the standard narrative of early Christian history. Eusebius, watching the Jews lose their independence and their holy city after the coming of Christ, denied them any place except as witnesses in the history of Christianity. Yet in later centuries, the church remembered that it had drawn vestments and institutions from the temple and the synagogue. By collecting these traditions systematically, Polydore transformed the problem of telling the Christian story: it could no longer be a narrative stripped of Jewish characters—even if the Jews sometimes transmitted earlier pagan ways, an origin story that would fascinate seventeenth-century scholars.[71] Both Boemus and Polydore showed that compilation could be more than a neutral assembly of information. Each of them made commonplacing into an epistemic tool. For Boemus, it traced networks of connections between Christianity and other religions: a process that could give rise to suspicions that Christianity was not so distinctive as its followers had believed. For Polydore, it showed that Christianity was itself a product of human effort in history: and perhaps one that, like so many other products of human effort, had declined over time.

But Polydore's collection of material not only had a larger historical point, it also had a polemical flavor. True, it is not easy to define Polydore's own religious views—or to follow them as they shifted after the outbreak of the Protestant Reformation. Writing in December 1517, before news of Luther's theses had traveled far, he explained his own enterprise to his brother. The language in which he described his intentions mirrored the complexity of his situation and, perhaps, his own desire to remain safe, while still issuing what amounted to a demonstration that many Catholic institutions were not of Apostolic origin:

> I have sweated through this task. Embracing all the institutions of our religion and other peoples, and examining their origins, wherever they were found, I stuck my results onto the previous edition. As the subject of this part is much more serious, so it has turned out much longer. Now, accordingly, everyone who cares about the religion that reconciles us to God and binds us to him by an indissoluble knot, can, as you requested, find out more easily from what source, and then through what streams—for it is always pleasant to know the origins of everything—ran that great river of ceremonies and rituals, in which at last all mortals may bathe, so that they can lead a peaceful and joyous life here and look forward in firm hope to a heavenly life elsewhere.[72]

When Polydore offered the image of a "great river of ceremonies and rituals," he sounded like an Erasmian or Lutheran critic, using colorful language to show how the accumulation of forms of worship coincided with the decline of Christianity. But a very different image followed: one of mortals immersing themselves in this river for purification and sanctification. Was Polydore a man in a thornbush, angered by many facets of the Christianity he served, but unable to utter a full-throated denunciation of it? Or was he a critical scholar who played it safe, walking one step backward for every two forward?

In later editions of the enlarged *De rerum inventoribus*, Polydore emended his letter to his brother. He made clear that Jesus had transformed the meaning of the Jewish ceremonies he retained:

> Christ our Saviour, as he himself bears witness, came to us mortals not to revoke the law but actually to confirm it. From the start he made everything that the Jews, following the shadow of the law, had tinged, dyed, and adulterated, pure, naked and transparent. Whatever they had abated, and whenever they had introduced less piety and more ceremonies, he restored, and wanted there to be more piety and fewer ceremonies.[73]

He removed his list of important practices added to Christianity and deleted the metaphor of the river of ceremonies that had accompanied it in the first version. At the end of the letter, moreover, though he left the original date unchanged, he added a passage that seems to take the sting out of the demonstration that Christians had borrowed their practices: "I showed that the Fathers acted piously and with reason. Since they were eager to lead even barbarous peoples to the cultivation of true piety, they thought it best to handle them with the seasonings of humanity. Since they were not terrified by their customs, they did not abolish them, but improved them, so that no danger to religion would arise."[74] Here as elsewhere, however, Polydore danced to the tune of "Two steps forward, one step back." He still found it necessary to observe that after the time of Jesus, "this forest of Jewish ceremonies has gradually taken over the field of the Lord."[75] As these swerves suggest, Polydore himself may not have had—or may not have revealed—a fixed goal. Censors repeatedly demanded the elimination of individual passages from *De rerum inventoribus*. But they could not eliminate the book's charge of polemical energy: its apparent proof that Christianity had learned a great deal from the Jews.

FROM INVENTING RITUALS TO HISTORICIZING CHRISTIANITY

Polydore set a new agenda for every church historian who came after him. The first great Lutheran Church historian, the southern Slav Matthias Flacius Illyricus, translated and commented on two chapters from *De inventoribus rerum.* He did so, he explained, in order to prove from the testimony of a "Papist" that the Mass was actually a late addition to Christian ritual, and a corruption of original purity.[76] But he and his associates had more direct access to Jewish traditions than Polydore had had. Flacius himself taught Hebrew at Wittenberg from 1544 to 1549. After he broke with Wittenberg, members of his circle still discussed the questions that occupied Christian students of Judaism everywhere. For example, they debated the value—if any—of the compendious and revelatory-seeming *De arcanis catholicae veritatis* (1518) of the Franciscan Pietro Galatino, a work that remained on scholars' desks for a century and more, thanks to its long quotations from Talmudic passages and its efforts to establish the exact relationship between Judaism and Christianity. Gottshalk Praetorius, rector of the Magdeburg Gymnasium in the 1550s and one of the organizers of the Magdeburg Centuries, remarked to another member of the Magdeburg circle that "Galatinus takes a great deal from Porchetus [the fourteenth-century Carthusian author of *Victoria Porcheti adversus impios Hebraeos*]: so much that sometimes whole pages can be shown. But he makes almost no reference to the name."[77] He was half a century ahead of Joseph Scaliger, whose accusations of plagiarism against Galatino became famous.

One of Flacius's Wittenberg colleagues showed the way to integrate specialized knowledge of Judaism into the history of Christianity. Paul Eber, an astronomer and historian, gained renown chiefly for his calendars, which replaced the saints' days that had filled Catholic calendars with the dates of important battles, births, and deaths in biblical, classical, and modern history.[78] In 1547, he issued another pioneering little book: a history of the Jews, from the Babylonian exile to the fall of Jerusalem. He gave his colleague Flacius a copy of it.[79]

Eber's history examined Second Temple Judaism in some detail. His account of the sects—he first treated the Pharisees and Sadducees, then the Essenes—made clear that the Judaism that Jesus encountered was not uniform.[80] And though he treated both the Pharisees and the Sadducees with disdain, he cast his account of the Essenes in a very different key. Following Philipp Melanchthon, he argued that the very name the Essenes had adopted revealed their special approach to the religious life:

> They called themselves Essenes, that is workmen, and by this name they referred both to what they criticized in others and to the way in

which they hoped to outdo others. They fled, that is, the profane license of the Sadducees, and they did not approve of the histrionic pretending of the Pharisees. But they would do useful works, those that were divinely commanded.[81]

Himself an eager naturalist, Eber appreciated the close attention the Essenes had brought to the study of nature and the care they had expended on treating patients, even those who suffered from disgusting ailments.[82] He praised their deep passion for learning and their ascetic pursuit of virtue. And he suggested, not for the last time, that the ways of the Essenes might have become the ways of the Christians as well:

> This college was so severe, that if someone cheated others, or lied, or polluted himself in his passion, they immediately removed him, by the agreement of all, from the whole community. And they observed the ancient custom of the Synagogue, which is discussed in Mark 18 [18:15–18]. For no new rule is made there: rather, an old custom is recited, and passed on by the first Fathers. Its traces had always persisted in the Church.[83]

Even the Essenes, Eber admitted, had failed in their principal duty: "firm training deserves praise, but let there also be true recognition of the son of God."[84] Yet he had nothing but praise for their learning, their self-discipline, and their courage in the war against the Romans.

When the group of scholars whom Flacius gathered and inspired wrote up the first volume of their history of the church, they insisted that the historian of Christianity must survey the Jewish beliefs and institutions that Jesus had known: "Christ arrived at a time when the Jewish religion was still in some sense intact. Therefore he used certain ceremonies, especially those that God established through Moses, and did not use others, such as the traditions of the elders, which had elements of superstition. Accordingly, before we go over the new and splendid rituals that Christ established, we will describe the received and customary ceremonies of the Jewish people."[85] They followed Eber in treating the existence of the rival groups of the Pharisees, Sadducees, and Essenes as the basic fact about Judaism in the last centuries BCE. The Magdeburg Centuries were produced by compilation, as young men filled prepared notebooks with the excerpts from which the final text was drawn. They pulled passages from Eber's book—some of which, lightly disguised by elegant variation, found a place in the finished volume 1 of the Centuries.[86]

The Centuriators did not accept all of Eber's theories, which described the Pharisees and Sadducees as new sects. They, by contrast, followed Josephus, who had characterized all three sects as very old. Where Eber treated the form of excommunication practiced by the Essenes as the origin of the Christian practice, the Centuriators noted its terrible consequences: "they expelled those who were caught in their sins from their congregation. And those condemned in this way generally died a terrible death. Since they remained bound by those sacraments and rituals, they could not use any food that others offered them. They picked grass like cattle as they were eaten away by hunger, and the ruin spread through their limbs."[87] On the whole, though, they followed his general approach even when they disagreed with him about important facts. Though they despised the Wittenberg theologian Philipp Melanchthon, they followed Eber in accepting Melanchthon's view that the name of the Essenes derived from the Hebrew verb *asah*, which meant "make" or "produce."[88] And they fully shared his glowing admiration for the pious "colleges" that the Essenes had created. Suddenly, Jews were playing a visible—and even a partly laudable—role in the drama of early Christianity.

Not all later church historians followed this lead. Even those who did not, however, had to explain their decision. The Lutheran scholar Lucas Osiander, who issued what he described as an epitome of the *Centuries* in 1592–1599, suggested that the Centuriators had wasted too much time on Jewish sects. "The countenance of God's church was sorrowful in those days," he explained, and after a very brief account of the Pharisees, Sadducees, and Essenes, he passed rapidly on to the life of Jesus.[89] But Cesare Baronio, who committed himself to confronting the Centuriators and defeating them, text by text and line by line, emulated them in this respect as in many others. Baronio investigated Jewish life and institutions with considerable care and seriousness. He, too, examined at length the major sects and a host of minor ones, including the Samaritans, Hemerobaptists, and Herodians. As the Centuriators had used Josephus to fill in and sometimes to qualify the narrative given by Eber, Baronio drew on a wealth of Jewish sources to establish his own command of Jewish traditions. The margins of his book swarm with references to the Alfasi, a summary of the Talmud; the Code of Maimonides; and the Talmud itself, which he often quoted in the original. The comparative principle, in other words, was established in ecclesiastical scholarship well before the great seventeenth-century age of Christian rabbinical scholarship had dawned. Those who applied it cast their nets widely and brought up a new catch.

Early comparatists asked a wide range of questions of a wide range of sources. They took their inspiration where they found it, as much in the traditional, but potentially explosive, sources of ecclesiastical scholarship as in the cutting-edge studies of the antiquarians. Sometimes, as Smith argues so powerfully, comparison narrowed the historian's empathy and the theologian's imagination. Yet sometimes it opened both to new possibilities. And gradually, in the study of early Christianity as in that of the origins of the world's peoples, comparative methods gained enough in precision and discrimination to yield powerful new histories.[90]

CHAPTER 5

Matthew Parker Makes an Archive

THE GREAT COLLECTORS of Renaissance Europe fostered conviviality as well as learning. Robert Cotton opened his library to visitors, many of whom he allowed to borrow books. By the end of Queen Elizabeth's reign, the Society of Antiquaries met at his house and its members knew his manuscripts well.[1] Thomas Bodley did the same with the public library that he created at Oxford. It too became a center for learned conversation. As Isaac Casaubon noticed, Bodley's policy of not allowing books to circulate meant that all the serious scholars in Oxford spent the day in his library, where a visitor could meet them easily.[2] Matthew Parker was less hospitable than his fellow library legends, yet he displayed some of his treasures to selected scholars. He showed the antiquary William Lambarde, who worked fairly closely with him, a manuscript of Homer and other texts that he thought had belonged to his seventh-century predecessor as archbishop of Canterbury, Theodore of Tarsus. As Lambarde recorded in the first draft of his *Perambulation of Kent*,

> The reverend father, and worthy prelate, Mathew, now archebiss-
> hoppe of Canterbyrie (whose care for conseruacion of Learned mon-
> uments can never be sufficiently commended) shewed me, not longe

128

synce, the Testament in Greke, and homers workes fayre written in thicke paper, with the name of this Theodore in the fronte, to whose Librarie he verely thinckketh (beinge therto reasonably ledd by greate shewe of antiquitie) that they somtyme belonged.[3]

This report was not completely accurate. In a second version of the text, which Lambarde submitted to Parker for correction, the titles of the texts in question were crossed out. Parker or one of his secretaries replaced them in the margin: "the psalter of D[avi]d and certen homelyes in greke, with Homer and some other greke authours."[4] Lambarde's text was emended again before it reached print.[5]

Even the corrected report was not complete. Lambarde did not mention most of the manuscripts that Parker thought had come to England with Theodore of Tarsus. Worse still, his episcopal informant led him into error. The Theodore who had owned the Homer before Parker was not the early medieval prelate but rather the fifteenth-century humanist Theodore Gaza, and the manuscript itself was written in the fifteenth century.[6] At least one period eye saw more clearly than Parker's. Bodley's first librarian, Thomas James, had examined many codices by the time he reached Cambridge. He repeated Parker's assertion in his union catalogue of Oxford and Cambridge manuscripts: "this book is of paper, and once belonged to Archbishop Theodore." But then he made his skepticism clear: "let the authority for this rest with the reader."[7] By the late seventeenth century, the brilliant paleographer Humfrey Wanley was making fun of the archbishop, claiming that the great collector of early codices had been "abused" because he had failed to realize that a "recent paper copie" could not be a manuscript from Theodore's time.[8]

Still, Lambarde made good use of his opportunities, and one of his finds is revealing. Later in his book on Kent, Lambarde discussed the status of lands in Kent held "by auncient tenure of Knights service" from the archbishop of Canterbury. He argued that they were "departible" (separable or divisible) and traced this condition to a grant that King John had made to his chancellor, Archbishop Hubert Walter, "the tenor whereof (being exemplified out of an auncient roll, late remaining in the handes of the deceased Reuerend father, Mathew, the Archbishop) hereafter followeth." The Latin charter that Lambarde then printed is genuine: a notification to the bishop that he had the right to convert gavelkind holdings into knights' fees, dated May 4, 1202. It is a little paradoxical that this charter does not appear in one of the early charter rolls that constitute the official records of the Court of Chancery, for Hubert's services to his king as chancellor included reforming the archives and, very likely, compiling the first rolls of charters.[9] In this case, however, as in many others, no extant roll preserves the document. Instead, two medieval copies of it appear in a manuscript in Lambeth Palace Library.[10]

Lambarde's description of the document is anything but clear. He describes it as "exemplified out of an auncient roll": which normally would be the description of an official copy.[11] The newer of the two Lambeth copies, which was written at the end of the thirteenth century, has a contemporary note reading "h[ec] est duplicata," which could mean that Lambarde was identifying it as his source.[12] But Lambarde's full sentence reads, "being exemplified out of an auncient roll, late remaining in the handes of the deceased Reuerend father, Mathew." This could mean that Lambarde himself or a scribe made a copy of the charter from a roll, now lost, which then formed part of Parker's collection. In short, we cannot be sure exactly what Parker showed Lambarde—any more than we can be sure if the archbishop described his holdings accurately. But we can be sure of something else: when Parker discussed his collection with collaborators and visitors, they looked at official documents as well as manuscripts and treated his collection, in our terms, as an archive as well as a library.[13]

Parker's collection embraced more than the hundreds of books and manuscripts he gave to Corpus Christi College: he donated twenty-five manuscripts and seventy-five printed books to the University Library in 1574, and other manuscripts that once belonged to his library can be found not only in Oxford and London, but also from Aberystwyth to Princeton. Its contents included not only the historical, theological, and liturgical manuscripts that fascinated Parker most, but also charters and other documents. What we do not know, from Parker himself, is how exactly he viewed his collection. Did he himself see it as a library or an archive? Did he consider it a semiprivate possession or a public resource? Richly documented studies by R. I. Page and Mildred Budny, Timothy Graham and Jennifer Summit, and many others have illuminated the ways in which Parker collected and used the manuscripts that survive.[14] Drawing on this wealth of Parkerian scholarship, I hope to come closer than we have until now to understanding exactly what Parker thought he was doing, and why, when he built his collection.

PARKER THE COLLECTOR

A clever boy from Norwich, who was born in 1504, Parker made his way up the greasy pole of preferment, first at Cambridge and then outside. When Queen Elizabeth and William Cecil took over, they appointed him archbishop of Canterbury, much against his will, and entrusted him with the task of constructing a new church but not the power to do so. The Presbyterians made his life a torment, and his term of office, from 1559 to his death in 1575, was largely consumed by controversies that he could not resolve.[15]

But as an impresario of scholarship, Parker achieved a great deal. He built up a team of scholars, who rapidly acquired books on his behalf.[16] One member of this team, Stephen Batman, recalled that he had "gathered within foure yeares . . . sixe thousand seauen hundred Bookes, by my onelye trauaile."[17] Soon the floors of Lambeth Palace were heaped with folios. And these resources were exploited. One of the central products of Parker's enterprise was the massive *De antiquitate Britannicae ecclesiae* published under his name in 1572. This was a history of the English Church, in the form of a collective biography of the archbishops of Canterbury. But it was also the harvest of Parker's collecting: a huge collage or mosaic, as Graham nicely describes it, of passages from primary sources assembled to tell a particular story.[18] Like many of the rich products of Renaissance methods of compilation, this book too became the armature for further compilation in its own right.[19] Parker's son John, his chief secretary, John Joscelyn, and others turned a copy of the *De antiquitate*, now preserved as Lambeth Palace Library MS 959, into a stunningly rich and complex record of the work they had done. They added relevant materials, including both original documents with seals and their own versions of archival information; entered notes in the margin; and clarified part of the history of the book itself.[20] On the title page of the printed text, Joscelyn identified himself as one of the "antiquaries" whom Parker had hired. He also claimed to have been the main author of the actual book.[21] Joscelyn did not exaggerate. The British Library preserves many of the manuscripts and copybooks in which Joscelyn did preparatory work for this great enterprise. Collecting in Parker's circle involved active comparison and analysis as well as accumulation and storage, all to serve the needs of composition.[22]

Parker and his men, accordingly, did their best to transform the materials they collected into tools. They added titles and pagination; they assessed age and quality.[23] They also inserted headnotes that indicated the nature and uses of particular texts. In a manuscript of William of Malmesbury's *History of the Kings of England* that is now in Princeton, as in many other manuscripts, Parker himself added page numbers in red chalk. Joscelyn noted missing passages and inserted replacements for them, neatly written, in all cases but one, on paper, so that no one could take them for part of the original.[24]

The aim of these activities was clear. Parker wanted to show that the Anglican Church had restored the usages of the early church: in particular, the Anglo-Saxon Church. This goal generated headlong activity, as he and his men scoured the columns of each text for references to precedents. Parker strongly defended clerical marriage. The point to be noted in the ritual for priestly ordination in Parker's Canterbury Pontifical, accordingly, was clear: "In the prayers, in the instructions, and in the blessings there is no mention of celibacy."[25] Every early manuscript could supply another stone for the church Parker hoped to build.

Under Parker, Lambeth Palace buzzed so loudly with scholarly activity that it reminded one observer of an academy of learned men.[26] His men amassed—or reconstructed—forms of technical knowledge that had been lost with the monastic libraries. Medieval monks had been connoisseurs of older scripts—especially when they had to fake older documents that confirmed a privilege of their community.[27] Parker's antiquaries became almost equally deft. They produced facsimile leaves and inserted them into some of the most magnificent and historically important of his manuscripts—such as the eleventh-century Canterbury Pontifical that may have been used for the installation of Lanfranc, a figure who mattered greatly to Parker.[28] More striking, though, is Parker's heavily abbreviated fourteenth-century codex of the thirteenth-century writer Gervase of Tilbury. Across from the first recto, one of his men has supplied a transcription of the heavily abbreviated text. Its title reads: "For the benefit of those who have not had practice with abbreviations like these, which the ancients used."[29] Original and transcription face one another, as in one of the plates in Mabillon's *De re diplomatica* of 1681, that great summa of premodern archival science, or in a modern manual of paleography.[30] Here knowledge of the ancient script serves purely scholarly ends. Parker and his men sought, not just to curate ancient manuscripts, but also to add value to them.

PARKER'S MODELS AND PRACTICES: COLLECTING FOR A PURPOSE

Some people are born collectors, and some have collection thrust upon them. Traditional accounts suggested that Parker belonged to the latter group. On becoming archbishop in 1561, Parker found himself confronted with two pressing problems. He had to construct—or reconstruct—a Protestant Church. This in turn must show as much fidelity as possible to the teachings and practices of Jesus, Paul, and the Fathers, and the early traditions of English Christianity, while not rejecting contemporary practices unnecessarily. He also had to fashion histories of that church, which would provide charters for its independent existence and its distinctive practices.[31] From the start, Parker felt the hot breath of competitors and worried about the inadequacy of his source base. The feisty and energetic Matthias Flacius Illyricus was hard at work in Germany, organizing the multivolume history of Christianity now known as the Magdeburg Centuries. To support his arguments about the degeneration of the church, he energetically collected medieval histories, letters, and other documents.[32] Flacius wrote to the English court in 1560 and to Parker himself in 1561. He asked for support, which Parker provided, and for manuscripts of Matthew Paris—which, Parker explained, he did not have. Helpfully, Flacius listed the sorts of materials he needed: unpublished histories of the church; lives of the popes and councils; letters of popes, bishops, famous teachers, and rulers; canon law texts from before the time of Gratian; old missals; inquisitions; and much more.[33] With this template in his hands, Parker began a systematic hunt for sources.[34]

For further guidance Parker turned to a great if opinionated bibliographer: the former Carmelite and fierce Protestant John Bale, who commanded the history of ecclesiastical writing in England and elsewhere as few others could. Bale had surveyed collections and scoured documents, keeping a beady eye out for references to other texts and, if possible, their locations. He had come into contact with the Centuriators during his time as a Marian exile on the Continent and appreciated their comprehensive efforts to collect materials. And he had discovered that the problem of recovering the documents was complex. English monks, whose libraries had contained the core texts and documents Parker needed, had been "more dedicated to their bellies and gullets than to books or letters." They had allowed the books in their care to be eaten by insects and worms—or, at least, had allowed them to lose the vital first pages that identified them.[35] After Henry VIII and Cromwell closed the monasteries, moreover, most of the books that the monks had bothered to preserve were either destroyed at home or shipped abroad to equally dubious fates.[36] The heritage of medieval English Christianity, good and evil, was being dissipated or even destroyed just when it was most needed. Bale—who had lost his own library in Ireland—devoted his last years to compiling information about English churchmen and the texts and documents they had written. Some of this material he published in a biographical compendium on English writers, and some of it he synthesized in a long letter to Parker after Elizabeth's accession to the throne. The archbishop and his assistants followed Bale's guidance, using his printed bibliography as well as his letter, as they explored the churches, colleges, and other collections where the sources they needed could best be found.[37]

Parker's collection, in other words, was built in haste, as his agents bought and borrowed and his friends and colleagues sent him manuscripts. And an air of improvisation hung about the enterprise to the very end of his life. Parker found a brilliant way to ensure that his manuscripts would not suffer the fate of those of the ancient monasteries. He exploited those strongest of academic emotions, jealousy and Schadenfreude, to preserve what he had brought together from the attacks of future generations of Counter-Reformers, not to mention managers or consultants. Parker left the core of his collection to Corpus, the college that had formed him and that he had served as master. Every year, he stipulated, the librarians of Gonville and Caius and Trinity Hall must inspect the Parker collection. If more than twelve items went missing, Gonville and Caius would take over the rest; and if more than twelve items went missing there, Trinity Hall would provide a home while Corpus waited in the wings in case losses took place there. It all sounds admirably precise and deliberate.[38]

Yet a secretarial note in Parker's manuscript of Homer tells a very different story:

> This book of Theodore's was found in Saint Augustine's monastery at Canterbury after the dissolution, and, so to speak, thrown away amid the torn-up charters of that monastery. A certain baker who had once worked for that very monastery examined the heap of charters and found it. Since the monks and other inhabitants of that monastery had either been expelled or were departing from it, he took it home. But happily this book came at length into the possession of Matthew, archbishop of Canterbury. He keeps it with him as a great treasure, and intends to deposit it either in the public library of Cambridge University or in the faithful keeping of the master of our college (which at the time would be that of Corpus Christi and the Blessed Mary) there.[39]

Cast in the melancholy key of one of Bale's lamentations for lost books and then changing to a more joyous vein, this note suggests that Parker may have been inspired by his ownership of Theodore's Homer to think about finding an official way to deposit his books. It also suggests that his thinking on the subject was no more systematic than his division of the actual books into those that went to Corpus and those that went elsewhere. He started with one book that he misidentified and built on that small basis, in what must have been a very short time, the more comprehensive plan that he finally put into effect.

Still, the standard version of Parker's development, as Graham has pointed out, cannot be the whole story. It seems to be true that he did not start collecting manuscripts in a big way until he could mobilize the resources and power of his archbishopric. But Parker bought, read, and annotated dozens of printed books, forming himself as a scholar long before he became archbishop. A famous example is his copy of that egregious manual of the witch hunters, Nider's *Formicarius*. Parker inscribed a lapidary judgment in it: "egregius fabulator."[40]

PARKER AND THE PAST

Parker did more than collect sources. He also established two basic habits: that of doing elaborate research into the richest sources he could find for the practices and the theology of the early church and that of collaborating with a secretary or assistant. In the late 1530s, as new editions of the Fathers streamed from the presses at Basel and elsewhere, Martin Bucer began to compile a florilegium: a systematic compendium, topically organized, of the opinions of the Fathers on such vital issues as the nature of the Eucharist, the liturgy, clerical celibacy, prayer, and images.[41] Bucer and Parker became close during the last two years of Bucer's life, when he held the Regius Chair of Divinity at Cambridge. Parker delivered the eulogy at Bucer's funeral. He also evidently inherited Bucer's unfinished collection of research materials. Set free from practical tasks when Mary became Queen and he was stripped of his benefices and offices, Parker devoted himself to finishing the work.[42] In its pages he appears filling in a missing quotation from Ambrose about the frequency at which masses should be held and having a secretary fill in another one, this one from a sermon by the Cistercian Guerric d'Igny.[43] Not surprisingly, Parker had the same secretary add long passages to those that Bucer had collected on celibacy and clerical marriage.[44] He not only added excerpts, moreover, but also gave strikingly precise references to the sections and page numbers where they appeared in original works. Parker was, in short, a seasoned explorer of sources before Elizabeth became queen.

More important, Parker knew before he uneasily took over the See of Canterbury that scholarship about the history of the church would play a central role in defining or subverting current practices. No aspect of church discipline stirred up more controversy, in the 1550s and after, than the question of clerical vestments. In this case, up-to-date scholarship helped to destabilize church life. In the second, longer edition of his *De rerum inventoribus,* which appeared in 1521, the Italian humanist Polydore Vergil crafted, as we have seen, what was in effect the first modern history of Christianity. Working topic by topic, he investigated the origins of church and mass, hierarchy and Eucharist—and vestments.[45] The systematic comparison of customs and garments, a practice learned from such earlier antiquaries as

Flavio Biondo, enabled him to show that Christian priests had borrowed their albs and surplices from their Jewish predecessors, as they had borrowed other adornments from pagans.[46]

In 1550, John Hooper refused to accept consecration to the see of Gloucester because it would force him to wear vestments that were "Romish" or of "Aaronic nature." He had learned from Polydore Vergil and Vergil's sources that the standard vestments were derived from those of Aaron. Hence, they were not consistent with the priesthood of Jesus, who had died naked on the cross.[47] Ridley wrote a reply, in which he accepted Polydore's history of Catholic vestments, but rejected the consequences that Hooper drew from it.[48] The debate went on, and challenges to the traditional vestments revived—after the Marian period—in the 1560s. In a pamphlet printed in 1566, Robert Crowley, vicar of St. Giles Cripplegate, denounced the wearing of vestments and refused to allow a minister who conformed to hold services in his church. Like Hooper, he used Polydore's historical arguments to support his position: "all men may see, that the ministring garments of the Popes Church, were taken partly from the Iewes, and partly from the gentiles. And as Polidorus Virgilius, dothe note in his fourthe booke, De inventoribus rerum, they came from the Egyptians by the Hebrues."[49] Parker contemptuously rejected all efforts to show that traditional vestments must be rejected simply because they came from pagan or Jewish sources: "the Apostles used long after Christes ascention the Ceremonies of Moises, and that in the Temple, to wynn to Chryst the obstinate Iewes."[50]

Moreover, he argued, the best traditions of the British Church were on his side: "The histories Ecclesiasticall also haue divers experiences, howe much our auncient fathers increased Christes Churche by such godly policie. Hence it was, that they plucked not downe all the Jewyshe Sinagoges and Heathenyshe Temples, but turned them to the seruice of God." A marginal note made clear which history ecclesiastical Parker had in mind: "Note this place of Bed. Eccl. hist. lib. 1. cap. 30. and expende his reasons."[51] This chapter of Bede's history consists of a letter that Pope Gregory sent to Mellitus in AD 601, as the latter was on his way to England. It instructs him not to destroy, but rather to appropriate and transform, the temples of the pagans.[52] Parker's hunt for precedents in doctrine and liturgy in manuscripts and documents formed a natural extension of his early interests and beliefs and a vital support for his practical efforts as archbishop.

At times, scholarly questions seemed very urgent indeed to Parker. He enjoyed the personal favor of Elizabeth. But she firmly disapproved of clerical marriage—including Parker's happy one, for which he had sacrificed much under Mary. After one of the queen's visits to the archbishop's house, she thanked him "and then, looking on his Wife, and you (saith she) Madam, I may not call you, and Mrs. I am ashamed to call you, so as I know not what to call you, but I do thank you."[53] Catholic polemicists never ceased beating the same drum. Parker, accordingly, took it personally when Fredericus Staphylus showed that two letters in defense of clerical celibacy, ascribed by Luther and others to Ulricus, a tenth-century bishop of Augsburg, could not be by him, since they were dedicated to the ninth-century Pope Nicholas I. Parker's copy of the texts in question, now in Gonville and Caius library, contains detailed notes by him and one of his secretaries. The manuscript, which they took—probably correctly—as coming from St Augustine's, Canterbury, ascribed the texts to Volusianus.[54]

Parker leaped on this new ascription like hunger on a loaf, in the words of Benvenuto Cellini, even though he was quite uncertain about the author's identity. The testimony of an incorrupt manuscript was exactly what he needed. In his own 1569 edition of the text, he argued that the name of Ulrich had been deliberately substituted for that of the true author, which was attested by his manuscript. In this case, as in others, excitement carried Parker considerably beyond the point that his evidence would have allowed him to reach. He described his manuscript as "antiquissimum," "written before William I held the reins of government in this kingdom."[55] Moreover, he convinced his closest allies that he was right. Foxe wrote:

> As touching the antiquitie of thys epistle above prefixed, it appeareth by the copie, which I have seene, and receaved of the right reverend . . . Matthewe Archbyshop of Canterbury, to be of an old and auncient writing, bothe by the forme of the characters and by the wearing of the Parchment almost consumed by length of years and tyme.[56]

John Jewel recalled that "I have seen the same epistle unto P. Nicolas, together with another epistle to like purpose, written in old vellum, of very ancient record, under the name of *Volusianus*, the *bishop of Carthage*."[57] Another set of lost conversations comes back to life—eager ones, in which the proud collector and his friends examined the little manuscript, leaf by leaf, and failed, one and all, to realize that it had actually been written in the late twelfth or the thirteenth century.

"JUST LET ME INVENT THE EVIDENCE AND I'LL PROVE MY POINT": PARKER AND THE MANUSCRIPTS

For all Parker's passion for history and its sources, he and his men treated many of the primary sources they collected in a strikingly arbitrary way: they inserted inappropriate decorations. Parker's Lambeth Palace housed a staff of book artists, who were experts at script, illumination, and binding. Sometimes, as we have seen, they worked with discipline and precision. Sometimes he turned them loose to do their worst. In a letter to William Cecil, Parker noted that he had thought of having an illustration for the start of Cecil's manuscript of the Psalter in Old English "counterfeited in antiquity" by his illuminator, one Lylye. By doing so he would have gilded that magnificent eighth-century lily, the Vespasian Psalter, one of the glories of pre-Conquest Britain.[58] His team added opening pictures, both taken from the same thirteenth-century Psalter, to an eleventh-century manuscript of vernacular homilies and a twelfth-century manuscript of a Latin history, with no evident worries about whether he was corrupting their authenticity.[59]

On occasion Parker's men seemingly ignored the historical contexts in which, they knew, particular scripts had actually been used. For example, Parker had the Latin text of Asser's life of King Alfred printed in Anglo-Saxon type. The preface suggested that he meant to imitate the original: "though the text is Latin, I have seen to it that it was printed in Saxon characters, because of my special veneration for the original MS."[60] He knew the codex was old and possibly contemporary, as he explained, since he had compared it with copies of Alfred's version of Gregory the Great's *Pastoral Care*, "which were written at the same time and survive today, copied out in the same characters."[61] Yet he misrepresented it to his readers. The manuscript from which Parker worked, Cotton Otho A XII, was destroyed in the Cotton Library fire in 1731. But an eighteenth-century facsimile shows that it was actually written in Roman script, except for the Anglo-Saxon words and names that appeared in the text from time to time.[62]

In other cases, Parker deliberately changed documentary evidence that he thought important. In order to show that the Anglo-Saxon church of the early Middle Ages had shared vital doctrines with his own Protestant church, in 1566 he printed the Easter sermon of the erudite tenth-century cleric Aelfric, in the original Anglo-Saxon, with a facing English translation. Parker hoped to prove that Aelfric had denied transubstantiation and accepted clerical marriage: and thus confirmed a major Anglican doctrine and practice. Carefully placed glosses substantiated this reading. Only a few scholarly adepts, some of whom worked for Parker, could actually judge the text and version. In order to guarantee their accuracy, Parker held a conference with his bishops. They went through the entire work. They attested that the texts were "truely put forth in Print without any adding, or withdrawing any thing, for the more faithfull reporting of the same." And they signed their names, which Parker printed.[63] There was considerable pathos in Parker's emphasis on the accuracy of his publication. The original list of signatures of the bishops who approved of Parker's Aelfric survives, in a copy of the printed text, which itself thus became a sort of archival document.[64] Comparison shows that the printed version of the list— which was presented as a surrogate for their original signatures— silently omitted two names.

Is it anachronistic, as some have argued, to criticize Parker and his men for these practices? That is not necessarily the case. Parker's dealings with some of his texts curiously resemble the deceptive practices engaged in—so Protestant scholars suspected—by Jesuits and other Catholic editors. Thomas James set up teams of collators in the Bodleian library, hoping to show that Catholics had systematically interpolated the texts of the Fathers that they published (Bodley, rightly, urged him to calm down). In 1612 James vividly described practices at the living center of Catholic scholarship as the mirror image of Parker's. He did not mean this as a compliment:

> In the Vatican Library, there are certaine men maintained onely to transcribe Acts of the Councels, or Copies of the Fathers Workes.

These men, appointed for this business, doe (as I am credibly in-formed) in transcribing bookes imitate the letter of the auncient copies, as neere as can be expressed. And it is to be feared, that in copying out of bookes, they doe add, and take away, alter and change the words, according to the pleasure of their Lord the Pope. And so these Transcripts may within a few yeares (by reason of their counter-faiting the auncient hands) be avouched for very old Manuscripts; de-luding the world with a shew of Antiquitie. The danger is the greater, because there may bee an Index Expurgatorius (for ought that wee know) for purging the Manuscripts, as well as the Printed bookes.[65]

The well-known scholar and exegete Franciscus Junius told similar tales of Catholic perfidy.[66]

Parker and his men nourished similar suspicions of Catholic scribes and scholars: especially those who had lived and worked in more re-cent, and more corrupt, times. In 1570, they printed an edition of a chronicle compiled originally at St Albans and then extended by many writers, the *Flores historiarum*. Their preface described the work as based on a "very ancient MS of the history" and as radically different from the known text. Many texts, after all, had undergone radical al-teration over time at the hands of Catholics determined to suppress inconvenient truths. Bale had criticized monks for losing or concealing books. Parker and his men raised the philological stakes: "For such was the wickedness of those times, so unrestrained was the passion for con-cealing the truth, that in order to blind the minds of men, they did not hesitate to insert, erase or change whole sentences in the old writers, and much less when it came to individual words, just as each one wished."[67] The Carolingian theologian Hrabanus Maurus discussed the nature of the sacrament in his treatise *De ecclesiasticis officiis*. Parker owned a manuscript of this text. In the margin of the passage in ques-tion, a modern note makes an accusation: "there is an omission here, which the scribe seems to have made deliberately."[68] The passage in question is entered in the margin above it. In the preface to the *Flores historiarum*, Parker described this manuscript and treated it as a case in point of the old church's general effort "to bind the minds of men." Happily, he explained, the full text could be found "in every copy put into circulation before the time of William the Conqueror."[69] Evi-dently Parker's beloved Anglo-Saxon Christians had copied their texts

honestly. The same could not be said for the Anglo-Norman scribes
who came after them, however.

Moreover, Parker—or rather Joscelyn, writing as Parker—made clear
in one particularly prominent place that sources must be reproduced
accurately. The *De antiquitate,* as Joscelyn acknowledged in his preface,
drew heavily on texts by the corrupt monks and ignorant theologians
whose traditions the Reformers had rightly rejected. He read—as one
might now say—against the grain, finding evidence of wrong practices
and beliefs in the very texts that described and praised them. To use
the testimony of his enemies credibly, Joscelyn argued, the historian
must take extra care to quote it accurately:

> We have generally used the very words with which those old writers
> portrayed the customs and events of their times. This we did delib-
> erately, to prevent anyone from raising the suspicion that we our-
> selves invented or corrupted the sins of the Papists, which those
> monks and ancient writers recorded and described in such a remark-
> ably clear way, and to avoid any suspicion that we could seem to have
> departed from what they meant to say.[70]

Parker and his followers believed that any suspicion of tampering with
their texts would destroy their credibility. They identified deliberate
alteration of texts as a feature of Catholic practice, which they denounced. And yet, given the chance, they tampered away.

PARKER AND THE ARCHIVES

Parker collected documents of the sort that went into archives—and
not only the archiepiscopal one. His extensive archival experience
began in his own college. As master of Corpus he devised a new system
for keeping the college's accounts in order, revised its statutes, and assembled a "Black Book," which today is still kept in the college archive,
of documents related to college and university business.[71] Parker's official manuscript of the revised college statutes, also known as the
Black Book, shows the care with which he identified those who carried out the revision and the visitors who signed it (and those who did
not).[72] In the early 1560s, he worked closely with the English martyrologist John Foxe. Foxe, as Elizabeth Evenden and Thomas Freeman

have shown us, filled his *Acts and Monuments*, the great, formative martyrology, with primary sources: official reports on the interrogation of Protestant heretics, first-hand accounts of their heroic martyrdoms, and personal letters.[73] Parker owed much of his early religious inspiration to one of the most appealing early Protestant martyrs, Thomas Bilney, who was burned in August 1531. He preserved Bilney's letters so that Foxe could integrate them into his work.[74] And Parker took the *Acts and Monuments* very seriously indeed. In the *Canons* for clerical life and behavior that he issued in 1571, he ordered that "[e]very Archbishop and bishop shall have in hys house the holy Bible in the largest volume, as it was lately printed at London, and also that full and perfect history, which is intituled Monumentes of Martyrs, and other suche lyke bokes, fit for the setting forth of religion."[75] Other contemporary materials that Parker collected included the manuscripts, notebooks, and records of his predecessor, Thomas Cranmer.[76] Though he begged and borrowed manuscripts from cathedral libraries and other collections across Britain, moreover, he made serious efforts to see to it that when documents related to specific institutions turned up in manuscripts of largely different content, they were restored to the institutions in question—even as he cannibalized other documents to serve as bindings and endpapers.[77]

Parker carefully documented turning points in his own career. An elegant scribal copy of the record of his consecration as archbishop—which two notaries attended—went to Corpus.[78] Gilbert Burnet found it there, and he used a precise copy, bearing notarial attestations of its own, to disprove the canard that Parker had been consecrated in a pub, the Nag's Head.[79] A second copy went into Parker's archiepiscopal register.[80] All this, as Robert Masters, the historian of Corpus, realized, was performative archiving at its best, designed to show the "plainness and simplicity" of the rites and ceremonies used, "in opposition to those vain and superstitious ones, ever heretofore in use."[81] Parker's collections were meant to—and did—nourish the writing of "full and perfect" histories of the church by feeding their authors with original sources.

More striking, Parker knew—and employed—standard archival practices, such as the procedures for ensuring that a copy could actually serve in place of its original. In 1419, King Arthur's charter for the

University of Cambridge and the bulls of Popes Sergius and Honorius in its favor—medieval forgeries, created to fill the lacunae in the university's early history—were displayed in Great Saint Mary's Church. An apostolic notary named Thomas de Ryhale carried out an official exemplification of the documents. He copied them in the presence of witnesses, whom he named, and adorned the copy with his sign. Parker collated a copy of his document, now in the Parker library, with the original, now in the Corpus archive, and gave it his own official attestation: "This matches. Matthew of Canterbury."[82] Parker's vision of the archive, in other words, was traditional in one crucial respect: he saw it, not as a place where texts were preserved in the closest possible approximation to their original state, but as one where texts were "renewed" or "exemplified" and replaced whenever practical needs required it. In his edition of Aelfric he applied the same procedure to a new end: listing reputable witnesses to give authority, not to a handwritten copy, but rather to a text and translation. He thus transformed an ordinary printed edition into something like a renewal of the original source: here we see old archival procedures transformed by the touch of new media. Yet we also see archival procedures used to achieve the opposite of what one anachronistically considers their intended effect: to make a falsified piece of evidence look genuine.

Parker and his group enunciated principles, but their own practices did not reliably match them. If Parker's standards of documentary editing dissolve in something like contradiction, however, it may still be possible to fix his ultimate goals as a historian and manager of other historians more precisely. The main products of Parker's workshop were a series of histories. These included the *De antiquitate,* which appeared as his work, and several editions of medieval chronicles: the *Flores historiarum* and the works of Matthew Paris, the spurious Matthew of Westminster, and Thomas Walsingham. It seems possible, at least, that Parker and his men saw these books, in their own way, as an official, irrefutable archive of English history: especially ecclesiastical history.

True, Parker and his men regularly referred to archives in the modern sense: as repositories of records, in the Tower of London and elsewhere. In the preface to Asser, Parker evoked the "many extant diplomas and monuments of older times, both before and after the

Normans arrived in England, and the royal charters that are kept in the archives."[83] In a proof version of *De antiquitate*, Joscelyn printed a major document, the 1072 Accord of Windsor between the dioceses of York and Canterbury, in full, including all the names of signatories.[84] Then he changed his mind. In the definitive version, the list of names is sharply abridged. A marginal gloss informs the reader that the rest can be found "in the archives."[85] References like these make a simple, transparent impression: when Parker and his associates mentioned archives, they referred to the repositories of power and government, secular and ecclesiastical—those repositories whose history have recently become a focus of historians' interest and research.[86]

Plenty of evidence, however, suggests that early modern collectors and readers of manuscripts and documents took a broader view of archives. The Bolognese bishop Baldassare Bonifacio, whose little treatise of 1632 surveyed the subject, demonstrated that no clear lines could be drawn between different forms of collections: a library could consist of an archive, a person with a good memory, the knotted cords used in the Andes, the clay tablets used in ancient Babylon, or the brick and stone pillars of Seth, the latter of which had supposedly preserved the knowledge of the antediluvian patriarchs. These last showed, Bonifacio argued, that archives went back to the creation of the world—though the Egyptians and Chaldeans had clearly invented their fabulous claims to have archives that covered tens or hundreds of thousands of years.[87] In early modern Europe, scholars and natural philosophers cocooned themselves in papers, ordinary citizens chronicled their own lives, and fashion plates recorded their every change of costume. Even marginalia in printed books could serve—for a professional reader like Gabriel Harvey—as a form of historical record. We should not too rapidly decide what form of record might be seen—as archival records have been in the world of post-Rankean historiography—as bearing the stamp and weight of an official origin.[88]

CAN A BOOK BE AN ARCHIVE? THE VIEW FROM 1572

The *De antiquitate*, as we have seen, bulged with quotations from primary sources. Joscelyn, in his preface, boasted that readers would find his history of the archbishops of Canterbury, "which is taken and drawn from a range of ancient authors, so properly and harmoniously assembled here, that the authorities and quotations drawn from many may seem rather to be the consistent work of one writer."[89] But he also insisted, quite accurately, that he had quoted the exact words of his sources. And he evoked the examples of earlier ecclesiastical historians: Eusebius, Socrates, and Sozomen, all of whom filled their works with literal quotations of letters, decrees, and narratives by other writers.[90]

The connection between archives and this sort of church history was equally traditional. Eusebius, the creator of Christian church history, quoted documents from the "public records" of the city of Edessa (Eusebius, *Historia Ecclesiastica* [hereafter *HE*] 1.13.5). True, these were letters between King Abgar of that city and Jesus, which were abject forgeries. But he also cited many other documents. When defaming a heretic named Alexander, for example, Eusebius wrote, "I don't have to say this: the back chamber contains it (*HE* 5.18.6)." The ὀπισθόδομος, or Back Chamber, was an Athenian archive on the Acropolis. Eusebius's Latin translator Rufinus rendered this term as "acta publica." Further evidence came from what Eusebius described as "the public archive of Asia" (*HE* 5.18.9). He also mentioned a letter written by Serapion against a particular heresy. This bore the "autograph attestations"—Rufinus translated this as "subscriptiones"—of several bishops, which Eusebius listed, which served as a clear charter for the inclusion of similar documents, and lists of signatures, in later histories, down to Matthew Paris and Parker himself (*HE* 5.19.3-4). Eusebius also compiled documents—especially verbatim accounts of martyrdoms—in his own library at Caesarea Maritima and visited other Christian archives at Jerusalem (renamed Aelia Capitolina) and elsewhere.[91]

Medieval continuators of the tradition followed Eusebius's example. The Venerable Bede, for example, compiled his brilliant ecclesiastical history of the English nation in the early decades of the eighth century. He never left his monastery at Jarrow. But Albinus sent him primary sources from Canterbury, via Nothelm, who was later to become archbishop of Canterbury. Later on, Nothelm carried out archival research on Bede's behalf in the "scrinium" of the Vatican. Bede's acknowledgment of this help, in the preface to his work, is the first instance in the entire historical tradition of an author thanking a curator and a research assistant.[92] Clio is an ironist: the texts in question were not all genuine.

Yet ecclesiastical historians were seldom explicit about where they found the documents they quoted (often, when they were, they had forged the texts themselves).[93] And they were understandably ambivalent about whether the safest archive was the physical place where the documents were stored or their own texts. Eusebius—who filled his life of Constantine with what we now know were accurate transcripts of official documents—wrote that he cited one of these texts "so that it might survive in the interest of history and be protected for our posterity, and also so that the quotation of the edict might confirm the truth of my present narrative. The text is quoted from an authenticated copy of the imperial statute preserved in my possession, on which the subscription, by Constantine's right hand, signifies its testimony to the trustworthiness of my speech like some sort of seal."[94] Apparently Eusebius believed that his text might well outlive the imperial archives, which housed the official copies of imperial statutes. He was, of course, quite right.

PARKER AND HIS MODELS: DOCUMENTARY
HISTORIANS PAST AND PRESENT

It seems likely that Parker saw himself as emulating Eusebius. In the 1560s, Parker and John Foxe worked very closely together. When the first edition of Foxe's *Acts and Monuments* appeared in 1564, his preface made clear that he saw a strong resemblance between his own work, which was stuffed with primary sources and dedicated to the modern Christian prince, Elizabeth, and the Church history of Eusebius, which was similar in form and dedicated to the ancient savior of Christianity, Constantine. One striking point in his description of Eusebius applies better to Parker than to Foxe himself, or indeed to the historical Eusebius. Constantine, wrote Foxe, told Eusebius to ask for anything that might be useful for the church. Eusebius, who despised honors and possessions,

> made this petition, onely to obtaine at his maiesties hande, vnder his
> seale and letters autentique, free leaue and license through al the

monarchie of Rome, going to all cōsulles, Procōsulles, Tribunes and
other officers in all cities and countries, to searche out the names,
sufferinges and actes, of all such as suffered in al that time of persecution before, for the testimonie and faith of Christ Iesus.[95]

No surviving document records that Eusebius made this precise request. Jerome, or someone writing under his name, provided the inspiration for Foxe's tale of a public commission in a letter quoted by the
early sixteenth-century humanist and encyclopedist Raffaele Maffei,
better known as Volaterranus:

> When Constantine the Great had come to Caesarea and asked Euse-
> bius what he needed, he answered, nothing at all, since your gener-
> osity fills all my needs. But here is what I most want: give orders
> throughout the world that the deeds of the martyrs and everything
> that Christians have done be gathered everwhere, from public and pri-
> vate records, and brought to me. And that is how he afterwards be-
> came the author of so universal a history.[96]

But Parker—like Foxe's Eusebius—tried to take even more direct action than this text described. He did not ask the state and its masters
to collect sources for him. Instead, in 1561, he asked the Privy Council
to provide official support for his own quest for sources (seven years
later, the council finally empowered him to search for texts). Given
Eusebius's many references to official sources, it seems quite possible
that Parker modeled his own petition for assistance on Eusebius's plea
to Constantine.

Parker was even more prone to admire the example of the medieval
chroniclers that he studied so avidly. They too had cited documents
freely, even exuberantly. When Joscelyn incorporated the Accord of
Windsor into the *De antiquitate,* as we saw, he changed the list of signatories. Here he followed the example of that uniquely critical
twelfth-century philologist and historian, William of Malmesbury.
Like Joscelyn, William made a habit, not only of citing, but also of editing and abridging, primary sources. William, as Joscelyn knew well,
inserted the accord—with its full list of signatories—into his *History
of the Kings of England.*[97] But he also quoted it in another form—along
with other documents that provided its context in Lanfranc's struggle
for authority—in his *History of the Prelates of England,* as Joscelyn

pointed out in a marginal note.[98] Materials had flowed freely, in the English Middle Ages, among cartularies, registers, and chronicles—all of them often created by the same individuals (rather like the various versions of Matthew Paris that Parker and his men took as individual chronicles). The Croyland Chronicle, for example, offered a glowing description of the "very beautiful charters, written in *litera publica* and adorned with golden crosses and lovely images and precious substances" that the monastery's archive had contained until it burned, as well as the texts of many documents.[99] The description and the documents were equally fictional, but Parker had no way of knowing that.[100]

Substantial evidence suggests that Parker came to see the Anglo-Norman chronicles as an official archive in their own right. The central distinction in modern (as opposed to postmodern) historical scholarship is that between historical sources and the historical narratives that rest on them. Parker, for all his emphasis on the archive, regularly elided this distinction—just as he elided the differences, or tried to, between archival documents and printed reproductions. Where Eusebius and many later ecclesiastical historians had woven archival narratives, Parker read particular narratives as archives. In particular, he argued that the monasteries of Anglo-Norman England had been the official repositories of memory, which they had preserved in official chronicles. In his 1570–1571 edition of the thirteenth-century Benedictine chronicler Matthew Paris, Parker made clear how much he liked and admired that stout medieval critic of the papacy. More striking still, he suggested that Matthew's chronicle formed part of a longer tradition of official histories commissioned by the kings of England, which were composed and preserved at the Monastery of St Albans.[101]

To support this argument, Parker drew on the preface to the British history of the Bellunese humanist Ludovico Da Ponte (in Latin, Ponticus Virunius).[102] Learned historians, Parker claimed, had recorded and then archived contemporary history:

> It was our law that the monasteries and ecclesiastical colleges, especially Saint Albans, should be a sort of common treasury, where all the historical events of this kingdom that were worth remembering were recorded. This was also noted by Ponticus Virunius, in his British history, in which he attests that it was the custom of western rulers to have scholars with them who could master their excellent

sayings and deeds exactly and by heart. But they did not want to publish these splendid deeds, while they or their sons lived.[103]

Da Ponte, who rewrote Geoffrey of Monmouth, shored up the credibility of his narrative by evoking, ". . . the custom of western kings, of having with them men who would record their deeds, with particular accuracy, but not to reveal them in their lifetimes or those of their sons, for it would be shameful to state what they had not been able to achieve with such great authority. They kept them for posterity in the royal archives."[104]

A sequence of arguments that were strikingly similar to Parker's had appeared previously in his friend John Caius's little book of 1568 about the antiquity of Cambridge University. First Caius conjured up the Saint Albans chronicles, presenting them as a sort of official or national archive: "Edward I ordered the monastery at Rochester to record the events of his times, as they happened, and he chose that monastery, with many others, and especially St Albans, as if for a treasury of memorable things, as Matthew of Westminster and the author of the Rochester chronicle write."[105] Then he drew on Da Ponte to set this particular form of history writing into a larger context:

> For it was once the custom of kings in the western regions, to have with them men who would accurately record the events of each year as they happened. But they did this without making them public in the time of the king or his sons, but passed the histories that were composed into the royal archives, where they were preserved for posterity, as Virumnus Ponticus explains in his history of the Britons.[106]

Caius greatly esteemed Da Ponte's book. Far more sharply than Parker, moreover, he defended Geoffrey of Monmouth's history of early Britain, which Da Ponte summarized.[107] Parker's vision of an archive seems to have taken shape in the course of a dialogue with Caius: someone who saw his own work on Cambridge, in part, as a reliable repository of primary materials.

The thesis that Caius formulated this view might help to explain why it first appears in writings connected with Parker in 1568, after Caius's *De antiquitate Cantebrigiensis academiae* reached completion. The Privy Council's printed letter of that year awarded Parker "a speciall care and oversyght" over historical records and monuments and ordered all who possessed such materials to make them available to Parker.[108] This letter stated explicitly that the monasteries had served as the official custodians of English records—secular as well as religious: "Auncient recordes and monumentes . . . heretofore were preserved and recorded by speciall appoyntment of certaine of her auncestours, in divers Abbeyes, to be as treasure houses, to kepe and leave in memorie such occurentes as fell in their times."[109] In some cases, arguments about medieval historians that appeared under Parker's name were formulated by others. A list of contents in the British Library copy of the *Flores historiarum* ascribes the preface, not to Joscelyn, but rather to "Roffensis"—that is, Edmund Gamaliel Gheast or Guest, bishop of Rochester and chaplain to Parker.[110] In April 1570, Caius tells us, he had a literary discussion at the table in Lambeth Palace with the two men.[111] Parker's vision of chronicles—the monastic ones and his own—as a sort of continuous, authoritative archive was probably hammered out in the course of conversations like that one.[112] The culture of conversation based on Parker's collections involved more than displaying treasures to his trusted friends. It also helped the archbishop himself assess the nature of the traditions he collected.

CHAPTER 6

Francis Daniel Pastorius
Makes a Notebook

A MAN OF TRADITION IN A NEW WORLD

FRANCIS DANIEL PASTORIUS loved to make jokes.[1] Once he had made them, he tried to preserve them—even at the cost of defacing the beloved books in his library. Among his favorite writers was the Leiden University historian Georg Horn (1620–1670), who attracted attention in the 1650s and 1660s for his polemical works on the origins of the American peoples and his surveys of European history and politics.[2] In 1666 Horn brought out a typically short textbook on a typically big subject, the history of nature and God's relation to it. He gave it the catchy title *Arca Mosis, sive Historia mundi* (*The Ark of Moses, or the History of the World*). The engraved title page depicts Pharaoh's daughter as she discovers the infant Moses. Turning toward a bare-bellied companion while her serving women watch, she holds the baby up in what the British still call a Moses basket. Pastorius's copy of the 1669 edition, like a number of his other books, is in the Library Company of Philadelphia.[3] Writing in a sinuous loop that follows the highlighted section of the Egyptian princess's legs and then moves onto the surface of the Nile, Pastorius has entered a line of Latin: "Est mihi namque domi pater, est crocodilus in illo/et ipse"—either "I have a father at home, there's a crocodile in it too," or "I have a father at home, and he's also a crocodile."

The remark seems mysterious. But its obscurity was deliberate: it was an allusion, deliberately designed to challenge the reader. In the third of Virgil's great pastoral poems, the *Eclogues*, the shepherd Menalcas refuses to bet one of his sheep against the rival piper Damoetas. As he explains:

> est mihi namque domi pater, est iniusta noverca,
> bisque die numerant ambo pecus, alter et haedos.
> For I have a father at home, there's a mean stepmother,
> and they both count the flock twice a day, and one
> of them counts the kids.[4]

Evidently something about the illustration reminded the German in Pennsylvania about the ancient Roman epic poet. Perhaps, as a good Christian humanist, Pastorius meant to suggest that Virgil's imaginary shepherd and Pharaoh's daughter both struggled with problematic families. Each had a harsh father, the one counting sheep and kids and the other mistreating Jews. While Menalcas had to deal with a wicked stepmother, Pharaoh's daughter confronted a sharp-toothed reptile. It is hard to imagine a less convincing punch line. Perhaps you had to be there.

Yet Pastorius's bad joke is more than a tiny, learned puzzle. As Robert Darnton argued long ago, it is precisely when historical actors say or do strange and paradoxical things that we need to work hardest at interpreting their actions and sayings.[5] Our bafflement may mean that we have encountered a genuinely strange belief or practice: a clue that may help us to experience the true foreignness of the past. Pastorius was an eminently practical man. He founded Germantown, drew up its legal codes, compiled its register of properties, and served the settlement in several legal and political capacities. Why, then, did he amuse himself with erudite Latin games like this one? What did they mean to him and to others?

Pastorius believed that the Latinate scholarship that he practiced as a reader retained utility and value in the practical life that he led in Pennsylvania. In fact, the learned practices he brought with him from Europe remained central to his day-to-day work, helping him deal with the personal and intellectual challenges with which the New World presented him—from deciding whether Christians could hold slaves to working out how to describe the Lenape Indians, near whom he spent much of his adult life—and enabled him to build communities. And that is less surprising than it may seem. Erudition still mattered, after all, in the late seventeenth century. Reading and writing in particular, highly skilled ways were intimately connected with membership in the intangible but powerful community known as the Republic of Letters, which stretched across the Atlantic, as it did across political and religious borders in Europe.

From the start of Pastorius's time in America, knowledge of Latin literature cemented relationships that mattered deeply to him. Pastorius met William Penn and Thomas Lloyd on the ship that brought him to the New World. He and Lloyd began what became a lifelong friendship—Pastorius became a mentor to Lloyd's children and grandchildren as well—while speaking Latin (Pastorius and Penn spoke French). What really won Penn's affection for Pastorius, however, was the slightly grandiose Latin inscription that the German placed over the door of his first small house in Pennsylvania, which was only "thirty shoes long, fifteen wide, with oiled paper windows for lack of glass." "Parva domus sed amica bonis, procul este prophani," wrote Pastorius: "It's a little house but welcoming to good people: profane men, keep your distance."[6] The second part of this inscription was a quotation from Virgil's *Aeneid*. In book 6 of the epic, Aeneas and the Trojans come to Cumae, where the Sibyl explains to him how he may descend to the Underworld. As priests perform sacrifices to the chthonic gods, Pluto and Proserpine, the Sibyl cries "procul, o procul este, profani . . . totoque absistite luco" (Keep your distance, profane men . . . and shun this whole grove; *Aeneid* 6.238–239). Apparently the incongruity of the high sentence over the low doorway of a naïve domestic house charmed Penn. According to tradition, he even laughed when he saw it: one of two occasions in his life when he laughed.[7]

When Pastorius showed off his Virgilian learning in what now seems a curious way, he was declaring his allegiance, as he did in many other ways, to a world of bookish traditions in which he had been formed, and which he continued to draw on and use throughout his life in Pennsylvania. Doing so, as Penn's response shows, was a practical as well as a spiritual exercise. Soon he and Pastorius were embarked on the walks and rides in which they explored their common interest in such questions as maintaining peace with the Indians and building a godly society. Yet as we will see, the practices of erudition that Pastorius knew were neither uniform nor unchanging. The German Enlightenment emerged, in large part, from the same learned world that produced Pastorius, and his ways of reading texts, for all their seeming quirkiness, in fact identify him as a characteristic figure of a particular cultural landscape, and even a characteristic member of a single intellectual generation.

Born a Lutheran in the Franconian town of Sommerhausen, Pastorius came from a well-off family and studied law at Altdorf, Strasbourg, and Jena. Inspired by the Pietist Philipp Jakob Spener, Pastorius came to America in June 1683, in pursuit of a simpler, more pious life. But simplicity proved elusive. Pastorius spent his life in what became Pennsylvania, working hard at his various professions and trying to keep his head above the surface of a flood of information. His legal and political work as an agent of the Frankfurt Company and bailiff, committeeman, clerk, and burgomaster in Germantown required him to master the laws of Pennsylvania.[8] His passionate religious convictions inspired him to find and study every Quaker text he could—especially in his early years in America, when Quaker works in English were more accessible than other books.[9] Much of Pastorius's note taking and writing served immediate, practical ends. His *Young Country Clerk's Collection* collected the details of the Pennsylvania legal practice that he knew at first hand, and his primer reflected his experience as a teacher in Germantown and Philadelphia.

Yet Pastorius read far more than his practical duties required. As the supply of books available in Philadelphia gradually expanded, his irrepressible curiosity pushed him to explore everything from Renaissance works on world history and natural philosophy to contemporary discussions of the diseases prevalent in his part of the world and the therapies that might be available for them—not to mention alchemy, which fascinated him as much as it did Governor John Winthrop Jr. of Connecticut, one of the few earlier inhabitants of the colonies who had been Pastorius's match for cosmopolitan erudition.[10]

OF MAKING MANY NOTEBOOKS

Pastorius's mind—or at least his books—buzzed with poetry and prose, proverbs and biblical verses, visions of edible legumes and rules for surveying, bibliographies and stories about authors. He stored all this material for use, by himself and his sons, in the margins of the books in his library and in magnificent information retrieval machines, the grandest of which is his *Bee-Hive*, the immense commonplace book that is one of the glories of the Van Pelt Library at the University of Pennsylvania.[11] If Pastorius's books reflect complex patterns of reading and sociability that seem unfamiliar in the age of the Kindle, his commonplace books are even more disorienting. Reading one of them resembles entering a carnival fun house where texts of all kinds— excerpts and stories, jokes and reflections, history and alchemy, stories about horses and dogs—take the place of distorting mirrors. Subjects and languages blur into one another in a continual process of metamorphosis. Associations served Pastorius very much as links serve us, both tempting and enabling him to leap from one text or subject to another. Every small tag from a great text had associations for him, which spurred him to call up and write down passages from other texts.

The marginal notes and manuscript compilations on which Pastorius lavished so much time and effort challenge modern disciplinary boundaries. How are we to map this extraordinary unknown territory? Scholars have taken two paths in recent years and found gold at the end of each. Historians, legal scholars, Germanists, and others have read their way into Pastorius's manuscript compilations and finished writings, tagged and identified many of their sources, and re-created the larger social and cultural worlds within which he lived, worked, and read. Thanks to Alfred Brophy, Patrick Erben, Margo Lambert, and others, who have illuminated Pastorius's thought in these ways, we know how he explored the magnificent labyrinths of Quaker thought and spirituality, how he developed his ideas about language and other central themes, and how he practiced as a lawyer, served his community, and taught.[12]

Historians of the book have also begun to look seriously at Pastorius's books and at his magnificently weird devices for textual storage and retrieval. Edwin Wolf collected the evidence for Pastorius's own library, showing that it was probably the largest in Philadelphia before James Logan built his collection.[13] More recently, Brooke Palmieri has laid out, in gritty, granular detail, exactly how Pastorius made and expanded his notebooks and sorted and indexed his excerpts. She has shown how Pastorius, as he worked, updated, and personalized the methods for commonplacing that Renaissance humanists like Erasmus had laid out in textbooks that reached a vast readership.[14] The digital version of the *Bee-Hive* now available on the web site of the University of Pennsylvania libraries will enable many more scholars to make direct excursions into this rough intellectual country.[15]

Much remains to be done. One major task is simply to describe Pastorius's ways of reading and connect them with their sources in learned tradition. For generations, the learned humanists of Europe had covered the title pages of their books with everything from signatures that declared their ownership to mottos in learned languages—not to mention allusive comments on the texts that followed. The sublimely erudite Huguenot Hellenist Isaac Casaubon filled his printed working copy of the Greek historian of Rome, Polybius, with so many handwritten notes that the Bodleian Library classifies the book as a manuscript.[16] He too made jokes on the title page: in his case, jokes that reflected serious thought about his author. Casaubon described the Greek historian's frequent digressions on historical method as a bug, rather than a feature, of his style: "Note: one thing we do not like in this author is that he repeats, and sets out, his plans, his goals, and his ends, so many times. Why bother to do this? Did he think he was going to be read only by Greek soldiers and centurions who smelled like goats?"[17]

Gabriel Harvey, the Cambridge professor of Greek and counselor to Philip Sidney and other great men, was not simply eccentric when he used the title pages of his books to record his autobiography as a reader or when he wreathed the texts of Livy, Guicciardini, and many others with notes reminiscent of Pastorius in their obsessive concern with detail, their pedantic playfulness, their multiple languages, and their wonderfully legible handwriting.[18] He was carrying on a tradition of annotation deeply rooted in the world of manuscript books. Different versions of it had served Francesco Petrarca, Angelo Poliziano, and Niccolò Machiavelli in their turn when each of them set out to master texts and make them his own.[19]

Notebooks were also traditional. Even wide margins were not wide enough to contain everything that annotators wanted to record, in an age when books were the prime sources of knowledge. By their nature, moreover, as expert humanists noted, marginal notes were hard to review and index.[20] Ann Blair and other historians of information management have shown that many of those who seriously wanted to survey a province of the world of books did so by keeping either adversaria—random notebooks in which they entered extracts as they read—or commonplace books—systematic notebooks in which they organized extracts under topical headings.[21] Some, like Casaubon, kept both. When the young Sir Julius Caesar—like Pastorius, a humanist and a lawyer—set out late in the sixteenth century to master the humanities and the law, he bought a ready-made commonplace book—a set of blank pages with categories already printed on them and a preexisting index, published by the martyrologist John Foxe in 1572. Caesar showed patience and practiced a clear handwriting that matched those of Pastorius as he filled 1,200 large pages.[22] Like Pastorius, Caesar both collected passages from many languages and traditions and assembled materials of practical use to a British lawyer and statesman. He thus created, in William Sherman's words, "a powerful tool that anticipated the kind of indexed archive now being delivered to anyone with a computer by Google and its associates": an information recovery machine that, like the *Bee-Hive*, used verbal associations as its links.[23]

LIFE IN THE MARGINS: READING AS
A CRAFT AND A CALLING

Each of these men turned reading into a formal craft and practiced it with articulate self-consciousness. Each of them stated the rules of the game of interpretation and note taking, in advance, as he saw them. Each of them documented his own life with books with great precision and in a highly legible form, embracing with muscular willingness a vast effort of personal and physical self-discipline. For each of them saw reading as a deeply serious enterprise: vital for the practical affairs of everyday life and for the forging of a religious identity, for the amassing of a kind of cultural capital and for the making of links to other passionate readers. Each of them knew, and stated, that he was doing more than memorialize an apparently fleeting experience: he was carving a niche of his own in a humanistic tradition. These men dramatized reading as an act to be carried out in conditions of strenuous attentiveness, preceded by rituals and attended by elaborate equipment. Casaubon made a point of combing his hair every morning before he went upstairs to his study to speak with the ancients; Jacques Cujas worked with a book wheel and a rotating barber's chair, so that he could whirl from project to project.[24] And they valued their readings and the notebooks in which they recorded them. One of the standard handbooks for early modern readers, the *Aurifodina* (*Gold Mine*) of the Jesuit Jeremias Drexel, shows two sorts of mining on its title page. On one side, three literal miners dig for material gold in a cavern. On the other, a lone scholar mines gold from his book by taking careful notes. Drexel left his reader in no doubt as to which sort of mining yielded the greater and more lasting riches.[25]

Pastorius's prized copies of several books by Georg Horn, now in the Library Company of Philadelphia, reveal how closely he adhered to these traditions. True, these books are not festooned with notes, as Harvey's were. But they show every sign of engaged reading in the fullest traditional style: one that combined marginal annotation with commonplacing in a single, complicated system of information storage and retrieval. Pastorius regularly entered Latin mottos—appropriate to a student reader proud of his knowledge—on their title pages. By the image of ship in full sail at the start of the *Orbis imperans*, Pastorius wrote, "Quo me Fata trahunt: retrahuntque" (Wherever the Fates drag me, and then drag me back), very likely a saying he had found in an earlier collection.[26] He also provided guidance to their contents—as in the note that summed up in advance the providential natural history that underpinned Horn's *Arca Mosis*.[27]

Above all, Pastorius maintained an active dialogue with his books. Sometimes his comments took the modest form of dry Latin jokes and puns. When Horn mentioned Charles V's reform of the Imperial Chamber Court, which he moved to the city of Speyer (Spira in Latin), Pastorius noted: "in qua plurimae lites spirant, sed non exspirant" (here many lawsuits breathe, but never breathe their last).[28] Sometimes he responded directly to the text: as when he came across a passage in the *Orbis Politicus* in which Horn described Quakers, Shakers and Fifth-Monarchy Men as sectaries of essentially the same kind. Pastorius crossed out this passage and commented, at the end, "haec ultima falsa" (the last bit is false).[29] Here he put himself in a tradition that stretched all the way back to Petrarch, who regularly discussed matters with the ancient authors he read, and even sent formal letters to Cicero and Virgil, in which he rebuked the former for his involvement with politics and expressed his regret that the latter had lived too early to be saved by Jesus.[30] Yet Pastorius was not finished with these books once he had marked his progress through them. He listed some of these books among his special favorites and copied excerpts from them in the *Bee-Hive*. Horn noted, for example, that "the skin of the Ethiopians is soft and porous, because the sun has consumed its stiff grains."[31] Pastorius put a line beside the passage, and later copied it into the entry entitled "Negro" in the *Bee-Hive*.[32] Pastorius's ways of using his books mark him off as an inhabitant of a world we have lost: a world of relative textual scarcity, in which each book was a precious possession that must serve multiple functions—and in which someone who lived in a slave society and could have examined black men and women directly still found information that he saw as useful in a Latin compendium written decades before his time.

Sadly, we do not have an inventory of Pastorius's library. But the evidence of his surviving books makes clear that he reveled in the multiple uses of print. The title of a Jesuit encyclopedia stimulated him to set off a fireworks display of Latin jokes and quotations, as well as a fancy version of his signature.[33] A satire on scholars and their ways by the Utopian Johann Valentin Andreae provoked sardonic remarks about the spread of both belief and deceit in an age when new inventions like the telescope, which called perception and knowledge itself into question, were multiplying.[34] And a wry remark about the way that medical men's rivalry spurred them to offer competing remedies, regardless of their utility to the sick, inspired a paradoxical reflection: "So many are helping me that I am quite overwhelmed."[35] As Pastorius read one book after another, he turned them into something like tiny chapters of his autobiography as a reader, each of them distinctive and each of them—at least for those who knew and appreciated him and his learning—potentially valuable.[36]

These considerations were not purely theoretical. Pastorius's circle of friends included James Logan, the ruthless trader and fantastically erudite scholar who, in the face of considerable practical obstacles, built up the largest library in the English colonies.[37] Logan loved obtaining rare books, such as the early printed edition of Ptolemy that a German friend gave him, and in return for which he sent his benefactor a buffalo robe.[38] He took pleasure in the fact that some of his books came, directly or indirectly, from Pastorius, and recorded it with precision. On the flyleaf of one of them Logan wrote: "I bought this book from Phillip Monckton, to whom it was sold by the son of my great friend Francis Daniel Pastorius of Germantown, 15 November 1720."[39] For his part, Pastorius seems to have liked borrowing books from Logan—at least to judge from the epigram in Latin and English that he addressed to Logan when he returned his friend's copy of the political emblem book of Diego de Saavedra Fajardo, with its impressive vision of a Christian prince.[40] It seems quite likely that Pastorius thought with pleasure about a time after his death when friends and later scholars would collect and examine his books, and remember him and these transactions.

Not all such exchanges were commercial. By giving or lending a book, or indeed by borrowing one, one acknowledged the other party's citizenship in the Republic of Letters. Pastorius arranged his friendships deliberately so that only those who deserved to become his intimates could do so.[41] This did not mean that he bonded only with other males. Like a number of his contemporaries, he saw women as eminently capable of citizenship in the Republic.[42] He made this view clear when writing to a younger friend, Lloyd Zachary, in Latin, to excuse himself for having held on for far too long to a female friend's copy of volume 4 of the *Spectator*: "I humbly beg for the forgiveness of the owner, who is quite right to be annoyed, and I hope your intercession will keep her from denying me volume 5."[43] Evidently Pastorius, his correspondent, and the book's owner all belonged to a world of learned, skeptical readers, who helped one another keep abreast with the newest arrivals from London.

If Pastorius cared about the printed books that he customized, he cherished his commonplace books. A graphomaniac, he copied everything he could, including the journals of friends (whom he reprimanded when he felt that their diaries included so much boring, repetitive detail that it taxed even his patience): "now a days most Readers loath Superfluities in all sorts of Writings, and much more those to whose

Task it falls to copy or transcribe them."[44] When a friend fell ill, his first thought was to copy out the perhaps valuable remedies that he had stored up over the years: "I heartily sympathize with thy lameness, and forasmuch as I collected out of several experienced authors many good Remedies agt bodily distempers let me know, if thou please, what you properly call it, and I shall very willingly transcribe what I find in my book."[45] Pastorius literally believed that the results of all his toil were priceless. He urged his sons not to part with the greatest of his notebook-making feats, the *Bee-Hive,* "for any gold or red Dust of this world."[46]

PASTORIUS AND THE ELDER PLINY: A CASE STUDY

It is not easy to know what to call the results of Pastorius's active and multiple ways of reading: certainly not a textual interpretation in any simple sense—and far less the sort of simple, straightforward reading of texts that early Quakers had preferred to the subtleties of the learned.[47] An analysis of one phrase will give a sense how reading and writing, tradition and the individual talent interacted as Pastorius sat over his books and his excerpts from them, crafting, not only a body of notes, but also a classical identity. When Pastorius began to copy out *The Young Country Clerk's Collection,* he reflected, in a nicely characteristic mixture of Latin and English, that "Ingenuum est fateri per quos profeceris according to Plinius" (it is honorable to acknowledge the sources through which you have derived assistance, according to Pliny).[48] Here he quoted the preface to one of the largest and most diverse compilations in classical literature, the *Natural History* of the elder Pliny. This Roman lawyer, official and military commander, who died while inspecting the eruption of Mount Vesuvius in 79 CE, completed his vast rag and bone shop of ancient learning, thirty-seven books long, not long before his death. Early modern printers often called the book *History of the World,* a title that gives some idea of its scope.[49] The author's nephew, also named Pliny, described his uncle's masterpiece as "a massive and learned work, as crammed with incident as nature itself."[50] In fact it was something like a classical *Bee-Hive:* a large-scale work of compilation. The elder Pliny, as his nephew explained, laid the foundations of his own scholarship by an ascetic regime of reading. He rose at midnight or a little later, visited the emperor

Vespasian before dawn, did his official job in the imperial administration and the law—and then lay in the sun and ate his meals while books were read to him. "He made extracts of everything he read, and always said that there was no book so bad that some good could not be got out of it."[51] At his death in the eruption of Vesuvius, he left his nephew "160 notebooks of selected passages, written in a minute hand on both sides of the page, so that their number is really larger than it seems. He used to explain that when he was serving as procurator in Spain he could have sold these notebooks to Larcius Licinus for 400,000 sesterces [an ancient Rome coin], and there were far fewer of them then."[52] To mention either Pliny, in the context of reading and note taking, was to call this story to mind. No wonder Pastorius wrote early in the *Bee-Hive* that he wanted "my two sons, not to part with it. . . . But rather Continue it by the help of this following Table. Because, The Price of Wisdom is aboue Rubies."[53] Later in the eighteenth century, Americans would imagine themselves as citizens of the Roman Republic as they wrote their political treatises. Pastorius portrayed himself as an American Pliny and his commonplace book as the American counterpart to those marvelous notebooks that the original had compiled.

For decades, modern scholars criticized Pliny for relying on books rather than the informants with practical experience whom Aristotle and Theophrastus had regularly consulted.[54] In fact, Pliny made no bones about the fact that his work chiefly consisted of facts extracted from texts. He insisted on the value of information of this kind, and remarked that his predecessors had not read and commonplaced with his meticulous integrity.[55] As he noted in his preface:

> You will be able to judge my taste from the fact that I inserted at the beginning, the names of my authors. For I consider it to be pleasant and to indicate an honorable modesty, to acknowledge the sources whence we have derived assistance, and not to emulate the majority of those whom I have examined. For please be aware that when I compared authors with each other, I discovered that some of the most grave of our recent writers have transcribed the ancients word for word, without mentioning their names.[56]

Contemporary scholarship on Pliny is duly appreciative of the richness of the material he had collected, and its appropriateness to the tastes of his contemporaries. Pastorius would certainly have agreed.

In practice, Pastorius emulated Pliny in two ways: he not only identified the primary sources which he used, but also cited Pliny as his warrant for doing so. At the same time he changed Pliny's words even as he quoted them, shortening "est enim benignum, ut arbitror, et plenum ingenui pudoris fateri per quos profeceris" (for I consider it to be pleasant and to indicate an honorable modesty, to acknowledge the sources whence we have derived assistance) to "Ingenuum est fateri per quos profeceris according to Plinius" (it is honorable to acknowledge the sources through which you have derived assistance, according to Pliny). In the section on letter writing that appears later in the *Collection*, Pastorius cited Pliny's thought again, translating the beginning of the original Latin literally while adding a further suggestion for elegant variation later on: "it indicates an ingenuous modesty, to acknowledge the sources whence you have derived assistance. Pliny. From which you have copied."[57] In this practice of deliberate variation Pastorius followed a standard precept of classical rhetoric. The well-educated man should take care to misquote, slightly, when he brandished a quotation from an older text: to practice elegant but apparently inadvertent variation. By doing so he showed that he quoted from memory—the proper way for a gentleman to access his texts—even as he admitted that in practice he took extensive written notes.[58]

COMMONPLACING PRACTICES AND THEIR MEANINGS

Even when Pastorius compiled an eminently practical book, in other words—a collection of model legal documents and passages from letters—he played the elaborate, self-conscious games of humanism, even playfully assuming a classical persona. He borrowed his description of the proper way to borrow from the ancient whose note-taking prowess inspired him, and then made it his own by altering its form. In the *Bee-Hive*, he used the same tactics even more elaborately, creating a colorful patchwork of sayings about indebtedness and note taking:

> I acknowledge, with Macrobius, that in this Book all is mine, & Nothing is mine. *Omne meum, nihil meum.* And though Synesius says, It's a more unpardonable theft, to steal the labours of dead men, than their garments, *Magis impium Mortuorum lucubrationes, quam*

vestes, furari, Yet the wisest of men concludes, there is no new thing under the sun, *Nihil novi sub Sole,* and an other, that nothing can be said but what has been said already, *Nihil dicitur quod non dictum prius.* Seneca writes to his Lucilius that there was not a day in which he did not either write some things or read & epitomize some good author.[59]

This whole passage on acknowledging what one has borrowed is, appropriately enough, a series of borrowings. In this case, Pastorius drew the sayings he ascribed to Macrobius and Synesius not from their own writings but from the address to the reader, signed Democritus Junior, in Robert Burton's *Anatomy of Melancholy,* itself one of the seventeenth century's masterpieces of compilation.[60]

The source of the last saying, which Pastorius attributes to Seneca, is especially revealing. At the end of this passage, most of which is in English, appears a phrase in Latin: "Vide omnino Spectator num. 316" (See to be sure Number 316 of the *Spectator*). Here Pastorius cited an article by John Hughes, a poet, musician, and librettist, in Joseph Addison's periodical. Hughes denounced his contemporaries for their idleness and offered the commonplace book as a remedy:

> Seneca in his Letters to Lucelius assures him, there was not a Day in which he did not either write something, or read and epitomize some good Author; and I remember Pliny in one of his Letters, where he gives an Account of the various Methods he used to fill up every Vacancy of Time, after several Imployments which he enumerates; sometimes, says he, I hunt; but even then I carry with me a Pocket-Book, that whilst my Servants are busied in disposing of the Nets and other Matters I may be employed in something that may be useful to me in my Studies; and that if I miss of my Game, I may at the least bring home some of my own Thoughts with me, and not have the Mortification of having caught nothing all Day.[61]

This passage is suggestive in more than one way. It shows that Pastorius—like most commonplacers—took his quotations from intermediary sources as well as from originals. It indicates that one could conceive of commonplacing, not only as an artificial memory—the way in which Pastorius himself described it—but also as an ascetic discipline, a way of forming a moral, hard-working self. And it reminds us that in the late seventeenth and early eighteenth centuries, the methods and meanings of commonplacing continued to evolve, and that cutting-edge intellectuals played a role in that process. No less a modern than John Locke devised a new method for making them.[62] They were so trendy, in fact, that self-proclaimed traditionalists who proclaimed their own independence of such aids to learning denounced them. In the preface to his 1711 *Tale of a Tub*, Jonathan Swift joked that he had planned to expand his satire with a panegyric to the present and a defense of the rabble, "but finding my Common-Place-book fill much slower than I had reason to expect, I have chosen to defer them to another Occasion."[63] When Pastorius used Seneca to support his view that reading and writing, excerpting and composition, were closely connected, he was not harking back to the Latin works of Erasmus, much less his classical sources, but rather citing a current periodical.

The *Young Country Clerk's Companion* and the *Bee-Hive* were both meant to serve practical purposes: the former was a guide to legal practice in Pennsylvania, the latter an aid to full mastery of the vast vocabulary of English. Yet both of them also offered Pastorius opportunities, of which he took exuberant advantage, for the same sort of humanistic play in which he engaged on the title pages of his Latin books. To some extent, as we have seen, his ways of playing would have been familiar to others who were well read in the English literature of his day.

Still, in the English-speaking world around 1700, Pastorius stands out as a compiler for his riotous polyglot learning and his manically associative habit of mind. To enter the *Deliciae hortenses* (Garden delights) or *Voluptates Apianae* (Bee-keeper's pleasures), a collection of sayings and poems that Pastorius assembled late in life, is to be swept away by Pastorius's virtuosity. A skillful gatherer-hunter-collector of others' phrases, he was equally deft at ringing multiple changes on them. He could turn one tag into rhyming or rhythmic phrases in multiple languages and find in all of them food for contemplation of God's ways in nature. A single thought—"Only the bee stores up honey"—could pass through seven languages as Pastorius worked his way to the maxim that God's word is even sweeter than honey:

Μόνη ἡ μέλισσα τιθαιβώσσει
Sola Apis mellificat. Die Bien allein trägt Honig ein.

Het honigh komt alleen Van Biekens by een,
Solamente le Pecchie fanno Mele. Seulement les Abeilles font du miel.
The Bees alone bring home   Honey and honey-Comb.
The Bee is little among such as flie, but her Fruit is the Chief of sweet
    things. Syrac. 11:3.
Qu. What is sweeter than Honey? Judg. 14:18.
Answ: God's Word. Psal. 119:103. etc.[64]

Marc Shell and Werner Sollors did not exaggerate when they canon-
ized Pastorius as the first of America's multilingual writers.[65] Collections like his, with their complicated games of variation and their
pursuit of symbols and messages, were as foreign as many of the texts
he quoted.

PASTORIUS'S INHERITANCE: LATE HUMANISM
IN THE GERMAN WORLD

Pastorius's practices came with him from Europe to Pennsylvania.The
best way to understand more precisely what he hoped to accomplish
through this vast accumulation of texts and sentiments is to follow
him back into the intellectual territories in which his mind was formed:
the world of German schools and universities in which he grew up, became a learned man, and developed his particular passions. Pastorius
grew up in Windsheim, where he attended the local Gymnasium. From
1668 he studied at a whole series of German universities before he took
his degree in law at Altdorf in 1676. Like so many German males from
the urban patriciate, in other words, he joined the Gelehrtenstand:
the social order of the learned. Doing this meant mastering a foreign
language and culture, since the learned used Latin as their primary
language in academic exercises and publications.[66] "In Winsheim,"
Pastorius recalled in the autobiographical narrative in the *Bee-Hive*,
"I had good Schooling, and mostly twenty or more young Earls, Bar-
onets, & Noble mens Children for School fellows, there being then an
excellent Rector of the Gymnasium by name Tobias Schumberg, a
Hungarian by birth, who could speak almost no Dutch, so that it was
not allow'd, to use any other Language but the Latin."[67] Though he
studied French, and perhaps other modern languages, at Strasbourg, he
had to defend his dissertation—and the set of theses appended to it—in
public in Latin.

Fluent Latin was not easy to attain. In theory, as Erasmus advised in his ever-popular textbook *On Copiousness*, the young student should simply read all the Latin and Greek authors, entering excerpts in a commonplace book until he had made a rich vocabulary and a wide range of allusions his own and could deploy them deftly. In practice, though, as Erasmus knew perfectly well, most students would never even attempt this. The very work in which he explained how to make notebooks, *On Copiousness*, offered sprawling lists of examples that readers could plunder as they wished: hundreds of ways to say "Thank you for the letter" in good Latin, for example, and dozens more for saying, "So long as I live, I shall remember you." Erasmus's *Adages*, which appeared in 1508, offered potted essays on thousands of subjects, each inspired by a pithy and quotable ancient saying.

These books became best sellers on a pan-European scale. Learned men and women across Europe used Erasmus's words as they assured one another that the friendships they had made and hoped to sustain across the vast distances and uncertain postal services of a warring world would last forever. Ambitious writers emulated Erasmus's magnificent effort to command a vast vocabulary, to weave a tissue of words, myths, and allusions that allowed—as Erasmus himself had shown—for play of many kinds.[68] But the majority, who harbored more modest literary goals, put on the Erasmian language of allusion, much as modern individualists wear black, as a straightforward way of asserting their membership in a literary world.[69] Pastorius's creatively configured quotation from Pliny may well come from Erasmus or another popular compiler, for it appears, in a similarly simplified form, in Cotton Mather's *The Christian Philosopher* and also in a letter of July 25, 1744, from the Dutch scholar J. F. Gronovius to John Bartram.[70]

To set Pastorius's work of compilation before this background is to see it in a clearer light. He actually set out to do what Erasmus had recommended and later Central European scholars had practiced: to read his way into a vast body of literature in many languages and make it his own, as Erasmus had eloquently advised, by excerpting and organizing it under his own categories. As always, though, Pastorius updated and reconfigured what he borrowed from others. The Baroque poets of the Germany Pastorius knew as a young man had cultivated many languages at once, producing verse in set forms in Latin, Italian, French, and other languages, especially in their youth, because their poetry could serve as their ticket of admission to academies or courts.[71] Pastorius focused especially on English, the language of his new community, in which his sons would live, and decanted his other languages into it. He made this clear when he described his immense—and multilingual—*Bee-Hive* as his "English Bee-Stock, which being the largest and best Manuscript, I in my riper years did gather out of the most excellent Authors," and left it to his sons as a precious possession.[72] Like the clear-minded late-humanist pedagogues who were inspired and informed by Erasmus, but set their own sights lower, Pastorius offered young lawyers in the New World not a straight replication of the rich humanistic and legal education he had enjoyed in Germany, but something more practical, designed for his new world: model letters and contracts for replication and adaptation and a mass of tags and anecdotes, recipes and remedies in English that could serve both their practical needs and any literary ones that might arise. Yet he never abandoned his love for polyglot wordplay. And this—like the forms of literary gathering, hunting, and collecting that he practiced— gives us a first clue to the identity of the scholars on whom Pastorius modeled himself.

The dominant figures in the intellectual world of the Holy Roman Empire that Pastorius knew at first hand—who were known, in their own time, as polyhistors—look, nowadays, like scholarly dinosaurs— especially when they appear next to nimbler contemporaries like René Descartes, whose ideas, we know in hindsight, had the future on their side. They took all knowledge as their province: past and future, nature and culture, history and astronomy. The Jesuit Athanasius Kircher, for example, traced the history of the world's peoples from before the Flood to his own day, deciphered Egyptian hieroglyphs, clambered into the crater of Vesuvius to study the mechanism of volcanic eruption, adhered to the Copernican system at a time when Catholics were forbidden to advocate it, played football against the Dominicans, and imagined the cat piano. Moreover, he presented his discoveries not only in a stately series of Latin folios, but also in the magnificent material form of the museum housed in his rooms in the Jesuit Collegio Romano.[73]

The polyhistors' reach often exceeded their grasp. The Hamburg scholar Peter Lambeck, for example, never managed to complete the "history of literature" that he outlined and planned to compile, in some thirty-eight volumes, and no wonder. This enormous work would have collected information about the lives and works of all significant authors from the Creation down to his own time, as well as about the institutions of intellectual life: from the contests at which ancient Greek poets competed, through the universities of the Middle Ages, to the academies of his own day.[74] But Lambeck's failure did nothing to dissuade others from attempting the same enterprise: all the way down to Nicolaus Gündling, who in the 1730s published a history of erudition that was almost 7,700 quarto pages long. The index alone stretched for over 900 pages.[75]

As one might expect, methods of compilation interested these men greatly. Vincentius Placcius (1642–1699), a professor of rhetoric at Hamburg, published an extensive manual on making notes in 1689. This included the first publication of a design for a "scrinium litteratum," or note closet: a piece of study furniture equipped with hooks on which the reader could fix and arrange excerpts on thousands of slips of paper. Though the plan was actually drawn up by Thomas Harrison, an English member of the circle of Samuel Hartlib, it is characteristic of the German world Pastorius knew that it was published there—and that Leibniz actually owned and used one of these scrinia, "though it apparently had little impact on the messiness of his papers."[76]

Other German savants specialized in bibliography rather than straightforward compilation. But the ways in which they gathered, processed, and displayed their materials have a clear kinship with Pastorius's methods. In Germany, a nation that was impoverished following the Thirty Years' War, few students could afford many books. (This was the world in which the writer Jean Paul Richter imagined an impoverished schoolmaster, Maria Wutz, who would compose the books he imagined when he read their titles in the Frankfurt book fair catalogue, but that he could not afford to buy.) Professors offered formal courses on "literary history." They would reprint the inventory of a major library or print a list of writers, distribute it to their students, and then dictate comments on it. These courses—a Baroque counterpart to Pierre Bayard's *How to Talk about Books You Haven't Read*—offered a rich mix of basic bibliographical information, critical judgments, and literary gossip, much of it unreliable. The influential Wittenberg professor Conrad Samuel Schurzfleisch, for instance, told his pupils of a rumor that the great philologist Joseph Scaliger had been castrated by his father in order to ensure that he not marry and discredit his illustrious family. There is no further evidence in any source to support this story.[77]

Students copied out what their teachers told them. Sometimes the teachers then recycled their students' notes as printed textbooks, which other teachers in turn made the objects of their own lectures. Compilation and excerpting, recompilation and commentary followed one another in a seemingly endless cycle.[78] The texts of these compilations grew as slowly and inevitably as glaciers, with a thin crust of slick textual ice covering a deep, dark rocky mass of footnotes. Christoph August Heumann of Göttingen surveyed all the knowledge that counted in a *Conspectus*, five hundred pages of Latin thrilling enough, or useful enough, that the book went through seven or eight editions.[79] Gottlieb Stolle of Jena offered courses in which he used Heumann's book as the textbook and dictated comments on it. Then he published his own lectures. Some student readers had their copies of Stolle on Heumann interleaved so that they could add still more information of their own.

Biographical evidence identifies two of the ways in which Pastorius may have encountered these methods and one of the teachers who may have helped him master them. Pastorius's own father, the jurist Melchior Adam Pastorius, was a compiler on the grand scale and a versifier almost as obsessive as his son. In 1657 he issued a massive study of the election and coronation of the Holy Roman emperors. Here he gathered, not only a vast amount of information about the preparations and ceremonies that had attended the most recent election in 1653, but also an emperor-by-emperor account of Imperial history from ancient Rome to his own time, with supplementary material on the electors.[80] Very late in his life, in 1702, Melchior Adam served as the publisher as well as the author of *Franconia rediviva*, a weighty anthology of lists and documents regarding the noble families and monasteries, cities, and institutions of the Franconian Kreis of the Holy Roman Empire.[81] Each of these books must have rested on systematic compilation—as did the extensive manuscript collections of Melchior Adam's verse, interspersed with curious illustrations, that survive in Philadelphia collections.[82]

In the *Bee-Hive,* Francis Daniel Pastorius recalled that he had learned some of the principles of public law from "the renowned Dr. Boeckler at Strasbourg."[83] It is likely that Pastorius learned some law from the elderly jurist Johann Heinrich Boecler (1611–1672). But it is even more likely that he learned a great deal about compiling and managing information. Boecler was not only a lawyer of reputation but also a master practitioner of literary history, an expert at manipulating the rococo information machines that took in names and titles, anecdotes and maxims, and spat out textbooks and courses. At the request of Leibniz's patron, Johann Christian von Boineburg, Boecler drew up a crisp little manual of the history of letters, from the Creation to the present, for young students. It bore the modest title *A Curious Historical-Political-Philological Bibliography That Reveals the Merits and Defects of Each Writer.*[84] Far longer—though still less than 1,000 pages—was the *Critical Bibliography of All the Arts and Sciences* that Boecler also composed, and that continued to be reprinted after his death.[85] Johann Gottlieb Krause, who edited this work after Boecler's death in 1715, ransacked Boecler's other works for relevant passages and added them to give the book more depth and heft, intervened where he thought editorial care could improve the exposition, and turned the original, skeletal work into a relatively content-rich guide to the world of learning.[86] In his original sketch of literary history, Boecler had said of the Greek historian Herodotus that he was not a liar and of Thucydides that he was very noble.[87] In Krause's elaborated version, the reader encountered Boecler explaining that modern travel accounts confirmed Herodotus's stories about gold-digging ants the size of wolves and noting that Thucydides's account of the Greek states at perpetual war with one another shed a powerful light on the fragmented, militaristic Holy Roman Empire of his own day.[88] When Pastorius listed topics, entered excerpts, and drew up indexes, treating compilation as a central and valuable part of scholarly work, he practiced skills that he had encountered in his youth and mastered through the long years of his university training.

Material evidence confirms that Pastorius began to master these techniques as a student. Pastorius owned a linked set of textbooks, which are now in the Library Company of Philadelphia. They include chronological tables for world history from the Creation to the present by a Braunschweig theologian, Christoph Schrader; introductions to the tradition of historiography from antiquity to modernity and to the genealogy of rulers from ancient Rome to the present; and a short textbook on geography by a Gymnasium professor, Heinrich Schaevius. Pastorius signed and dated the last of these in 1674.[89] The books themselves, annotated sparsely but systematically, show how he read his way into mastery of a world of scholarly methods and materials. Schrader's chronological tables, which presented world history in the skeletal form that was normal at the time, were dated, in the traditional way, from the Creation forward: Pastorius followed the custom that had become widespread in the seventeenth century and added a BC date, reckoned backward from the Incarnation, for the start of world history. Where Schaevius, whose brief handbook of geography Pastorius read, mentioned Pliny's *Natural History* as a model compilation on cosmography, Pastorius added a marginal reference to the Renaissance classic in the field, the work of Sebastian Münster.[90] And where Schaevius discussed systems for describing the world's landmasses, Pastorius noted, in very up-to-date terms indeed, that "the whole landmass of the world can also be divided into three parts, or great islands, around which the ocean flows: the first contains Europe, Asia, and Africa, the second America, and the third the Magellanic lands that are also called Austral [southern] and unknown."[91] Most revealing of all, though, is the list of writers on the early church, starting with the apostles and including pagans as well as Christians, that Pastorius copied into one of these books from the dissident Pietist historian Gottfried Arnold's book on the history of Christianity.[92] Every book invited the reader to engage in bibliographical compilation; every ancient authority invited the reader to make comparisons with modern counterparts.

Pastorius not only applied the techniques of the polyhistors, he shared their tastes. Like Kircher, the Jesuit Michael Pexenfelder, whose odd little encyclopedia of the arts and sciences Pastorius owned, took an interest in ciphers and other forms of writing designed to conceal one's meaning from curious readers.[93] He described Steganography as "a clandestine form of writing, which uses secret signs that a few have agreed on." These could be letters, standing in for one another, or numbers, or "new characters."[94] Here Pastorius wrote, "see the next page, near the bottom."[95] He covered the next opening, which deals with the use of metal characters in printing, with ingenious prints of many different kinds of leaf. In the bottom margin he wrote that characters could be "natural, the progeny of the gardens and the fields, some of which appear in the margin, or artificial. Of the first category, absinth stands for A, beta for B, the crocus for C, ferns for F, and so on. Botanists understand this very well."[96] Here we see that Pastorius's fascination with language, in all its texture, richness, and variation, was rooted in the culture of the old Holy Roman Empire—a world in which cryptography offered the possibility of sending secret messages, something every chancery and resident ambassador regularly did, and inspired the production of a rich body of poetry by a kind of combinatorics—rather like modern language poetry. Pastorius's mystical vision of language had its roots in a very particular milieu and moment.

This was not the only case in which Pastorius drew on the mysterious codes and emblems of the Baroque: the very element in which polyhistors like Kircher had lived, moved, and had their being.[97] At one point in the *Bee-Hive*, he reflected that human affairs always move in a circle: "The Revolution or Changeable Course and Recourse of this present World, viz., all Empires, Kingdoms, and Prouinces thereof, Yea of all particular Inhabitants of the same, [can be] prefigured in a Wheele of Seuen Spokes, called *Omnium Rerum Vicissitudo*." Poverty, Pastorius explained, created Lowliness, and that in turn Peace. Thanks to Peace, Traffick (or trade) increased, and created Wealth. But Wealth instilled Pride, which led to War and then back to Poverty.[98] Here Pastorius reconfigured an image coined, over a century before, by the Catholic Kabbalist and historian Michael von Aitzinger. A writer with an eye for the visual presentation of evidence, Aitzinger invented the popular image of the Low Countries as a lion, which played a very large part in Dutch visual propaganda during the war with Spain. Aitzinger also laid out the cycle by which societies passed from poverty through wealth to poverty again, on the title page of his history of the Dutch Revolt, to suggest a way of understanding the narrative that followed.[99] True, his cycle had only six phases rather than seven: perhaps this was another instance of Pastorius's desire to modify the treasures he collected. Basically, though, Pastorius was learning from Baroque tradition how to cope with rapid modern social change.

Even what may seem to be Pastorius's most characteristic and original writings drew nourishment from roots set deep in the layers of traditional scholarly practice. Consider, for example, the letters that he sent back to Germany, in which he described the new world that he found around him in Pennsylvania. These texts eventually became the groundwork for his most famous work, the *Umständige Geographische Beschreibung Pensylvaniæ* (*A Detailed Geographical Description of Pennsylvania*), which was published in Leipzig in 1700. One of the preparatory letters, written in Latin and dated December 1, 1688, was directed to Georg Leonhard Modelius. A friend of Pastorius's who was then at the university of Altdorf, Modelius eventually became rector of the Gymnasium in Windsheim that Pastorius had attended. He had asked Pastorius, in a letter we no longer have, for a description of Pennsylvania, both for himself and for his colleague Johann Christoph Wagenseil, a professor of Oriental languages—the period term for Hebrew and Arabic—at Altdorf still famed for his publications both on the Meistersinger of Nuremberg and on Jewish blasphemies against Jesus. The text pleased its recipient so much that he communicated it to one of the new journals of the period, aimed at a literate and alert lay public.[100] It appeared in Wilhelm Ernst Tentzel's *Monatliche Unterredungen einiger guten Freunde von allerhand Büchern und andern annehmlichen Geschichten* (*Monthly Conversations among Good Friends on All Sorts of Books and Other Pleasant Stories*) in April 1691.[101]

It is a charming text. Pastorius instructs his readers, first to use their maps to zero in on the Delaware and on Philadelphia, and then to imagine themselves there in the flesh, recovering from seasickness and eagerly welcomed by Pastorius. He invites them to enter his house, pointing to the inscription that offers hospitality, and shows them Germantown, with its rapidly growing population: only thirteen inhabitants in 1683, but now over fifty. Pastorius displays the prosperous houses and farms that the citizens of the new community have built, notes that they have no need as yet of a wall, and suggests that he and his guest walk out of town to see the Indians.[102] Pastorius apparently shared William Penn's sympathy for the Lenape Indians, which made possible the early "long peace" between them and white settlers. He describes the Indians admiringly and at length, noting their intelligence, their use of canoes and tobacco, the personality traits and behavior of males and females, their ways of courting and marriage, their religious rituals, and their ways of caring for the sick and burying the dead. The letter winds up with a list of phrases in the Indian language and in translation. Pastorius comments: "If you can divine the origins of these Indians from these bits of evidence, or from the fact that they call their mother *ana*, their wife *squáa*, their old woman *hexis*, their devil *menitto*, their house *wicco*, their land *hockihóckon*, their cow *muss*, their pig *Kuschkusch*, I will admit you're a really good philologist."[103] This letter adumbrates, not only Pastorius's future achievements as culture broker and populist, but also, more generally, the ethnographic writings of men like Lafitau and Lahontan and their successors.[104] Indeed, with its almost obsessive emphasis on the observer's intellectual resources and point of view, it seems to belong to the new travel writing of the eighteenth and early nineteenth centuries. And that impression is strengthened by a passage toward the beginning of the letter. Here Pastorius, as he takes Modelius on his imaginary walk, says, "So that we don't walk in silence like sheep, let's talk a little about the origin of the Nile—or, what is equally obscure, that of our Indians. Some think, not without plausible clues, that they are the descendants of the Hebrews. But their native language suggests that some of those who live farther from here come ultimately from Wales. Your Polyhistor in Altdorf [Wagenseil] will work out for you the dates and details of their navigations across the Atlantic. But I, since I have hardly a single book, will not myself take part in this dubious battle."[105] Here, so it seems, Pastorius ironically distanced himself from the culture of the learned in their universities. Implicitly, at least, he emphasized the superiority of direct experience of the present to book learning about the past.

It is always hard to decode the jokes and irony of past actors. Georg Horn spent much of his life devising ways to intercalate the history of China and the New World into the traditional narrative of world history, centered on the Mediterranean and Western Europe. He not only composed original textbooks, but also carried on long debates with colleagues about the origins of the Indians and the paths by which they had arrived in the New World after the Flood.[106] In recent years, Sanjay Subrahmanyam and Daniel Smail have advanced powerful programs for decentering our histories, by abandoning our obsessions with narratives centered in Mesopotamia, the Mediterranean and Western Europe and by combining scientific with historical evidence.[107] Horn was their seventeenth-century revisionist counterpart. Yet Pastorius, much as he admired Horn's books, made light of the complex historical genealogies and itineraries that filled their pages, as an outworn, obsessively bookish form of knowledge.

In offering an account of local Indian society based on direct experience, as in reading Horn's overviews of institutions and national histories, Pastorius did not rebel against the world of learning as he had known it in Germany. Rather, he carried on one of its central traditions. In the *Bee-Hive*, after all, Pastorius told his sons that they should record "all remarkable words, Phrases, Sentences or Matters of moment, which we do hear and read"—a clear instruction to combine experience and witnesses' accounts with reading.[108] From the sixteenth century onwards, humanists had argued that travel, and the direct experience of other countries and mores that it afforded, was essential to anyone who hoped to attain distinction in scholarship or politics. But travel, like reading, had to follow strict protocols if it was to profit those who undertook it. As we have seen, Theodor Zwinger, Thomas Turler, and many others drew up manuals of what they dubbed the "methodus apodemica" or formal art of travel.[109] Dozens of writers and hundreds of young men bore these instructions in mind (and the books that transmitted them in their pouches), as they compiled guides to the states of Europe, memoirs of their travels, or imaginative works of literature, like George Barclay's *Euphormionis Satyricon*, that turned on knowledge of the national characters of the different European peoples.

Pastorius's connections to this tradition were deep and organic—so much so as to make his own career as a travel writer seem almost over-determined. Travel writing was an early pursuit. Pastorius recalled that he kept "a peculiar Manuscript Journal . . . in 8°" of his travels down to 1682, when he arrived in Frankfurt.[110] It was also inherited. His own father, Melchior Adam Pastorius, compiled a detailed journal of his early education in the German college in Rome, his later travels, and his self-discovery in Paris, as a Protestant.[111] It is a charming medley of prose and verse, full of vivid recollections. The opening poem makes a boldly self-conscious allusion to Odysseus. Melchior Adam vividly describes how melancholy he felt when he was left on his own in the great city of Ferrara, and had nothing to do but visit churches, and how strange he found it that Italian nuns were surprised that he did not speak their language. A good polyhistor, Melchior Adam took a special interest, when he traveled, in the learned men who had adorned particular cities: for example, the Flemish Tacitist and ancient historian Justus Lipsius, whose house he visited in Louvain.

As a grown man, Francis Daniel continued to share his father's interests—even as he made gentle fun of them: "Here we should be wanting to ourselves," he writes in the *Bee-Hive*, "to the Memory of Justus Lipsius (oh quantum nomen! to which we dare not presume so much as to aspire) if we should not insert into these our Remarks the Inscriptions and Descriptions of his three most beloved dogs, whose Counterfeits or Resemblances still are to be seen at Louain, a City in Brabant, in the very house, wch this transcendingly learned man did inhabit . . . he names them Sapphirus, Mopsulus, and Mopsus."[112]

He also continued to respect books from the learned tradition of travel literature, such as Barclay's *Satyricon*, which he warmly recommended to Lloyd Zachary as late as 1717.[113] Once again, material evidence proves especially revealing. Pastorius's books in the Library Company of Philadelphia include a detailed guide to the sights and antiquities of Italy, region by region, illustrated with crisp views of the major cities. Written by the Antwerp lawyer Franciscus Schottus, the book was edited after his death by his brother Andreas, a Jesuit scholar, and had a long career as a learned person's guide to Italy.[114] It begins with a set of instructions for travelers on what to observe, neatly set out in diagrammatic form. Set topics include the geographical region, the name of the place and its founder, geographical features such as rivers and mountains, public and private buildings, political institutions, schools, and then "the customs of the ordinary people: including their ways of earning their living, their clothing and their crafts."[115] Pastorius's Latin report on Pennsylvania followed this outline with striking precision.

CRITICS OF TRADITION: PASTORIUS AND
HIS GERMAN COUNTERPARTS

In his systematic effort to use and to update the traditions of human-istic scholarhip, Pastorius reveals his kinship to a particular set of con-temporaries who remained in old Europe. Pastorius did not say any-thing very flattering in his autobiographical notes about the universities he attended. All of the academies he visited—and none of which he re-mained at for very long—had one thing in common: a love of hier-archy and ceremony. Johann Burkhard Mencke, the editor of the Leipzig periodical *Acta eruditorum*, described the etiquette of the erudite with biting wit in two satirical orations on *The Charlatanry of the Learned* in 1713 and 1715. He made brilliant fun of scholars' lust for honorific forms of address: "you see many demanding to be called *Clarissimus* who are absolutely unknown outside the walls of their city; *Magnificus*, who are oppressed by poverty; *Consultissimus*, who have little or no advice to give." He mercilessly ridiculed the elaborate Latin titles by which scholars tried to make humdrum books impressive: for example, "Public Law, or Medical Theses on Headache." And he sketched un-forgettable, acid pen-portraits of self-absorbed scholars like Johann Seger of Wittenberg:

> He had an engraving made on copper, showing the crucified Christ and himself. From his lips came the words, "Lord Jesus, do you love me?," and from the lips of Jesus came the answer, couched in the most laudatory terms: "Yes, most eminent, excellent and learned imperal poet laureate and rector of Wittenberg University, I do love you."[116]

Pastorius looked back without affection to the "impertinent Ceremo-nies" he had undergone as a beginning student at Altdorf.[117] His books in the Library Company show that complaints about the tediousness of traditional forms of learning and satires of the erudite piqued his interest.[118] He insisted on the central importance of English when he educated his own sons, and even if they inherited the *Bee-Hive*, they practiced crafts rather than pursuing erudition. And in the preface to his published description of Philadelphia, he stated formally that he rejected the learned institutions of Europe. Though he deplored the wickedness he saw around him in Pennsylvania, he wrote, "Nevertheless I hope things here will never be conducted in a way so unbecoming men, as in those universities in Europe, in which a man must learn for the most part things which are to be utterly forgotten. Many professors waste their time on useless questions and clever trifling tricks, and while they detail the minds of the learners on empty questions they prevent them from aspiring to more solid matters." He rebuked the learned for preferring Greek mythology to Christ, using Aristotle to explicate Scripture, and wasting their time on "utterly useless questions and trickeries," such as looking "among the Greek declensions for the ablative case" (Latin, not Greek, has an ablative case).[119]

The indictment and the rejection of erudite pursuits sound as unsparing as Mencke's. And that is precisely the point. Mencke denounced the universities because he hoped to improve them—as he tried to do, as professor and, eventually, rector of the University of Leipzig and editor of the major periodical his father had founded, the *Acta eruditorum*. Much evidence suggests that Pastorius, too, when he was not proclaiming the merits of life in fertile Pennsylvania, criticized the learned world, not in order to destroy it, but in order to save it. In the *Bee-Hive*, which he compiled in the last decades of his life, he continued to show an interest in Gottfried Arnold, the church historian who resigned his professorship at Giessen even before he published his history of the church and its heretics, which used the records of the past to challenge what he saw as a sterile orthodoxy in his own day. Pastorius also regularly noted books that contained information about the new university at Halle, and the Pietist Orphanage and mission to the Jews there: new intellectual foundations that deliberately departed from the traditions of the past and created new forms of learning and teaching.[120]

Pastorius's impatience with Latin and ceremony did not lead him to turn his back on the ceremonious, Latin-speaking world of learning. Like Gottfried Arnold, he wanted, not to abandon erudition, but to reconfigure it. And in that respect he resembled no one more than his close contemporary, the jurist Christian Thomasius (1655–1728). In many respects, to be sure, the elegantly coiffed Thomasius, who summoned his fellow German professors to learn to behave as if they were proper courtiers, seems sharply different from Pastorius, with his Quaker-inspired belief in equality and his love of fishing and gardening, yet the two men shared experiences and qualities. Both were trained as jurists and belonged to a larger wave of learned lawyers committed to reforming the law and the institutions that sustained it.[121] Both came under the influence of Philipp Jakob Spener and rejected the Lutheran orthodoxy in which they had been raised. Both were steeped in the traditions of erudition. And though Thomasius sharply criticized these traditions, more often he turned them to new ends. Thomasius attacked the universities' monopoly on learning and promoted modern studies. He broke with tradition and lectured publicly in German at Leipzig; he recommended the cultivated French way of life as superior to the German, pedantic one; and he founded a monthly periodical for the cultivated urban reader. But in doing so, he hoped to make the sterile culture of erudition fertile again.[122]

Lutheran theologians claimed the right to determine what could be taught and learned at universities. They tested every proposition against what they described as the immutable truths of orthodoxy.[123] Thomasius, by contrast, argued that the intelligent, cultivated person should receive all philosophical systems with the mild, reasonable skepticism they deserved. By doing so, one could find a middle path, between the absolutist follies of the Aristotelian scholastics and the overly strong prejudices of the Cartesians. The only royal road to wisdom lay in informing oneself about all the schools of philosophy, from the very beginning of human history—and then making an informed, eclectic choice among their principles.[124] For the human mind was simply incapable of creating a single, universally valid system, and as Thomasius reflected, it was better to have a refitted and rebuilt ship that could sail than one that had never been repaired and was full of cracks and falling apart.[125]

Thomasius's call for a reasonable eclecticism gave a new meaning to the polyhistors' pursuit of learning in general and "literary history" in particular.[126] Francis Bacon had suggested that a vital way to reform learning in the present was by composing a "just story" of its vicissitudes in the past. An analytical history of philosophy and the sciences, he believed, would show both which principles and which institutions had proved most productive over time. The passages in which Bacon made this argument had long inspired compilers like Lambeck.[127] Thomasius—and his disciples, such as Gündling and Stolle, who became the most renowned compilers of their day—seized upon them as the key to creating a literary world in which every new thesis would be seen against the proper, full background, traced to its roots, and fairly judged. As Martin Gierl has shown, what looks from the outside like formless erudition spilling down the thousands of pages of the literary histories actually represented a sustained effort to lead readers out of the maze of opinions that bewildered them. Erudition and eclectism were the keys, in Thomasius' view, to creating a critical public sphere: one in which the true, spiritual understanding of Christianity would come naturally to fruition.[128]

ERUDITION AND CRITICISM

This comparison can help us to dig down below the buzzing polyglot surface of the *Bee-Hive* and detect some of the deeper motives that underlay its creation. Pastorius himself described his commonplace books as memory theaters, and that they certainly were: cultural capital ready to be invested. But Isaac Casaubon also described his commonplace books as mnemonic devices.[129] And yet, as Joanna Weinberg and I have tried to show, they were also analytical tools, in which he showed how to analyze texts historically and philologically. It was there that he recorded the impressive Talmud lesson he received from a Jewish friend, Jacob Barnet, who had shown him how to surf the oceanic contents of that most complex and rebarbative of texts, moving from the text to the margins, identifying commentators, and noting discrepancies between editions.[130] When Pastorius addressed his readers, he instructed them, not just to memorize, but also to revise, his collections:

> Sis mihi Corrector, resecando superflua Lector; Veraque digneris, quae desunt jungere Veris
>
> [Be my corrector, reader, cutting what is superfluous, and deign to add the truths that are lacking to the truths that are here].
>   Read not to contradict, nor to Believe; But to weigh & Consider. Fr. Bacon.[131]

Similarly, Thomasius urged his readers to read his *Introduction to Courtly Philosophy* critically, in the hope that their corrections would make later versions of his arguments more rigorous.[132] Both treated erudition, not as a stock of material to be drawn on, or a cultural bank account, but as a challenge to the reader's intelligence: as a challenge to develop prudence and discrimination. And both proved eminently capable of examining and rejecting long-established beliefs and practices. Thomasius rejected the prosecution of witches and the use of torture, using comparative arguments to show that the custom of accepting evidence obtained by torture, though old, was neither universal nor founded in reason.[133]

On February 12, 1688, Pastorius and three friends examined the custom of slaveholding that many Quakers accepted and practiced. We do not know which of them wrote which parts of the document. But it seems likely that it was the cosmopolitan Pastorius, reader of Georg Horn and student of world systems of law and warfare, who criticized Christian slavers as resembling the Turks who enslaved Christians. It seems likely, too, that it was Pastorius, who was concerned for the reputation of Pennsylvania in Europe, and who argued that the colony would discredit itself in Germany and Holland by holding slaves. Perhaps he was the one who suggested that the slaves would have as good a "right to fight for their freedom" as Quakers could possibly have to use the sword against them.[134] At all events, Pastorius showed that he was the sort of critical, independent thinker that he hoped to find among his readers. And he never stopped worrying about the issue, as is clear from the fact that he put notes on "Negroes" in the *Bee-Hive*.

In this context, it is easy to understand why even in the last years of his life, Pastorius never ceased writing Latin epigrams to celebrate homely occasions like the staking of his grapevines. For, like Thomasius and other European reformers, he believed that tradition still had its value; indeed, that tradition, rightly updated, was modernity at its best. One scholar whom both Pastorius and Thomasius respected was the Franeker jurist Ulrich Huber, whose magnificent rectoral speech *On Pedantry* Thomasius reprinted twice. Thomasius denounced those "pretentious" scholars who "cite verses, proverbs, Latin, Greek and Hebrew words, scholastic technical terms, laws, medical rules, and other evidences of their learning when they serve no purpose."[135] Like Thomasius, Huber ridiculed the pedants who insisted on speaking Latin to people who lacked the competence in the language, or the confidence, to reply. But he insisted that Latin still had its uses as "a common chain that links the Christian peoples together," and its unique position as "the language of the people that ruled all the rest," and he urged the learned to continue to use it.[136] The fluent Latinist could communicate both with the learned of other nations and with the learned of the past. For Huber, Latin still embodied an intellectual cosmopolitanism that deserved to be honored and preserved. It was in the same sense, as Patrick Erben has suggested, that Pastorius prefaced his highly practical collections of laws, legal documents, and deeds in German, Dutch and English with grand title pages in which he used bold, sharp Latin axioms to give them a larger philosophical setting.[137] It was in the same sense, I would argue, that Pastorius used Latin and other elements of erudition: to maintain contact with learned friends in Europe; to make friends with William Penn, Isaac Lloyd, and James Logan; and to include younger friends like Young's grandson Lloyd Zachary in what Pastorius continued to see as the charmed world of a millennial conversation.

Pastorius's methods derived from a broad culture, which was Catholic as well as Protestant. He learned them from the Jesuits he disliked as well as the Protestant sages he admired. And he undoubtedly derived elements of his practice as a reader·and recorder—like his belief in writing down both good and bad arguments and letting the reader decide between them—in part from the Quakers he so admired, and into whose world he plunged in America, as well as from the scholarly traditions he came from.[138] But he seems to have had most in common with the particular brand of late humanism that flourished in Halle and elsewhere in North Germany in the years of his, and Thomasius's, maturity. The similarity between the literary histories compiled by Thomasius and his disciples and Pastorius's efforts to amass the treasures of Quaker spirituality, European learning, and modern medicine and alchemy for his sons seems clear. In Germany as in Philadelphia, the culture of erudition was both troubled and inspired by a pervasive dissatisfaction with existing customs and institutions. And in Germany as in Philadelphia, the combination of a strong religious motivation and a vast scholarly arsenal proved potent. In Philadelphia as in Halle, the foundations of the Enlightenment's true Holy City were located in the realms of erudition and religion—both of them, of course, defined in historically particular ways.[139]

If Pastorius had stayed in Europe, he might well have become a reforming Roman lawyer, like Thomasius. As it happened, however, he discovered America and helped to build a new world there. But his American life, for all its local particularity, also represents a fascinating chapter in two larger stories, which are only now beginning to be told: that of the practices of erudition in its early modern heyday and that of how the Enlightenment grew in part from roots deeply set in an older world of European learning and Christian belief.[140] Joannes Boemus and Polydore Vergil were not the last scholars to find, and show, that the making of excerpts from canonical sources could trigger uncanonical thoughts. Pastorius's annotated books and notebooks may seem to be unlikely avatars of Enlightenment thought. When set before the proper background, they suggest that the Enlightenment, at least in Pennsylvania, took more forms and drew on more traditions for inspiration than are suspected in our historical philosophies.

CHAPTER 7

Annius of Viterbo Studies the Jews

THE PRINCE OF FORGERS

WHAT DID HE KNOW, and when did he know it? Whenever a scandal breaks out, we ask these questions about its subject. Often, however, no answer comes, or at least no certain answer. Scandal has swirled around Giovanni Nanni, or Joannes Annius, of Viterbo, for six centuries. Many scholars would like to find out, in detail, what this most mischievous and creative of Renaissance historians actually knew about the past: to trace the ways in which he gained access to the ancient and medieval sources that he copied and condemned with equal zeal. For the moment, however, we cannot know. Condemned by the state of scholarship, we wander the labyrinthine pages of early editions of his work like shades in the Inferno, endlessly complaining about the ignorance to which we are apparently condemned. The present investigation of one small aspect of Annius's thought and practices will certainly reveal more than one dark area. Perhaps, however, it will also suggest some of the benefits that precise contextual study of the way he worked can still yield.

Scholars have established a good many facts about Annius's life: for example, that one more miracle, in addition to the one actually recorded in the *Acta sanctorum*, might have made him the patron saint of forgers. Born in the 1430s, he led a peripatetic career in the Domin-

ican order, teaching and doing rather unsuccessful astrological consul-
tations.[1] When Annius settled down in his native Viterbo around
1490, he fascinated his fellow citizens and prominent visitors alike by
showing them wonderful inscriptions and other Etruscan antiquities—
some of them, he claimed, discovered by a peasant who followed a
hare down its hole. His treatise on these inscriptions—which, in fact,
he had forged—was the first full-blown study of epigraphy to be composed during the Renaissance. It marked the beginning of a short but
dazzling career that would raise Annius to one of the highest offices a
Dominican could hope for, the position of Magister sacri palatii, or
papal theologian. He served until Cesare Borgia poisoned him in 1502.
Annius's crowning work, a massive collection of *Antiquitates*, was
published in Rome, with Spanish financial support, in 1498.[2]

This supremely Borgesian book was inspired by the fragments of
ancient historians whose full works were lost. These texts were embedded in longer works by Josephus and Eusebius—themselves, in some
cases, newly translated into Latin in the fifteenth century. Annius
claimed that a fellow Dominican had discovered and given him a series of interlocking narratives, mostly ascribed to shadowy but impressive ancients like Berosus the Chaldean, Manetho the Egyptian,
and Metasthenes the Persian (this last was his version of the real
name of a Greek historian of Persia, Megasthenes). Together they told
a labyrinthine tale of the origins of ancient civilization in Italy, where
Noah—also known as Janus—arrived after the Flood. The texts were
short, like their models. Annius chopped them up into even smaller
bits, which he laid out, like so many islands, on a sea of commentary
printed in smaller type. The devil, as always, lurked in the small
print. As Walter Stephens and other intrepid explorers have discovered
when they ventured into these dark realms, Annius's critical notes
and genealogical diagrams were even more ingenious than the fake
ancient texts they surrounded. This complex, dizzyingly self-referential
apparatus identified the faked authors' sources, coordinated their
voices, and made them accessible to readers, who used them for many
purposes.

Like any good Dominican theologian, Annius knew how to couch
an argument. In his commentary, he insisted, again and again, that the
only historians who deserved *fides* (formal belief) were those who wrote

on the basis of official records, like the cartularies kept by the public notaries of Italy in his own time.[3] In antiquity, the priests of the great kingdoms of Babylon, Egypt and Persia—Berosus and colleagues—had drawn their chronicles from the public records. They had also pointed out, explicitly, that they had done so, in helpful passages that Annius repeatedly cited. His text of Metasthenes, for example, began by insisting that ancient priests like Berosus were the only authoritative historians because only they sourced their chronicles in the archives.[4] These men's narratives neatly confirmed one another's truthfulness and authority. And they refuted the fanciful stories cooked up by the historians of *Graecia mendax* (deceitful Greece): individualists like Herodotus, who had made up their stories out of whole cloth instead of drawing them, as they should have, from the archives.[5] Edition after edition came from the presses, handsomely printed and equipped with detailed indexes and the other mod cons of the printing house.

The most obvious problem Annius's collection raised—as philologists noted within a few years after it appeared—was that though his historians supposedly represented many different ancient nations and languages, one and the same writer had composed, not only their texts, but also the commentary, in a recognizably uniform Latin style. As the great Beatus Rhenanus remarked, appositely citing an adage of his friend Erasmus, "one of them milks the he-goat; the other holds the sieve."[6] Like Erasmus, Rhenanus probably did not like being reminded that he himself, in an off moment, had cited the Annian texts as more or less authoritative.[7] As details underwent close scrutiny, increasing numbers of contradictions also emerged between Annius's texts and the remainder of the historical record. Annius, it seems, took a characteristically perverse pleasure in varying and transforming the information that he took from genuine sources. Josephus and Eusebius, the Jewish and Christian writers who preserved the major fragments of Berosus, noted that he had composed his account of antiquities in three books. Annius's Berosus wrote five. By the middle of the sixteenth century, any number of philologists and historians compiled lists of these discrepancies, which they used effectively to argue that the Annian texts could, or must, be fakes.[8]

Nonetheless, Annius's magnificent Rube Goldberg contraption rolled on like a juggernaut through the sixteenth century and beyond.

Multiple editions and rewritings helped his lurid histories play central roles in the early chapters of world and national chronicles, the pageantry of royal entries and the early stages of royal and noble coats of arms, from Iberia to Scandinavia, for well over a century. Though historians and librarians gradually learned to recognize the Annian fakes, however well disguised, and condemn them, the texts never lacked respectable, or at least semirespectable, defenders. As late as the 1920s, a very learned Harvard professor of Slavic languages, Leo Wiener, argued in his magnificent four-volume *Contributions to the History of Arabo-Visigothic Culture* that Annius—like his brother in forgery, the Benedictine Joannes Trithemius—had only published, and not created, his texts, and that in reality, they had been forged in the eighth or ninth century. "The works of Annius," Wiener reflected, "show stupendous learning even at a time when the polyhistorians were abroad. . . . It is sheer madness to accuse such a man of willful forgery."[9] Wiener may not seem like a very serious witness to the surviving credibility of Annius. After all, he also exposed Tacitus's *Germania* as a forgery—or at least believed that he had done so. Even his loving son, the infinitely more famous Norbert Stuart Wiener, admitted in his autobiography, *Ex-Prodigy*, that philology and history had not been his father's long suit.[10]

ANNIUS AND THE JEWS

Yet Wiener's arguments deserve a moment's attention, for he called attention to aspects of Annius's work that have not been fully explored. Annius, Wiener pointed out, used, not only Greek and Latin sources, but Semitic ones as well. He peppered his commentary with Hebrew and Aramaic words and phrases, which he usually explained. This material, as Wiener explained, came from a native informant, "his friend Rabbi Samuel, the Talmudist, obviously Samuel Zarfati, the court physician of Alexander VI, a most learned Spanish Jew," as well as from two other unnamed Talmudists.[11] Wiener had mastered Hebrew and Aramaic as a yeshiva student in Europe and taught Yiddish as well as Russian at Harvard. He felt confident when he claimed that Annius had had the help of Jews who had enjoyed the fifteenth-century counterpart to his own Jewish education: systematic training in the study of the Talmud, the great compilation of Jewish law, custom, history, and tradition. He confirmed his verdict by noting that another informed and serious scholar had put it forward long before. In the middle of the sixteenth century, the eminent Basel Hebraist and geographer Sebastian Münster had defended Annius in his widely read *Cosmographia:* "However it may be, I know this much, that as far as the Hebrew words are concerned, of which there is a great number in these fragments, no deception can be discovered, and I am obliged to have faith in the book and the author, because at the time when Berosus was published by a certain monk, there was no one among the Christians who was expert in Hebrew."[12] Did Münster and Wiener have a point? Did Annius channel to Christians the deep Semitic knowledge of a learned Iberian rabbi?

No. Both Wiener and Münster based their arguments on a general proposition that we now know was wrong. Protestant scholars, especially Reformed ones, insisted that they were the first Christians since the ancient world to study Hebrew or compare the Vulgate Old Testament with its Hebrew original. "Two hundred years ago," Joseph Scaliger told the French students who lodged in his house in Leiden from 1603 to 1606, "if anyone had taught or known Hebrew, he would have been considered a heretic."[13] Recent scholarship has revealed that medieval monasteries and mendicant houses harbored circles of active Hebrew scholars. They learned the language and created a wide range of aids for others, from bilingual texts and grammars to dictionaries and commentaries stuffed with Hebrew learning, like those of Nicholas of Lyra. In the early sixteenth century, Robert Wakefield, England's most skillful Hebraist, ransacked the Hebrew text of the Bible for evidence that would support the plea for a royal divorce. His mastery of Hebrew still rested in part on foundations laid two and three hundred years before.[14] Plenty of monks could have given correct explanations of the words that Münster cited: which included such elementary terms as *Maia,* for water, and *Ruah,* for spirit.

But Annius did more than cite a few Hebrew words. Names were the focus of Annius's philological efforts. Give him the name of a city or a nation, as Christopher Ligota showed long ago, and it was the work of a moment for him to perform the magic of *aequivocatio:* inventing a founder with a similar name.[15] That was how he conjured up, from the Latin name of the Lombards, or Longobardi, those of their founders: two gentlemen named, appropriately, Longo and Bardus. In the years that led up to the composition of the *Antiquitates*, as Annius elaborated his argument that Noah himself came to Italy and founded its ancient civilizations, he made increasing use of what he described as Hebrew and "Araratheic" etymologies. In his view, these onomastic studies proved beyond a doubt that his histories of the ancient world were true.

ANNIUS AND JEROME: ETYMOLOGY, COMPILATION, AND REVISIONIST HISTORY

Yet as Walter Stephens proved in his dissertation, the learning that underpinned Annius's Hebrew origin tales for place names was neither accurate nor his own.[16] In his commentary on the histories that he ascribed to Myrsilus of Lesbos, Annius had to discuss the people that the text called the "prisci Umbri" and located on the Tiber. He explained that in the *Itinerary* of the emperor Antoninus, he had found a list of the stages by which one traveled from Rome, on the Tiber, to Gaul. This list included a city named "Saleumbrona." "Now Sale," Annius wrote, "in the Aramaic tongue, means someone's origin and departure." He ascribed this information to Rabbi Samuel, to whom we shall return. But he also cited a Latin source to confirm what his Jewish informant told him: "Similarly, Saint Jerome, in his book on the meanings of names, says that Sale means departure." Therefore, Annius neatly concluded, "Saleumbrona is the place mentioned by Herodotus and others, where the Umbri had their original dwelling, from which they originate, and from which they departed, to spread through Tuscany to the sea and across the Tiber to the mountains of Umbria."[17]

As happened so often, here too Annius concealed his sources and method by identifying them for the reader, rather as the blackmailer in Poe's "Purloined Letter" concealed a document by leaving it in plain sight. More than a millennium before Annius, as Jerome of Stridon worked up his knowledge of Hebrew to translate and comment on the Old Testament, he came across a Greek text that explained the meanings of Hebrew names and words in the Bible. Helpfully entitled "A Book on the Interpretation of Hebrew Names," it was ascribed to the Alexandrian Jew Philo. At first Jerome found this book helpful, and he translated it into Latin. Later he decided that some of the material in it was not trustworthy and revised it.[18] This well-known text recorded that "Salec means departure."[19] Unfortunately, Annius did not realize, as an educated Jew would have, that the Latin name in Jerome's text, Salec—not Sale, as he had it—was actually a transliteration of the Hebrew name Tselek. Tselek the Ammonite was mentioned in 2 Samuel 23:37 and 1 Chronicles 11:39. In neither form, Hebrew or Latin, was his name a plausible origin for the euphonious, if imaginary, Saleumbrona.

Jerome's book, it seems, inspired Annius to believe that Semitic lexicography could provide a key, not only to the Scriptures, but also to the names that the Jews had assigned to cities and other places as they spread through the world after the Flood. More important, Jerome gave Annius, not only his tools, but also the bulk of his raw materials— though he did his best, as always, to disguise them. Consider one more example. In his discussion of the early history of Florence, Annius echoed the long discussions that had taken place in Florence itself about the city's origins. He described the city as relatively new and mentioned that it had conquered and taken over the much older city of Phesulae (Fiesole). Here too, Annius used the definitions of two Hebrew names to explain one old Italian one:

> *Phese* means crossing over, and *ulai* means swamp, as my friend Samuel explained, and Saint Jerome agrees in his book on the interpretation of names. Hence Phesulai, in the Aramaic form, and Phesulae, in the Roman form, means a crossing over from the swamps. For the plain beneath was swampy.[20]

Here too Annius drew both explanations from Jerome's informative book:

> *Fase* means a passing over or crossing, in place of which we read Pascha. *Ulai* means swamp.[21]

The two comments referred, respectively, to Luke 2:41, where the Greek word πάσχα appears, and Daniel 8:2, which mentions "the river of Ulai": two texts unconnected with one another or with Fiesole. Once again, Annius's lightning philological imagination must have supplied the missing links. And once again, it is hard, if not impossible, to imagine an actual Jew deriving the name Fiesole from the term פסח (*pasah*, pass over, which is the verbal origin of *pesah*).

Not all of Annius's histories of names have turned up yet in Jerome's little book. But enough of them have been discovered to confirm Stephens's thesis that the Dominican needed no knowledge of Hebrew to create them. Annius collected interpretations from Jerome and then mixed and matched them with the place names he wanted to explain. In fact, Annius admitted as much before he ever published the *Antiquities.* Around 1494, Annius dedicated to Pope Alexander VI some pseudo-Etruscan texts and elaborate fake inscriptions in Greek characters, along with his own commentary.[22] He explained with almost perfect frankness how he arrived at his explanations of the mysterious words they contained: "My constant frequenting of Talmudists and experts on languages has yielded some understanding of the original mixed Etruscan language. Then if I remain in doubt, my copy of Saint Jerome *On the Meanings of Hebrew Names* is right there."[23] We need only turn Annius's sentences around—imagine him consulting Jerome first and fishing in deeper waters only later—and we have what must be an accurate account of his method.

ANNIUS'S JEWISH FRIENDS?

Yet the story is not so simple. Here and elsewhere, as Wiener, Stephens, and others have noted, Annius advertised his close connection with Talmudists, one of whom was named Samuel. How should we understand these references? Most Dominicans were not known, in this period, as Philo-Semites. Just a few years after Annius died, the Dominicans of Cologne collaborated with a converted Jew, Johannes Pfefferkorn, who set out to confiscate and destroy the books of all the Jewish communities of the Holy Roman Empire.[24] Franciscans like Thomas Murner, who published the first printed edition of the Passover Haggadah in order to show that it contained no support for the blood libel, and Pietro Galatino, who defended the Kabbalah, took such positions more often than Dominicans did. Leo Wiener confidently identified Annius's informant as the papal physician Samuel Zarfati. But Zarfati did not come to Rome until 1498—years after Samuel and other unnamed Talmudists supposedly began helping Annius do his scholarly homework.

Roberto Weiss and Amanda Collins have pinned down, in classic articles, the date at which Annius began to claim acquaintance with

Rabbi Samuel. In his little treatise on fake inscriptions, Annius stated that Rabbi Samuel had translated the "Araratheic words" "in the presence of the vice governor, lord Prospero Caffarrelli." Caffarrelli, Weiss explained, served as vice legate (or governor) of the Patrimony of Saint Peter in Tuscia, "the capital of which was Viterbo, in 1485 and again from 1492–94." In the *Antiquitates*, moreover, Annius described how, after the inscriptions came to light, "triumphales statuae" were excavated in the land of Cybele and in the presence of Alexander VI and the papal curia.[25] Alexander spent time in Viterbo between October and December 1493, hunting hares. If Annius was telling the truth, it would have been then that he met Samuel and asked his help in deciphering the puzzling "Araratheic" inscription.

In fact, Annius invoked the authority of experts on the Talmud in many passages of the *Antiquities*, and the forms he used in doing so raise multiple questions about the identity and number of his informants. Sometimes he cited "a Talmudist" or "a certain Talmudist," sometimes "Talmudists," and sometimes "Hebrew Talmudists."[26] At times, as Wiener noted, he wrote with a more personal touch of "Samuel," "Samuel the Talmudist," "Rabbi Samuel," or even, in various forms, "our Talmudist Samuel."[27] In these cases, the term "Talmudist" apparently referred to a contemporary Jew who was an expert on the Talmud. In other cases, however, Annius applied the term to the ancient authors of the Talmud rather than its modern interpreters.[28] In many instances he cited Jerome and the Talmudists together, as if he saw a connection between them.[29] At least once he gave an opinion that he ascribed to "Hieronymo de interpretatione nominum Hebraeorum et aliis Talmudistis" (Jerome in his work on the interpretation of Hebrew names and other Talmudists), a formula that suggests that for Annius, a Talmudist might be an ancient Christian as well as an ancient or modern Jew.[30] Was Samuel Annius's only expert adviser?

And what sort of expertise did Samuel offer? Was it reliable? In most cases, Annius treated the Talmudists he cited as authorities. Sometimes he even praised "a learned Talmudist," or "skillful" or "learned Talmudists."[31] In other cases, however, he took the more conventional, opposite tack. He decried the "myths and errors of the Talmudists" and the "Pharisaic Talmudic vanities," which, as Paul's testimony showed, had infected the early church (Annius did not explain how Christians contemporary with Paul could have known the Talmud, which, in his view, was compiled in the second century CE).[32] He also described the Talmudists as "corruptors of sacred scripture" and recorded that their opinions, and those of Josephus, were rejected in the study of chronology.[33] Annius, in short, seems to have been quite conflicted, both about the Talmudists' actual identity and about the value of their scholarship.[34]

He was also evasive and inconsistent about the sort of knowledge that they could provide. In his short text on the inscriptions discovered in Viterbo, Annius claimed that he needed help from Samuel with "Araratheic" words. This term suggests he was engaging in the sort of calculated indirection that he used when he called the Persian priest whose writings he forged Metasthenes rather than Megasthenes. The nonsense name "Araratheic" looks as if he derived it from "Aramaic," perhaps in the intention of drawing a connection between Mt. Ararat, which is traditionally identified as the place where Noah's ark came to rest, and Aramaic. And the inscription that Samuel helped Annius to decode was written, by Annius's own admission, in Greek rather than Hebrew characters, in what he called a mixture of Greek and Araratheic words. In fact, the inscriptions would have baffled the most learned Jewish scholar, since the words in them that are not Greek are gobbledygook. But in the *Antiquities*, a few years later, Annius cited the opinion of "the learned Talmudists," not on a question of Hebrew or even Araratheic, but on the origin of the name Inghaevon: an invented name, clearly derived from that of the Istaevones, which is mentioned by Tacitus in chapter 2 of his *Germania*.[35] History records some Talmudists who read Tacitean Latin: Christian ones in the sixteenth and seventeenth centuries, Jewish ones as well in the nineteenth century and after. But it seems safe to infer that Samuel the Talmudist and his fellow fifteenth-century Jewish students of Araratheic inscriptions and Tacitus were figments of Annius's lurid imagination.

Most striking of all are two other passages in the *Antiquitates*, in which Annius vividly described his actual discussions with his informants. In the *Quaestiones Anniae*, Annius recalled that he had conducted an elaborate discussion with "Rabbi Samuel and two other Talmudists" five years before, "in the Octaves of Easter for the last five years": that is, either in the eight-day period from Easter Sunday to

Low Sunday, or on the latter day itself, starting (if we may trust his dates) in the period from April 7 to 15, 1493.[36] Easter was normally a time of tension between Jews and Christians.[37] Just before Easter in 1475, a boy named Simonino was found stabbed to death in Trento. This terrible find prompted accusations of ritual murder against the Jews of Trent, some of whom admitted to the crime under torture, and led to a number of executions.[38] Yet Annius claimed to have spent his Easter weeks chatting with Talmudists. In the other passage he stated that "in the Aramaic language, and in Hebrew before Greek," the term *fanum* meant a place where prophecy took place. Samuel, he explained, had confirmed this by "citing Genesis 32, where it is written that Jacob, predicting the coming victory and fate and the change of his name by the angel, called the name of that place, in Hebrew, Fanuel, that is, the *fanum* of God. He said, 'I have seen the lord face to face.'"[39] In fact, the Hebrew text of Genesis 32:31 states that Jacob called the place in question Peniel, "for I have seen God face to face (*panim el-panim*) and my life is preserved." Evidently, the learned Talmudist with whom Annius bandied onomastics, year after year, did not understand—as Annius clearly did not—the Hebrew text's explanation of the origin of the word Peniel. The first of these passages is socially implausible, and the second is linguistically even more so. Samuel and his colleagues, it seems safe to infer, were some of Annius's many imaginary friends—or perhaps avatars of his acute multiple persona disorder.[40]

ANNIUS'S JEWISH SOURCES

Yet ridding the record of Annius's Talmudists does not remove all its mysteries. Leo Wiener noticed something much more striking in the *Antiquities* than Annius's glossing of individual names. More than one of Annius's references to Jewish sources reveal direct knowledge of material that he could not have drawn from Jerome, for the simple reason that it did not yet exist in Jerome's time. Annius cited, not only the etymologies of supposed Talmudists, but also passages from the Talmud itself, which were traditionally dated a century after Jerome (and probably later still).

Some of these references are strictly technical. One of Annius's forgeries, a history of the Jews ascribed to Philo, dealt with questions of Jewish chronology and history in the age of the Second Temple: the period for which the Old Testament itself offered little by way of connected narrative history. In his commentary, Annius quoted the Talmudic treatise Avodah Zarah (Foreign worship, i.e., idolatry) to establish the duration of the Hasmonean dynasty: the line of high priests and kings descended from Matthias, father of Judah Maccabee, which ruled Judea from 142 to 63 BC. Pseudo-Philo made the dynasty rule 129 years. Annius's gloss read: "Josephus says that the Hasmoneans ruled for 127 years. But the Talmudists, in Aaboda Zara, in the chapter beginning Lipfne Idiem, say: Rabbi Joseph relates that the kingdom of the Hasmoneans lasted 103 years."[41] Annius's reference was both precise and correct. The relevant section of Avodah Zarah reads: "For R. Jose b. Rabbi taught: Persian rule lasted thirty-four years after the building of the Temple, Greece ruled one hundred eighty years during the existence of the Temple, the Hasmonean rule lasted one hundred three years during temple times, the House of Herod ruled one hundred three years" (8b–9a). Annius even quoted further information from the twelfth-century commentary of Rashi on this passage.[42]

In the same section of the *Antiquities*, Annius recorded a Talmudic story about the massacre of the Jewish high court or Sanhedrin:

> The Hebrews write in the Talmud, in the book Bava Batra, in chapter Assufatin, on the destruction of the Sanhedrin. Herod the Ascalonite, he says, was a servant of the Hasmoneans. Once he had attained power by force, he killed all seventy judges of the Sanhedrin. One, named Bab the son of Bota, he preserved, but he gouged out his eyes.[43]

Again, Annius's reference was both precise and correct. The original reads: "Herod was a servant of the Hasmonean family. He cast his eyes upon a young maid [of that family]. On a certain day he heard the *Bath Kol* [a voice from heaven] saying, 'Whatever servant will now rebel shall prosper.' He arose up against his masters, and slew them all. . . . Herod said, Who is there that interprets these words, 'Thou shalt set a king over thee out of the midst of thy brethren?' (Deut. 17:15) The Rabbis [interpreted the words]. He rose up and slew all the Rabbis, leaving only Baba Ben Buta, with whom he consulted" (Babylonian Talmud Baba Bathra 3b).

In these and other cases, the material that Annius or Samuel quoted in Latin was anything but ordinary. The Babylonian Talmud, of course, is a work of great mass, density, and difficulty. At its core is the Mishnah: a codification of Jewish law in Hebrew, traditionally ascribed to Judah haNasi and dated around the year 200 CE. In the Talmud, the Mishnah is cut into segments, each of them followed by the relevant passage of the Gemara: a much longer body of rabbinical discussion largely in Aramaic, sprinkled with words from Persian and even Greek, narrated by a voice of uncertain identity. Even in modern printed editions of the entire text, both segments of the text appear without vowels. It is easy to imagine Annius collecting glosses from Jerome and ascribing them to an imaginary Talmudist; it is much harder to imagine him reading the actual Talmud, even in its modern printed form.

In the fifteenth century, moreover, that printed form did not exist. Daniel Bomberg, the great Christian printer, assembled the full corpus of the Babylonian Talmud and published it as a single work in the 1520s. Before that, parts of the Talmud usually circulated separately, in manuscript or in print.[44] Very few Christians knew the text directly. The German Hellenist and Roman lawyer Johannes Reuchlin studied Hebrew and Aramaic as rigorously as any Christian in the first twenty years of the sixteenth century. In 1512 he obtained, apparently with difficulty, a copy of tractate Sanhedrin of the Jerusalem Talmud: the version created by the rabbinical schools of Palestine, a little before the Babylonian Talmud took shape.[45] But in 1516, when he issued a powerful defense of the right of the Jews to keep their copies of the Talmud, he stated that he had no copy of the full text and did not know the work directly. In a vivid passage he went on to make clear just how alien and difficult he found its mixture of languages:

> And I know no Christian in all of Germany who has himself actually studied the Talmud. Never, moreover, in my lifetime has there ever been a baptized Jew in the German realm who could either understand or read it. . . . For although the Talmud is written in Hebrew letters, its language is not pure Hebrew, as we find in the Bible, but rather, we find in its phrasing diverse strains from other Oriental languages, that is, among others, from the Babylonian, Persian, Arabic and Greek. It also contains countless abbreviations, so that great effort and lengthy study is required of the reader, which is why not many Jews can understand the Talmud, not to speak of Christians.[46]

Through much of the sixteenth century, even Christians who knew Hebrew and Aramaic well often admitted that they could not decipher the Talmud. Guillaume Postel, for example, translated the key text of the Kabbalah, the Zohar, from Aramaic into Latin. But he confessed to the Zurich Hebrew professor Konrad Pellikan that he could not make head or tail of the Talmud, and asked to use Pellikan's version.[47] For many Christian scholars, the widespread tales of defamatory statements about Jesus appearing in the text—which had led to burnings of the Talmud in the thirteenth century and would do so again in 1553 and after—sufficed to suppress any interest.

THE TALMUD AND ITS READERS IN ANNIUS'S WORLD

There were exceptions, however. Individual experts like Pellikan and the convert Paulus Riccius translated parts of the Talmud for Christian readers.[48] More relevant to our purposes, Rome and the papal curia actually harbored scholars who claimed to find materials in the Talmud that, when rightly studied, could profit Christian scholarship in vital ways. Around 1487, for example, a converted Jew named Paulus de Heredia published a Latin letter ascribed to one Neumia son of Haccana. R. Nehuniah ben haKanah was a historical figure of the first century. His supposed letter contained a set of queries from "Antoninus, consul of the city of Rome," and answers from "Rabbenus hacchados": a partly Latinized version of the phrase "our holy Rabbi," the traditional Jewish way of referring to Judah haNasi. The rabbi, living before the incarnation, prophesied both the coming of Jesus as the Messiah and, more astonishingly still, the discovery of the True Cross in Palestine by the Emperor Constantine's mother, Helen. The text—which became very influential when Galatino included extracts from it in his own book of 1518 on the secrets of Christianity—reflected real knowledge of the Talmud. Tractate Sanhedrin contains a dialogue between the rabbi and Antoninus, which must have served as Paulus's model.[49]

Another Jewish convert—the formidably learned Sicilian Guglielmo Moncado, who took the name Flavius Mithridates in token of his command of many languages and translated Kabbalistic texts of great difficulty for Pico della Mirandola—looks even more like Annius's fictional Samuel. In 1481, Flavius held a Good Friday sermon for the papal curia. Speaking for two hours, he enchanted the prelates with his elegant pronunciation of Hebrew and Aramaic. These included what Flavius described as passages from the "vetus Talmud" (the old Talmud): quotations in real Hebrew and Aramaic that confirmed the Messiahhood of Jesus and the doctrine of the Trinity. The Jews, Flavius explained, had suppressed the genuine Talmud by replacing it with their own Babylonian and Jerusalem Talmuds, which concealed the vital fact that the best of the rabbis in the time of Jesus had recognized him as the Messiah and accepted central Christian teachings. Like Annius (or Samuel), Flavius took care to name the sources from which he drew his texts.[50] Evidently, then, when Annius published a book that cited the Talmud, in Rome, with papal support, he knew that he would not offend anyone. The papal curia was already alert to the fact that arcane Jewish texts might deserve study. Flavius Mithridates acted as an adviser and interpreter to Pico della Mirandola and other Christian scholars: exactly as, in Annius's account, Samuel did for him.[51] The parallels are striking.

It even seems possible that the historical figure of Flavius Mithridates lurks somewhere behind the imaginary one of Annius's friend Samuel. Flavius was recognized as an expert not only on Hebrew and Aramaic, but on other Oriental languages as well, from Arabic to the invented "Chaldean" (Hebrew and Aramaic words written in Ethiopic characters) that he taught to Pico della Mirandola.[52] Annius described Samuel as "nostro linguarum interprete Talmudista Samuelle" (Samuel the Talmudist, our translator of languages).[53] Flavius, the son of a rabbi who sold magical amulets to Christian women, was a great expert on the Kabbalah and took a deep interest in the magical powers of words. Annius described one of the inscriptions he and Samuel translated as an example of magical epigraphy. Look at it one way and no writing appeared; look at it in another way and from one direction the letters seemed to be incised in the stone, while from another they appeared to stand out in relief. "These variations are revealed in turn," Annius remarked, "as in a chameleon."[54]

At one point in his commentary on Sempronius, a forged text that discussed, among other topics, the horoscope of the city of Rome, Annius described the Roman legends about the changes that the name of the city had undergone.[55] The Etruscans, he explained, had a special method for concealing the name of the god that protected the city:

> The Etruscans' method for concealing this was to draw out another name from the god's own name, by a certain mystery and certain letters. Only the Talmudists and Cabballarians [Cabballarii] use this ritual and mystery now. This is the teaching that is now called Caballa.[56]

Here, as Annius connected his Talmudists with the study of Kabbalah, he sketched something like a portrait of Flavius Mithridates—though, so far as is known, Flavius never claimed that the Kabbalah had its origins in Etruria.

In one vital technical way, however, Annius's practices diverged from those of Paulus de Heredia and Flavius Mithridates. Paulus and Flavius invented the passages they cited, exactly as Annius did when he composed the works of Berosus and colleagues. But Annius cited real passages from the Babylonian Talmud. And that, as we have seen, was not easy for any Christian to do in Annius's time. How did he manage it? Annius himself offered an explanation in 1494, when he presented his Araratheic inscriptions to Alexander VI. Using one of the standard keys in which forgers pitch their messages—that of false modesty—he admitted that "I have a very rough knowledge of Aramean and Hebrew words, as I dallied for only a few months with the Hebrews of Viterbo in their schools as a boy."[57] Annius claimed, in other words, that he had attended a Jewish heder or yeshiva, if not both. No wonder he knew the Talmud. Only a supremely imaginative Christian scholar with his eye on the curia could conceivably have boasted, in these years, that he had attended Jewish schools in his native Italian city. Yet his ignorance of Semitic languages reveals that this tale—like his talk of Samuel—was not a record of experience but a product of his native wit.

CHRISTIAN COMPILATIONS AND JEWISH LEARNING

It is to Walter Stephens and Carlotta Dionisotti that I owe, not the exact answer to my question, but the vital suggestion about where to find it. Both of them have emphasized that Annius was a late medieval mendicant, steeped in an existing Dominican culture of erudition and compilation.[58] It was in the literary world in which he came to maturity that Annius found his genuine Talmudic material. Controversies between Jews and Christians had blazed up in the thirteenth century, leading both to formal disputations and to bonfires of the Talmud. A Spanish Dominican, Ramon Martí, or Martini, set out to examine the traditions that the Jews defended so fiercely. He learned both Hebrew and Aramaic. He examined passages from the Talmud, the Targum and other Jewish works, at first hand: not, probably, in their full contexts, but in anthologies. And he compiled his results in the *Pugio fidei*, a massive, systematic effort to demonstrate that the Talmud and related texts were sewers—but also that Christians needed to explore them. Like sewers, these texts contained jewels that could be fished out and saved.[59] Martí's long and demanding book did not reach print until the middle of the seventeenth century, though Galatino's rewriting of it, the *De arcanis Catholicae veritatis*, opened up much of its content to hundreds of readers after 1518. But Annius must have gained access to a manuscript of the *Pugio fidei*. The passages that he quoted from the Babylonian Talmud had already appeared in Latin translation, two hundred years before, in Martí's book.[60]

Always resourceful, always on the lookout for new material, Annius dug for treasure in recent works as well as older ones. At least once he found a vital piece of evidence about the Talmud in a text by a writer closer to his own time than Martí, which he probably encountered in a printed edition. In his commentary on his own forged *Breviarium* by Philo, Annius argued that in times of necessity, non-Jews could not only convert to Judaism, but also become teachers of the Jewish law. In fact, he argued, this was how the Talmud itself came into being, after Herod had slaughtered the members of the Sanhedrin:

> For after Herod killed the teachers of the law and the Sanhedrin, he established a Sanhedrin of neophytes and proselytes, who were called the Pharisees and Scribes. Accordingly, Mayr, who was the author of the whole doctrine of the Talmud, was an Idumean, converted to Judaism, as is reported in passages scattered through the Talmud, and as Maimonides relates in the prologue to his Summa on the authority of the Talmud.[61]

The Talmud does state that Meir, a wonder-working rabbi of the second century CE, was the son or descendant of a convert.[62] And Maimonides accorded Meir a fairly prominent role in the transmission of Jewish law, as Annius stated, in the prologue to his *Mishneh Torah*, a codification of the Jewish oral law:

> Ribbi Yishmael and Ribbi Meir, the son of a righteous convert, received it from Ribbi Aqivah. Ribbi Meir and his colleagues also received it from Ribbi Yishmael. Ribbi Meir's colleagues were Ribbi Yehudah, Ribbi Yose, Ribbi Shim'on, Ribbi Nehemyah, Ribbi El'azar son of Shammua, Ribbi Yohanan the sandal maker, Shim'on son of Azzai, and Ribbi Hananya son of Teradyon.[63]

Yet Maimonides did not identify Meir as an Idumean or make him the principal author of the Talmud. Unlike his Arabic *Guide for the Perplexed*, moreover, the Hebrew *Mishneh Torah* was not translated into Latin until the seventeenth century, when it became a favorite text for Christian students of Jewish law and tradition.[64]

Here, too, Annius drew on a Latin source. Paul of Burgos (d. 1435), a rabbi and learned Talmudist, converted to Christianity and became archbishop of Burgos and a renowned Christian exegete of the Bible. He drew up a set of *Additions* to Nicholas of Lyra's *Postillae* on the Bible, in which he frequently cited Jewish sources and traditions that were otherwise closed to Christians. And in his Addition on Isaiah 34:1, he not only used Maimonides's statement about Meir but amplified it in ways that prove that Annius used his work:

> The Jews relate and strongly believe that their evil doctrine of the Talmud was given orally by God to Moses on Mount Sinai. But this false and Pharisaic doctrine was actually redacted in written form by someone whom they call Rabbi Judah haNasi. He received that whole doctrine from someone called Rabbi Mayr, on whose authority that whole doctrine depends. But it is established by their testimony that that Rabbi Mayr, who was the chief author, was an Idumean by nation, and he received the faith and the rituals of the Jews in the time after Christ's passion. Hence they call him an Idumean convert, all of which can be found in various passages in the Talmud, and this is also laid out in a systematic fashion in the summa of Maimonides,

which has the highest authority among them, in his preface, where
he deals with the authority of the Talmudic doctrine.[65]

Like Annius, and unlike Maimonides, Paul treated Meir or Mayr as
the chief compiler of the Talmud and identified his convert father as
an Idumean: Paul's own derogatory term. It seems certain, then, that
Annius found his information in Paul's *Additions*. Once again, apparent evidence that Annius knew Jewish sources at first hand dis-
solves on acquaintance with a Latin volume: in this case, one well
known and widely accessible in late fifteenth-century Europe.

   The identification of Annius's sources for Talmudic erudition removes any last shred of a reason to believe that a Jewish scholar or
scholars provided him with information. Personal connections with
Jews seem as evanescent, in Annius's life, as those with the informants,
a monk named George from Armenia and William of Mantua, who,
he recalled, brought him his texts. And yet more than one mystery remains about Annius's intellectual relations with the Jews. I conclude
with one of them.

THE TALMUD AS A SOURCE: HOW ANNIUS AND OTHERS COMPARED ANCIENT INSTITUTIONS

In his commentary on Philo, Annius discussed the Jewish high court
at length. First he defined it:

> But the term Sanhedrin, which often crops up, is interpreted by the
> Talmudists as meaning the collective body that controlled the scepter
> and public power for the whole realm. This belonged to seventy el-
> ders from the more distinguished members of the tribe of Judah and
> the other tribes, over whom a single king presided. . . . But the Tal-
> mudists say, in the book Sanhedrin, that this was the public scepter
> that God established in the desert, according to Numbers 11.[66]

Then, as always, he expatiated at greater length on the name, and other
questions of terminology:

> The [members of the Sanhedrin] are called, using a conventional
> term, elders: but in the Roman language they are called Senators, in
> the Aramaic and Etruscan language Lucii, with the accent on the last

syllable, and in Greek Palei. Moreover, they must be masters, that is, men of the word, whose word is obeyed. From their imperious word the Romans named them Dictatores, and by a single common term, Magistrates. Therefore among the ancient Hebrews as well, the body with public power was called the Senate of masters; among the Romans, the ruling Senate; among the Etruscans, the Lucumonium; among the Greeks, the Paleologum. Accordingly, we find that the names that indicate public power among the ancients are all composed from two words, one of which means age and antiquity, the other the word and imperious statements. Among the Hebrews, this is Sanhedrin; among the Romans, the decreed Senate; among the Greeks, the Paleologus, from paleos, meaning old, and logos, meaning reason and word; among the Etruscans, Lucumonium, from lucu, meaning old, and moni, meaning reason and word.[67]

Even for Annius, this passage seems an unusually wild series of associative leaps. His etymology for Sanhedrin is wrong, of course: the word really comes from the Greek *synedrion,* or council. Even stranger is the term he applies to the Greek—presumably Athenian—council: Paleologus. This was, of course, the family name of the last dynasty of Byzantium, which Annius had somehow mixed up with the term for the ancient Athenian aristocratic court, the Areopagus.

Still, even as Annius piled misinformation for misinformation, he was on to something profound. Probably he hoped to show that all the great political institutions of the ancient world derived—like the ancient peoples themselves—from the Jews, and to make that point with special emphasis on the Etruscan and Roman inhabitants of ancient Italy. But what he suggested, to alert readers, was something more general as well as more radical: that the institutions of the Jews were just as ancient and just as worthy of study as those of the Greeks and Romans, and that the despised Talmud and other rabbinical texts offered the only direct access to them.

One scholar's response to Annius's work supports this reading. In 1566, the French jurist Jean Bodin published his *Methodus ad facilem historiarum cognitionem.* It was a guide to the study of ancient and modern historians, designed to help readers obtain reliable information about the constitutions they described.[68] At times, Bodin showed an imaginative flair in reconstructing the past that was worthy of

Annius himself. More important, he not only used the Annian forgeries: he quoted as authoritative the rules that Annius had formulated for deciding which historians deserved belief.[69] Yet Bodin did
more. He made clear, in the preface to the *Methodus,* that the only
way to understand how constitutions and institutions operated was to
study all of them: Jewish as well as Greek, Roman, and French. Bodin
promised to draw all the necessary information to elucidate the
Jewish Sanhedrin from what he called "the Pandects of the Jews": that
is to say, the Babylonian Talmud, which, like the Pandects, or Digest,
that forms part of the Roman *Corpus Juris,* was a compilation of jurists' dicta and verdicts. And like Annius, he named the scholars who
would help him carry out this comparative operation: not Jews, in this
case, but Jean Mercier and Jean Cinquarbres, two leading French
Christian Hebraists.[70]

Apparently these men did work together. The second edition of
Bodin's book, which appeared in 1569, contained detailed discussions
of the Sanhedrin and its powers, which he compared to those of the
Roman Senate. Bodin continued on this line in his *Six Books of the
Republic,* first published in 1576.[71] So—as Eric Nelson has shown in
his recent, important study of *The Hebrew Republic*—did a whole series of late sixteenth- and seventeenth-century political thinkers, such
as Petrus Cunaeus, Hugo Grotius, and John Selden.[72] For all their disagreements, these men agreed on using a comparative method, on
treating ancient Jewish institutions as valuable political models, and
on insisting that the rabbinical texts that described them were vital
sources. If Annius did not pioneer in intercultural collaborative study
of the Bible and the Talmud, as he claimed to, he did pioneer in the
sort of comparative research that would become a central form of political and historical writing and argument in the centuries after his.[73]

Annius caused the scholars of his own time and later generations
endless trouble. But he also gave them endless stimulation. And sometimes—as in this case—he was the first to break the intellectual land
that much more celebrated and respectable thinkers would settle and
cultivate. We still have much more to learn about Annius and his
Jewish friends, real or imaginary—and, above all, about the complex
combination of reading and imagination that led him to spin his webs
of references. It will not be easy to learn as much as we want to about

what he knew, and when. We lack—and need—a critical edition of Annius's texts and commentaries and a full commentary on Annius's sources.[74] Once they take shape, they will reveal, again and again, that Annius was as brilliant and prescient—and as diligent in exploiting the materials available to him—as he was wicked. The forger who knew Jewish scholarship through compilations, intermediaries, and inventions helped inspire a great wave of Christian scholarship on Jewish law, history, and religion. Surely even the greatest of forgers could not ask for more than that from his loyal, if baffled, readers.

CHAPTER 8

John Caius Argues about History

A MEDICAL MAN AND A SCHOLAR

IN 1568, John Caius was the master of all he surveyed. The most celebrated medical man in England, he was also one of his country's very few philologists of European reputation.[1] He spent his days productively, rebuilding his college into a humanistic machine for character formation, which was carefully designed to stamp its inmates with good morals as well as good learning. Undergraduates were to enter it through a "Gate of Humility"; pass through a "Gate of Virtue" every day during their years in college; and finally leave for the Examination Schools through a "Gate of Honour." When students or fellows defied him, Caius found a simple remedy. He put them in the stocks and beat them.[2] But now he ventured into history, with a short, polemical book, *De antiquitate Cantebrigiensis academiae.* It was more or less a flop at the time, and over the centuries even his most enthusiastic modern admirers have found little or nothing to praise in it. The historian of his college, who admired Caius enormously, called this book "a farrago of invention and credulity."[3] Truth be told, it is a very odd little work.[4]

Caius (1510–1573) came from Norwich to Gonville Hall in 1529. This small establishment was, in the 1530s, as much a monastic community as a college. Evidently the new member did not make much of an impression at first, at least to judge from the variety of ways in which the bursar spelled his name in the account books. But brilliance and a mastery of Greek and Hebrew soon set him apart, first at Cambridge, where he graduated at the head of the list of BAs in 1532–1533, and then, in 1539, at Padua, where he roomed with Vesalius, studied medicine, and stayed on to teach. Caius won a European reputation as a Galenic scholar and academic physician. He produced some impressive critical editions before working his way home to England, library by library, collating manuscripts as he went. A close friendship developed between Caius and a fellow medical man, humanist, and bibliographer, Conrad Gessner. Until Gessner's death in 1565, which Caius mourned, he sent his friend numerous descriptions and images of animals.[5] From 1547 on Caius practiced medicine in London, where he rebuilt the reputation of the Royal College of Physicians, which he served repeatedly as president. He also held anatomical demonstrations in the Hall of the Barber-Surgeons, "reveiling unto this fraternity," in the words of William Bulleine, "the hidden jewels, and precious treasures of CL. Galenus."[6]

As Bulleine's description suggests, Caius was not an innovator on the model of Vesalius but rather a devotee of the humanistic medicine practiced by Thomas Linacre, whose monument in St Paul's he restored.[7] He believed that Vesalius and other heralds of change had not so much found errors in Galen as misread him: better philology was needed more than better anatomy.[8] After ten years or so, his practice had made him rich, and in 1557 he offered to refound his college. Caius's proposal found acceptance, he himself was elected master, and he devoted himself to equipping what became Gonville and Caius College with new statutes, new landholdings, new plate, and new buildings.[9] Caius would remain a man of tradition and the book to the end of his days. His onetime student Thomas Muffett warned:

> Furthermore care is to be taken of their health, that give us milk; for as an unclean and pocky nurse (which woful experience dayly proveth) infecteth most sound and lively children; so likewise a clean sound and healthful nurse recovereth a sickly and impotent child. . . . What made Dr *Cajus* in his last sickness so peevish and so full of frets at Cambridge, when he suckt one woman (whom I spare to name), froward of conditions and of bad diet; and contrariwise so quiet and well when he suck another of contrary disposition? verily the diversity of

their milks and conditions, which being contrary one to the other, wrought also inn him that sucked them contrary effects.[10]

Marsilio Ficino had recommended, in his *De triplici vita*, that old scholars drink the blood of young men or the milk of young women.[11] It seems utterly characteristic of Caius that he went to his grave still trying to make practical use of that proverbially erudite, even recondite book—itself compiled from a vast range of ancient and medieval sources—on how scholars should maintain their health.

Caius's history of Cambridge is perhaps even more fantastic than his effort to save his life through the help of wet-nurses. Still, he took the enterprise very seriously. Alfred Hiatt, Ad Putter, and James Carley have brilliantly illuminated the later medieval background of Cambridge's mythical history.[12] Cambridge needed a long, unbroken history to prove that it was a real university, which had translated its studies from the proper academies in the past and deserved to enjoy independence from outside jurisdictions in the present. Oxford had claims to greater antiquity, which needed to be refuted. External authorities—notably the Bishop of Ely—claimed the right to try members of the university and to confirm the election of the Chancellor-elect, which must be appealed to Rome. Proofs were needed, and in short supply. Cambridge also suffered an archival trauma during the Peasants' War in June 1381, when "all of the university's charters, and other membranes and ordinances, and the statutes of the university" were burned outside Great Saint Mary's church. As Matthew Parker eloquently told the story,

"At the end, when everything had been consumed to ashes, a certain raving mad old woman named Margaret Stars gathered the ashes and then threw them into the winds and scattered them, crying aloud 'Away with the skills of the clerics,' 'Away with the skills of the clerics.'"[13] Nonetheless, it seems that strange and wonderful documents, created in the late thirteenth or early fourteenth century, reappeared in the fifteenth: in time to be displayed, archived and used. These documents, their modern students have shown us, were fakes. But they also represented a serious effort to invent necessary traditions—even when their inventors showed their high spirits and revealed their creative hand at work. It is in this empathetic spirit that I hope to shed some new light on Caius.

THE UNIVERSITIES AT WAR

De antiquitate sprang from a strange but recognizable form of academic politics.[14] Queen Elizabeth loved pageantry, which both universities provided in lavish style. In 1564, a Cambridge orator informed her that his university was much older than the other place. But in 1566 the queen graced Oxford with her presence. By a strange chance, John Caius's namesake, Thomas Caius, a fellow and warden of All Souls College and Register of the University of Oxford, composed an "Assertion of the Antiquity of Academy of Oxford," which he presented to her majesty.

Thomas Caius had not meant his work for general circulation. But Elizabeth's court was a hive of information masters, above all William Cecil. Cecil was a Cambridge man and a friend and ally of Matthew Parker, another Cambridge man and Caius's closest friend. Networks buzzed, messages flew. As the antiquary John Strype told the story in the early eighteenth century, "This MS. as it seems by the Secretaries means, a *Cambridge* man, coming into the hands of the Archbishop, a *Cambridge* Man also, was transcribed, and communicated by him unto another *Caius,* and a learned *Antiquarian* of Cambridge; the Archbishop exhorting him to consider well the Book, and to vindicate his University."[15] One of the copies that came into circulation remains in the Parker Library.[16] John Caius was one of many early modern medical men who did systematic historical research, as Nancy Siraisi has shown.[17] But this was a special case: Caius the historian was taking part in a wider confrontation, one university against the other, when he sent his little book to be printed in London together with the work by the other Caius, which was prefaced by a short imaginary history of Oxford taken from the Oxford proctors' book. It was the pedant's version of the Boat Race. Caius put up a feeble pretense of impartiality by calling himself "the Londoner," but he soon admitted that everyone had seen through it. Not many seem to have taken John Caius's side. The antiquary William Lambarde was a trusted friend and assistant of Matthew Parker, the archbishop of Canterbury and Caius's close friend. Yet all he found to say was that he left the points at issue "to Doctour Caius of Cambridge and Maister Key of Oxforde to be disputed, and to indifferent readers to be adiudged."[18]

The controversy went on for another fifty years. Generations of scholars expended energy worthy of a better cause on the quintessential learned activity of belaboring one another with slapsticks and bladders. The arguments involved were relatively simple. Oxford was clearly the older of the two universities. The city, after all, had been founded by Good King Mempricius, only a century after Brutus the Trojan first came to Britain. It was known as "Beaumont" due to its handsome setting. Later on, the Greek scholars who had accompanied Brutus to England and settled in Cricklade (Greeklade) migrated to Beaumont. This move took place not long before the Saxons settled in England. Their King Alfred formally called the university into being in 873, when he restored the schools that had long flourished near Oxford and appointed St. Grimbald as its first chancellor. This was the tale summarized in the Oxford *Historiola,* or narrative of university origins, which Thomas Caius excerpted from the official proctors' book.

Cambridge was also clearly the older of the two universities. It was founded by Cantaber the Spaniard. He belonged to a group of Spanish exiles whom King Gurguntius Brabtruc encountered as they sailed in Scottish waters. Cantaber married the king's daughter and founded a city on the river Cant, which was named after him. His son Grantinus, who bridged the river, provided names for both Grantchester and Cantbridge, or Cambridge. Cantaber gathered scholars around him. In the course of time, both Anaximander and Anaxagoras visited his city. In the second century, local scholars helped convert Good King Lucius of Britain to Christianity. This was the narrative of the Cambridge *Historiola,* which was composed by the Carmelite Nicholas Cantilupe in the fourteenth century.

THE DOCUMENTS IN THE CASE

So far, one might think, so silly: time for something completely different. And that materialized on cue. By the time the quarreling historians reached the early Middle Ages, detailed documents began to accumulate: the very forged documents that we have already encountered. These may have appealed to Caius because they seemed to resemble the documents, not all of them genuine, that he knew from Bede's *Ecclesiastical History of the English Nation.* In 531, King Arthur granted Cambridge a charter. On February 7, 624, Pope Honorius I issued a bull in favor of the university, in which he recalled that in his youth he too had spent time there. On May 3, 699, Pope Sergius I issued another bull, which also evoked his happy younger days in Cambridge. More recently still, as further documents showed, two fifteenth-century popes, Martin V and Eugenius IV, had recognized the validity of the documents—even though, as both of them noted, the university could not produce the fragile originals, only copies.

When John Caius fought against Thomas Caius, in other words, he used these documents as his weapons. He quoted them at length, and took care to locate the repository where he had found them: "the black book of the university"—that is to say, the black parchment book of documents which now bears the signature Collect. Admin. 9 (2) in the University Archives.[19]

Only two flies marred the ointment. As Caius himself knew better than anyone, the material documents in question were not ancient. They had been added to the Black Book "by that venerable old man, who is still well remembered, William Buckenham, Master of Gonville and Caius College at Cambridge, when he was Vice-Chancellor [1508–10]."[20] Buckenham left Cambridge for Norwich, where he might have talent-spotted the young Caius and sent him to his old college (he might also have talent-spotted the young Matthew Parker). His own list of the contents of the Black Book includes the bulls and the *Historiola*, and makes no claim that they were originals.[21] One of the later documents in the Black Book—the bull of Martin V—included a suspiciously circumstantial explanation for the fact that the original documents, fragile with age, had vanished.

Worse still, the greatest of all authorities on early Britain had denounced the early history of Cambridge as a tissue of fantasies. John Leland's book on the British universities disappeared at his death. But he had mentioned Cambridge and its founding in his poem on the Thames, the *Cygnea Cantio*, published in 1544. Leland had taken notes on the *Historiola*, which he described as an "old but fabulous book of uncertain authorship." In his printed commentary on his poem, he revealed exactly what he thought about the standard account of Cambridge's early past: "[t]here exists in the archives of Cambridge a little history written by an unknown author and of very uncertain credit. . . . Truly I have never read anything more empty, more foolish or more stupid."[22] Thomas Caius knew a lot about original documents. He did research in the archives of University College to support his reconstruction of Oxford's past.[23] So he not only quoted Leland's condemnation of the stories about Cantaber and the Pre-Socratics, but also took a malicious pleasure in pointing out that Cambridge had defended these evident untruths "with the authority of her Black Book."[24] From a modern standpoint, of course, he was absolutely right.

As the best—or perhaps the only—form of defense, Caius mounted a sharp preemptive attack on the arguments that might be obviously be used against his documents:

> If the color offends you, if you think it's silly because it's black, we'll produce a white one. . . . If paper suggests the novelty of the argument, we'll show you it to you in hide, even that of the she-goat Amalthea. If its ink makes it seem recent, we'll show you a version elegantly worked with red and gold, written by a skillful old hand.[25]

Caius meant to make two points here: that the documents he produced were credible even though they were only preserved in the plain, modern form in which they were found in the Black Book; and that proper new copies of the documents would in fact soon be provided. In 1590 another antiquary and product of Caius's college, Robert Hare, officially presented the university with a new "Register," as he called it, of all the documents that supported the liberties and privileges of Cambridge. He had a skilled scribe and illuminator reproduce the charter of Arthur and the bulls of Honorius and Sergius, in each case adding a little side note that read "ex archivis universitatis" ("from the archives of the university"), to assure readers of the documents' genuineness—in a certain sense. These texts were colorful enough already, but Hare had them decorated with miniatures of no small splendor—presumably to enhance the impression of antiquity and authority that he vainly hoped they would make.[26] Elisabeth Leedham-Green has argued that Hare actually began work on this work of restoration in much the same period that Caius was compiling his book.[27] If so, there is every reason to think that he meant it as a fulfillment of Caius's promise.

STANDARDS OF PROOF

Was it reasonable, by the standards of the time, for Caius to build his argument on these materials? Contemporary opinions differed. Richard Willison of Sugwas, Heredfordshire, a native of Norwich who attended school and university with Caius, professed nothing but respect for the erudition deployed in the *De antiquitate:*

> I thanke you for your booke of th'antiquitie of Cambridge. In myne opinion the Universitie can not geave you too much honor. I mervailed much in the reading, how you were hable to gather suche a fardell of straunge Antiquities together, being otherwise occupied in weightie affaires. But you were ever Helluo Literarum, & that the worlde may well understande.[28]

Thomas Caius, not surprisingly, adorned his copy of *De antiquitate* with sharp criticisms. Before he died in 1572, he also wrote an extensive reply, which Thomas Hearne eventually transcribed and published, along with his marginalia.[29] Thomas had a sharp eye for John's shaky assumptions and weak arguments. John wrote that "I call the Cambridge *Historiola* old, because it did not just come into being, and was not invented by the Cantabrigians to glorify themselves."[30] "It's not old," Thomas replied, "if Cantilupe was its author. . . . Nor does it matter much how new or old the history is, but how true it is, and how far it agrees with the writings of the ancients."[31]

Another copy of Caius's book, now preserved in the Beinecke Library at Yale, bears even more revealing marginalia. At the first mention of the Black Book the reader—clearly an Oxford man—entered a superb rant:

> Why is it called the black book? Because of its black color? To frighten the Oxonians? Because of the black morals of its author? Or because Caius possesses no more candour than he does virtue? Because it is close to the vanity of a lie? Or because it smacks of the devil, who was a liar from the beginning?[32]

More substantive, and more effective as criticism, were the darts that the reader plunged into Caius's documents and the inferences he drew from them. The bull of Honorius not only evoked his own time as a Cambridge student, but also mentioned that an earlier pope,

Eleutherius, had favored the university. Eleutherius—as Felicity Heal has explained—converted King Lucius to Christianity, late in the second century.[33] Here, Caius assured the reader, was clear evidence that "the university existed in the time of Honorius and long before him, in the time of Eleutherius."[34] "A ridiculous and impudent invention," noted the Oxonian.[35] When Honorius forbade "any archbishop or bishop, or other ecclesiastical or secular person," to do something, the commentator immediately pointed out the anachronistic terminology that revealed the document to be a fake: "this just wasn't the style used by the popes in that century."[36] And when Caius trotted out the explanation that the original bulls had been "consumed by antiquity" and hence could not be found, much less used, the reader waxed sarcastic, and by doing so showed his knowledge of the rhetorics normally used by forgers: "Cambridge is indebted to those moths and bookworms [who ate the original forgeries]."[37]

CAIUS AND PARKER: COLLABORATION IN RESEARCH

From the standpoint of these contemporary readers, Caius had picked up not the wrong end of the stick, but the wrong stick. Were they right? When it came to medieval texts and traditions, Caius knew his way around. His treatise is stuffed with information of a kind not found in the rest of his works: quotations from documents preserved in the Cambridge archives and the Tower of London and the Latin and many others from a vast range of medieval historical texts. These came from one of the richest repositories of medieval documents to be found anywhere in Europe. A dense bibliography lists Caius's sources.[38] Most of these works were unpublished in 1568—as most of them still were in 1574, when the posthumous second edition of the work appeared, with a better organized bibliography. And a great many of them—as M. R. James pointed out a century ago—were available in a single collection: the massive manuscript library at Lambeth Palace in London, which Matthew Parker and his secretaries created, and much of which is now to be found in the Parker Library at Corpus Christi College Cambridge. Caius and Parker both came from Norwich, and remained close friends in later life. Just as Thomas Bodley allowed one friend, Henry Savile, to have special privileges—including the right to borrow books—at his library in Oxford, so Parker evidently allowed Caius the run of his materials. The Parker Library was larger then than it is now: it included many of the Cotton MSS that Caius also used.[39]

Strype's conclusion is lapidary: "from the first, to the last, the Archbishop's Influence and Assistance, ran through this curious Work."[40] And it is true: the archbishop's fingerprints appear again and again in the doctor's book. Parker himself printed the second, posthumous edition of *On the antiquity of Cambridge,* and distributed presentation copies to the good and the great.[41] His son John went on doing the same long after his father's death. He had a copy with a special illuminated title page made up for King James I, who remarked, "What shall I do with this book? Give me rather Caius *De Canibus* [On English dogs]."[42] A manuscript in Lambeth Palace Library includes a copy of Parker's printed work on Cambridge, which lists contemporary senior members of the university and describes his building projects at the university. Marginal notes add material from Caius's book.[43]

Most suggestive of all, Parker's printer added a cautionary note to some copies of the second edition of Caius's book, on the verso of the title page. It explained that Caius had been less interested in carrying on a polemic with his namesake in Oxford than in using a wide range of "ancient monuments" to establish Cambridge's privileges. This was a hopeful gesture toward peace—a typical Parkerian effort to damp down controversy and emphasize the importance of primary source research, at a time when—as Nicholas Popper has shown—many similar enterprises were taking shape.[44] Caius, moreover, did not have to depend on the busy archbishop alone for technical assistance. Parker, as we have seen, had assembled a whole team of younger scholars. These men, like Parker, regarded Caius as a colleague and his project as connected organically to their own efforts.

Manuscript evidence shows in more detail how Caius worked with Parker and his secretaries. In the body of his work, Caius said almost nothing about the Parker collection: a point to which we shall return. But a note by one of Parker's secretaries in Corpus Christi College Cambridge MS 10 reveals a pattern of friendship, collaboration, and benefaction:

> Note that Gonville and Caius College has a scroll or roll written in parchment, given to that College by Sir Robert Hare in 1568. This roll deals in particular with the church of Winchester . . . it also gives the chronology of the British, Saxon and Norman kings, down to the

beginning of Henry V. It also gives an account of the origin of
Cambridge University, that is, telling about Cantaber etc. And it
is this scroll that Dr Caius mentions in his book on the Antiquity of
Cambridge.[45]

The imposing document in question is a handsome and colorful
fifteenth-century chronicle in roll form, now Gonville and Caius College Library 717/717. A neat presentation inscription identifies Hare
as the donor. Notes by Caius reveal the careful scrutiny to which he
subjected this document, which, he thought, Thomas Hoccleve had
translated and supplemented.[46]

The manuscript included a version of the standard history of Cambridge's origins: "Cambridge was founded by Duke Cantaber in the year
of the world 4095 and frequented by philosophers in the year 394 B.C.,
2425 years from the arrival of Brutus and 2430 from the building of
London."[47] Its author also stated as an established fact ("constat") that
Cambridge had been a university for 1825 years in the year when he
wrote.[48] Caius cited the roll at length in *De antiquitate*. He also described it in unusual detail, as the work "of an author of uncertain name,
but great authority, written in 1447 on parchment with red and black
ink."[49] And he laid special weight on the text's wording, calling attention to the fact that the author called Cambridge a "university" and
claimed that its age was established ("that's the very verb he uses," says
Caius, triumphantly).[50] The note by Parker's secretary shows that he
knew who gave the MS and to which Cambridge library—a detail Caius
himself omitted—and that he had a full sense of its contents—which
Caius did not describe. This short text vividly evokes the sort of detailed textual discussions that Caius and Parker's helpers must often
have held.

Late in the *De antiquitate*, Caius used the testimony of Alfred the
Great to argue that Oxford could not have existed in the king's time.
His source was the letter prefixed to the Anglo-Saxon translation of
the *Cura pastoralis* of Gregory the Great. Here, as he pointed out,
Alfred described his intention to send one book to every diocese in his
kingdom. Given the very modest dimensions of this effort, Caius felt
justified in arguing that "at the time of Alfred, there was not a single
school of grammar in the whole western kingdom."[51] In this case, Caius
cited one of the documents dearest to Parker's heart. Parker stated, in

his 1574 edition of Asser, that he had "ancient manuscripts" of Alfred's work, "written in his own time."[52] Trinity College Cambridge MS 5 22 bears a note by one of Parker's secretaries, which identifies one segment of it as a presentation copy, from Alfred to Sherborne, of his version of Gregory's *Cura pastoralis*.[53] Parker included a text and translation of Alfred's preface from this manuscript—which he identified, again, as contemporary with its author—in his edition of the life of the king ascribed to Asser. Here and in many other cases, Parker and his men seem to have fed Caius his materials, explaining their finds as they did so. Medieval scholarship—like the collation of ancient manuscripts—was a highly social process, and one that Caius knew very well. It took a village to produce his little book.[54]

Unfortunately, Caius did not always cite his sources as fully and precisely as he could have. In the *De antiquitate*, for example, Caius cites what he calls the "very old Annals of Burton," which recorded that nine scholars and doctors at Cambridge were baptized in AD 141.[55] He inferred from this text both that Christianity reached England even before the reign of Good King Lucius, and "that there were doctors in those days."[56] The text in question is now Corpus Christi College Cambridge MS 281, a fourteenth-century chronicle of St Andrew's in Northampton. An ownership label pasted onto the first leaf reads: "This book belongs to the society of Burton: let anyone who removes it be anathema. Amen."[57] Evidently Caius himself did not read far enough to see that the text had been misattributed. He then exaggerated its age. More surprisingly still, he omitted to mention that the note he cited on conversions at Cambridge was not even part of the original fourteenth-century text but rather a scrawled addition in a later hand.[58] (This could, of course, mean that he took the testimony of one of Parker's secretaries on faith—again, something he would have regarded as problematic practice in his other, classical world of scholarship.) Other contemporary antiquaries, such as Lambarde, who also regularly visited and used the Parker Library, were less sparing with such significant details.[59] When Caius's attention was engaged, he had a sharp eye for detail. Writing to Gessner about a pet puffin, he vividly described its behavior:

When there was nothing for it to eat, it would beg for food with a natural word that it repeated, in a humble tone: pupin, pupin. I kept one at my house for eight months. It enthusiastically bit anyone who gave it food or touched it, but in a gentle and innocent way. A very small amount of food was enough to satisfy it.[60]

Caius's references to historical sources and the manuscripts that contained them had none of the immediacy, the sense that a shrewd observer notes and preserves the apparently insignificant, that pervades his tales of animals.[61]

CAIUS THE PHILOLOGIST

Caius's systematic silence on the locations of the Parkerian manuscripts that he quoted in *De antiquitate* and his laconic or nonexistent descriptions of them, contrast strikingly with his own practice when citing readings from manuscripts or classical texts. Caius was a philologist of formidable skill. Vivian Nutton has revealed the care with which he collated the manuscripts of Galen that he consulted in Italy and elsewhere in his extraordinary copy of Galen's works, which is now housed in Eton College.[62] True, Caius's practices were not always innovative or distinctive. When he remarked that older manuscripts of Galen preserved the text in a more intact form than later ones, he was echoing the conventional wisdom of contemporary critics.

Sometimes, though, he showed remarkable precision: in the collations that he entered in the margins of a copy of his own 1544 edition of Galenic texts, he attached sigla to particular manuscripts.[63] In his working copy of Galen in Eton, he dated his consultation of the one that belonged to Edward Wotton. It seems likely that he learned these techniques, not from his teachers, but from contact with the school of Italian humanists who, in the late fifteenth and early sixteenth centuries, insisted that proper editing must rest on full recension and collation of identified manuscripts. Angelo Poliziano, the founder of this school, left a characteristic note in one of his manuscripts of Galen, which is now known as Laur. 75,8: "This book belongs to Angelo Poliziano. It was bought from the heirs of Paolo the medical man. I, Angelo Poliziano, had worked through it at my little country house at Fiesole, on June 14, 1487."[64] In his study of his own books—a bibliographic autobiography modeled on that of Galen—Caius recorded this information while urging potential editors of Galen to hunt up this publicly available resource and use it. The Biblioteca Laurenziana, he explained, held:

> Two books [on the making of drugs], bought by Angelo Poliziano, the tutor of Pope Leo, in his little country place at Fiesole, on June 24, 1497—so that if anyone wishes to copy and publish them, or use them to correct the Greek works of Galen, he may seek them there.[65]

True, Caius mistranscribed the date when Poliziano made his note, but his interest in the Florentine scholar's practices is unmistakable. More remarkable still, when Caius described what he saw as his most notable achievements, he included among them "the apparatus and, so to speak, commentary toward a future castigation of Galen's works in Greek (for they are very corrupt), if the fates allow, partly based on the old books that we have in Britain, partly on the ancient books of Italy, where I traveled in Italy, in order to see the customs of her people, cities, and libraries."[66] When Caius insisted on the unique value of his notes and collations—the raw materials, as he believed, for a truly critical edition—he spoke the language of Pier Vettori, the self-made disciple of Poliziano who was teaching in Florence when he lived in Italy, and Antonio Agustín, who was in Florence in the same year when Caius was, carrying out an elaborate study of one of the most famous manuscripts in Europe, the sixth-century Florentine Pandects.[67]

Caius's interest in criticism was not only textual. He tried to sort out the titles and orders of fragmentarily preserved works by Galen and Hippocrates, and he knew how to cast his net widely when looking for historical and bibliographical context. In 1557, for example, he gave his college library a Hebrew manuscript containing all the books of the Hebrew Bible except the Pentateuch, which was annotated in the thirteenth century and which he considered highly valuable.[68] At the start he had entered an elaborate discussion of the number and order of the books. Here Caius carefully noted differences between the Hebrew and Christian canons, and discussed the authorship of apocryphal works found only in Greek:

> Nowadays, the book of Wisdom is accepted for use in the church. Some suspect it is by Philo the Jew.[69]

He also noted that the Jews had no knowledge at all of many of the Christian apocrypha. The note shows the range of Caius's reading. Jerome had stated in his preface to the three books of Solomon, Proverbs, Ecclesiastes, and the Song of Songs that Wisdom was a pseudepigraphic work: "it was never known in Hebrew, for its very style bespeaks Greek eloquence; and some of the older authors affirm that it is a work of Philo the Jew."[70] As to Jewish ignorance of the apocrypha, Caius mentioned one exception—and in doing so cited the very up-to-date source of his knowledge: "Though they have something about the Maccabees, whom they call Hasmoneans, in their histories, which [Sebastian] Münster recently published in his edition of the little text known as the Josippon."[71] A final, retrospective note, cast in the third person, recalled that "Caius wrote this when he was still young, and studying Hebrew, at Cambridge."[72] In fact, Münster's edition and translation of the Josippon, with a detailed prefatory discussion of the text, appeared at Basel in 1541. Caius's memory may well have been imperfect (Gabriel Harvey often noted the years when he had studied his books—without realizing that they clashed with the evidence of his own later marginalia).[73] Still, Caius's note impressively documents the range of his knowledge and the sophistication of his bibliographical equipment.

CAIUS ON LIBRARIES AND RESEARCH

A library rat, Caius liked to brag about his very bookish adventures. He took clear pride in telling his readers, in his 1570 *De libris propriis*, about the contrasting conditions that awaited scholars at the Biblioteca Laurenziana, which was open to all, thanks to the generosity of Cosimo de' Medici, and the library in Urbino, which was very user-unfriendly.[74] He not only explained that he had created an apparatus for future work on the text of Galen, but surveyed a whole series of Italian libraries where he had collated his manuscripts.[75] More important still, as a philologist Caius knew that location and provenance mattered to experts on manuscripts. In his collations of manuscripts of Galen, he noted some of the owners of the manuscripts he studied and even dated some of his working sessions with them: this was vital information for later editors, which was rarely supplied by scholars at this time (Parker and his secretaries seem almost never to have done so).[76]

Caius thought it important that England develop research libraries. In his posthumously published *History of Cambridge*, he excoriated the inhabitants of Oxford for neglecting Duke Humfrey's library: "it took such a short time for negligence to destroy gratitude and sink benefactions in oblivion" (he was an experienced academic administrator).[77] Then he drew up a detailed list of the books in Cambridge University Library: this was the first printed catalogue, as David McKitterick and others have pointed out, of an English library.[78] Caius insisted repeatedly in his polemic against Thomas Caius that his arguments deserved belief because he had used very few recent texts, "just as I used few printed texts, but used all the other manuscripts, which are my principal delight, as exemplars of pure and venerable antiquity."[79] Yet nowhere in his works in defense of Cambridge did he so much as mention Parker's collection—much less make clear that he had done the vast majority of his research there.[80]

CAIUS AND HISTORY

More striking still are the differences between the historical sensibility that Caius displayed and that of his critics. An antiquary as well as a medical man, Caius compiled a work, now lost, on the ancient cities of Britain.[81] When in Rome, he studied the columns of the emperors attentively enough in 1543 that he remembered a sculpted goat almost thirty years later.[82] Like most well-schooled students of ancient remains and institutions, Caius knew all too well that time changes everything in human life, from institutions to customs. He made this point often, usually while complaining that students no longer acted as they had in his youth. "Young men now-a-days," he wrote to Parker in 1567, "be so negligent that they care for nothing."[83] In his *History of Cambridge University*, composed at the end of his life, he inserted a long passage in which he mourned for the austere Cambridge of his youth: "no fancy caps were worn at disputations, no clothing of uncertain identity, no ruffled shirts, no round caps, no barbered frivolity, no bearded vanity, no jollity, no arms, no dice, no dances, all of which the laws of the university then prohibited, no haughtiness in dress and bearing, in which many shine with a borrowed light, like the moon."[84] It seems all the more striking, then, that Caius's comments on the documents he mustered show so little evidence of a sense of change over time.

Thomas Caius thought it obvious that the stories in the Cambridge *Historiola* belonged to the realm of mythical history. Caius defended them, in part, by citing the Renaissance's greatest single spinner of historical myths, the brilliant forger Annius of Viterbo, whose considerable gifts did not include a sense of anachronism. The annotator of the Beinecke copy of Caius's book saw at once that references to a second-century university or to seventh-century British prelates were out of place and time, yet Caius quoted them with every evidence of confidence.

At times, Caius could practice historical criticism in its most up-to-date form. When he attacked his namesake, he wielded sharp critical tools. Thomas Caius regularly cited what he presented as several modern writers, Leland, Bale, and Lily, who had rejected the mythical history of Cambridge. John neatly pointed out that Thomas was really citing only one witness, since "all of them are following Polydore Vergil as their source."[85] He also showed that his opponent cited texts in deceptively incomplete forms.[86] Yet Caius himself piled up endless citations from multiple sources. Only rarely did he consider their genealogical relations: as when he argued that Hoccleve had translated Robert Hare's genealogical and chronological roll.

THE AUTHORITY OF DOCUMENTS

It seems possible to account, at least in part, for Caius's faith in one set of texts: the supposed charters and bulls that he printed and defended. Why did he repose such confidence in material texts that, by his own admission, had been copied quite recently? One partial answer has to do with the way in which they were copied. When Buckenham and Hare renewed documents that were meant to serve as historical and juridical evidence, they followed standard archival and notarial practice. As Petra Schulte has shown, in theory an original document had a unique authority: it "generated" copies, while copies "were generated." The *exemplar generans*, not the *exemplar generatum*, had *publica fides*: authority. Everyone knew, moreover, that copying often made things worse, yielding documents written in worse ink, on worse parchment, which were less capable than their originals of offering proof.

Notaries, accordingly, developed procedures of replication and verification, carefully designed to produce copies that could effectively stand in for their originals. The notary should transcribe the document word for word on a parchment of the proper size. Then he should read the text aloud, in the presence of a representative of the government and five notaries, two to follow along with him as he read aloud from the original and three to follow in the copy. Only then should the witnesses enter their attestations, in the proper form.[87]

The documents on which Caius relied were produced—as he knew—by this very process. In 1419, the Arthurian charter and the papal bulls had been displayed in Great Saint Mary's church. Thomas de Ryhale, a papal notary, made an official copy of them. He took every precaution to give it authority, naming the witnesses and attesting the document with his official sign. The original of this document survives in the archive of Corpus Christi College. A partial copy—it includes Thomas's list of witnesses and his sign—is in the Parker Library. Parker himself—as a marginal note shows—collated it with the original.[88] The whole archival document, notary's sign and all, is reproduced in the second edition of Caius's book.[89]

Caius himself, moreover, was an expert on the restoration of documents. Both at the College of Physicians and at his own college, he set about renewing the archives. At both institutions, he directed that charters and other important documents be collected in miscellanies that he called "Pandects."[90] He himself collected all the documents he could find, while complaining that at Gonville and Caius, many "evidences" had been scattered among the fellows' rooms. These had to be recopied onto the proper material, vellum, and stored.[91] Caius, in other words, had faith—by modern standards, too much faith—in the normal practices of documentary renewal. Richard Serjeantson and others have taught us to see the assessment of testimony, in these years, as depending on the status and credibility of the witness.[92] In something of the same way, Caius's assessment depended, not on the content of the document or its material form, but on the process by which it came into being. Caius was by no means the only scholar in his world who thought that a historian could—even should—also be a notary.[93]

Caius could see time at work all around him, slowly but relentlessly destroying stones and documents alike. That frightening vision is the antiquary's lot, after all. But he was also a historian of a special kind, one who specialized in institutions. At both his colleges, Caius himself compiled annals: year-by-year accounts of institutional history. In these he transcribed the most important legal documents that he could find. The originals were stored in parallel volumes called Pandects—and became, in a sense, marginal to the institution's functioning and history, despite their unique authority.

Caius put his *De antiquitate* together in much the same way that he had assembled the annals of his two colleges. He copied documents and entered them, in their entirety, in the text. He assumed that if they came from a credible source, they were credible. And he saw the past that he was reconstructing from the standpoint of the creator of annalistic institutional histories: flattened out and continuous, without historical breaks except when some aspect of the system had malfunctioned. Compilation, in a world poor in information, had a value that it can be hard to appreciate in the world of Google.

Recovering that particular point of view helps to explain why Caius simply piled up the documents without worrying about editorial details. The text he printed of Thomas Caius's *Assertion of the Antiquity of Oxford* infuriated its author, since John refused even to correct the obvious slips that Thomas had already detected. Thomas described Alcuin as an associate of Alfred, for example, but then expunged the name in his manuscript. Caius simply printed the text as it stood and set the correction in the margin, ignoring his namesake's dotted line.[94] Thomas Caius and Thomas Hearne both complained bitterly about John's editorial conduct.[95] When seeing as an annalist, Caius could pick out the details in an early papal bull or a late medieval chronicle that gave especially strong support to his arguments. But he could not see that these documents themselves did not fit the periods they supposedly came from. Perhaps conservation simply mattered to him more than criticism.

THE ANTIQUARIAN AND THE SENSE OF THE PAST

Yet there is a little more to the story than that, and Caius's sense of history and change also played a part in it. Caius had a deep love for ancient traditions. Others at Cambridge did as well. The antiquary

Christopher Watson, as Warren Boutcher has shown, recalled how in the 1560s he had frequented

> an antiant bwildinge) behinde S. Johns Colledge, whether [(]yett a novice and abecedarie ther) often resorted (as to the ruine of wisdom) withe my companion and fellowe student M^r henrie Medforde with no small delighte (as to remember him now comfortes me) wh[ere] we together devised, howe ye worthy M^r and his scholers sat ther (in ould time) to reede and dispute; The house at this day is called Pithagoras schoole; Nor was this onelye oure conjecture, for in publique assemblyes and oulde pamphlets the same hath bine harde and reede.[96]

This direct contact with an ancient Cambridge strengthened his faith in the stories told by that "diligent historiographer" Nicholas Cantilupe.

Every good Cambridge man loved Pythagoras's house. But Caius went further. He took a deep interest in Catholic traditions that were supposedly obsolete and definitely dangerous in his day, and in the objects that embodied them. Like the seventeenth-century antiquaries so vividly evoked in classic studies by Margaret Aston and Alexandra Walsham, he felt a considerable interest and affection for textual and material remains that more strenuous Protestants—such as Matthew Parker—wanted, not to collect, but rather to destroy.[97] Dissident members of Caius College reported to the Bishop of London that the Master "mainteyneth wythin his colledge copes vestments albes suinches sensors crosses tapers also all kinde of Masse bookes Porteses pies grales processionalls wth all massinge abominations and termeth them the college treasure."[98] The vice-chancellor, the master of Trinity, and the provost of Kings demanded an inventory of this "treasure" from the college. On December 13, 1572, all of these items that could be found were confiscated and burnt.[99] Either Caius or Legge, his successor as master, described the event in the college annals. The iconoclasts spent an exhausting three hours burning it all—and breaking up whatever would not burn with hammers. Caius or Legge recorded in the language of M. R. James, that God had punished those who roused the mobs against the master with death "or removed them in other ways."[100]

From Caius's own time on, informed observers have suspected him, with good reason, of being a crypto-Catholic.[101] Yet he dined with Matthew Parker, no friend of Recusants, at Lambeth Palace as late as 1570 and continued to exchange warm letters with him after that. Parker's record of the expenses for his funeral shows every evidence of continued affection and sincere mourning.[102] In any event, the old Caius was a man out of place. As a young man, he had lived through the dissolution of the monasteries and the destruction of their traditions and their libraries. As an old man and master of his college, he witnessed his university undergoing another set of rapid, radical changes. New ideas flooded in, upsetting traditional ways: for example, of practicing anatomy and astronomy. New young men also streamed in: the sons of the gentry, who drank, strutted, and fought instead of turning to their books and crowded out the poor, able boys for whom the colleges had originally been intended.

Caius himself rejected all such innovations, including the Erasmian pronunciation of Greek. He denounced the ingenious paradoxes with which so many authors of his time tried to make their names:

> Nonetheless, there is no projector of any new thing, however foolish or impudent or tasteless he may be, who will not have patrons and supporters for his stupidity: half-grown youths or the foolish rabble, but not a single serious man who has real judgment. Unless they are perhaps doing this in order to show off their wit, as Isocrates did when he praised Busyris, Libanius Thersites, Lucian a fly, Favorinus the quartan fever, Synesius of Cyrene baldness, Dio Chrysostom hair, and in our own time, Copernicus when he wrote a work on the movement of the earth and the immobility of the heavens, and Erasmus when he wrote short texts on fever and Phalarism. For rhetoricians often amuse themselves by dealing with disreputable topics, and practice by proving an ignoble thesis.[103]

As a good humanist, Caius recalled the example set by the Romans, who "felt that whatever was introduced contrary to the customs and traditions of their forefathers was neither acceptable nor proper."[104] As a good college man, he praised the old traditions of university life, however irrational they seemed:

> the schools of English public law can in no way be prevailed upon to forsake their octaves; or certain schools of the university to abandon their socks when candidates are to be admitted Master of Arts, or their leggings when they are to be distinguished by the degree Doctor

of Sacred Theology, or their eggs prepared in various ways when in the determinations the new BAs greet the seniors of their rank at meals. Nor can they be persuaded that in disputations, when the participants have been seated, the auditors should not sit on the ground on a thickly strewn layer of rushes. Nor will the Spaniards of the University of Bologna abandon their hood and their scapular, which they call "staminea," a garment worn only by the Fellows of the Spanish college at Bologna. All of these I applaud, for they are not driven inconstantly hither and thither for trivial reasons. They are not pulled away from their ancient custom, nor do they abandon it easily, as is the tendency in some universities, where a childish superficiality very rashly exchanges the large for the small, the square for the round, and one form for another, preserving no order, custom or dignity.[105]

Moreover, he consistently denounced, with special venom, the new ways of the young men of property who treated Cambridge as a humanistic finishing school, wearing fashionable clothing rather than the prescribed academic garments:

> our young men . . . embrace vices in place of virtues. This is the way the mobs of courtiers behave, when they don shirts with ruffs and corked shoes for the sake of fashion. These were first devised for everyday use in order to conceal sickly shanks and necks. For once upon a time, in living memory, when healthy practices reigned, they did not use high-heeled boots, and their necks were left bare to the chest, and their chests were laid bare to the breast (to use Plautus's term), and uncovered down to the nipples, even in winter.[106]

Caius hit the mark with these last remarks. Only a few years after he wrote, the university condemned the colleges for

> suffering of sondry yonge men, being the children of gentlemen and men of welth, at their coming to the same Universitie, contrarie to the auncient and comely usage of the same, to use very costly and disguised manner of apparrell and other attires unseemely for students in any kinde of humaine learning, but rather mete for riotuos, prodigall, and light persons.[107]

Special criticism was meted out to students who wore "any excessive ruffs in their shirts," or carried swords or rapiers.[108] Torn by nostalgia for past austerity and past learning, passionately committed to "the auncient and comely usage" of the universities, schooled to believe that institutional archives held valid sources, Caius had to believe the sources he published. If he had not found them in existence already, the logic of his situation would have forced him to invent them. Faced with revolutions, the student of history invented traditions—and cast his lot with those who had done so in the past. This advanced humanist's preferences among the sources for Cambridge history and his reactions to them had a certain logic. In the archive and in the history based on it, Caius believed, he could avenge himself and the institutions he loved for the blows of time and ignorance. That helps to explain how the most straightforward of historical genres, the short and simple annals of an institution, turned in his hands into what now seems so strange a polemic.

Mysteries remain. If Caius exaggerated the virtues of the Cambridge of his youth, he nonetheless diagnosed the social and cultural changes it was undergoing in his time with considerable precision. In doing so he showed considerable powers of observation and a sharp sense of historical change. He was as aware as contemporary social and cultural historians of the ways in which garments should reflect the position of their wearers. Like them, he knew that changes in fashion, far from being trivial, reflected changes in society.[109] When he collected sources to buttress the antiquity of Cambridge, by contrast, he made no effort to situate them in time or to assess their reliability. Violating a principle enunciated by one of his models of humanistic philology, he did not weigh his sources, but rather counted them.[110] It was not easy, in Caius's time, to date a manuscript. But efforts to establish authorship, fix dates, and even assess scripts formed a core part of historical scholarship as Parker and his secretaries practiced it. In this respect, he and his friends and allies differed sharply.[111]

Distance was lacking: not historical but emotional distance. Caius clearly found it easier to postpone drawing conclusions from the manuscripts of Galen than from fourteenth- and fifteenth-century chronicles. Proving that England had an independent tradition of learning, rooted in antiquity, mattered deeply, and Caius's passion diminished his ability to read critically. Faith, by contrast, was present: all too powerful a faith in the ability of scribes and notaries to refresh their archives without changing or adding to their contents. And Caius, as Randolph Head has shown, was far from the only early modern expert who preferred notarial standards of documentary validity to philological ones.[112] Still, it seems remarkable that Caius, as gifted and experienced a student of the material remains of antiquity as any of his contemporaries, paid so little attention to the materials and ages of his sources. Confirmation bias hung like a scrim between him and his sources, and all his skillful efforts to collect the evidence went for nothing when he laid it out in support of an argument to which it added little weight.

A copy of the 1568 *De antiquitate,* owned by someone well-disposed to Caius—at least to judge from the few trefoils that appear in the margins—is now in the library of the New York Academy of Medicine. A brief judgment appears, scrawled on the top of the title page: "Antiquitati maxima debetur veneratio" (Antiquity deserves the deepest reverence).[113] Caius could not have asked for a better epitaph.

CHAPTER 9

Baruch Spinoza Reads the Bible

VISIONS OF SPINOZA

A VISION OF SPINOZA—of the sort of man he was, the life he led, the way he worked—has often dominated efforts to interpret his works. Spinoza had a gift for friendship. Still, it has seemed natural—and is by no means wholly wrong—to see him as a rather solitary figure, a heroic individualist who lost some of his closest friends to the religious intolerance he fought. And it has seemed normal to read him as a rather solitary intellectual, who, like Descartes, cut his own paths, making as little use of others' writings as his very sparing citations suggest. Many books and articles offer interpretations of the *Tractatus theologico-politicus,* or parts of it. Relatively few of them connect the book systematically with earlier efforts to lay out principles of biblical interpretation, and those that do so often concentrate on a few works that have become more or less canonical in this connection. In 1666, Spinoza's friend Lodewijk Meijer published *Philosophia S. Scripturae Interpres* [*Philosophy as the Interpreter of Holy Scripture*]. This rationalizing interpretation of the Bible helped provoke Spinoza to offer his own radically different view of how to read the text. Another friend, Adriaan Koerbagh, recorded the two men's discussions of the Bible and much else in his *Ligt schijnende in duystere plaatsen* [*A Light Shining in Dark Places*] before he was imprisoned.[1] Most interpreters of the

Tractatus theologico-politicus discuss these texts. Only a few scholars in recent years—notably J. Samuel Preus, Noel Malcolm, and Susan James—have introduced further materials into the discussion.[2]

In the 1930s a brilliant and exuberant Jesuit, Stanislaus, Graf von Dunin-Borkowski, took a very different approach as he prepared to climb this mountain. He assumed that Spinoza's writings on biblical criticism and interpretation formed part of the larger movement of humanist philology that arose in Renaissance Italy and developed further in France, the Netherlands, the Holy Roman Empire, and Britain. He worked his way through a vast number of primary sources—editions of and commentaries on texts, treatises on antiquities and chronology, and the philological miscellanies that served, in the absence of scholarly journals, as a medium for publishing small, new results. And he produced both a rich panorama of early modern scholarship and a distinctive context for Spinoza. He portrayed the author of the *Tractatus* as a figure in period style rather than an isolated hero striding along the mountaintops. Von Dunin-Borkowski paid too little attention to central questions of method: above all, that of whether any evidence confirmed that Spinoza had read and responded to the vast mass of philological literature from which he blew the dust of centuries.[3] But his spirited and erudite book offers another way of reading Spinoza, and this chapter attempts both to channel and to discipline his spirit. I will ask what difference it makes if we imagine Spinoza in dialogue with a rather large and diverse crowd of Jews and Christians, both imaginary ancients and troubling moderns. What, if anything, did he take from the learned traditions that surrounded him? And what did he refuse or fail to take?

LEARNED CRITICISM:
TRADITION AND TRANSFORMATION

Around 1650, Henri de Valois began to write a treatise on the art of criticism in the ancient world and after. A lawyer by training, Valois was an erudite humanist, a lover of granular and intricate textual arguments who did pioneering work as an editor of ecclesiastical histories. He dedicated one passage in his *De critica* to a brief manifesto that sounds, in part, very like Spinoza. Valois insisted that the critic abandon all presuppositions when studying a text—including the assumption that a text by a famous or an antique author must be profound or valuable: "Above all we must take care that we do not set out to read with our minds already fixed in an attitude of respectful submission, so that we do not allow the authority or the antiquity of the writer to fool and make sport of us."[4] But he also set boundaries for the movement of the critical intellect: clear ones, which appeared exactly at the point where Spinoza accepted none: "Only the divine books enjoy the right to demand that we read them with our minds as if enslaved, and renouncing freedom of judgment. We must acquire the habit of pronouncing judgment on all other books as we read them."[5]

Ninety years or so later, a very different scholar, the busy Dutch historian and print impresario Pieter Burman, edited and published Valois's text. He treated the Catholic scholar with respect, comparing him to such heroes of Protestant erudition as Isaac Casaubon and Joseph Scaliger. But when he came to Valois's profession of unwillingness to read the Bible critically—as Benedetto Bravo noted in an important essay—he revealed some skepticism:

> I am not sure that Valois spoke his mind fully in this passage. True, I think no sane person will challenge the principle that all who offer their obeisance to decent thought owe honor and reverence to the meaning and contents of the sacred pages. But since the value of criticism is the point at issue here, no one will maintain either that it should never be applied, in a modest and appropriate way, to the holy books. For those who passed them down to posterity by copying them had hands that could make mistakes, as happened to the scribes of other authors, and scholars of distinction have used the aid of true criticism to remove these.[6]

Burman clearly saw the task of criticism in such a different light than Valois had that he could not imagine his predecessor had been sincere. The contrast between the original text and the editor's note suggests that much had happened between 1650 and 1740. A series of intellectual storms—sketched brilliantly in a single great book, eighty years ago, by Paul Hazard, and surveyed in breathtaking detail, more recently, by Jonathan Israel—had burst upon the canons, both scriptural and classical. They reduced what had seemed authoritative texts to battered fragments and stripped them of their cultural authority.[7]

SPINOZA'S CRITICISM OF THE HEBREW BIBLE

None of these storms was more violent or killed more trees than the one caused by Spinoza's *Tractatus theologico-politicus*. More than any single other work, so it seems, Spinoza's book made it impossible for a cutting-edge intellectual—even one like Burman, who was fascinated by the intellectual traditions of late humanism—to imagine living with the sort of mental reservation that had seemed natural to Valois. After all, he had argued—powerfully enough to inspire radicals and to worry conservatives—that Ezra, not Moses, was the true author of the core of the Old Testament. More important still, Spinoza showed, Ezra's crude and unpolished compilation clearly did not offer guidance to the secrets of metaphysics or of natural philosophy, as many thinkers held. The Bible was not an encyclopedic and authoritative description of the universe but rather a rough guide to morality, put together quickly to serve the needs of a primitive people.[8]

No one who studies the scholars of this period can ignore the liberating effect of Spinoza's clear and radical statement of the case against the coherence and authority of the Old Testament—or the courage that propelled him and friends like Koerbagh to explore these dangerous realms. No encomium can do them justice. That is fortunate, since historians should not compose encomia. Instead, I propose to do for Spinoza, on a tiny and partial scale, what he proposed to do for the books of the Bible as a whole: to sketch the way to write a new "history," not of his entire text, but of the central chapters, 7–10, that deal with hermeneutics and Scripture. I will try, that is, to establish, as he did for Ezra, some of the circumstances in which he framed his ideas, the sources on which he built, and the sources on which he did not build. By doing so, I hope to suggest that he was not quite the isolated figure that so many portraits of him depict.

SPINOZA AND EARLIER TRADITIONS OF CRITICISM

The *Tractatus* offered, not only arguments about how to read Scripture, but also a full-blown theory about the origins of the text. Like the theologians and humanists who made library shelves bend under polyglot editions of the Bible, treatises on how to interpret it, and massive commentaries on each book, Spinoza did more than think about the Bible itself. He gathered bits of evidence from multiple sources and fitted them into place in a mosaic of his own composition. Moreover, sometimes he did so in a very distinctive and unexpected way. No earlier reader of the Bible mattered more to Spinoza than the twelfth-century commentator ibn Ezra—who, Spinoza wrote with some exaggeration, argued "that it was not actually Moses who wrote the Pentateuch but some other person who lived much later, and that the book Moses wrote was a different work."[9]

In that light, Spinoza's interpretation of ibn Ezra's comment on Deuteronomy 1:2 seems all the odder. There ibn Ezra told the reader that if he understood "the secret of the twelve" and a number of phrases from Deuteronomy, he would "know the truth." The phrase "the secret of the twelve" almost certainly refers to the last chapter of Deuteronomy, 34, which describes Moses's death and burial in twelve verses that Moses himself presumably could not have written. Spinoza held, much less plausibly, that ibn Ezra's words referred to the altar on which the original book of Moses was inscribed (Deuteronomy 27:8). According to the rabbis, this consisted of only twelve stones.[10] In this and in other cases, as Warren Zev Harvey has argued, Spinoza might have drawn inspiration from other, unmentioned Jewish commentaries.[11] Identifying which learned works Spinoza actually read and what, if anything, he took away from the traditions of learned criticism that they purveyed is no simple task.

To support the possibility of applying rational criticism to the Bible, Burman quoted two scholars of different older vintages. Isaac Vossius, in his 1684 edition of Catullus, had invoked the testimony of "those who handle books and collate old manuscripts with one another." Clearly defined scribal errors, he argued on their authority and his own, occurred as often in manuscripts of the Bible as in those of secular texts: "Everywhere—and even in all the sacred writers—we can notice that when similar or identical words appear, the scribes omit what is found between them. No scholar is unaware of this or denies it. But certain fools and incompetents, who nonetheless want to appear as theologians, do not grant this, and would prefer that the sacred books were immune from corruption. Accordingly, they conjure up imaginary scribes who were holy and never made mistakes."[12] Vossius, as

Burman admitted, had sprinkled some salt on his remark (and the wounds of his opponents). But his general point was valid.

Isaac Casaubon, a far more moderate figure, had argued decades before Vossius that while the core of biblical doctrine had survived the centuries intact, the texts had been quite labile: "In Greek the matter is obvious, many things have undergone small changes, and some have been more seriously corrupted, but in such a way that the truth remains unshaken. In Hebrew we can have no doubt at all: the whole Masorah [the textual apparatus of vowel signs, accents and marginal notes] offers absolutely certain testimony on this point."[13] Casaubon, as Burman knew, had intended to write a full-scale study of ancient textual criticism in which he compared the methods of the Jewish Masoretes of Palestine, who redacted the text of the Hebrew Bible, to those of Alexandrian Greek and Latin scholars, who redacted the texts of Homer and many other writers.[14] He clearly assumed that all manuscripts, whether Latin, Greek, or Hebrew, were products of human industry and could be victims of human incompetence. Burman did not exaggerate when he traced the roots of his own critical attitude to texts to the traditions of late humanism. He saw the critical attitude that he missed in Valois, not as something that had just been invented, but rather as part and parcel of a philological tradition that began long before Spinoza wrote.

What access did Spinoza have to these traditions of learned criticism? And what resources did he find in them? The postmortem inventory of his library is suggestive.[15] Machiavelli—perhaps the most thoroughgoing naturalist to publish a commentary on an ancient text before Spinoza—was there, ready to inspire anyone who did not believe that miracles had sustained biblical leaders. So, more unexpectedly, was the Paduan scholar Lorenzo Pignoria, who in 1611 had published a provocative edition of an Egyptian cult object, the bronze Isiac Table.[16] The erudite but fanciful chancellor of Bavaria, Herwart von Hohenburg, and others read complex philosophical and theological allegories into its designs. Pignoria, by contrast, told his friend Marx Welser that he "hated the excessive and usually irrelevant interpretations of this sort of object that Platonists have imported into them, to shore up their collapsing myths, ignoring the doctrines of their own teacher."[17] Like Spinoza, Pignoria sought to read a glittering and supposedly profound ancient document without presuppositions. The philological tradition thus offered some aid and comfort for a reader like Spinoza, one who insisted on sweeping away the traditional commentators and reading with fresh eyes and critical reason.

CRITICAL CONVERSATIONS? HUMANIST CRITICISM IN SPINOZA'S WORLD

Spinoza could have taken in scholarly arguments like these not only from books, but also from the atmosphere he breathed. For the air, in the Amsterdam of the 1660s, was filled with provocative comments about the status of Scripture, and so were the bookstalls. Spinoza and his friends were talking, in the 1660s, about the questions he would attack in the *Tractatus*. In his book of 1666, Lodewijk Meijer recorded a remark by someone he described as a distinguished man who was expert in these matters. Meijer indicated that he offered a direct quotation by printing the passage in italics. Pretty much every manuscript of the Bible, this man claimed, whether in Hebrew or in Greek, had been corrupted by the interventions of the evil-minded. This expert on criticism went so far as to say that "the rabbis themselves admitted that there were so many and so confused variants in the Hebrew Bible, that it was hard to tell the true ones from the false." He also insisted "that if someone collated and examined all the manuscripts of the New Testament, he would find almost as many discordances as words."[18] Some scholars have identified the gentleman in question with Spinoza.

The evidence suggests a more complicated story. In 1659, long before Isaac Vossius edited Catullus, he set off a great debate on biblical chronology. Vossius pointed out that the credible annals of Chinese history, newly brought to Europe and translated by Martino Martini, stretched back so far into the past that the Hebrew Bible, which set less than 4,000 years between the Creation and the Incarnation, could not accommodate them. Happily, he explained, the longer chronology of the Greek Old Testament, the ancient version known as the Septuagint, could contain the Chinese past without difficulty. To accept his solution, scholars must simply realize that the Hebrew text was manifestly unreliable, and follow the Greek.[19] As in the later comment Burman quoted, here too, the tone of Vossius's argument matters as much as its content. "It would be wonderful," he wrote scornfully, "if we had the autograph of Moses. But is anyone so lacking in judgment as to think that God always stood next to the Hebrew scribes and guided their hands and pen?"[20] Clearly, the excursus on the unreliability of scribes that Vossius added to his late edition of Catullus would not have surprised his longtime readers: for decades, after all, he had taken a similar view on the textual transmission of the Bible. Vossius considered it certain that Ezra, when collecting and editing the Bible after the Babylonian Captivity, had abandoned the old Hebrew alphabet, which he took as identical to Samaritan, in favor of Aramaic letters. Later, the Masoretes—the Jewish grammarians of the period from the seventh to the eleventh century—equipped the text with further signs. Moses himself, Vossius quipped, "if he came back to life, wouldn't be able to decipher a single accent mark in the books of the Jews: for they received their letters from the Chaldeans and their vowel points and accents from the Masoretes."[21]

These arguments reflected a long tradition of erudite debate about the different versions of the Old Testament. But Vossius made them, as Adam Sutcliffe pointed out some time ago, in a brusque, punchy tone, and cast them in short, punchy pamphlets—one of which was even translated into Dutch.[22] Moreover, he used them to undermine what contemporaries saw as a fundamental part of the content of the Hebrew Old Testament text: the chronological backbone of world history. Unlike Spinoza, moreover, Vossius insisted that the manuscripts of the New Testament were just as full of errors as those of the Old. His views became the talk of more than one town. When Meijer's friend evoked the pullulating variants to be found in the manuscripts of the New Testament, he was, in fact, repeating, partly word for word, what Vossius had already said about them in his own pamphlet: "in these there is such variation in the readings, that if someone collated all of the manuscripts with one another, he would find almost as many discordances as words."[23] Three possibilities suggest themselves. Perhaps Meijer was quoting Spinoza; if so, however, Spinoza himself was quoting Vossius. More likely, Meijer was citing Vossius directly. That could show that Vossius participated in the discussions that took place in Meijer's—and Spinoza's—circle. In the dedication of his pamphlet to Govert van Slingelandt, Vossius mentioned that it treated questions that had first come up in conversations between the two men.[24] Or it could reveal that Meijer and others in Spinoza's immediate circle read Vossius's little book. In any case, one path by which Spinoza and his associates had access to the conclusions of learned criticism has now been traced.

In the later 1660s, moreover, Vossius did something even more mischievous, from the standpoint of undermining biblical authority, than writing a disturbing pamphlet about the age of the world. He printed the *Secunda Scaligerana*—the table talk of Joseph Scaliger, the greatest of chronologers, from the years 1603 through 1606, when the French students who lodged in his house in Leiden took down his remarks in a savory mixture of French and Latin. Scaliger had long struggled with the contradictions and cruces of biblical chronology. Some of these did not greatly worry him. Scaliger wrote to his Leipzig colleague Seth Calvisius, for example, that "no one of sound mind" could hope to put the kings of Israel and Judah into a single coherent chronological order.[25]

But as Scaliger worked on his last great synthesis of sacred and secular history, the *Thesaurus Temporum* (1606), he found himself acutely aware that some significant contradictions could neither be resolved nor ignored. Traditionally, as Noel Malcolm has shown in a rich and wide-ranging essay, Catholic scholars had been willing to accept the possibility that the Old Testament text was far from perfect. But in the years leading up to 1600, Protestant divines insisted more and more pertinaciously that every word of Scripture, as transmitted, was inspired.[26] In his garden and chimney corner, Scaliger confided his worries to the French students who boarded with him, Jean and Nicolas Vassan. They recorded his remarks, in the collection that Vossius published, rearranged, and alphabetized.[27] The account of Herodias and the death of John the Baptist offered in Mark 6 disagreed with that given by the Jewish historian Josephus (*Jewish Antiquities* 18.116–117). Scaliger thought Josephus must be right, since he was usually precise and claimed to have derived his information from official sources, rather than the evangelist. And he was horrified by his own conclusion: "This is a terrible thing. Who would have induced him to lie? . . . Josephus is a very accurate historian, and more accurate than any other author, and very faithful; he says he took this from the

Acta [diaries] of Herod."[28] Scaliger concluded that deliberate falsification had taken place: "The early Christians added a great deal to the New Testament. They could have changed that too."[29] The moral was clear: human hands had recorded the text of the Bible, and human hands could slip or introduce changes deliberately: "Copies could be corrupted, then as now. What is written on paper could always be corrupted."[30] The changes in question, moreover, were not mere textual variants. Some of them affected the content of the New Testament. The Gospel of John states that Mary Magdalene came to the sepulcher of Christ "early, when it was yet dark" (20:1). Matthew, by contrast, reports that she and the other Mary came "as it began to dawn" (28:1): Mark, that she, Mary and Salome came "at the rising of the sun" (16:1-2). Luke does not give the time when "they" came to the grave (24:1). And even though Scaliger tried to convince himself that the scribes were at fault, he clearly revealed his anxiety that something deeper was at work:

> As to the fact that one of the Evangelists says that the women came to the tomb very early in the morning, as the sun rose, this is an error and a scribal corruption. I don't know what to say. Ambrose, Augustine and Chrysostom tormented themselves, with no result.[31]

In language very different from that of Henri de Valois, Scaliger admitted that he would speak critically about the Scriptures if he dared, but found the topic too hot to touch in public: "There are more than 50 additions or changes to the New Testament and the Gospels. It's a strange thing, I don't dare to say it. If it were a profane author, I would speak about it in a different way."[32] Scaliger, in other words, did more than argue that individual witnesses to the text of the New Testament were imperfect. In private, he worried about the truthfulness of the Gospels, in their transmitted form—and insisted that their early Christian readers, who had passed them down to posterity, had also corrupted them. He dared to say, if not to write, what Valois, half a century later, did not dare to think. By the 1660s Vossius could print his comments.

The sharp remarks—and in Scaliger's case, the agonized admissions—of Christian believers about the conflicts between reason and biblical authority were part of the wider cultural debate before Spinoza wrote. When Spinoza described the Hebrew Old Testament as full of corruption and error, he knew that some Christian scholars agreed with him—and that they had made these points quite directly, in the teeth of opposition from theologians.

LEARNING FROM THE OPPOSITION: SPINOZA AND HIS SOURCES

What in particular, then, did Spinoza draw from the various traditions of learning as he framed his formal theory? The *Tractatus*—like many other great, explosive works—was deeply overdetermined. As Malcolm has revealed, Spinoza pulled together ideas about the authorship of the Old Testament that had already been widely diffused for decades and in some cases for centuries, clarifying their implications and giving them a dramatic new expression.[33] But his few references did not pin down the sources on which he drew, and even Malcolm's skillful detective work has not identified all of them. As Yosef Kaplan and others have revealed, Spinoza often alluded to and worked with texts that he did not explicitly name, and that did not form part of his library as inventoried at his death.[34] It will take time, luck, and imagination to establish exactly what he knew, when he knew it and how he used it.

One case will suggest some of the complexities of these questions. Spinoza himself cited the Jewish scholar Jacob ben Chajim ibn Adonijah's introduction to Daniel Bomberg's second edition of the Rabbinic Bible, published in 1524–1525. He probably read the text in the Rabbinic Bible printed by Johann Buxtorf and Abraham Braunschweig at Basel in 1618–1619, a copy of which he owned. Spinoza quoted only one line, in which ibn Adonijah admitted that: "it is the habit of the Talmud [the great code of Jewish law] to contradict the Masoretes [the grammarians who had compiled the marginal apparatus of the Hebrew Bible]" about individual readings.[35] He used this evidence to argue that more biblical variants had existed in the past than were attested to in the Masoretic Bible. The text of the *Tractatus* does not suggest that Spinoza learned much from ibn Adonijah. Spinoza described the earlier scholar, contemptuously, as "the superstitious corrector" of Bomberg's Bible—without making clear whether ibn Adonijah was superstitious because he thought the Masorah ancient or because he converted to Christianity.[36] He did not discuss the long argument that followed the remark he quoted, in which ibn Adonijah tried to show that the Masorah was often right and the Talmud wrong. Instead, he used ibn Adonijah's remark to support his general argument that ancient biblical texts had swarmed with variants: more than the modern apparatus recorded.

Yet this was not the only point that Spinoza gleaned from ibn Adonijah.[37] He needed to explain why, if variants had been so profuse as he claimed, the Masorah normally gave only two readings for any given word. To explain how this had happened Spinoza quoted a passage from a post-Talmudic tractate: Soferim (Scribes) 6.4.[38] This relates that three Bibles with distinctive readings had been found in the Temple court. Where they disagreed, someone (evidently someone in authority) decided that the majority should rule, and accepted the variant found in two of the three. "They maintain," Spinoza wrote, referring to the authors of the passage, that the three manuscripts were "found in the time of Ezra, claiming that the notes were added by Ezra himself."[39] Since there were only three manuscripts, Spinoza reasoned, it was natural that two of them would agree against the third—and hence that there would be only two versions of each reading that varied at all.[40]

Spinoza misrepresented the text of Soferim, which does not connect the discovery of these manuscripts with Ezra or claim that he added the notes. And it is easy to see how this happened. Ibn Adonijah, in the text Spinoza used, quoted the passage from Soferim. More important, he made clear that in his view, the story showed that Ezra had regarded all the variants concerned as "the law of Moses from Sinai." Otherwise, he explained, Ezra would simply have decided to "expunge the reading of the one copy, and adopt that of the majority of codices."[41] Spinoza connected the three manuscripts of the Temple court with Ezra, not because he thought the evidence over systematically but because ibn Adonijah had already done so. It seems highly likely, then, that Spinoza found the basic elements for his history of the biblical text in later times, not by carrying out research into a wide range of sources, but by reading the erudite Bible on his own shelf.

Thinkers learn from those they disagree with and even those they despise, as well as from those they reflect. Long ago, Michel Foucault argued that intellectual historians should cease to use the term and concept of "influence," which reflected the ancient superstitions of the astrologers.[42] In fact, the astrologers believed that malevolent as well as beneficent planets shaped human lives. They had their own kind of wisdom, which intellectual historians might do well to ponder. Early modern radicals learned much from orthodox Christian thinkers, as Alan Kors and Dmitri Levitin have taught us.[43] Through a meticulous analysis, James Preuss showed that Spinoza learned from Lodewijk Meijer's hermeneutics and the responses they provoked from liberal Calvinist theologians like Ludwig Wolzogen and Lambert van Velthuysen, even though he agreed fully with none of these writers. By subjecting the Bible to the authority of philosophy, Meijer made clear that he did not see it as an absolute authority in its own right. Wolzogen and van Velthuysen insisted that Scripture was as much a historical text as Livy's Roman history. No biblical book could properly be understood except in terms of its original context and its peculiar "mental framework." Yet Meijer insisted that the truths of Scripture matched those of rationalist philosophy, and the liberals held that Scripture spoke directly to each present generation. Spinoza took what they had to offer, used and sharpened their language—and radicalized their message so successfully that few could recognize its partial sources.[44]

In the same manner, it seems likely that a particular work of Protestant biblical scholarship inspired Spinoza. Nothing has excited readers more in Spinoza's work, from his own time to this, than his demand for a "history of Scripture."[45] To study nature, he explained, one had to construct a natural history and then draw the definitions of natural things from it. Similarly, to study Scripture, one must begin by creating a "pure history" of it, and using that to work out the ideas of the text's authors.[46] This history must be drawn from the Bible alone: a peculiar principle, which Spinoza did not observe in practice, and to which we will return.[47] And it must describe the language of the text, collect and compare all passages on such subjects as the nature of God, identify the author and occasion of each book and trace its transmission and reception.[48] When Jean Le Clerc dissected Richard Simon's *Critical History of the Old Testament* in 1685, he began by stating that it simply did not amount to a full history—that is, though he did not say so, a history in Spinoza's sense, which would describe the full origins and later histories of each biblical book.[49] In recent years, debate has centered on the question of what sort of history Spinoza had in mind: a Baconian one, like one of the Lord Chancellor's natural histories, built up by collecting all the evidence, or an ancient one somehow rebuilt on Cartesian principles, which moved from clear and distinct general principles to the local level of facts and texts.[50] The answer— so far as the origins of the enterprise is concerned—is not quite either. As so often in early modern Europe, in this case too, the "history" that inspired Spinoza was an Aristotelian project for collecting all the information about a particular question, and the source through which Spinoza gained access to it was modern.

Johann Buxtorf, the Basel Hebrew professor whose edition of the Rabbinic Bible Spinoza owned, described his *Tiberias*, the book in which he gave his formal account of the Masorah, on its title page, as a "history of the Masoretes."[51] He assembled, collated, and interpreted all the information he could find in Jewish sources, including the Talmud, the Masorah itself, and later Jewish writings, on the origins, development, and terminology of the textual apparatus that accompanied the Hebrew Bible. The textual history that Buxtorf traced was Aristotelian in form as well as name. He divided the rich material he collected into sections that revealed in the most traditional way the material, efficient, formal, and final causes of the biblical apparatus.[52] Spinoza, in radical contrast, described his history as a multilevel empirical inquiry into the language, origins and reception of the biblical text, book by book. Still, the similarities between the arguments of these two very different histories are striking. Like Spinoza's history of the Old Testament text, Buxtorf's history of the Masorah rested on painstaking collection of primary evidence. Any defects in his arguments, he insisted, reflected the failings of his sources and of those who should have preserved more of them.[53] Like Spinoza's history, too, Buxtorf's made clear that firm conclusions were premature, since any conclusion must rest on the evidence collected, and that did not provide conclusive proof. Spinoza admitted that in taking Ezra as the author of the Bible, he was not offering definitive proof but rather putting forward a hypothesis.[54] Buxtorf had admitted his uncertainty on the history of the biblical text, especially the age of the vowel points, long before in private letters, though not in public.[55] In the *Tiberias* he acknowledged that he could only put forward the strongest arguments he could frame for Ezra as the creator of the Masorah, not prove them, "given the great lack of ancient histories and the sparseness of authors."[56] Spinoza would certainly have described Buxtorf as part of his credulous opposition; but that is no reason—as Susan James has suggested in a different context—for assuming that he could not have learned from or be provoked by the Basel professor, as he was by Lodewijk Meijer and the liberal Utrecht theologians who criticized his work.[57] When Spinoza called for a history of the Bible and its terminology, he referred to an exercise that he had already seen performed by others.

SPINOZA AND BIBLICAL AUTHORSHIP

Most striking of all, however, is the way in which older works of learning helped Spinoza to carry out a crucial part of his critical task. Readers of the *Tractatus* in recent decades have emphasized that Spinoza's work was "historical" in a radically modern sense. Spinoza, they point out, insisted that the only way to determine the meaning of a biblical book was to work out the exact circumstances in which its author had written and the intentions and resources with which he did so. While true, such claims are more than a little exaggerated. When Spinoza insisted on identifying the author and occasion of every biblical book, after all, he was not making an iconoclastic point but rather applying the ancient tradition of the *accessus ad auctores*, which had long since led medieval exegetes to set the books of the Bible, so far as they could, into their historical contexts.[58] He showed more originality when he insisted on following the later histories of the biblical books. In any event, experts on Spinoza, like many students of the history of hermeneutics, have shown more interest in his principles than in their application. They have devoted little attention to the considerable effort Spinoza expended to situate Ezra's project in time, space, and culture. When and where, exactly, did Spinoza think Ezra did his work? And why did he place and date it as he did?

Spinoza argued that the "historian," the true author of the Bible whom he identified as most probably Ezra, had woven together from existing sources most of the text, starting from Genesis and coming down to the end of 2 Kings. Here we learn that Evil-Merodach, king of

Babylon, released Jehoiachin, the king of Judah whom his troops had captured when they took Jerusalem, from prison in the thirty-seventh year of his captivity. Evil-Merodach treated the Jewish ruler well, giving him a pension and showing him great respect (2 Kings 25:27–30). Since the historian's text ended here, Spinoza argued, "it follows that no one before Ezra could have been this historian."[59] After all, he noted, "Scripture tells us of no one living at that time other than Ezra (see Ezra 7.10) who set himself zealously to seek out and organize the law of God; it also relates that he was a scribe (Ezra 7.6), well-versed in the Law of Moses."[60] With these points—both based on chapter 7 of the biblical book of Ezra—Spinoza evidently thought he had made his case as solid as he could, and concluded: "Hence, I cannot surmise that anyone but Ezra wrote these books."[61]

The problem here is simple. The fall of Jerusalem and the captivity of Jehoiachin or Jechoniah took place—according to the standard computations of sixteenth- and seventeenth-century scholars, as of contemporary ones—early in the sixth century BCE. Spinoza seems to have thought that Ezra lived and worked close to those events. But chapter 7 of the Book of Ezra dates Ezra himself to the time of a Persian king named Artaxerxes, usually taken to be Artaxerxes I, who ruled in the middle decades of the fifth century BCE. When did Spinoza think Ezra wrote? One suspicion immediately arises. Rabbinical chronology drastically shortened the history of Persia in order to accommodate what seemed to be Daniel's statement that the kingdom would have only four rulers. A standard summary, the *Seder olam rabba*, claimed that Persia had existed for only thirty-four years.[62] In the sixteenth century, Christian chronologers like Matthieu Béroalde and Hugh Broughton accepted the Jews' argument even though it contradicted the evidence of Herodotus and other Greek historians. These men forced the history of the ancient world into a Procrustean bed and lopped off a segment of it. They moved Cyrus—the Persian king who allowed the Jews to return from their Babylonian exile to Jerusalem—from the middle of the sixth century to the middle of the fifth.[63] Did Spinoza too collapse time?

Spinoza was much happier when rejecting rabbinical tradition than when embracing it. In this case, too, he defied the rabbis and radically extended their Persian history: "For it was the first Persian king, Cyrus, who gave the Jews permission to rebuild the Temple, and it was more than 230 years from his time to that of king Darius, fourteenth and last king of the Persians."[64] The biblical book of Ezra, he argued, was not even written under the Persians, but in the Hellenistic age, after Judah Maccabee restored worship in the Temple. Spinoza ascribed it to the same writer who produced Nehemiah and Daniel, who wanted to offer "an orderly narrative of the affairs of the Jews from the time of the first captivity."[65] As to the historical Ezra and Nehemiah, Spinoza made fun of the idea that they could have lived long enough to write their books: "No one supposes, I imagine, that Ezra or Nehemiah were so long-lived as to outlive the fourteen kings of Persia."[66] The gap between the historical Ezra and the book of Ezra had to be long: long enough to accommodate the Persian dynasty list.

Why, then, did Spinoza connect Ezra with the composition of the first set of biblical histories, and why did he connect the composition of those histories with the fall of Jehoiachin? No biblical source provides a clear source for this idea. But one passage in the *Tractatus* suggests an answer. Spinoza argued that the biblical Psalms were collected in five books in the period of the Second Temple. And he cited evidence—in this case, extrabiblical evidence—to support his view: "The Psalms were collected and set out in five books in the Second Temple. According to the testimony of Philo the Jew, Psalm 88 was published when King Jehoiachin was still in prison in Babylon, and Psalm 89 after the same king had regained his liberty."[67] Philo thus tied the production of dateable parts of the Bible to the lifetime of Jehoiachin, just after the fall of Jerusalem: each Psalm reflected a particular moment in the king's life. Could Spinoza have spun his little web of data about Ezra from these brief and cryptic skeins of textual reference? It seems likely that he did. For when Spinoza quoted Philo, he went on, in a way highly unusual for him, to insist on the solidity of his bit of evidence. He described it as "something I do not think Philo would have said, were it not either the received opinion of his time or had he not received it from others worthy of credence."[68] This statement is not only emphatic but also distinctive: Spinoza rarely argued for the credibility of a particular source.

As Carl Gebhardt and others showed long ago, Spinoza was not really following Philo here—not, that is, the Alexandrian Jewish Neo-Platonist whom we know as Philo.[69] The text he quoted was Philo

"On Times"—one of the many interlocking forgeries created and published, at the end of the fifteenth century, by Annius of Viterbo.[70] Spinoza did not read Annius's forged Philo directly, and the nature of his secondary source is also suggestive. He found the text, translated into Hebrew, in the work of a sixteenth-century Jewish scholar, Azariah de' Rossi: the *Meor einayim* [*Light of the Eyes*].[71] In this controversial work, published in 1573–1575, Azariah argued—against rabbinical tradition—that the chronology and history of the Jews in the age of the Second Temple could not be reconstructed from the Bible alone. To reach the truth the historian must collate the biblical narratives, and the rabbinical chronologies that rested on them, with the works of the pagans and their modern commentators.[72] In chapter 34 of his book Azariah laid out the chronology of Persia, from the Christian writer Eusebius. He listed fourteen Persian kings from Cyrus to Darius, and supplemented this material with citations from other Christian sources.[73] After exhaustive analysis of the conflicting sources, Azariah explicitly rejected the foreshortened chronologies of the rabbis: "it appears that Rabbi Jose's span of 34 years is too short for accommodating all the kings of Persia who ought to be counted from the time of the building of the Temple until their defeat at the hands of Alexander."[74] De' Rossi's work sparked controversy—many rabbis in Venice and elsewhere objected to parts of his argument—and he revised it as it went through the press to take account of the technical criticisms of Moses Provenzali and others. Yet it retained its reputation as a potentially dangerous book.[75] The *Meor einayim* was, in short, radical in its own fashion. When Spinoza made fun of the idea that Ezra could have written the book that bore his name, because the chronology of Persia was longer than traditionalists realized, he was not doing something new but accepting one of de' Rossi's dangerous ideas: and one that rested, as his own arguments did not, not on the Bible alone but on a collation of the Bible with other sources.[76]

Spinoza's arguments about the value of Philo's testimony look strange and arbitrary now. Why claim that an Alexandrian writer of the first century CE—a writer who, de' Rossi himself had argued, could not read Hebrew—had preserved vital information about the production of the Hebrew Bible centuries before?[77] Yet there may be a reason why Spinoza found Philo's testimony about the origin of Psalms important enough to defend. As he reimagined the history of the biblical text, setting it into the period after the kingdoms of Israel and Judah were destroyed, Spinoza might have seen Philo's words as a precious testimony about the sources from which it had been compiled. The Bible, viewed through Spinoza's lens, was a mosaic, composed of fragments of memory and history. It offered, not a true history, but rather a "vision of the vanquished," which revealed only a few small facts about the actual past of the Jews.[78] Every clue that connected a particular segment of the text with actual events was valuable. If Spinoza was thinking in these terms, then Philo's statement must have seemed the most precious of clues, and worth defending: both in itself, and as a clue to when the historical Ezra had done his work.

My point here is certainly not to criticize Spinoza, whose radical insight and Roman integrity need no defense from me. As a philosopher, he could reasonably think that the part of his argument that mattered was that in which he sketched out how and why the Bible, as he and others knew it, had come into being, rather than the details of when and where it all happened. It is, instead, to suggest that Spinoza described his own work in a way that has sometimes, quite inadvertently, deceived modern readers. He argued that scriptural and natural histories must follow the same method. This statement of principle implied, he thought, that, as all the evidence for a natural history must come from nature, all the evidence for a scriptural one must come from Scripture. If the history of Scripture was to be put on an empirical, or historical, basis, it must rest on the Bible alone. In fact, though, no one could write even a provisional history of Scripture without drawing evidence from multiple sources—and, to some extent, returning to traditional forms of learning. Spinoza himself drew, in a selective and appropriative way, on many products of earlier Jewish and Christian erudition, some of them now largely forgotten. And he found stimuli and suggestions in them that helped to shape his work.

WHAT SPINOZA MISSED

Yet Spinoza also missed a great deal, and the gaps in his knowledge must be tallied up more precisely than they have been, for they too help to assess exactly what Spinoza could, and could not, offer by way of an innovative, critical assessment of the history of the biblical text. Fortunately, a learned contemporary identified some of the gaps in Spinoza's technical equipment. When Leibniz annotated the first copy of the *Tractatus* that he saw, in 1670–1671, he noted that Spinoza seemed to possess a great deal of Oriental learning, and worried that only someone of comparable expertise could refute his frighteningly radical theories. But he also recorded his own skepticism about Spinoza's elevation of Ezra to the role of primary author. Spinoza, as we have seen, claimed in theory that a history of the Bible must rest on biblical evidence alone. Christian humanists, however, had set the textual history of the Bible into a much wider context. Scaliger and Casaubon, for example, called attention to what they saw as similarities between the fortunes of the Bible and those of Homer. They used both Greek and Hebrew evidence when they compared the work of the ancient scholars who had redacted both texts.[79] Leibniz found this comparison enlightening. He himself likened the textual work done by Ezra to that of the most influential Alexandrian and Latin grammarians, whom no one identified as the creators of the *Iliad*, the *Aeneid*, or the *Eunuchus*: "this compiler doesn't seem any more an author to me, than Aristarchus is the author of the books of Homer, and Tucca and Varius of the verses of Virgil, and Calliopius of the plays of Terence."[80] A look at comparative evidence—a step that Scaliger and others had long since taken, on a path that Spinoza did not follow—suggested that for all the force of Spinoza's analytical arguments, he exaggerated the precision and power of his results. He did so partly because he was not familiar with evidence well known to any well-trained philologist. In other marginal notes, Leibniz pointed out that Spinoza often drew unnecessarily extreme conclusions from his evidence, not all of which suggested that the main content of the Old Testament was late and inauthentic.[81]

Leibniz was not the only scholar to read this copy of the *Tractatus*. His patron, Johann Christian von Boyneburg, who owned the book, also responded to it. As Henk Nellen has discovered, he pointed out in a letter that Ezra could not have "imposed" his Bible on the whole Jewish people. Vast numbers of Jews never went into captivity in Babylon and instead lived in largely independent communities, across the Mediterranean world and beyond, even after the return from exile.[82]

One man's efforts could never have fixed the text of the Bibles used across so wide a geographical area:

> It is certain from Nehemiah, Ezra, Zachariah, Hagar, the Maccabees, the Gospels, Acts, and finally the Talmud, that, already in the times of Ezra and in the few centuries that followed before the appearance of Christ our Savior, the whole people, scattered throughout all of Asia (which was full of Jews even before the second destruction of the Temple, as is clear from the Acts of the Apostles), was firmly convinced that these books were legitimate and divine. But that contemporaries and near-contemporaries did not notice such an obvious innovation, that they did not contradict it, that they did not even feel any suspicion about the poorly fitting seams of such an obvious and crude device, let him believe who wishes to—even then I will not manage to persuade myself.[83]

Leibniz entered this text, with small changes, into the copy of the *Tractatus* now in Erfurt. The neatness of his written version suggests that he copied what his patron had already written about Spinoza.[84] The Erfurt *Tractatus* may well record not only their separate responses to Spinoza's arguments, but also the echoes of their long-lost conversations about Spinoza. Separately or together, the two German polymaths pointed out—implicitly but clearly—further lacunas in Spinoza's knowledge of contemporary scholarship.

Spinoza portrayed the Jews as a lonely, isolated people, whose scriptural canon one man could have created or reshaped. He thus showed that he had not taken on board the revisionist work of sixteenth- and seventeenth-century scholars such as Scaliger, Drusius, and Selden. These late humanists drew on the New Testament, the books of Maccabees, and the Talmud to re-create an ancient world in which vast numbers of Jews, many of them Greek-speaking, rubbed elbows from Asia Minor to Gaul with Greeks and Romans. Ancient Jews, they argued, were as diverse in their textual practices as in the languages they spoke. Many read their Bibles and prayed in Greek.[85] One wonders if Spinoza deliberately rejected this approach: and, if so, whether he was influenced in doing so by the Protestant theologians who refused to use extrabiblical evidence. If so, opposites touched, and in a very curious way. The great deconstructor of biblical authority seems to have had a surprising amount of common ground with radical biblicists such as David Pareus, whom Scaliger dismissed as lunatics and "prophets," since they believed that chronology must rest on the evidence of Scripture alone, taking no account of astronomical data or comparative evidence from pagan texts.[86] This was, of course, far from the only case when Spinoza used the languages and concepts of Christian theology. Many Calvinist theologians insisted that a truly virtuous state must draw its laws from the Bible. Spinoza, of course, rejected the idea that this primitive ancient document could serve as the framework for a modern constitution. But he might have assumed that he could not hope to convince his opponents if he did not argue his radical case on grounds that they could see as reasonable.

The *Tractatus theologico-politicus* still needs a full Spinozan history of its own, one that will track the author's faltering but fascinating progress through the Hercynian forests of early modern humanistic learning, both Christian and Jewish; make clear to whom he saw himself as speaking while he did so; and explain how he found some of the golden apples at the center, which more learned explorers had missed—but he missed others, which his predecessors had already found. For the moment, though, this very preliminary study may help to locate Spinoza's place in the long and complex evolution by which the critical scholarship of humanists and forgers, ecclesiastical historians and eccentric critics helped to give birth to Enlightenment—and to suggest that his conceptions were no more immaculate than those of his Christian contemporaries and readers.[87]

CONCLUSION

What the Ink Blots Reveal

SOME OF THE scholars examined in this book were innovative philologists and historians, who collected texts with energy and precision and devised sharp tools for dissecting them. Some of them were traditionalists, who thought that properly executed notarial documents could prove a historical thesis even if their content was manifestly implausible. Some were fantasists, who worked by a principle crisply formulated long ago by the Chicago critic Wayne Booth: "Just let me invent the evidence and I'll prove my point." Some proudly offered conjectures where a manuscript contained corrupt readings or a historian made obvious errors. Some refused to divine words or facts unattested in the record, insisting that scholarship must end where the preserved evidence gave out. Some worked unwillingly in spaces that they had to share with artisans. Others took pleasure in learning from hornyhanded sons and daughters of toil. Most remarkable of all, several played multiple roles, some of which seem manifestly incompatible now, as practical needs or polemical points dictated. These chapters provide little support for arguments that humanism was a uniformly radical, modern movement, or that it was not substantially different from its medieval predecessors: though some of my protagonists looked eagerly forward, and others faithfully backward.

What does seem clear, however, is that the scholarship of the humanists was a form of work: one that required drudgery. Even the most elevated of the thinkers discussed here, Marsilio Ficino and Benedict Spinoza, worked their way through complex texts, collected evidence as systematically as they could, and based their arguments on it. Even the most fantastic of fantasists, Annius of Viterbo, searched through compendia to learn about the Talmud. The making of notebooks began at school and served, at first, as a way to gain a mastery of ancient languages and literacy in ancient cultures. As scholars matured, however, it became something more. The notebooks of specialists turned into equally specialized paper tools, designed, not only to store information, but also to process it. Moreover, processing was not always a peaceful, quiet process. It often involved confronting excerpts from ancient sources with scenes from contemporary life. As texts and facts encountered one another in the labyrinths of a Zibaldone, explosions sometimes took place. Belief in the superiority of Christianity and Latin culture was chipped away by new information about the world outside Europe, which could call the purity of traditional Christianity and the validity of traditional ideas into question. Men of tradition and makers of notebooks told their readers that the wildest African and Asian countries were no stranger than the Germanic lands of Central Europe and reported and relied on personal experience even when it forced them to abandon traditional practices.

Like many other forms of knowledge-making in Renaissance Europe, humanism was deeply embodied. The work its protagonists did ranged from copying inscriptions in the hot sun or heavy rain to filling notebooks with texts and excerpts from texts, and from collating texts to comparing ancient precepts and examples with contemporary realities. Some humanists struggled to gain access to manuscripts and chronicles; others, to correct proofs that compositors tried to snatch away from them so that they could begin their work. But all of them were doing a combination of physical and mental labor: eye-stinging observation of the minute ways in which manuscripts of the same text or accounts of the same event differed, and hand-cramping recording of whatever they found in reference books. Much of their work was boring: constant deep dives into texts that had none of the sheen of a newly discovered work by Lucretius or Jerome but that could yield startling facts when read, deftly, against the grain. Often limits were set by the hard realities of practical life: the deadlines and marketing strategies that governed publishing could shape methods of research and practices of editing.

Humanists were artisans as well as thinkers. They lived in a world of ideas, but one made of books and parts of books. To make ideas new, they had to work with the skill of lute makers who bent wood and tightened string. Only the most skillful cutting and pasting could make the new patterns that they saw as they contemplated the past take on the material forms, handwritten or printed, that could, in turn, reach and convince others. Watching them at work, we see them touch, as well as read, the texts and other forms of evidence that mattered most to them and make, as well as compose, the books that changed the world. Often, humanists proudly emphasized the social and cultural distance that separated them from men who worked with their hands. Yet they worked in crowded shops as well as in quiet studies. Texts and experiences, words and things, collided around them. Even those who insisted that they had found everything they knew in books also pursued knowledge at rituals and in households. Even those who claimed that they had found new ways to read books without accepting ancient prejudices and errors trawled the margins of learned editions. The conditions of learned life and the techniques of writing and printing both limited and expanded the humanists' consciousness. By remembering to place the humanists in the worlds where they worked, to examine their descriptions of their methods while also comparing them to their practices, and to set their finished books in the conditions that so often shaped them, we can hope to know them and their books better than we have in the past.

NOTES

ACKNOWLEDGMENTS

INDEX

NOTES

1 The most up-to-date summary of what is known about Boemus is Hartmut Kugler, "Boemus, Johannes, Aubanus," in *Deutscher Humanismus 1480–1520: Verfasserlexicon*, ed. Franz Josef Worstbrock (Berlin and New York: Walter de Gruyter, 2005), 1:1, 209–217. See also Erich Schmidt, *Deutsche Volkskunde im Zeitalter des Humanismus und der Reformation* (Berlin: Ebering, 1904).

2 Joannes Boemus, *Omnium gentium mores leges et ritus* (Augsburg: Grimm and Virsung, 1520; repr., Lyon: Gryphius, 1541).

3 Ptolemy, *Geographicae enarrationis libri octo*, ed. Willibald Pirckheimer (Strasbourg: Grieninger, 1525), maps of Europe, Africa, and Asia. Unlike Boemus, Pirckheimer also included maps and treatments of the New World in his atlas.

4 Good general treatments include Margaret T. Hodgen, "Johann Boemus (Fl. 1500): An Early Anthropologist," *American Anthropologist*, new series, 55, no. 2 (1953): 284–294; Klaus Vogel, "Cultural Variety in a Renaissance Perspective: Johannes Boemus on 'The Manners, Laws and Customs of all People,'" in *Shifting Cultures: Interaction and Discourse in the Expansion of Europe*, ed. Henriette Bugge and Joan-Pau Rubiés (Münster: Lit, 1995), 17–34; Massimo Donattini, *Spazio e modernità. Libri, carte, isolari nell'età delle scoperte* (Bologna: Clueb, 2000); Andreas Motsch, "La collection des moeurs de Johannes Boemus ou la mise en scène du savoir ethnographique," in *Le théâtre de la curiosité*, ed. Frank Lestringant (Paris: Presses de l'Université Paris-Sorbonne, 2008), 51–65; and Diego Pirillo, "Relativismo culturale e 'armonia del mondo': L'enciclopedia etnografica de Johannes Boemus," in *L'Europa divisa e i nuovi mondi: Per Adriano Prosperi*, ed. Massimo Donattini, Giuseppe Marcocci, and Stefania Pastore (Pisa: Edizioni della Normale, 2011), 2:67–77.

5 Boemus, *Omnium gentium mores leges et ritus* (1520), fol. II^v: "Quapropter ornatissime domine Doctor scripta haec nostra, quae ex multis praeclarissimis rerum scriptoribus, iam triennio ferme non sine maximis laboribus in librum istum collegi, congessi, & quantum ingenio atque industria potui,

augmentavi, a me obvijs manibus & serena fronte suscipere velis, susceptaque tanta diligentia, tanta fidelitate perlegere, perlustrare, examinare, ab omnique macula expurgare: ut nihil usquam praetermittatur, nihil praeterfluat, quod secum minutuli quippiam subripiat involvatque, quod postea a lynceis vitiligatorum obstrigilatorumque oculis inventum, sphingeis unguibus enodatum, vippereis linguis compunctum, exibilatumque, in famae & nominis nostrorum amborum dispendium, atque obfuscationem in omnibus trivijs pro fabula iactetur."

6 Ibid., fol. IIII^r: "Memorabiliores gentium mores, ritus, leges, locorumque ubi degunt situs, quos historiae pater Herodotus, Diodorus Siculus, Berosus, Strabo, Solinus, Trogus Pompeius, Ptolemaeus, Plinius, Cornelius Tacitus, Dionysius Apher, Pomponius Mela, Caesar, Iosephus: & ex recentioribus nonnulli, Vincentius, Aeneas Sylvius, qui postea Pij secondi pontificis maximi nomen tulit: Antonius Sabellicus, Ioannes Nauclerus, Ambrosius Calepinus, Nicolaus Perottus in Cornucopijs: alijque permulti clarissimi rerum scriptores in commentarijs suis diffuse & ceu per partes celebravere: ut in uno libro conscriptos haberes, facileque quando usus deposceret invenires, historiarum lector cultorque studiosissime, per ocium succisivis horis undique conquaesivi, collegi, & in diarium hunc conscripsi, digessi."

7 Ibid., fols. II^v–III^r:

BOEMVS DOCTORI SVO SACRVM.
Hos hominum mores ritusque situsque locorum
  Acceptos a me splendide Doctor habe:
Tris totos annos ex magnis scripsimus illos
  Authorum magna sedulitate libris:
Gnaviter evolvas foliatim cuncta: sequetur
  Non minus insignis lausque decusque tibi
Quam quondum erranti per mundum cessit Vlyssi
  Aeneaeque pio Thyrsigeroque deo.

Note also the verses of Ioannes Hiersdorf, ibid., fol. III^r:

                                             nec ullo
  Tale quidem in lucem tempore venit opus:
Quale vides praesens: brevibus nam plurima: sparsim
  Nempe alias magno lecta labore: tenet,

And Ioannes Clavus, ibid.:

Pluribus e gravibus scriptoribus ista fateris
  Te sumpsisse brevi conspicienda libro
Perpetuas igitur lectores dicere grates
  Debebunt merito docta Boeme tibi.

8 Ibid., fol. LXXXI^r: "Quoniam vero propter impedimenta plaeraque aetate maxime nostra omnibus hoc non concedatur, ut non minus illa haec in patrio sinu quiescendo cognoscerentur elaboravit Boemus hic meus Lit-

erarum humanarum scientissimus ex innumeris classicis scriptoribus conscriptum praesens opus."

9 Ibid., fol. II^r: "Verum quod te materia ea haud mediocriter delectari notanter ex eo cognoverim, quod anno superiori similes libellos duos, unum de septentrionalibus gentibus, cuius author Matthias de Michau, alium de meridionalibus cuiusdam Ludovici de Bononia, impresseris, meque librum praesentem in Germanicam linguam nostram transferre interpretarique adhorteris."

10 Ibid., fol. II^{r-v}: "Quod ita comparatum sit, ut illis, qui extra patrios agros ad secundum vix lapidem unquam pervenerint, quique ingenuorum morum & artium in iuventute parum aut nihil perceperint, quamvis naturae suae bonitate opulenti, facundi & solertes satis superque in patriae sinu populos moderentur et urbes: tantum tamen felicitatis adiuvatur eis, ut propemodum pro despicatis quicquid dicant faciantque ab omnibus habeatur. Ædiverso alijs, qui peregre aliquando profecti, sub fidelibus & eruditis praeceptoribus in claris probeque institutis urbibus egregia multa viderint didicerintque, tantum gloriae & maiestatis adijciatur, ut nihil ab eis attentetur, nihil fiat, quod non secus, quam a divinissimo oraculo praeceptum alacriter non amplexetur: cunctisque non summe placeat."

11 Ibid., fol. II^r: "Et hoc dignissime: quippe, qui optime diu antea haec atque alia, quae de externis nationibus memorantur, omnia cognoris, sciasque: licet non ex levibus circulatoribus, non ex vagis mendicis, qui ut vulgo admiratiores acceptioresque sint, adeo nefandissime absque omni verecundia plaerunque mentiuntur: ut non ipsis modo non fides etiam minima habeatur, verum omnibus iuxta, qui aliquid de his aut scribunt, aut recitant: Sed ex gravium fide dignissimorum authorum scriptis, quibus perdius et pernox tu quoque quandocunque a medicis curis vacari datur, operam summam impendis. Atque ex hinc homini in publica praesertim administratione constituto nihil utilius, nihil gloriosius iucundiusque magis esse, quam veraciter aut legendo aut peregrinando cognoscere, qua religione, quibus moribus, qua regiminis forma, quibus legibus institutisque aliae per orbem gentes vitam traducant."

12 Ann Blair, *Too Much to Know: Managing Scholarly Information before the Modern Age* (New Haven: Yale University Press, 2010). See also Martin Mulsow, *Prekäres Wissen: Eine andere Ideengeschichte der frühen Neuzeit* (Berlin: Suhrkamp, 2012); and Helmut Zedelmaier, *Werkstätten des Wissens zwischen Renaissance und Aufklärung* (Tübingen: Mohr Siebeck, 2015). For an exemplary edition and analysis of a schoolboy notebook, see Jean-Claude Margolin, Jean Pendergrass, and Marc Van der Poel, *Images et lieux de mémoire d'un étudiant du XVIe siècle* (Paris: Guy Trédaniel, 1991).

13 Roberto Weiss, *The Renaissance Discovery of Classical Antiquity* (Oxford: Blackwell, 1969; 2d ed., Oxford: Blackwell, 1988), chap. 11.

14 Rocco Di Dio, "'*Selecta colligere*': Marsilio Ficino and Renaissance Reading Practices," *History of European Ideas* 42, no. 5 (2016): 595–606.

15 Anthony Grafton and Joanna Weinberg, "Johann Buxtorf Makes a Notebook," in *Canonical Texts and Scholarly Practices: A Global Comparative Approach*, ed. Anthony Grafton and Glenn W. Most (Cambridge: Cambridge University Press, 2016), 275–298.

16 Boemus, *Omnium gentium mores leges et ritus* (1520), I.1, "De origine hominis opinio theologorum vera," fols. VI^v–VII^r.

17 Ibid., 1.2, "De origine hominis opinio ethnicorum falsa," fols. VII^{r–v}.

18 C. Philipp E. Nothaft, "The Early History of Man and the Uses of Diodorus in Renaissance Scholarship: From Annius of Viterbo to Johannes Boemus," in *For the Sake of Learning: Essays in Honor of Anthony Grafton*, ed. Ann Blair and Anja Goeing (Leiden and Boston: Brill, 2016), 2:711–728.

19 British Library MS Add 41,086A. See Nella Giannetto, *Bernardo Bembo: Umanista e politico veneziano* (Florence: Olschki, 1985), 359–393.

20 Klaus A. Vogel, "Schedel als Kompilator: Notizen zu einem derzeit kaum bestellten Forschungsfeld," *Pirckheimer Jahrbuch* 9 (1994): 73–97.

21 Boemus, *Omnium gentium mores leges et ritus* (1520), II.4, "De Iudaea & Iudaeorum vivendi ritibus, legibus ac institutis," fols. XIX^v–XXII^r, at XIX^v: "Existimabat eximius ille theologus Moses nullam civitatem sine iuris & aequitatis cultu diutius consistere posse."

22 Ibid., fol. XXI^r: "De Iudaeis & Mose duce eorum Etnici scriptores ab Ecclesiasticis dissentiunt."

23 Tacitus, *Histories* 5.3–5.

24 F. F. Bruce, "Tacitus on Jewish History," *Journal of Semitic Studies* 29, no. 1 (1984): 33–44.

25 Tacitus, *Histories* 5.4, quoted by Boemus, *Omnium gentium mores leges et ritus* (1520), fol. XXI^r: "Profana illic omnia, quae apud nos sacra, rursum concessa, quae nobis incesta."

26 Ibid., fol. XXI^v: "Haec & multa alia Cornelius Tacitus & Trogus lib. xxxvi. scribunt." Boemus actually refers to Justin's epitome of Pompeius Trogus, 36.2–3.

27 Ibid., fols. XXI^v–XXII^r.

28 Joannes Boemus, *Mores, leges et ritus omnium gentium* (Lyon: Gryphius, 1541), Henry Haule's copy (private collection), 75. On Henry Haule, or Halle, see Peter Clark, *English Provincial Society from the Reformation to the Revolution: Religion, Politics and Society in Kent, 1500–1640* (Hassocks: Harvester, 1977), 183, 272, 276, 287, 288, 292, 365, 385.

29 Boemus, *Mores, leges et ritus omnium gentium* (1541), Haule's copy, 73–74.

30 Di Dio, "'Selecta colligere,'" 597.

31 See the classic study of François Hartog, *Le miroir d'Hérodote: Essai sur la répresentation de l'autre* (Paris: Gallimard, 1980); and James Redfield, "Herodotus the Tourist," *Classical Philology* 80, no. 2 (1985): 97–118.

32 Boemus, *Omnium gentium mores leges et ritus* (1520), fol. X^r: "Eorum foeminae olim negotiari, cauponari, institoriaque obire munera consueverunt. Viri intra murorum parietes texere: hi onera capitibus gestare, mulieris humeris: illae stantes micturire, hi sedentes: domi vulgo ventrem exonerare: in vijs comessari."

33 See, e.g., Vogel, "Cultural Variety"; and Joan-Pau Rubiés, *Travel and Ethnology in the Renaissance: South Asia through European Eyes, 1250–1625* (Cambridge: Cambridge University Press, 2000), chap. 4.

34 Saskia Metan, *Wissen über das östliche Europa im Transfer: Edition, Übersetzung und Rezeption des "Tractatus de duabus Sarmatiis" (1517)* (Vienna, Cologne, and Weimar: Böhlau, 2019), chap. 3.

35 See Rubiés, *Travel and Ethnology in the Renaissance*, chap. 4; Stephanie Leitch, *Mapping Ethnography in Early Modern Germany*, New Worlds in Print Culture (New York: Palgrave Macmillan, 2010).

36 See Metan, *Wissen über das östliche Europa im Transfer*, 256–258.

37 Boemus to Althamer, 1520, in Johann Arnold Ballenstedt, *Andreae Althameri vita* (Wolfenbüttel: Meisner, 1740), 61–62, at 61: "Salue, mi Palaeosphyra: Quod nomini meo adeo studiosus, adeo deditus mihi es, gratias quoque maximas tibi habeo, daboque operam omnem, ut epistola haec tua aliquando libro nostro addatur: multo enim magis mihi placet, quam alia, quam ex Reutlinga ad me dederis, quod plus olei in ea, quam in alia absumseris, quadragesimae utpote diebus illam, hanc larvalibus insanisque scriptam. . . . Falsissimus et invidentissimus hac tempestate mundus est, nusquam tuta fides: Momo omnia plena: et tu ausus eras, in faciem mihi invocare, omnia operis mei contenta in aliis contineri, cum ego tantum elaboravi, tantum meo ingenio adieci, ut nisi amicitia nostra, ex qua te hoc dixisse cogitaram, obstitisset, benigne profecto non tulissem."

38 Boemus (1520), fol. LXXXI^(r–v): "Quoniam vero propter impedimenta plaeraque aetate maxime nostra omnibus hoc non concedatur, ut non minus illa haec in patrio sinu quiescendo cognoscerentur, elaboravit Boemus hic meus Literarum humanarum scientissimus ex innumeris classicis scriptoribus conscriptum praesens opus. In quo tres terrae partes, partium regiones, & loca, locorum homines, hominum mores & ritus memorabiliores explicantur omnes, tanta diligentia, tanta arte, quanta a nemine ante eum unquam prius pertractati dinoscuntur. ex racematione diligenti vindemiam, ex spicilegio messem foecit, succosum non minus quam Iucundum, nec Iucundum minus, quam utilem atque pernecessarium librum."

39 Ibid., fol. IIII^r: "Cognoscasque mi lector quam pulchre & feliciter hodie, quam item inculte & simpliciter olim primi mortalium, a creatione sua ad generale diluvium usque & ultra multis saeculis per terram vixerint." On Boemus's view of the early history of humanity, see Nothaft, "The Early History of Man."

40 Boemus, *Omnium gentium mores leges et ritus* (1520), fol. IX^r: "Et talis fuit ab initio, & iam ante multa saecula Aethiopiae status: hi gentis ritus & mores. Hodie vero, ut se Marcus Anthonius Sabellicus, ex quo maiorem partem eorum, quae hic, & in sequentibus a nobis dicuntur accepimus, ab ipsis locorum illorum indigenis cognovisse dicit, Aethiopiae Rex, quem nostri Pretoianem voant, ac sacerdotem Ioannem sive Ianem: illi Giam, id est potentem, tam potens est, ut duobus & sexaginta aliis regibus imperitare praedicetur."

41 Ibid., fol. XLII^v: "Efferunt autem promiscue voluntarij quique vel cives vel hospites, foeminis propinquitate coniunctis ad sepulchrum eiulantibus, conduntque in publico monumento, quod est iuxta monumentum Callisti, apud suburbana, ubi semper eos sepeliunt, qui in bello ceciderunt, praeterquam, qui in Marathone, quorum singularem fuisse virtutem existimantes, eodem in loco sepulchrum foecerunt: postea vero quam eos humaverunt, aliquis ab ipsa civitate delectus vir haud quaquam pro inconsulto habitus, & cui pro dignitate conveniat, super eos orationem habet, qualem decet de eorum laudibus: qua habita disceditur. Hoc quidem more sepeliunt, quo per omne belli tempus, quoties id accidit legitime utuntur."

42 Ibid.: "Caesos in bello Thucidide authore in hunc modum sepeliunt: facto ante triduum tabernaculo, mortuorum ossa proponuntur, & suorum quisque reliquiis, si quid lubeat, imponit: quum efferuntur singularum tribuum singulas tribus suae quanque tribus ossa continentes vehicula portant." Boemus quotes Thucydides 2.34 and 2.46.

43 Valla rendered the passage thus in the manuscript of his translation that he deposited as an official "archetypus" in the Vatican Library: Vat. lat. 1801, fols. 35ᵛ–36ʳ.

44 Pius II, *Historia rerum Friderici tertii Imperatoris* (Memmingen: Albrecht Kunne, not after March 1491), sig. e2ᵛ: "primi quos adii ex lituanis. serpentes colebant. patresfamilias suus quisque in angulo domus serpentem habuit. cui cibum dedit. ac sacrificium fecit in feno iacenti. hos Hieronimus iussit omnes interfici. & in foro adductos publice cremari. Inter quos unus inventus est maior ceteris. quem sepe admotum ignis consummere nullo pacto valuit"; Pius II, *Europe (c. 1400–1458)*, tr. Robert Brown, ed. Nancy Bisaha (Washington, DC: Catholic University of America Press, 2013), 144.

45 Pius II, *Historia*, sig. e2ᵛ: "Post hos gentem reperit. que sacrum colebat ignem. eumque perpetuum appellabat. Sacerdotes templi materiam ne deficeret ministrabant. hos super vita egrotantium. amici consulebant. Illi noctu ad ignem accedebant. Mane vero consulentibus responsa dantes umbram egroti apud ignem sacrum se vidisse aiebant. Que cum se calefaceret signa vel mortis vel vite ostentasset. victurum egrotum facies ostensa igni. Contra. si dorsum ostentasset. moriturum portendit. Testari igit. & rebus suis consulere suadebant delusionem hanc esse Hieronimus ostendit. Et persuaso populo deleto templo ignem dissipavit Christianos mores induxit"; Pius II, *History*, tr. Brown, 144–145.

46 Pius II, *Historia*, sig. e2ᵛ: "profectus introrsus aliam gentem reperit. que solem colebat. & malleum ferreum rare magnitudinis singulari cultu venerabatur. Interrogati sacerdotes, quid ea sibi veneratio vellet. Responderunt. olim pluribus mensibus non fuisse visum solem. Quem Rex potentissimus captum reclusisset in carcere munitissime turris. Signa zodiatica deinde opem tulisse Soli, ingentique malleo perfregisse turrim. Solemque liberatum, hominibus restituisse. Dignum itaque veneratu instrumentum esse. quo mortales lucem recepissent. Risit eorum simplicitatem Hieronimus. Inanemque fabulam esse monstravit. Solem vero & Lunam et stellas creatas esse ostendit."

47 Boemus, *Omnium gentium mores leges et ritus* (1520), fol. XLVIIIʳ: "Hieronymus Pragensis, qui Eugenij quarti pontificatu in ea terra evangelium praedicavit, quique gentis illius ritus & mores ad id tempus minus notos nostris hominibus demonstravit, dicebat Lithuanorum quosdam, ad quos primum pervenisset domesticatim serpentes habuisse: quibus per se quisque ut diis penatibus sacrificabant: caeterum tenuisse se, ut praeter unum, qui cremari non potuit, a suis cultoribus interficerentur."

48 Ibid.: "alii ignem colunt, captantque ex eo auguria."

49 Ibid.: "Solem nonnulli mallei ferrei specie immani magnitudine proprium ducem habent, quem Magnum vocant."

50 Pius II, *Historia*, sig. e3ᵛ: "hec nobis Hieronimus constanti multu [read vultu] nihil hesitans. ac per iuramentum affirmavit. dignum fide. & gravitas

sermonis & doctrina ostendit. & viri religio. Nos que accepimus immutata retulimus. veri periculum non assummimus. persuasi tamen & nos & comites ab eo recessimus"; Pius II, *Europe*, tr. Brown, 146–147.

51 Boemus (1520), fol. XXXV^r: "In capite mitris utuntur velis ipsis superpositis, ita, ut decenter hac involutae, una veli extremitas a dextro aut sinistro capitis parte dependeat, qua, si domum exire, vel in domo in virorum conspectum prodire debeant, sine mora totam faciem praeter oculos velare possint. Nunquam audet foemina Sarraceni ubi virorum congregatio est apparere. Forum adire, vendere aliquid aut emere omnino foeminis illicitum. In ecclesia maiori locum a viris longe remotum habent, & adeo occlusum, ut nemo introspicere possit, nec aliquo modo intrare. . . . Collocutio viri & mulieris in publico adeo rara est, adeo praeter consuetudinem, ut si inter eos per annum integrum morareris, semel vix videre posses."

52 George of Hungary, *Tractatus de moribus, condictionibus et nequicia Turcorum*, ed. and tr. Reinhard Klockow (Cologne, Weimar and Vienna: Böhlau, 1994), 250–252: "In capite utuntur mitris superpositis velis ita, ut involuta diligenter et decenter mitra, extremitas veli dependens remaneat ad dexteram faciei; quam si domum exire vel in domo coram viris apparere contingat, statim circumducere et totam faciem velare exceptis solis oculis possit. Sed hoc de omnibus etiam villanis et simplicioribus dico. In civitatibus vero magnum nephas putaretur, si uxor alicuius notabilis extra domum nisi tota facie cum subtili serico ita velata. ut ipsa alios videre. a nemine autem facies eius videri possit, exire compertum fuisset. Nunquam audet femina, ubi est congregatio virorum, comparere et forum adire; vendere aliquid vel emere feminam apud eos omnino illicitum est. In ecclesia maiori locum longe a viris habent separatum, et sic secretum, quod nemo potest introspicere vel aliquo modo intrare. . . . Collocutio viri cum muliere in publico ita rara est, ut, si inter eos per annum esses, vix semel experiri posses." The authorship of the *Tractatus* is not certain, though George of Hungary is the likeliest candidate. See Klockow's introduction, ibid., 11–29.

53 Ibid., 224–226: "Omitto multa, que de eo audivi, quomodo sit affabilis in collocutione, maturus et benignus in iuditio, largus in elemosinis et in aliis actibus suis benivolus. Unde fratres in Pera dixerunt eum intrasse ecclesiam eorum et sedisse in choro ad videndum cerimonias et modum officii. Unde etiam ipsi missam coram eo ipso sic volente celebraverunt et hostiam non consecratam in elevatione demonstraverunt, volentes eius curiositati satisfacere nec margaritas porcis prodere. Qui etiam dum cum eis de lege et ritu Christianorum colloquium habuisset et audisset, quod episcopi praeessent ecclesiis, voluit, ut ad consolationem Christianorum aliquem episcopum adducerent: cui ad omnia suo statui necessaria promisit se favorem et auxilium sine defectu praestiturum. Quis autem audiens a longe victorias, bella et exercitus multitudinem, gloriam et magnificentiam talem in eo possit simplicitatem suspicari vel auditam non admirari."

54 Boemus, *Omnium gentium mores leges et ritus* (1520), fol. XXXIV^v: "Religionem seu sectam suam abnegare Sarraceni neminem cogunt, nec istud alicui persuadere conantur, quamvis Alcoranus praecipiat, ut adversarios prophetasque eorundem perdant & omnibus modis persequantur: unde fit

ut in Turcia omnium sectarum gentes habitent, & quaeque, ut solet, suo deo sacra faciat."

55 Boemus, *Mores, leges et ritus omnium gentium* (1541), Haule's copy, 127: "Quaeque gens in Turcia suam religionem colit."

56 George of Hungary, *Tractatus*, ed. Klockow, 272: "nam in maximis frigoribus hiemis ipsi nudato toto corpore incedunt et non sentiunt, et hoc similiter in caloribus estatis."

57 Ibid., 278–280: "Vocatur autem festivitas eorum "machia" et ludus "czamach." Qui fit quadam tocius corporis regulata et bene modificata agitatione cum honestis et dignis et valde decentibus omnium membrorum motibus, secundum modulationem mensure instrumenti musici ad hoc convenienter aptate, et in fine per modum vertiginis quodam motu velocissimo circulari et rotatione vel revolutione, in quo tota vis ipsius ludi consistit. Nam ferventiores eorum in tanta velocitate revolvuntur, ut non possit utrum sit homo vel statua discerni ab intuentibus. Et ostendunt se in hoc quasi supernaturalem agilitatem corporum habere." For an expert analysis of George's account, which does justice to his misinterpretations of what he observed, see Mark Sedgwick, *Western Sufism: From the Abbasids to the New Age* (New York: Oxford University Press, 2017), 74–78; see also Klockow's introduction, in George of Hungary, *Tractatus*, ed. Klockow, 30–45. For the larger context, see Andrei Pippidi, *Visions of the Ottoman World in Renaissance Europe* (New York: Columbia University Press, 2013), esp. chs. 2–3.

58 Boemus, *Omnium gentium mores leges et ritus* (1520), XXXIV^v: "Sunt etiam in ea secta multi & varij religiosi, quorum quidam in nemoribus & solitudinibus vitam villatim ducentes hominum commercia effugiunt, quidam in civitatibus hospitalitatem exercentes peregrinos pauperes ad hospitia saltem recipiunt si non habeant quo reficere possint, ex mendicitate enim & ipsi vivunt: alii per civitates vagantes, in utribus quibusdam bonam atque semper recentem aquam portant, quam cuique petenti bibendam ultro offerunt, pro quo pietatis officio, si quid ipsis porrigitur, accipiunt, cupiunt nihil."

59 George of Hungary, *Tractatus*, 282: "Sunt enim tante exemplaritatis in omnibus eorum dictis et factis, in moribus et motibus quoque tantam preferentes religionis ostensionem, ut non homines sed angeli videntur esse."

60 Ibid., 284: "Si quis enim voluerit dicta eorum et facta privatim et in particulari perscrutari, tantam inveniet in eis ambitionem proprie reputationis et tantum spiritualis superbie venenum; ut hoc, quod dicitur: angelum sathane se transformare in angelum lucis proprie de ipsis potest intelligi."

61 Boemus, *Omnium gentium mores leges et ritus* (1520), fol. XXXIV^v: "tantam religionis ostentationem in dictis & factis, in moribus & gestis prae se ferentes, ut non homines, sed angeli credi possint."

62 Boemus, *Omnium gentium mores leges et ritus* (1541), Henry Haule's copy, note on p. 128: "157 lex Solonis." At p. 157 Haule has entered a cross-reference to p. 129.

63 Ibid., 111: "Incontinentissimi, Tartari. 129."

64 Ibid., 107: "220 francones. φιλαυτία Tartarorum."

65 Jean Bodin, *Methodus ad facilem historiarum cognitionem*, ed. and tr. Sara Miglietti (Pisa: Edizioni della Normale, 2013), chap. 5, 220.

66 Boemus, *Omnium gentium mores leges et ritus* (1520), fol. X^v: "Nam ut Philippus Beroaldus super Apuleianum Asinum scribit, plaeraque etiam ex Aegyptiorum religione translata in religionem nostram sunt, ut lineae vestes, derasa sacerdotum capita, vertigines in altari, pompa sacrificalis, musicae modulamina, adorationes, preces, aliaque id genus complura."

67 *Commentarii a Philippo Beroaldo conditi in Asinum Aureum Lucii Apulei* (Bologna, 1500), fol. 275^v. See Julia Gaisser, *The Fortunes of Apuleius and the Golden Ass: A Study in Transmission and Reception* (Princeton and Oxford: Princeton University Press, 2008), 210; and Konrad Krautter, *Philologische Methode und humanistische Existenz: Filippo Beroaldo und sein Kommentar zum Goldenen Esel des Apuleius* (Munich: Fink, 1971).

68 Boemus, *Omnium gentium mores leges et ritus* (1520), II.12, "De Christianis, eorumque origine & ritibus," fols. XXXV^r–XL^v.

69 Guillaume Durand, *Rationale divinorum officiorum* (Lyons, 1506), British Library C.77.d.17. On this and other evidence of Cranmer's reading, see David Selwyn, *The Library of Thomas Cranmer* (Oxford: Oxford Bibliographical Society, 1996); and Diarmaid MacCulloch, *Thomas Cranmer: A Life* (New Haven and London: Yale University Press, 1996), esp. 26–31.

70 Durand, *Rationale*, fol. lxxxix^r, col. 1: "<u>Ceterum in ecclesia generaliter nil canendum aut legendum est: quod a sancta romana ecclesia canonizatum et approbatum expresse aut pro patientia non sit. in primitiva tamen ecclesia diversi diversa quisque pro suo velle cantabant</u> dummodo quod cantabant ad dei laudem pertineret. Quedam tamen officia observabantur ab omnibus ab initio constituta vel ab ipso christo: ut oratio dominica. vel ab apostolis: ut symbolus. <u>Succedentibus vero temporibus</u> quia ecclesia dei propter hereses scissa est. <u>Theodosius imperator hereticorum extirpator rogavit damasum papam ut per aliquem prudentem & catholicum virum ecclesiasticum faceret officium ordinari.</u> Unde idem papa precepit Hiero. presbytero tunc in bethleem cum paula eustochio & aliis virginibus moranti: qui prius sub septem apostolicis viris rome vixerat. quatenus officium ecclesiae ordinaret." Underlining by Cranmer.

71 Ibid., fol. lxxxix^r, col. 2: "<u>Consequenter tamen beatus Greg. & gelasius orationes & cantus addiderunt et lectionibus & evangeliis responsoria coaptaverunt. gradualia vero tractus & alleluya Ambrosius Gelasius & Greg. admissam cantari instituerunt.</u>" Underlining by Cranmer.

72 Cranmer writes: "Orationes, cantus, Responsoria, Gradualia, Tractatus, Alleluya." Cranmer was not a credulous reader. On the same page, where Durand relates the miracle that prevented the replacement of the Ambrosian by the Gregorian Mass in Milan, Cranmer writes: "ffabula de officio Gregoriano & Ambrosiano." For excerpts from Durand in the Great Commonplace Books see British Library MS Royal 7B.XI, fols. 173^v–177^r; British Library MS Royal 7B.XII, fols. 11^r, 224^v–225^v.

73 See Chapter 4.

74 Boemus (1520), fol. XLVII^v: "Puellae a tergo capillum promittunt, caeterum matrimonio locatae sedulo abscondunt. Viri supra aures tondentur, datur probro huic sexui omnis capillorum cultus. Gens universa in Venerem prona, ac bibacissima."

75 Ibid., fol. LVIII^r: "Franconiae gens a caeteris Germanis & habitu & corpore
nihil differt: laboris patientissima est: in vinetis colendis tam viri quam
mulieres exercentur: nemini otium datur. Vinum quod inde percipit ob do-
mesticam egestatem vulgo vendit, <u>ipsa aquam</u> bibit. Cervisiam contemnit,
nec facile ad se deferri permittit." Henry Haule's underlining, in his copy
of the 1541 edition printed by Gryphius at Lyon (private collection). He also
entered a trefoil in the margin of his copy here.

76 Ibid., fol. LVIII^v: "Ad dei insuper cultum propensa est: duo tamen non me-
diocria vicia sunt, quibus plus satis hodie gens illa indulget, <u>blasphemia videlicet & latrocinium, illud decorum, hoc honestum reputans</u>, & sibi ex
longo usu licitum." The underlinings were made by Henry Haule in his copy
of the 1541 edition; he also entered a trefoil in the margin.

77 Ibid., fols. LVIII^v–LIX^r: "In Epiphania domini singulae familiae ex melle, fa-
rinae [ed. farina] addito zinzibere & pipere, libum conficiunt, & regem sibi
legunt, hoc modo: Libum materfamilias facit, cui absque consideratione
inter subigendum denarium unum immittit, postea amoto igne supra ca-
lidum focum illud torret, tostum in tot partes frangit, quot homines familia
habet: demum distribuit, cuique partem unam tribuens. Adsignantur etiam
Christo, beataeque virgini & tribus Magis suae partes, quae loco elehemo-
synae elargiuntur. <u>In cuius autem portione denarius repertus fuerit, hic Rex
ab omnibus salutatus, in sedem locatur, & ter in altum cum iubilo elevatur,
ipse in dextra cretam habet, qua toties signum Crucis supra in triclinij
laqueariis deliniat,</u> quae cruces quod obstare plurimis malis credantur, in
multa observatione habentur." Haule inscribed a large trefoil in the margin
here.

78 Ibid., fol. LIX^r: "Duodecim illis noctibus, quae Christi natalem Epiphania-
mque intercurrunt, nulla fere per Franconiam domus est quae saltem inhab-
itetur, quae thure aut aliqua alia redolenti materia adversus daemonum
incantatricumque insidias non subfumigetur. Quo item modo tres praece-
dentes quadragesimale ieiunium dies peragat, dicere opus non erit, si cog-
noscatur, qua populari, qua spontanea insania caetera Germania, a qua &
Franconia minime desciscit, tunc vivat. Comedit enim & bibit, seque ludo
iocoque omnimodo adeo dedit, quasi usui nunquam veniant, quasi cras
moritura hodie prius omnium rerum satietatem capere velit. Novi aliquid
spectaculi quisque excogitat, quo mentes & oculos omnium delectet, admi-
rationeque detineat. Atque ne pudor obstet, qui se ludicro illi committunt,
facies larvis obducunt, sexum & aetatem mentientes, viri mulierum vestimenta, mulieres virorum induunt."

79 Ibid.: "<u>Eodem tempore & talis mos observatur: intexitur stramine vetus una
lignea rota, atque a magno iuvenum coetu in aeditiorem montem gestata,
post varios lusus, quos in illius vertice illo toto die, nisi frigus impediat,
celebrant, circiter vesperam incenditur, & ita flammans in subiectam vallem
ab alto rotatur: stupendum certe spectaculum praebet, ut plaerique, qui prius
non viderint, Solem putant aut lunam coelo decidere.</u>" Underlining by Haule
in his copy.

80 Ibid., fol. LIX^v: "In nocte sancti Ioannis baptistae in omnibus fere per latam
Germaniam vicis & oppidis publici ignes parantur, ad quem utriusque sexus

iuvenes, & senes convenientes, choreas cum cantu agunt: multas etiam superstitiones observant."

81 Ibid., fol. LIX^r: "Quidam satyras aut malos daemones potius repraesentare volentes, minio se aut atramento tingunt, habituque nefando deturpant: alii nudi discurrentes Lupercos agunt, a quibus ego annuum istum delirandi morem ad nos defluxisse existimo. Non enim multum diversus est a Lupercalibus sacris, quae Lycaeo Pani in mense Februario olim a nobilissimis Rhomanorum iuvenibus celebrabantur: qui nudi, faciesque sanguine foedati, per urbem vagantes, obvios loris, cedebant, quos nostri saccis cinere refertis percutiunt."

82 Ibid., fol. LVIII^v: "Tunc etiam ex avita consuetudine ultro citroque munera mittuntur, quae a Saturnalibus, quae eo tempore celebrabantur a Rhomanis Saturnalitia, a Graecis Apophoreta dicta sunt."

83 Ibid., fol. LIX^r: "In die cinerum mirum est quod in plaerisque locis agitur, <u>virgines quotquot per annum choream frequentaverunt, a iuvenibus congregantur, & aratro pro equis adnectae tibicinem suum, qui super illud modulans sedet, in fluvium aut lacum trahunt.</u> [Haule entered a trefoil and wrote virginum expiatio here] <u>Id quare fiat, non plane video, nisi cogitem eas per hoc expiare velle, quod festis diebus contra ecclesiae praeceptum a levitate sua non abstinuerint."</u> Underlining by Haule in his copy.

84 Ibid., fol. LVIII^v: "Multos mirandos ritus observat quos ideo referre volo, ne quae de externis scribantur inanes fabulae aestimentur."

85 This side of Boemus's book has been somewhat neglected in recent literature. It is brought out by Schmidt and, in a context that makes the contemporary reader uneasy, by Richard Kohl, "Die geistesgeschichtliche Bedeutung der Deutschlandkapitel im Repertorium des Joannes Boemus Aubanus," *Zeitschrift für Volkskunde* 47 (1938), 191–200.

86 Boemus (1520), fol. LXI^v: "Gentis mores vivendique instituta ex legibus, quas orthodoxa fide recens suscepta habuere, cognosci possunt: tales fuere . . .".

87 Ibid., fol. LXI^r: "Verum enimvero non solum apud Suevos, sed & apud omnes fere gentes mutati sunt mores: & quod dolendum plurimum est, fere in peius."

88 Ibid., fol. LXI$^{r–v}$: "Privati Suevorum nulla alia re, nullo artificio magis occupantur, quam lini operatione, cui adeo incumbunt, adeo dediti sunt, ut in quibusdam Sueviae locis nedum mulieres & puellae, sed adolescentes & viri hyemis tempore <u>colo [the distaff] admoventur.</u> [Henry Haule writes: adolescentes & viri in lino operantur.] Panni genus faciunt cuius tela linea est, intextum bombycinum, Pargath illud vocantes: faciunt & totum lineum, quod Golsch appellant. Compertum habeo, apud Vlmenses solum quotannis utriusque generis pannos parari centum milia, ex quo quisque coniecturare potest quam incomprehensibilis incredibilisque summa in tota regione elaboretur. Ad remotissimas nationes isti panni transvehuntur, & maxime bis in anno ad Emporium franconafordense: ubi quam ingens vectigal Suevicae nationi accedit."

89 Ibid., fol. LXI^r: "quum id non minus opificibus & agricolis grave damnosumque sit, qui sua ante tempus gryphonibus istis ne potius dicam vel mercatoribus, vendunt quae postmodum necessitate cogente duplo aere re-

dimere ab ipsis debent, quam toti provinciae: quae, quibuscunque indiget, non apud vicinas gentes, a quibus minori pretio habere possit, accipere debet (sic enim a corruptis munere principibus imperatum) sed ab illis in Stutgardia, aut alias ubi emporia habent."

90 Ibid., fol. LV^v.

91 Ibid., fol. LVI^r.

92 Cf. Boemus's remark, ibid., fol. LXI^v: "Praeterea quoniam bonis mala commixta semper sunt: & nulla ex omni parte erecta: sunt Suevi in Venerem supra modum proni: foemineus sexus virili ad malum facile consentiens: immature uterque praevaricatur, sero resipiscit."

93 British Library MS Add 41,086A, fol. 142^v: "Exhibuit et Palatinis ingentes dapes. extis mullorum refertas. & cerebellis phoenicopterum: & perdicum ovis: & cerebellis turdorum et capitibus psytacorum.& fasianorum & pavonum. Barbas sane mulorum tantas iubebat exiberi. ut pro nastertis, apiasteris & faselaribus: vt foeno graeco. exiberet plenis fabatariis et discis. quod precipue stupendum est. Canes iocineribus anserum pavit. Habuit leones: & leopardos exarmatos in deliciis. quos edoctos per mansuetarios. subito ad secundam et tertiam mensam iubebat accumbere. ignorantibus cunctis. quod exarmati essent. ad pavorem: & ridiculum excitandum. Misit & uvas apamenas in presepia equis suis: & psittacis atque fasianis leones pavit." Bembo identified the source of this quotation in a marginal note: "ex Aelio Lampridio de helyogabali omnium deterrima vita": that is, the pseudonymous Aelius Lampridius, *Scriptores Historiae Augustae, Antonius Heliogabalus*, 20.6–21.2.

94 British Library MS Add 41,086A, fol. 142^r: "Veluti mihi contigit, Bernardo Bembo oratori, cum primum ad serenissimum Carolum, burgundiae ducem, prandenti assiderem. qui de improviso exarmatam leonam obviam attulit: qua re mirifice exorui: et palui ad multam chachinationem circumstantium aulicorum, anno salutis 1471. Augusti in Abbatis villa. Prouinciae Pichardiae."

95 British Library MS Add 41,086A, 190^r. Bembo's quotation reads: "Villam mire exaedificavit, ita ut in ea et provinciarum & locorum celeberrima nomina inscriberet: velut Licium. Achademiam. Pritanium. Canopum. Picilem. Tempe vocaret. Et ut nihil pretermitteret. etiam inferos finxit, & reliqua. In fine vite hadriani, per Helium Spartianum [*Scriptores Historiae Augustae, Hadrianus*, 28.5]." Bembo's comment reads: "Quam vidimus ipsi dum Ro. oratoria fungeremur. & structura et mollibus ac signisque impositis thalamis mire oblectaremur. anno christi 1487." See Giannetto, *Bernardo Bembo*, 191–192.

96 In addition to Blair, Mulsow and Zedelmaier, see Fabian Krämer, *Ein Zentaur in London: Lektüre und Beobachtung in der frühneuzeitlichen Naturforschung* (Affalterbach: Didymos-Verlag, 2014), and "Ulisse Aldrovandi's *Pandechion Epistemonicon* and the Use of Paper Technology in Renaissance Natural History," *Early Science and Medicine* 19 (2014): 398–423.

97 Di Dio, "'*Selecta colligere*,'" 596.

98 See the fine case study by Peter Fane-Saunders, *Pliny the Elder and the Emergence of Renaissance Architecture* (Cambridge: Cambridge University Press, 2016).

99 Grafton and Weinberg, "Johann Buxtorf Makes a Notebook."

100 Peter Burke, "The Uses of Literacy in Early Modern Italy," in *The Social History of Language*, ed. Peter Burke and Roy Porter (Cambridge: Cambridge University Press, 1987), 24–25.

101 Jacob Soll, *The Accounting: Financial Accountability and the Rise and Fall of Nations* (New York: Basic Books, 2014). See also the classic study of Iris Origo, *The Merchant of Prato: Daily Life in a Medieval Italian City* (London: Jonathan Cape, 1957; repr. London: Penguin, 2017), 257–284.

CHAPTER I · HUMANISTS WITH INKY FINGERS

1 Justin Stagl, *A History of Curiosity: The Theory of Travel, 1550–1800* (Chur: Harwood, 1995).

2 Theodor Zwinger, *Methodus apodemica* (Basel: Episcopius, 1577), 398–400.

3 Johan Gerritzen, "Printing at Froben's: An Eye-Witness Account," *Studies in Bibliography* 44 (1991): 144–163, at 149; for the original, see ibid., 162: "Quod officium docto alicui viro fere committi solet, qui cum judicio formas compositas relegat, recenseatque num recte omnes typi litteraeque sint conjunctae, syllabaeque ac orationes distinctae."

4 Ibid., 150; for the original, see ibid., 162: "Solentque in bene institutis officinis tres confici formae, ordineque singulae relegi, quo omni ex parte mendae vitiaeque expurgentur."

5 Jerome Hornschuch, *Orthotypographia*, ed. and tr. Philip Gaskell and Patricia Bradford (Cambridge: Cambridge: University Library, 1972), xvi, reproduced and analyzed in Percy Simpson, *Proof-Reading in the Sixteenth, Seventeenth and Eighteenth Centuries* (London: Oxford University Press, 1935), 126–134.

6 Ulinka Rublack, *Dressing Up: Cultural Identity in Renaissance Europe* (Oxford: Oxford University Press, 2010).

7 Martin Sicherl, "Aldinen (1495–1516)," in Dieter Harlfinger et al., *Griechische Handschriften und Aldinen* (Wolfenbüttel: Herzog August Bibliothek 1978), 119–149.

8 Geri Della Rocca de Candal and Paolo Sachet, "*Manus Manutii*: Corrections in the Aldine Press," forthcoming in *Printing and Misprinting: Typographical Mistakes and Publishers' Corrections (1450–1650)*, ed. Geri Della Rocca de Candal, Anthony Grafton, and Paolo Sachet (Oxford: Oxford University Press).

9 George Hoffmann, "Writing without Leisure: Proofreading as Work in the Renaissance," *Journal of Medieval and Renaissance Studies* 25 (1995): 17–31.

10 Rudolf Wackernagel, ed., *Rechnungsbuch der Froben und Episcopius, Buchdrucker und Buchhändler zu Basel, 1557–1564* (Basel: Benno Schwabe, 1881), 38, 40, 56, 72, 74.

11 Ibid., 20: "Leodigarius Grymaldus lector . . . Leodigario Grimaldo iterum pro indice Laurentii Justiniani operum et recognitione Agricolae de re metallica gallice."

12 Ibid., 58: "Bartholomeus Varolle corrigiert 24 wochen 2 tagk. . . . Eidem von dem exemplari speculi zůzůrüstenn . . . Eidem pro indice conscribendo in speculum iuris."

13 Note the complaints of R. B. McKerrow, Review of *Proof-Reading in the Six-teenth, Seventeenth and Eighteenth Centuries,* by Percy Simpson, *The Li-brary,* 4th ser., 16 (1935): 347–352; repr. in Percy Simpson, *Proof-Reading in the Sixteenth, Seventeenth and Eighteenth Centuries,* repr. with an intro-duction by Harry Carter (Oxford: Oxford University Press, 1970), v–viii.

14 Wackernagel, ed., *Rechnungsbuch der Froben und Episcopius;* Johann Amer-bach, *Correspondence,* ed. and tr. Barbara Halporn (Ann Arbor: University of Michigan Press, 2000); Edward Malone, "Learned Correctors as Technical Editors: Specialization and Collaboration in Early Modern European Printing Houses," *Journal of Business and Technical Communication* 20 (2006): 389–424.

15 *Das Chronikon des Konrad Pellikan,* ed. Bernhard Riggenbach (Basel: Bahn-maier (C. Detloff), 1877), 27: "Erat egregius praedicator et apprime doctus Mi-norita Franciscus Wyler, Basilensis, affinis Amorbachio, eundem obtinuit, ut brevia argumenta non libris sed capitibus praeponeret. Id egit per anni cir-culum, multos legendo et distinguendo in capitula, prius non distincta. sed sequenti anno loco motus, iterum solatio destituebatur impressor sanctis-simus. Convenit me juvenem quidem, sed laboriosum, rogavit ut in illius re-moti locum succedens, reliquos simili opera non distinctos, distinguerem in capita et distinctos argumentis praenotarem ad capita singula."

16 Ibid.: "Id invitus subivi, sed officiis et precibus expugnatus, acquievi, sicque residuos centum et quinquaginta Augustini libros ea ratione relegi, et ar-gumentis illustrare conatus sum, tam armatis precibus jussus, eos inquam libros omnes, in quibus invenit lector breviora argumenta: ubi autem pro-lixiora sunt, id factum est opera Francisci praedicti, brevitati enim studui pro virili." Arnoud Visscher was kind enough to inform me that Pellikan's copy of the edition survives in Leuven as Maurits Sabbebibliotheek, sig. P276. 567. 2 / Fo AUGU Oper 1505. The title-page in vol. 1 bears the inscrip-tion: "Dono assignati sunt hii Libri Fr[atr]i Conrado Pellicano Rubeaquen[si] Ordinis minorum Filio huius Conventus A m[a]g[ist]ro Iohanne Amorbachio pro immensis suis Laboribus quos pertulit in Distinctionibus Librorum per capitula argumentorumque prenotacionibus ingeniose docteque adhibitis Anno 1506." Pellikan's initials identify the "capitulorum annotatio" in many of the works included as his.

17 Martin Germann, *Die reformierte Stiftsbibliothek am Großmünster Zürich im 16. Jahrhundert* (Wiesbaden: Harrassowitz, 1994).

18 *Das Chronikon des Konrad Pellikan,* 27: "Fuit is Amorbachius doctissimus vir et mire diligens, libros suos corrigens magnis tam sumptibus quam la-boribus, adsistentibus sibi duobus vel tribus lectoribus, cum tot exemplar-ibus, ut nihil negligentia sua operi quomodocunque officeret, quin et ob un-amquamque dictionem, perperam impressam, maluit diurnum opus cum expensis repeti, ut patet, editionem attendenti diligentius." Though the phrasing of this passage is a little obscure, it probably means that Amerbach too put his texts through multiple proof readings (he may indeed have es-tablished the Basel tradition that Zwinger described in a later phase).

19 Madeline McMahon, "Polemic in Translation: Jerome's Fashioning of His-tory in the *Chronicle,*" in *Historiography and Identity, I: Ancient and Early*

Christian Narratives of Community, ed. Walter Pohl and Veronika Wieser (Turnhout: Brepols, 2019), 219–245.

20 Mark Vessey, "The History of the Book: Augustine's *City of God* and Post-Roman Cultural Memory," in *Augustine's* City of God: *A Critical Guide*, ed. James Wetzel (Cambridge: Cambridge University Press, 2012), 14–32.

21 For a reconstruction of Petrarch's notes from surviving copies see Giuseppe Billanovich, *Un nuovo esempio delle scoperte et delle letture del Petrarca: L' "Eusebio-Girolamo-PseudoProspero"* (Krefeld: Scherpe, 1954).

22 See generally Daniel Rosenberg and Anthony Grafton, *Cartographies of Time: A History of the Timeline* (New York: Princeton Architectural Press, 2010).

23 Peter Way, "Jehan de Mouveaux's *'Primum exemplar':* A Model Copy Made for Henri Estienne's 1512 Edition of Eusebius' *Chronicon*," *Quaerendo* 32, nos. 1–2 (2002): 60–98.

24 See E. J. Kenney, *The Classical Text: Aspects of Editing in the Age of the Printed Book* (Berkeley: University of California Press, 1974), 153, 156 (where Kenney remarks "possibly technical experimentation was in the air at Antwerp"); and more generally Luigi Battezzato, "Renaissance Philology: Johannes Livineius (1546–1599) and the Birth of the Apparatus Criticus," in *History of Scholarship: A Selection of Papers from the Seminar on the History of Scholarship Held Annually at the Warburg Institute*, ed. Christopher Ligota and Jean-Louis Quantin (Oxford: Oxford University Press, 2006), 75–111.

25 Poelman to Paul Chimarrhaeus, Antwerp, Museum Plantin-Moretus (hereafter MPM), MS M 229, I, 218: "Mitto ad te uti petis tua poematia, quae ad me dedisti, omnia, in quibus quaedam loca sunt, # hoc signo # in margine notata, a me parum intellecta; haec, si tibi non erit molestum, a te mihi explicari vellem. Notavi orthographiam, quam ego auctoritate doctissimorum hominum sequor; eam si tibi probabitur, imitare; si minus, quod non puto, abijce. Annotationes marginales omnes tollerem tum propter marginis angustiam, tum ut cuique liberum esset ascribere, quae vellet. Ostendi typographo Plantino Typum beneficiorum Christi, et Epitaphium Reginae: sed utranque chartam minoris duobus coronatis absque imaginibus se imprimere posse negabat etiam si illi privilegium non denegaretur. Quod scribis te omnia tua poemata ad me missurum ut meam censuram, prius quam edantur, subeant, [the page ends here]."

26 Schottus to Poelman, n.d., MPM MS Arch. 91, fol. 501ʳ: "Tandem contigit videre partum ex me natum, doctiss. et amiciss. Pulmane, quem mihi officii gratia filius tuus Methymna Campi misit: nondum enim quae frater misit, exemplaria, reddita: forte naufragium fecerunt: cumque recensere vellem magno meo dolore statim in limine impegi: et mendum statim obelo confodi: nam pag. 4. pro *cogitanti mihi*, excudendum erat *cogitavissem*, ut tres posteriores litterae evanescant, *ihi*. Damnavi meam ipsius oscitantiam; qui praesens non adverteram: nescio quid oculos meos fascinarat. Quivis facile non omnino rudis, negligentia, non imperitia peccatum, deprehendet. Ita fere fit, ut nosti: in alienis Lyncei; in nostris Lamiae sumus: quod quae memoria tenemus, ipsique composuimus, non tam accurate relegimus.

Mirabar equidem et Emendatorum doctiss. iuvenum oculos fugisse. Quare cum mea intersit plurimum in tanta exemplarium copia id corrigi, rogavi Plantinum obnixe, ut honoris mei caussa iuberet puerum aliquem horis aliquot, quae restant exemplaria, emendare: et Additamenta quaedam et Menda duabus paginis adderet: quod illum aegre facturum scio, sed honoris mei caussa tamen non detrectabit, ut confido: ego sumtus faciam: nec est necesse parentes resciscant, qui non intelligunt. Quae pagellae vendantur cum ijs quae restant, exemplaribus; mittanturque ijs qui plurima exemplaria coemerunt, et ad nundinas. Tu quoque si me amas, et litteras, huc hortare Plantinum; et me apud doctos purga, esseque operarum mendam: et corrige in illorum libris. [next sentence added in margin:] ego vero nescio quo fato hic labor meus in negligentissimum operarum incidit: alioqui elegantissime excusus Victor. Posthac cunctantius edam, quae molior: Paro enim Comm. in Hesiodum, sed premam ex Flacci praecepto, in annum nonum."

27 Anne Goldgar, *Impolite Learning: Conduct and Community in the Republic of Letters, 1680–1750* (New Haven: Yale University Press, 1995).

28 All these formulas come from the magnificent compilation of P. Gottfried Reichhart, O. S.B, "Alphabetisch geordnetes Verzechniss der Correctoren der Buchdruckereien des 15. Jahrhunderts," *Beiträge zur Inkunabelkunde* (Leipzig: Harrassowitz, 1895), 1–158, at 13.

29 Daniel Hobbins, *Authorship and Publicity before Print: Jean Gerson and the Transformation of Late Medieval Learning* (Philadelphia: University of Pennsylvania Press, 2013); Daniel Wakelin, *Scribal Correction and Literary Craft: English Manuscripts 1375–1510* (Cambridge: Cambridge University Press, 2014).

30 Palmieri's account of Lucius's conversion appears, for example, at Biblioteca Apostolica Vaticana, MS Pal. Lat. 817, fol. 94^r: "Lucius britanniae rex eleuterium pontificem baptisma postulavit: quod cum accepisset: brittani quoque fidem christi una susceperunt: & usque ad dioclitiani tempora inviolatam servaverunt." On the story of Lucius and Eleutherius, see Felicity Heal, "What Can King Lucius Do for You? The Reformation and the Early British Church," *English Historical Review* 120, no. 487 (2005): 593–619.

31 Vespasiano da Bisticci, *The Vespasiano Memoirs: Lives of Illustrious Men of the XVth Century*, tr. William George and Emily Waters (Toronto: University of Toronto Press in association with the Renaissance Society of America, 1997), 421–422.

32 Handsome copies of this text were much loved by Anglophone collectors. Examples include British Library Add MS 62994, Wellcome Library MS 591, Fitzwilliam Museum MS 178, Glasgow University Library MS Hunter 198 (U.1.2), and Beinecke Library Marston MS 217.

33 A still later continuation appears in Johannes Sichardus's edition, *Habes opt. lector chronicon opus felicissime renatum* (Basel: Petrus, 1536), fols. 211^r–221^v: "Nova temporum continuatio Germani cuiusdam."

34 MPM MS Arch 118, fol. 1^r: "Distinctiones exacte corrector observet, et assuescat ut (in legendo) una dictione lectorem antevortat. Lector etiam tardius legat, immo paulisper subsistat, si animadvertat correctorem erratorum multitudine obrui et detineri"; previously published and discussed by Henrik

Désiré L Vervliet, "Une instruction plantinienne à l'intention des cor-recteurs," *Gutenberg Jahrbuch* (1959): 99–103; by Martin Boghardt, "In-struktionen für Korrektoren der Officina Plantiniana," in *Trasmissione dei testi a stampa nel periodo moderno*, vol. 2: Il seminario internazionale, Roma—Viterbo, 27–29 giugno, 1985, ed. Giovanni Crapulli (Rome: Edizioni dell'Ateneo, 1987), 1–15; and by Dirk Imhof, "'Fauten des schrijvers, ende twee oft drij des druckers.' Proeflezen in de Plantijnse drukkerij," in *Por-tret van een Woordenaar. Cornelis Kiliaan en het woordenboek in de Ned-erlanden*, ed. Stijn van Rossem (Antwerp: Provincie Antwerpen, Departe-ment Cultuur, 2007), 73–85. It is also discussed and contextualized in Léon Voet, *The Golden Compasses: A History and Evaluation of the Printing and Publishing Activities of the Officina Plantiniana at Antwerp*, 2 vols. (Am-sterdam: Van Gendt; New York: Schram, 1969–1972), 2:174–193.

35 See the great study by Pierre Petitmengin and Bernard Flusin, "Le Livre an-tique et la dictée: nouvelles recherches," in *Mémorial André-Jean Fes-tugière. Antiquité païenne et chrétienne: vingt-cinq études*, ed. E. Lucchesi and H. D. Saffrey (Geneva: P. Cramer, 1984), 247–262.

36 For these and related materials, see Anthony Grafton and Megan Williams, *Christianity and the Transformation of the Book: Origen, Eusebius and the Library of Caesarea* (Cambridge, MA: Belknap Press of Harvard University Press, 2006), 184–187.

37 Alan Cameron, *The Last Pagans of Rome* (New York: Oxford University Press, 2011).

38 Johannes Elstius to Theodore Poelman, 1576, MPM MS Arch. R.91, 537, printed in Maurits Sabbe, "Uit de humanistenkring rond Plantin," *Verslagen en mededelingen van de Koninklijke Akademie voor Taal- en Letterkunde* (1922): 253–264; repr. in Maurits Sabbe, *Uit het Plantijnsche Huis* (Antwerp: Victor Resseller, 1924), 51–56, at 56: "Est Buseducis in conventu S. Gertrudis honesta matrona, tam bonis literis instructa, ut cum quovis grammatico audeat inire disputationes et putat sibi similem non facile reperiri posse aliam, memini me ex te Novimagi [at Nijmegen] audivisse de filiabus Plan-tini, eas non modo latine sed et grece et hebraice scire legere et scribere, id si verum est queso mihi perscribas si tibi satis est otij . . . MDLXXVI feria 4^a post pentacostam."

39 Poelman to Elstius in Nijmegen, 25 August 1576; MPM MS 229, I, p. 215, printed in Sabbe, *Uit het Plantijnsche Huis*, 56: "Suavissimae tuae fuere lit-tere, mi Elste, quod ex ijs te salvum et sanum intelligerem. quod autem matronam quandam ita bonis litteris imbutam scribis, ut cum quovis gram-matico de ea arte acute disceptare possit, non miror, cum ego Clementis Angli uxorem, et etiam filiam, qui cum Antverpiae aliquot menses haer-erent me ob nominis mei famam salutatum venerant, eas [MS and Sabbe eos] audiverim Graece et Latine loquentes, et non nulla veterum scriptorum atque etiam poetarum utpote Cypriani et Prudentij loca quaedam a se ob-servata et ex antiquis codicibus restituta mihi ostenderint. adhaec novi Joannem Hovium mercatorem Antverpiae qui filias duas et Graece et Latine doctas habebat. Plantini vero filia Hebraice Graece et Latine quidem expe-dite legebat: sed nihil intelligebat." There is a slightly different version in

MPM MS Arch. 91, 505 verso: "Plantini sane filia Hebraice, Graece, et Latine expedite legebat: verum non intelligebat."

40 MPM B.948.4 (proof copy of the Antwerp Polyglot later prophets), 73, at Isaiah 26.

41 A table of these correction marks appears in Hornschuch, *Orthotyographia*.

42 Quoted by Colin Clair, *Christopher Plantin* (London: Cassell, 1960; repr. 1987), 258n.16.

43 Ada Palmer, "The Recovery of Stoicism in the Renaissance," in *The Rout-ledge Handbook of the Stoic Tradition*, ed. John Sellars (New York: Rout-ledge, Taylor & Francis Group, 2016), 117–132.

44 This story has been well told by Winfried Trillitzsch, *Seneca im liter-arischen Urteil der Antike: Darstellung und Sammlung der Zeugnisse*, 2 vols. (Amsterdam: Hakkert, 1971), 1:221–250; and Lisa Jardine, *Erasmus, Man of Letters: The Construction of Charisma in Print* (Princeton: Princeton University Press, 1993), 132–136.

45 Gerritsen, "Printing at Froben's," 149; for the original see ibid., 162: "*Sigis-mundus Gelenius*, vir insigniter doctus, et longe meliore fortuna dignus."

46 Hornschuch, *Orthotypographia*, 27.

47 Zeltner, C. D. *Correctorum in typographiis eruditorum centuria* (Leipzig: Felscecken, 1718), 46–48.

48 Ibid., 528, 88–89.

49 Antwerp, Museum Plantin-Moretus, MS Arch 31, 84: "encores que ie luy eusse predict."

50 MPM MS Arch 786, fol. 15^r: "est parti malcontent et sans dire adieu etc."

51 MPM MS Arch 329, fol. 10^v: "Praescripta ego Philippus Jac. Noyens saepis-sime audivi a Praefatis viris et venerabilis D. de Kleyn a Domino Vanderw-eyden quoque Audivit Hieronimus de Brauio ab eodem vanderweyden quod correctores solerent quando fuissent per duos annos augmentari in pretio quod Noyens et praefatus de Kleyn etiam saepe audivere."

52 Poelman wrote "Vale, ex nostro Musognapheo"; see *D. Magni Ausonii Bur-digalensis Opera*, ed. Theodore Poelman (Antwerp: Plantin, 1568), sig. [*6]^r. In his copy, Bodleian Library Auct.S.5.22, Scaliger replied: "Vale, ergo, γναφεῦ."

53 Wackernagel, ed., *Rechnungsbuch der Froben und Episcopius*, 74 (March 1564).

54 Many of the basic sources are splendidly presented in Giovanni Andrea Bussi, *Prefazioni alle edizioni di Sweynheym e Pannartz prototipografi ro-mani*, ed. Massimo Miglio (Milan: Il Polifilo, 1978). For accounts of the epi-sode see Edwin Hall, *Sweynheym & Pannartz and the Origins of Printing in Italy: German Technology and Italian Humanism in Renaissance Rome* (McMinnville, OR: Bird & Bull Press for Phillip J. Pirages, 1991); *Gutenberg e Roma: Le origini della stampa nella Città dei Papi (1467–1500)*, ed. Mas-simo Miglio and Orietta Rossini (Naples: Electa Napoli, 1997); and Martin Davies, "Humanism in Script and Print in the Fifteenth Century," in *The Cambridge Companion to Renaissance Humanism*, ed. Jill Kraye (Cam-bridge: Cambridge University Press, 1996), 47–62.

55 Bussi, *Prefazioni*, 84.

56 Dati, note in Paris, Bibliothèque Nationale de France, Rés. C. 477, reproduced in *Gutenberg e Roma*, ed. Miglio and Rossini, fig. 19: "ab ipsis Theutonicis romae commorantibus qui huiusmodi libros non scribere, sed formare solent."

57 Leon Battista Alberti, *Dello scrivere in cifra* (Turin: Galimberti, 1994), 27–28: "Cum essem apud Dathum in hortis pontificis maximi ad Vaticanum et nostro pro more inter nos sermones haberentur de rebus quae ad studia litterarum pertinerent, incidit ut vehementer probaremus Germanum inventorem qui per haec tempora pressionibus quibusdam characterum efficeret ut diebus centum plus CCta volumina librorum opera hominum non plus trium exscripta redderentur dato ab exemplari. Unica enim pressione integram exscriptam reddit paginam maioris chartae. Hinc cum itidem aliquorum ingenia circa res varias laudaremus, vehementer admirari Dathum visus est eos qui fictis characterum inusitatissimorum significationibus litteras tantum ex composito consciis notas, quas cyfras nuncupant, suis scrutandi artibus compertum quid narrent, faciant atque explicent." On this text, see Arielle Saiber, *Measured Words: Computation and Writing in Renaissance Italy* (Toronto and Buffalo: University of Toronto Press, 2018), chap. 1.

58 Ian Maclean, "The Market for Scholarly Books and Conceptions of Genre in Northern Europe, 1570–1630," in his *Learning and the Market Place: Essays in the History of the Early Modern Book* (Leiden and Boston: Brill, 2009), 1–24, at 17.

59 Paul O. Kristeller, "De traditione operum Marsilii Ficini," in *Supplementum Ficinianum*, ed. Kristeller, 2 vols. (Florence: Olschki, 1937), 1:clxvii–clxxxi.

60 Rudolf Pfeiffer, "Küchenlatein," *Philologus* 86 (1931): 455–459.

61 See "A Biography of Gabriel Harvey," online, *The Archaeology of Reading*, https://archaeologyofreading.org/biography/, accessed October 2, 2019; and Lorna Hutson, *Thomas Nashe in Context* (Oxford: Clarendon Press, 1989).

62 Helene Harth, "Niccolò Niccoli als literarischer Zensor. Untersuchungen zur Textgeschichte von Poggios 'De Avaritia,'" *Rinascimento* 7 (1967): 29–53.

63 Silvia Rizzo, *Il lessico filologico degli umanisti* (Rome: Storia e Letteratura, 1973), esp. 249–268; see also Jardine, *Erasmus, Man of Letters*.

64 Francesco Rolandello, blurb to *Mercurius Trismegistus* (Treviso: Gerar. de Lisa, 1471): "Tu quicunque es qui haec legis, sive grammaticus sive orator seu philosophus aut theologus, scito: Mercurius Trismegistus sum, quem singulari mea doctrina et theologica, aegiptii prius et barbari, mox Christiani antiqui theologi stupore attoniti admirati sunt. Quare si me emes et leges, hoc tibi erit commodum, quod parvo aere comparatus, summa te legentem voluptate et utilitate afficiam."

65 Michele Ferno, "Campani vita," in Giovanni Antonio Campano, *Opera* (Rome: Silber, 1495), fol. [vii]ʳ: "Omnes eloquentiae parentem: oratorum poetarumque principem appellabant. Ad hunc quaeque illi condidissent tanquam ad communem censorem supremumque oraculum deferebant. Nemo litteratorum ausus eo tempore quicquam fuisset edere qui illius ante

iuditium sententiamque non explorasset. Magnam is labori suo gloriam addidisse ducebatur: cui huius commendatio accessisset."

66 For another such request on Pius's part, see his dedicatory letter in *Historia rerum Friderici Tertii imperatoris* (Memmingen: Albrecht Kunne, not after March 1491), ep. ded., sigs. a2^{r-v}: "Tu vale et si quid acerbius in quenquam scriptum offenderis, non tam mee nature quam stimulis padagre urgentis adscribe. Et quidquid inscite, inepte, absurde occurrerit, sumpto calamo dele."

67 Flavio di Bernardo, *Un vescovo umanista alla Corte pontificia: Giannantonio Campana (1429–1477)* (Rome: Università Gregoriana Editrice, 1975), 160–163.

68 Rome, Biblioteca Corsiniana, MS 147, fol. 361^v: "Facta est mihi ab eo potestas eiiciendi quae supervacua, corrigendi quae intorta viderentur, etiam illustrandi quae obscuriuscule dicta. sed ea visa est omnium elegantia, is splendor ut non solum aliena non aegeant manu ad augendam dignitatem sed manifestam efferant desperationem imitari cupientibus."

69 Concetta Bianca, "La terza edizione moderna dei *Commentari* di Pio II," *Roma nel Rinascimento* 12 (1995): 5–16.

70 See Rossella Bianchi, *L'"Eversana deiectio" di Iacopo Ammannati Piccolomini* (Rome: Storia e letteratura, 1984).

71 Ferno, "Campani vita," fol. [vii]^r: "Hinc iam nemo in tota impressorum Hesperia ea tempestate opus imprimendum suscipere velle videbatur cui illius commendationis epistola non praeluxisset. Adeo clarum et celebre apud omnes sanctumque et venerabile illius nomen habebatur. Vnde cum Vdalricus quidem Gallicus tunc qui formas in Vrbem literarias nuper intulisset interquiescere illum assiduis emendationibus non permitteret."

72 The Plutarch was printed by Ulrich Han in Rome in late 1469 or early 1470.

73 Douglas Duncan, *Thomas Ruddiman: A Study in Scottish Scholarship of the Early Eighteenth Century* (Edinburgh: Oliver & Boyd, 1965); see also Simpson, *Proof-reading*, chaps. 3–4.

74 See esp. John Monfasani, "The First Call for Press Censorship: Niccolò Perotti, Giovanni Andrea Bussi, Antonio Moreto and the Editing of Pliny's 'Natural History,'" *Renaissance Quarterly* 41 (1988): 1–31; and Ingeborg Jostock, *La censure négociée: le contrôle du livre a Genève, 1560–1625* (Geneva: Droz, 2007). On the imposition of Catholic censorship see Hannah Marcus, *Forbidden Knowledge* (forthcoming).

75 Joseph Scaliger, *Epistolae omnes quae reperiri potuerunt*, ed. Daniel Heinsius (Leiden: Elzevir, 1627).

76 See the excellent account by Paul Botley and Dirk van Miert on the website of their magnificent edition of Scaliger's correspondence, *The Correspondence of Joseph Justus Scaliger*, 8 vols. (Geneva: Droz, 2012), at http://warburg.sas.ac.uk/scaliger/indexjjscaliger.htm, accessed August 26, 2010.

77 Franciscus Raphelengius to Justus Lipsius, 7 November 1595; in *Sylloges epistolarum a viris illustribus scriptarum tomus I [–V]*, ed. Peter Burman, 5 vols. (Leiden: Luchtmans, 1727), 1:208. "Laudator et contemptor vehemens ac saepe eiusdem viri aut rei. Qui hodie Maraus, Asnes, Bestes, Ignorants etc. alias iidem erunt Galant-hommes, Doctes, Sçavants etc."

78 Martin Delrio, *Peniculus Foriarum Elenchi Scaligeriani pro Societate Iesu, Maldanato, Delrio* ([Antwerp]: n.p., 1609), 160–163.

79 Scaliger to Oldenbarvelt, 20 April 1599; Leiden University Library MS BPL 885: "Ego, quod scirem hoc ordinum non decretum, sed ipsorum professorum conspirationem, qui se levare, me onerare vellent."

80 Scaliger, *Epistolae omnes quae reperiri potuerunt*, ed. Daniel Heinsius (Leiden; Elzevir, 1627), 707. I owe this example to the Scaliger project website, http://warburg.sas.ac.uk/scaliger/moreimages.htm, accessed August 26, 2010.

81 Leiden University Library 754 G 36.

82 British Library 1086.b.1.

83 Gerardus Joannes Vossius to Franciscus Gomarus, 11 May 1627; Vossius, *Epistolae selectiores* (Amsterdam: Blaeu, 1699), 56: "Recte interim ac laudabiliter quod omnibus in locis, loco Juniani nominis, asteriscum posuere, uti et cum Manilius Junii, vel Tertullianus, vel Epistolae ejus ad Atticum taxarentur. Mallem tamen totos periodos omisissent. Nunc sic quoque intelligent non pauci, quid dicatur, idque ex iis, quae vel praecedunt, vel consequuntur."

84 Paul Dibon, "Les avatars d'une édition de correspondance: Les Epistolae I. Casauboni de 1638," *Nouvelles de la République des Lettres* 2 (1982): 25–63.

85 Angelo Poliziano, *Letters*, ed. Shane Butler (Cambridge, MA: I Tatti Renaissance Library, 2008–), 1:291–293.

86 In the holograph collection of Trithemius's letters, Biblioteca apostolica Vaticana MS Pal. lat. 730, ep. II.31, fol. 152^{r-v}, is headed "Epistola nicolai gerbellii phorcensis gymnosophiste in academia coloniana: ad ioannem tritemium abbatem"; this splendid title reappears at II.36, fol. 159^v: "presbyter et gymnosophista erpfordiensis." In the printed edition of the letters, Trithemius, *Epistolarum familiarium libri duo* (Haguenau: Brubach, 1537), this title disappears from the headings to the letters in question, though it reappears in the table of contents that lists all of them: mute evidence of a corrector trying to make the collection look more plausible.

87 Erasmus, *Opus epistolarum Desiderii Erasmi Roterodami*, ed. P. S. Allen et al., 12 vols. (Oxford: Clarendon Press, 1906–1947), 4:409.

88 Kathy Eden, *The Renaissance Rediscovery of Intimacy* (Chicago and London: University of Chicago Press, 2012).

89 Aldo Bernardo, "Letter-Splitting in Petrarch's *Familiares*," *Speculum* 33 (1958): 236–241; Hans Baron, *From Petrarch to Leonardo Bruni* (Chicago: University of Chicago Press for the Newberry Library, 1968), 7–101.

90 Nicholas Jardine, *The Birth of the History and Philosophy of Science: Kepler's "A Defence of Tycho against Ursus" with Essays on Its Provenance and Significance* (Cambridge: Cambridge University Press. 1984; repr. 1988).

91 Owen Gingerich, *An Annotated Census of Copernicus' De Revolutionibus (Nuremberg, 1543 and Basel, 1566)* (Leiden and Boston: Brill, 2002).

CHAPTER 2 · PHILOLOGISTS WAVE DIVINING RODS

Heartfelt thanks go to Christian Flow, Jill Kraye, and Glenn Most for comments and criticism.

1 Bodleian Library MS Casaubon 25, fol. 115ᵛ: "σὺν Θεῷ Kal. Aug. Narrabat hodie mihi rem miram reverendiss. Praesul D. Ep. Eliensis: quam ille acceptam auribus suis a teste occulato et auctore credebat esse verissimam. Est vicus in urbe Londino qui dicitur vicus Longobardorum. in eo vico παροικία est et aedes paroecialis, in qua fuit presbyter homo summae fidei et notae pietatis. anno 1563. quo anno, si unquam alias pestis grassabat per hanc urbem Lond. Narravit ig. hic paroecus et passim aliis, et ipsi quoque D. Episcopo, sibi hoc accidisse. Erat illi amicus in sua paroecia insignis, vir ut omnes existimabant probus et pius. Hic peste correptus advocavit presbyterum illum suum amicum, qui et aegrotanti affuit et vidit morientem nec deseruit nisi mortuum. ita demum repetiit domum suam. Post horas satis multas a morte huius quum ipse pro mortuo esset relictus in cubiculo, uxor illius idem cubiculum est ingressa, ut ex arca promeret lodicem sive linteamen ad ipsum ἐντολλιτεῖν ut est moris. Ingressa audit hanc vocem operi intenta. Quis hic est? terreri illa, et velle egredi. sed auditur iterum vox illa, Quis hic est? ac tandem comperto esse mariti vocem accedit ad illum, quid, ait, marite, tu ig. mortuus non es, at nos te pro mortuo compositum deserueramus. Ego vero, respondit ille, vere mortuus fui: sed ita Deo visum, ut anima mea rediret ad corpus. Sed tu, uxor, ait, si quid habes cibi parati da mihi. esurio enim. dixit illa vervecinam habere se, pullum gallinaceum, et nescio quid aliud. sed omnia incocta: quae brevi esset paratura. Ego, ait ille, moram non fero. panem habes, ait, et caseum? Quum annuisset atque ipse petiisset afferri, comedit spectante uxore. deinde advocato presbytero, et iussis exire e cubiculo omnibus qui aderant, narrat illi haec. Ego, ait, vere mortuus fui: sed iussa est anima redire ad suum corpus ut scelus aperirem ore meo manibus meis admis<sum>, de quo nulla unquam cuiquam nata est suspicio. Priorem nanque uxorem meam ipse occidi manibus meis, tanta vafritie, ut omnes res lateret. deinde modum perpetrati sceleris exposuit. nec ita multo post expiravit, ac vere tum mortuus est."

2 Bodleian Library MS Casaubon 28, fol. 125ʳ: "Σὺν Θεῷ. Rem miram mihi narrabat hodie D. Ep. Eliensis sanctae pietatis Antistes. Dicebat se accepisse a multis, sed praecipue a D. Episcopo Vellensi nuper mortuo: cui successit D. Montacutus: evenisse ante annos circiter XV. in urbe Vella, sive ea dicenda Wellas, die quadam aestiva, ut dum in Ecclesia Cathedrali populus sacris vacabat duo vel tria tonitrua inter plura audirentur supra modum horrenda. ita ut populus vnitus in genua μίᾳ ὁρμῇ procumberet ad illum sonum terribilem. Constitit, simul fulmen cecidisse, sine cuiusque damno tamen. Atque haec vulgaria: illud admirandum: quod postea est observatum a multis: repertas esse crucis imagines impressas corporibus eorum qui in aede sacra tum fuerant: Dicebat Ep.us Vellensis D. Eliensi uxorem suam (honestissima ea femina fuit) venisse ad se et ei narrasse fore grandi miraculo, sibi in corpore impressa [cross] signa extare. quod quum risu exciperet Episcopus, uxor nudato corpore ei probavit verum esse quod dixerat. Deinde ipse observavit sibi quoque eiusdem [cross] manifestiss. imaginem esse impressam in brachio opinor. aliis in humero, in pectore, in dorso, aut alia corporis parte. Hoc vir maximus D. Eliensis ita mihi narrabat, ut vetaret de veritate historiae ambigere."

3 M. Pattison, *Isaac Casaubon, 1559–1614*, 2d ed. (Oxford: Clarendon Press, 1875), 443–446, 473–474.

4 William Camden, *Epistolae*, ed. Thomas Smith (London: Chiswell, 1699), 342.

5 Ibid.

6 *A Letter of Mr. Casaubon* (London: Nicholas Okes for George Norton, 1615), bound with James Martin, *Via Regia. The Kings Way to Heaven. With a Letter of that Late Miracle of Learning, Mr. IS. CASAUBON* (London: Nicholas Okes for George Norton, 1615), sig. [A3]ʳ; for the original, see ibid., sig. [A2]ʳ: "Binas paucis diebus a te accepi: priores rei magnitudine quam narrabant dederunt me in stuporem: nam certissimum Miraculum quae scribis continent. Caeterum a Deone sit τὸ θαῦμα an ἀπὸ τοῦ Πονηροῦ nostrum non est pronuntiare, illorum est qui rei gestae fuerunt aut testes aut testium familiares, quique de eo quod accidit πληροφορηθέντος, peritiam habent voluntatis divinae circa miracula. Quare praestantissimis Theologis illustris Academiae vestrae hoc πρόβλημα relinquo tractandum: mihi volupe fuit cognoscere τὸ ὅτι: illi quaerant τὸ διότι. Quod si quid ab aliquo eorum fuerit super ea re sane mirabili scriptum, magnam inieris a me gratiam si id mecum communicaveris."

7 *Posterior Analytics* I.13, 78a22–24.

8 Thus Frank Kermode writes of A. E. Housman, "there is a more difficult and more interesting aspect of the switch to Manilius: how we should understand this life-absorbing passion for a craft that required not only a virtually unparalleled grasp of ancient languages and cultures but the possession of the exquisite divinatory intelligence required to make proper use of that knowledge?" ("Nothing for Ever and Ever," *London Review of Books*, July 5, 2007, 7–8, http://www.lrb.co.uk/v29/n13/frank-kermode/nothing-for-ever-and-ever).

9 Quoted in Anthony Grafton, *Joseph Scaliger: A Study in the History of Classical Scholarship*, 2 vols. (Oxford: Clarendon Press, 1983–1993), 1:134. For a good introduction to this text and its history, see the website of the Festus Lexicon Project at University College London, https://web.archive.org/web/20130112064549/http://www.ucl.ac.uk/history2/research/festus/index.htm, accessed August 23, 2018.

10 See Damiano Acciarino, "The Renaissance Editions of Festus: Fulvio Orsini's Version," *Acta Classica* 59 (2016), 1–22, 23, and fig. 1.

11 Robert Burton quotes the proverb in *Anatomy of Melancholy* 1.3, and I use his translation in the text; see *The Anatomy of Melancholy*, ed. Thomas Faulkner, Nicholas Kiessling, and Rhonda Blair, 6 vols. (Oxford: Oxford University Press, 1989), 1:424.

12 Verrius Flaccus, *Quae extant* (Geneva: Saint-André, 1575), Eton College Library Be.8.17., clxii; previously quoted in Grafton, *Scaliger*, vol. 1, chap. 5 (quotation on p. 149); note also Flaccus, *Quae extant*, cvii ("Divina Scal. coniectura").

13 Apuleius, *Apologia*, ed. Isaac Casaubon (Heidelberg: Commelin, 1594), 145: "Atque haec est nostro de hoc loco sententia: quam constanter & verecunde ideo proferimus, quia meminimus esse a te, Scaliger eruditissime, aliter pridem emendata ista & exposita. . . . Enimvero non is es tu vir nobilissime,

qui in hoc genere literarum, quod (ut de medicinae arte Celsus ait) coniec-
turale magnam partem est, tuas omnes sententias, ceu κυρίας δόξας velis haberi: quod falso nimis & improbe sycophantas quosdam, non Scaligeri nominis magis quam Musarum hostes dictitare non pudet." For medicine as
a conjectural art, see Celsus *De medicina*, Prooemium, 16–17: "Neque vero
infitiantur experimenta quoque esse necessaria, sed ne ad haec quidem ad-
itum fieri potuisse nisi ab aliqua ratione contendunt: non enim quidlibet
antiquiores viros aegris inculcasse, sed cogitasse quid maxime conveniret,
et id usu explorasse, ad quod ante coniectura aliqua duxisset. Neque inter-
esse, an nunc iam pleraque explorata sint."

14 Apuleius, *Apologia*, 149, on 47 (38.1–2): "LOCVS EX GRAECO) Quoties-
cunque in hac oratione fuisse aliquid recitatum, cum ea pronunciata est,
indicatur: eius quod lectum est titulum, inserendum ex ipsius authoris
verbis. Qua ratione quantum lucis orationi accedat, nemo non videt. Fuit
ea oratorum praesertim Graecorum consuetudo, ut in scribendis orationibus
quo quaeque loco litis instrumenta fuissent producta & recitata, titulo ap-
posito indicarent. Nulla fere hodie extat Graeca oratio, ubi indices istiusmodi plures non reperias. Male ergo meriti sunt de hac oratione, male de
nobis, qui hos titulos exemerunt: quos fuisse olim ab auctore appositos,
unicus saltem qui remanserat argumento sit. hunc dico qui in ipso fere fine
orationis habetur, TESTIMONIVM CASSII LONGINI, etc. [101.4 (Testimonium Cassi Longini tutoris et Coruini Clementis qR)] nam si illum Apuleius adiecit, cur solum? cur eum potissimum? cur non alios quoque omnes?
ille vero omnes ἀναμφισβητητῶς. Nemo igitur factum nostrum calumnietur:
quod non dubitaverim absque librorum auctoritate, aliena verba in con-
textum recipere. non enim ita est: sed inserta olim ab auctore, & male
postea sublata, in suum locum restituimus." In his working copy of the
book, British Library C.81.c.22., Casaubon changed "hac oratione" to "hoc
libro."

15 Anthony Grafton and Joanna Weinberg, *"I Have Always Loved the Holy
Tongue": Isaac Casaubon, the Jews and a Forgotten Chapter in Renaissance
Scholarship* (Cambridge, MA: Harvard University Press, 2011), esp. chap.1.

16 *Scriptores historiae augustae*, ed. Isaac Casaubon (Paris: Drouart, 1603), sig.
ij*v: "Atque ego non dubito Tribonianum istum cum hoc fecisset, visum sibi
bellum hominem, qui erat saperda merus."

17 For the attack on Tribonian, see, for example, Martin Loughlin, "The Historical Method in Public Law," in *The Oxford Handbook of Legal History*,
ed. M. D. Dubber and C. Tomlins (Oxford: Oxford University Press, 2018),
983–1000.

18 *Scriptores historiae augustae*, ed. Casaubon, sig. ij*v: "Quid fuerit consilii
collectionis huius auctori, quando in istam formam hoc corpus digessit, va-
tibus relinquimus divinandum."

19 Giovanni Boccaccio, *De montibus* (Venice: Vindelinus de Spira, 1473), fol.
75v: "Esto per coniecturas aliqua plura deprehendi possint: utputa quem Perusinum hodie lacum dicimus: transimenum fuisse coniecturamus: eo
quod flamineum consulem Hanibalem apud Aretium expectasse legimus:
et e vestigio secus trasimenum lacum conservisse. Et quia lacus alter praeter

perusinum Aretio propinquus non est: Satis illum percipimus transimenum
et sic de aliquibus fecisse fuerat possible. In reliquis potius divinare necesse
erat: quam alicuius posse imitari vestigium: quod quidem ego non didici."

20 Silvia Rizzo, *Il lessico filologico degli umanisti* (Rome: Storia e Letteratura,
    1973), 173, quoting Poggio's letter to Barbaro of 1417–1418: "Mitto ad te . . .
    Silium Italicum, libros V Statii Silvarum, item M. Manilium Astronomicum.
    Is qui libros transcripsit ignorantissimus omnium viventium fuit: divinare
    oportet, non legere. Ideoque opus est ut transcriberentur per hominem
    doctum. Ego legi usque ad XIII librum Silii, multa emendavi, ita ut recte
    scribenti facile sit similes errors deprehendere atque corrigere in reliquis li-
    bris." Rizzo shows, with characteristic precision, that Poggio was describing
    a particular manuscript and the difficulties it presented, and not, as Stangl
    thought, prescribing a rule for transcription.

21 Poggio, *Ep.* 3.17, quoted in Rizzo, *Il lessico filologico,* 327: "Philippicas Ci-
    ceronis emendavi cum hoc antiquo codice, qui ita pueriliter scriptus est, ita
    mendose, ut in iis quae scripsi non coniectura opus fuerit, sed divinatione.
    Nulla est femella tam rudis, tam insulsa que non emendatius scripsisset."

22 Cicero *ad Att.* 8.11.3, quoted in Rizzo, *Il lessico filologico,* 290: "Προθεσπίζω
    igitur, noster Attice, non hariolans ut illa cui nemo credidit, sed coniectura
    prospiciens."

23 Cicero *ad Fam.* 1.5b.1: "Hic quae agantur quaeque acta sint, [ea] te et litteris
    multorum et nuntiis cognosse arbitror; quae autem posita sunt in coniec-
    tura quaeque videntur fore, ea puto tibi a me scribi oportere."

24 Paolo Manuzio, *In Epistolas M. Tullii Ciceronis quae Familiares vocantur . . .
    Commentarius* (Frankfurt: A. Wechel, 1580), 70: "*Quae autem posita sunt
    in coniectura*] quae coniectura licet assequi: quae possunt e signis divi-
    nari. Coniectura & divinatio non idem sunt. Nam coniectura ducitur e
    signis, divinatio saepe signa non sequitur. Ita fit, ut omnis coniectura divi-
    natio sit, non contra."

25 As Pierre Bayle wrote: "Cicéron savoit les raisons fortes & subtiles dont *Car-
    neade* se servit en combattant la *divination*"; see *Dictionaire historique et
    critique,* s.v. Carneade, note I; 5th ed., 4 vols. (Amsterdam, Leiden, the
    Hague, and Utrecht: Brunel, Luchtmans et al., 1740), 2:62.

26 See, for example, Elizabeth Rawson, *Intellectual Life in the Late Roman
    Republic* (Baltimore: Johns Hopkins University Press, 1985); Mary Beard,
    "Cicero and Divination: The Formation of a Latin Discourse," *Journal of
    Roman Studies* 78 (1986): 33–46; and Malcolm Schofield, "Cicero for and
    against Divination," *Journal of Roman Studies* 78 (1986): 47–65.

27 Johannes Hartlieb, *Das Buch der verbotenen Künste: Aberglaube und Zau-
    berei des Mittelalters,* ed. Falk Eisermann and Eckhard Graf, with Chris-
    tian Rätsch (Ahlerstedt: Diederichs, 1989); and on this subject, see the full
    and judicious study by Frank Fürbeth, *Johannes Hartlieb: Untersuchungen
    zu Leben und Werk* (Tübingen: De Gruyter, 1992). Richard Kieckhefer sheds
    much light on the wider context in *Forbidden Rites: A Necromancer's
    Manual of the Fifteenth Century* (University Park: Pennsylvania State Uni-
    versity Press, 1998). Hartlieb's system of classification was not entirely new:
    Nicholas of Cusa and many others had followed Isidore of Seville in speaking

of the four arts of divination, aeromancy, geomancy, hydromancy, and pyromancy.

28 Hartlieb, *Das Buch der verbotenen Künste*, 162.

29 See Darrel Rutkin, "The Use and Abuse of Ptolemy's *Tetrabiblos* in Renaissance and Early Modern Europe: Two Case Studies (Giovanni Pico della Mirandola and Filippo Fantoni)," in *Ptolemy in Perspective: Use and Criticism of His Work from Antiquity to the Nineteenth Century*, ed. Alexander Jones (Dordrecht and New York: Springer, 2010), 135–149.

30 See, for example, Richard Kieckhefer, *Magic in the Middle Ages* (Cambridge: Cambridge University Press, 1989); the essays in *Conjuring Spirits: Texts and Traditions of Medieval Ritual Magic*, ed. Claire Fanger (University Park: Pennsylvania State University Press, 1989); and Frank Klaassen, *The Transformations of Magic: Illicit Learned Magic in the Later Middle Ages and Renaissance* (University Park: Pennsylvania State University Press, 2013).

31 See M. Moli Frigola, "*Iakobo*," in *Scrittura biblioteche e stampa a Roma nel Quattrocento: Aspetti e problemi*, Atti del Seminario 1–2 giugno 1979, ed. Concetta Bianca et al. (Vatican City: Scuola Vaticana di paleografia, diplomatica e archivistica, 1980), 183–203; and Anna Modigliani, "Testamenti di Gaspare da Verona," in *Scrittura biblioteche e stampa a Roma nel Quattrocento: Aspetti e problemi*, Atti del 2° Seminario 6–8 maggio 1982, ed. Massimo Miglio et al. (Vatican City: Scuola Vaticana di paleografia, diplomatica e archivistica, 1983), 611–627.

32 Rome, Biblioteca Casanatense, MS lat. 397, fol. 77^r: "[de sortilegiis multa dicta sunt in iure diuino. quae quidem sunt prohibita sicut et pleraeque species presagiendi ut necromantia chiromantia auguria extispitia pyromantia auspicia [et sic de singulis recte tractauit."

33 Ibid., fol. 77^{r-v}: "[comburi autem iussit quandam veneficam et necromanticam mulierem observandissimus d. Cardinalis firmanus quae in agro perusino eam detestabilem artem exercebat [nichil melius nichil iustius facere potuisset [ipse etiam est a vertice ad plantas iustissimus et prudentissimus simul et doctissimus altissimique consilii princeps: cuius verba aurea sunt quotienscunque leguntur: quem nil ob aliud amo colo et obseruo." See Modigliani, "Testamenti di Gaspare da Verona," 619.

34 Ibid., fol. 78^r: "Nescio quae fabula sit illa cum dicitur nunquam virgo pariet nisi dum templum pacis corruet vel dum virgo pariet templum pacis corruet. nam peperat maria virgo intemerata antequam esset vespasianus aut titus et antequam ipsum templum pacis de quo loquimur. Attamen sive credas sive non parvi facio cum non sit articulus fidei. In hac eadem mea sententia fuit leonardus aretinus vir litteratissimus, historicus non parvus itidem. sensit guarinus, conterraneus meus, necnon carolus compatriota leonardi praememorati. Immo et Io. Aretinus torquatellus familiarissimus mihi vir studiosissimus litteraturae omnium quos unquam noverim."

35 Ibid., fol. 26^v: "[carmina nunc sunt incantationes verborum [quomodo coquatur venenum illis relinquo quae faciunt. et ex medicina aliquid scio in hoc. quod tamen silentio penitus praeteribo."

36 Ibid., fol. 77^v: "[et ego vidi quosdam seniores in territorio seu agro patriae meae hoc est veronae, rusticos quidem qui siquis amisisset asinum vel

equum praesagiebant et videbant statim ubi esset res amissa. et dictis verbis et sacris suis perfectis, videbatur cadere stella quaedam certo loco in quo certa res quaerebatur et tandem inveniebatur [semel ex his quidam dum essent turbulentissima tempora, tonitrua, fulgura, imbres, pronosticatus est fulmen fore de subito, et casurum in cacumen cuiusdam montis [atque ita fuit ut praedixerat [agebat homo octogesimum annum illiteratus et indoctus."

37 Modigliani, "Testamenti di Gaspare da Verona," 618.

38 Ibid.

39 James Hankins, *Plato in the Italian Renaissance*, 2 vols. (Leiden: Brill, 1990).

40 Marsilio Ficino, *Opera* (Basel: Froben, 1576), 1616: "Inter haec expedit admonere multas in codice Graeco clausulas videri transpositas verbaque saepius permutata, haec equidem diligenter pro viribus emendavi, vatis (ut ita dixerim) potius quam interpretis officio fretus." See Denis Robichaud, "Working with Plotinus: A Study of Marsilio Ficino's Textual and Divinatory Philology," in *Teachers, Students and Schools of Greek in the Renaissance*, ed. Frederica Ciccolella and Luigi Silvano (Leiden: Brill, 2017), 120–154, whose translation of this passage I have adapted.

41 Rocco Di Dio, "'*Selecta colligere*': Marsilio Ficino and Renaissance Reading Practices," *History of European Ideas* 42 (2016): 595–606.

42 H. D. Saffrey, "Florence, 1482: The Reappearance of Plotinus," *Renaissance Quarterly* 49 (1996): 488–508 at 506–08.

43 Jan Machielsen, *Martin Delrio: Demonology and Scholarship in the Counter-Reformation* (Oxford: Oxford University Press for the British Academy, 2013), sec. 2, chap. 7.

44 Cf. Ada Palmer, "Humanist Lives of Classical Philosophers and the Idea of Renaissance Secularization: Virtue, Rhetoric and the Orthodox Sources of Unbelief," *Renaissance Quarterly* 70, no. 3 (2017): 935–976.

45 Desiderius Erasmus, *Adagiorum chiliades* (Basel: Froben, 1536), Adage III. vi.40, 766: "Refertur a Suida tanquam vulgo iactatum de divinatione, quae sumitur ab insomniis, superstitio multo omnium vanissima. Id tamen ita dictum est, quod mors finis sit omnium huius vitae malorum."

46 Keith Thomas, *Religion and the Decline of Magic* (New York: Scribner, 1971), 213–217, on the sieve and shears.

47 Erasmus, *Adagiorum chiliades*, Adage I.x.8, 329: "Κοσκίνῳ μαντεύεσθαι, id est Cribro divinare, est coniectura sagaci rem deprehendere." Aut stulte de rebus occultis divinare. . . . Porro genus hoc divinandi suspenso cribro, in hodiernum usque tempus durat apud quosdam superstitiosos. Apud veteres vaticinia peragebantur, cribro, lauro et tripode."

48 Ibid., Adage IV.iv.75, 937: "Vapula papyria, Sisinius Capito scribit proverbio dici solitum. Si quando volebant significare se negligere minas aliquorum: hoc tantum reperimus in fragmentis Festi Pompeij. Suspicor esse natum a Papyrio praetextato, a quo mater comminando plagas, frustra conata est exscalpere, quid actum esset in Senatu. Proinde Papyri legendum, non papyria, nisi mavis subaudire lege, ut sit comminantis poenam legis papyriae. Aut si magis placeat, ut intelligas de Papyria, uxore Pauli Aemilii, quae repudiata est a marito, cum repudij causam nemo scire potuerit. Quid enim facias? Divinandum est, ubi non succurrunt autores."

49 Ibid., Adage I.v.4, 160–161: "Extat apud Terentium in Phormione cum primis venustum adagium: Ita fugias ne praeter casam. Quo quidem admonemur, ne sic aliquod vitium fugiamus, ut in aliud maius incauti devolvamur. Nostrapte culpa facimus, inquit, ut malos expediat esse, dum dici nimium nos bonos studemus et benignos. Ita fugias, ne praeter casam, ut aiunt. Verba sunt Demiphonis senis semet accusantis, quod dum avari famam plus satis cupide studeret effugere, stulti reprehensionem incurrisset." See Terence, *Phormio*, line 768.

50 Erasmus, *Adagiorum chiliades*, 161: "Donatus adagio metaphoram hunc ad modum enarrat, si modo commentum hoc Donati videtur esse. Ita fugito, ne tuam casam praetermittas, quae sit tibi tutissimum exceptaculum. Aut ita fugias, ne praeter casam, ubi custodiri magis et prehendi fur et mulctari verberibus potest. Aut verbum erat, inquit, furem exagitantis, et interea providentis, ne ante casam transeat, ne in pretereundo etiam inde aliquid rapiat." The passage Erasmus quotes comes from *Aeli Donati quod fertur Commentum Terenti*, ed. Paul Wessner, 2 vols. (Leipzig: Teubner, 1902–1905), 2:473. The translation is from Martin Luther and Desiderio Erasmus, *Free Will and Salvation*, ed. E. Gordon Rupp and Philip Watson (Philadelphia: Westminster, 1969), 436.

51 Erasmus, *Adagiorum chiliades, Adagia*, 161: "Hanc veluti divinationem, incerta ac varia coniectantium quis ferret, nisi videremus et iuris interpretibus et Graecorum adagiorum enarratoribus hunc eundem esse morem. Primum interpretamentum mihi magis arridet. Quidam enim calore fugiendi, etiam ea praetercurrunt, ubi commode poterant quiescere." Translation from Luther and Erasmus, *Free Will and Salvation*, 436.

52 Jerome, *Contra Rufinum* 1.16. On the significance of this passage, see Anthony Grafton, "On the Scholarship of Politian and Its Context," *Journal of the Warburg and Courtauld Institutes* 40 (1977): 150–188, at 187–188.

53 Desiderius Erasmus, *Opera*, ed. Jean Leclerc, 10 vols. (Leiden: van der Aa, 1703–1706), IX, col. 139; *Opera omnia* (Amsterdam: North-Holland, 1969–), Ordo 9, IV, 101.

54 *L. Annaei Senecae Opera, et ad dicendi facultatem et ad bene vivendum utilissima, per Des. Erasmum Roterodamum ex fide veterum codicum, tum ex probatis auctoribus, postremo sagaci nonnunquam divinatione, sic emendata, ut merito priorem aeditionem, ipso absente peractam, nolit haberi pro sua. Confer et ita rem habere comperies* (Basel: Froben, 1529). On Erasmus's editions of Seneca, see Winfried Trillitzsch, *Seneca im literarischen Urteil der Antike: Darstellung und Sammlung der Zeugnisse*, 2 vols. (Amsterdam: Hakkert, 1971); Lisa Jardine, *Erasmus, Man of Letters: The Construction of Charisma in Print* (Princeton: Princeton University Press, 1993; repr., 2015); and L. D. Reynolds, "Beatus Rhenanus and Seneca, *De beneficiis* and *De Constantia*," in *Beatus Rhenanus (1485–1547): Lecteur et éditeur de textes classiques*, ed. François Heim and James Hirstein (Turnhout: Brepols, 2000), 101–115.

55 Jerome, *Epistolae* 107.1: "Iam candidatus est fidei, quem filiorum & nepotum credens turba circundat. Ego puto etiam ipsum Iouem si habuisset talem cognationem: potuisse in Christum credere."

56 *Omnium operum Divi Eusebii Hieronymi Stridonensis tomus primus [-nomus]*, ed. Desiderius Erasmus et al., 9 vols. (Basel: Froben, 1516), I, fol. 24ʳ: "Etiam ipsum Iouem. Non uidetur hic locus uacare mendo. Quorsum enim huc induceret Iouem? Verum diuinare possum, quid scribendum sit. Fortasse pro Iove legendum est proauum."

57 Erasmus to Gregor Reisch, September 1514, in *Opus epistolarum Desiderii Erasmi Roterodami*, ed. P. S. Allen et al., 12 vols. (Oxford: Clarendon Press, 1906–1958), 2:29: "Multa divinavimus, omnia non possumus." On the development and context of Erasmus's edition of the letters, see Eugene F. Rice Jr., *Saint Jerome in the Renaissance* (Baltimore: Johns Hopkins University Press, 1985), esp. 129–132; Ueli Dill, "Prolegomena zu einer Edition von Erasmus von Rotterdam, *Scholia in epistolas Hieronymi*," 2 vols. (PhD dissertation, University of Basel, 1997), published online, 2004, at https://edoc.unibas.ch/37684/1/Dill_Prolegomena_2004.pdf; Jardine, *Erasmus, Man of Letters*, 55–82; Mark Vessey, "Erasmus's Jerome: the Publishing of a Christian Author," *Erasmus of Roterdam Society Yearbook* 14 (1994): 62–99; Hilmar Pabel, *Herculean Labours: Erasmus and the Editing of St. Jerome's Letters in the Renaissance* (Leiden and Boston: Brill, 2008), chap. 3; Nicholas Naquin, "'On the Shoulders of Hercules': Erasmus, The Froben Press and the 1516 Jerome Edition in Context" (PhD dissertation, Princeton University, 2013), 1–174.

58 Erasmus, *Opus epistolarum*, 2:29: "In epistola ad Letham offendit locus, *Quibus corax, niphus, miles.*"

59 Jerome, *Opera*, 1516, I, fol. 24ʳ: "Verum hic locus ita depravatus est, ut ad restituendum, Delio quopiam sit opus. Nos tamen quantum assequi coniectura potuimus indicabimus. Corax.) Populus est inter Callipolim & Naupactum."

60 Erasmus, *Opus epistolarum*, II, 29: "Rursum in eadem, *Cibus eius olusculum sit et simila, caroque et pisciculi*, divino legi debere, *Cibus eius olusculum <sit> et e simila garoque pisciculi.*"

61 Jerome, *Opera*, 1516, I, fol. 25ʳ: "Cibus eius oluscu.) Satis constat hunc locum esse corruptum. Sic enim habebatur in plaerisque, Cibus eius olusculum sit & simila, caroque et pisciculi. Porro cum Hieronymus hic luxum dedocere conetur: si permittat carnem & pisciculos, quaeso quid omisit praeter placentas? Equidem conijcio legendum, Cibus eius olusculum sit, & e simila, garoque pisciculi: ut intelligas permitti olera, & pisciculos, sed non quoslibet, nec opipare conditos, sed minutos, ac uiles, eosque conditos garo & simila."

62 Ibid., sig. α3ʳ: "Quod superest, non depravatum erat, sed prorsus extinctum et oblitteratum: idque partim quidem illitteratorum vitio scribarum."

63 Ibid., sig. α3ᵛ: "Atqui super haec longe difficillimum est, aut ex varie depravatis, quid ab authore positum fuerit conijcere: aut ex qualibuscunque figurarum fragmentis ac vestigijs, primam divinare lectionem."

64 Bruno and Basil Amerbach, in their preface to the edition, also praised Erasmus's "in divinando cum res postulat, mira quadem sollertia." *Die Amerbachkorrespondenz*, ed. Alfred Hartmann (Basel: Universitätsbibliothek, 1942–), 2:65.

65 Erasmus's comment on the 1524–1525 edition appears in *Opus epistolarum*, 5:493: "Restant tamen adhuc loca, sed ea perpauca, in quibus mea divinatio non omnino satisfecit animo meo."

66 A. E. Housman, "The Application of Thought to Textual Criticism," in *The Classical Papers of A. E. Housman*, ed. J. Diggle and F. R. D. Goodyear, 3 vols. (Cambridge: Cambridge University Press, 1972), 3:1058–1069, at 1065.

67 Francesco Robortello, "De arte sive ratione corrigendi antiquorum libros," in Gaspar Schoppe, *De arte critica* (Amsterdam: Ploymer, 1662), 98–121; see esp. 104–119, on conjectural emendation, and see the praise of Poliziano, Valeriano, and Vettori at 119.

68 Klara Vanek, *Ars corrigendi in der frühen Neuzeit: Studien zur Geschichte der Textkritik* (Berlin: De Gruyter, 2007).

69 Aelius Lampridius, *Commodus Antoninus* 1.7–8: "Nam a prima statim pueritia turpis, improbus, crudelis, libidinosus, ore quoque pollutus et constupratus fuit, iam in his artifex, quae stationis imperatoriae non erant, ut calices fingeret, saltaret, cantaret, sibilaret, scurram denique et gladiatorem perfectum ostenderet." Translation from David Magie, tr., *Historia Augusta*, 3 vols. (Cambridge, MA: Harvard University Press, 2014), 1:264–267.

70 *Historiae Augustae scriptores VI*, 2 vols. (Leiden: Hack, 1671), 1:473: "Ut calices fingeret.) Lego, frangeret. De hoc genere παιδίας dictum aliquid ad Verum Imper. [*SHA Verus* 4.1.7] Est & calices fingere vinearii artificis potius quam ejus qui in imperatoria statione sit collocatus: sed eam lectionem refellunt sequentia."

71 Ibid.: "Sic [*ut calices fingeret*] quoque uterque Palatinus, & nescio quomodo placeat magis, quam divinatio aliorum *calices frangeret*, quam ipsam tamen non exsibilo, Vulgatam stabilit regum aliorum exemplum, qui aerariae artis fabricae se tradidere."

72 Joseph Scaliger, *Epistolae omnes quae reperiri potuerunt*, ed. Daniel Heinsius (Leiden: Elzevir, 1627), 60: "Dii boni. Plane me divinare et hariolari dixit quidam alius inter proceres rei literariae apud Italos primi nominis."

73 Polydore Vergil, *Adagiorum liber: Eiusdem de inventoribus rerum libri octo*, 2 vols. (Basel: Froben, 1521), V.6, II, fol. 56ʳ: "Post evangelicum dogma inter gentes publicatum, ubi loci prima aedes servatori nostro dicata fuerit pro certo ponere non ausim, ne divinare potius quam veritati inhaerere dicar."

74 Ibid.: "Sed in re parum nota conjectare licet."

75 Ibid., fol. 56ʳ⁻ᵛ: "Est tamen consentaneum credere, in remotis locis quo non facile pervaserat ille tyrannorum furor, phana aliqua interim aut aedificata, aut quae primum daemonum fuerant, Christo dicata ab Apostolis fuisse, qui ubique gentium ubique temporum propagandae fidei totis viribus incumbebant. Quod aut in Aethiopia a Matthaeo, aut in India citeriore a Bartholomaeo, aut in Scythia ab Andrea: quorum praedicatione his gentibus Christianae pietatis lux ab initio affulsit factum esse & crediderim & dixerim. Non abhorret praeterea a fide aliqua cellam fuisse primitus a Iacobo Hierosolymis deo dicatam, qui inibi cathedram primus locavit primusque rem divinam ritu apostolico facere coepit. Autor Eusebius." On Vergil as a historian of Christiuanity see Helmut Zedelmaier, "Karriere eines Buches. Polydorus Vergilius *De inventoribus rerum*," in *Sammeln—Ordnen—*

Veranschaulichen. Wissenskompilatorik in der Frühen Neuzeit, ed. Frank Büttner, Markus Friedrich, and Helmut Zedelmaier (Münster: LIT, 2003), 175–203; Catherine Atkinson, *Inventing Inventors in Renaissance Europe: Polydore Vergil's De inventoribus rerum* (Tübingen: Niemeyer, 2007).

76 *Carmina vetusta ante trecentos annos scripta, quae deplorant inscitiam Evangelii et taxant abusus ceremoniarum, ac quae ostendunt doctrinam huius temporis non esse novam. Fulsit enim semper et fulgebit in aliquibus vera Ecclesiae doctrina,* ed. Matthias Flacius Illyricus (Wittenberg: Rhaw, 1548), sig. A2^{r-v}: "Cantilenae hae Christiane Lector sunt (ut divinare ex minime obscuris signis licet) non minus quam ante trecentos annos compositae. Nam primum et Codex, ex quo eas depromimus, eam vetustatem prae se fert, ut videatur ante annos ducentos vel amplius scriptus. Postea sunt in eo non pauca parum emendate scripta, ut appareat, eum porro ex aliis vetustioribus codicibus transcriptum esse. Postremo et Musica, ad quam canuntur hae cantilenae, locupletissimum testimonium vetustatis praebere potest. Nam ea ante annos trecentos in usu fuit, iam vero a nemine intelligitur, quam ob hoc ipsum quod exoluit omisimus, quanquam et ipsum genus scripti non vulgarem vetustatem prae se ferat. Quis autem eas composuerit ignoramus, quandoquidem nomen adscriptum non est. Quicunque tamen composuerit, dubium non est, fuisse eum Christianum ac vere pium." On Flacius's medieval scholarship, see M. Hartmann, *Humanismus und Kirchenkritik. Flacius Illyricus als Erforscher des Mittelalters* (Stuttgart: Thorbecke, 2001).

77 BN Paris, MS lat 4855, fol. 82^r: "Diximus de imperii Ro. incrementis et omnes illius fere provincias sic recensuimus ut quo tempore quaequae subacta fuerit, per quos, quibusque de caussis bella excitata, quo denique tempore in formulam provinciae fuerit redacta notaremus. Nunc contrarium aggredimur, et demolitionem eius aedificii considerare paramus. Prius autem quam τὸ ὅτι pluribus explicem, quod nemini dubium est, τὸ διότι paucis considerabimus, et caussas eversi tanti imperii quaeremus."

78 Ibid., fol. 82^{r-v}: "Non enim tantum ἡ φύσις μάτην οὐ ποιεῖ οὐδὲν, sed etiam ἐν τοῖς πρακτοῖς nihil accidit cuius causae non praecesserint, sed quae saepe homines latent . . . [Casaubon's ellipsis] Nam eventus rerum fere sunt contra τὸ δοκοῦν πᾶσι. Vt Synesius ait p. 83. Inde est invectum in opinionem plerorumque illud volvi res humanas forte quae etiam Rota fortune quam appellant, de qua Marcellinus p. 1728 et 1833. Sed et illa, atque adeo fortuna omnis, opinione sola hominum constat οὕτως οὐδέν ἐστι. Neque propterea minus sunt certae rerum caussae quia illae sunt nobis saepe incognitae. Quare quaeramus tantae rei caussas veras."

79 Ibid., fol. 82^r: "Hic est illa virorum prudentium divinatio cuius passim auctores meminere. Qui ipsi φρόνησις est quaedam προνόησις et prudentiae providentia."

80 Ibid., fol. 84^v: "De luxu illorum temporum et fastu annotandi omnes loci Marcellini Synesij Basil. Etc."

81 See Isaac Casaubon, *Polibio,* ed. Guerrino Brussich (Palermo: Sellerio, 1991); and George Nadel, "Philosophy of History before Historicism," *History and Theory* 3 (1964): 291–315.

82 E. J. Kenney, *The Classical Text: Aspects of Editing in the Age of the Printed Book* (Berkeley: University of California Press, 1974), 147.

83 Carlo Ginzburg, "Morelli, Freud and Sherlock Holmes: Clues and Scientific Method," *History Workshop* 9 (1980): 5–36, esp. 14–16; Michael Fishbane, *Biblical Interpretation in Ancient Israel* (Oxford: Clarendon Press, 1989), p. 464: "Sometimes these [Mesopotamian prophecies] are merely playful *jeux de mots;* but, just as commonly, there is a concern to guard esoteric knowledge. Among the techniques used are permutations of syllabic arrangements with obscure and symbolic puns, secret and obscure readings of signs, and numerological ciphers. The continuity and similarity of these cuneiform cryptographic techniques with similar procedures in biblical sources once again emphasizes the variegated and well-established tradition of mantological exegesis in the ancient Near East—a tradition which found ancient Israel a productive and innovative tradent [i.e., transmitter of the received tradition]."

84 Kari Kraus, "Conjectural Criticism: Computing Past and Future Texts," *Digital Humanities Quarterly* 3 (2009) (http://digitalhumanities.org/dhq/vol/3/4/000069/000069.html). Kraus continues: "The pleasure George Ian Duthie, a postwar editor of Shakespeare, shows in permutating variants—juxtaposing and repeating them, taking a punster's delight in the homophony of stockt, struckt, and struck; hare and hart; nough and nought—finds its poetic complement in the metaplasmic imagination of Tom O'Bedlam in *King Lear* or the soothsayer Philarmonus in *Cymbeline.*"

85 2.54.3, trans. Thomas Hobbes.

86 Ginzburg, "Morelli, Freud and Sherlock Holmes," 16.

87 Robortello, "De arte sive ratione corrigendi antiquorum libros," 119: "Quanta fides, dii immortales, in Politiano! Cuivis intueri licet adhuc Florentiae, in Medicea et Marciana bibliotheca, manuscriptos libros, ubi publice asservantur, quibus usus est. Eadem fides in sanctissimo illo ac doctissimo sene, qui Vergilium ex Romano codice emendavit, Jo. Pierio Valeriano, viro dignissimo qui ab omnibus ametur et colatur. Nec secus egit Petrus Victorius meus. Qui ex hac emendandi professione non tam doctrinae magnae, quam magnae bonitatis et fidei laudem quaesivit. Quibus sit usus libris: ubi sint: Langobardicisne scripti an Romanis literis, semper patefecit."

88 Grafton, *Scaliger,* vol. 1, chap. 7.

89 See the wonderful case study by Reynolds, "Beatus Rhenanus and Seneca, *De beneficiis* and *De Constantia.*"

90 Samuel Johnson, "Preface," in *Johnson on Shakespeare,* ed. Arthur Sherbo, 2 vols. (New Haven: Yale University Press, 1968), 1:59–113, at 101, 104–105.

CHAPTER 3 · JEAN MABILLON INVENTS PALEOGRAPHY

My thanks to John Bidwell, Ann Blair, Lucio Del Corso, Christian Flow, Madeline McMahon, and Eleonora Pistis for information and criticism.

1 For a digital version, see http://digi.vatlib.it/view/MSS_Vat.lat.3225, accessed March 26, 2017.

2 Ingo Herklotz, "Late Antique Manuscripts in Early Modern Study: Critics, Antiquaries and the History of Art," in Amanda Claridge and Ingo Herklotz, *Classical Manuscript Illustrations*, The Paper Museum of Cassiano dal Pozzo. Series A—Antiquities and Architecture. Part Six (London: The Royal Collection and Harvey Miller, 2012), 60, quoting Biblioteca Apostolica Vaticana MS Ottob. Lat. 3059, 382 recto. This text is printed in *Antiquissimi codicis Virgiliani fragmenta* (Rome: R.C.A., 1741), iv.

3 Roberto Ribuoli, *La collazione polizianea del Codice Bembino di Terenzio* (Rome: Storia e Letteratura, 1981); John Grant, "Pietro Bembo and Vat. lat. 3226," *Humanistica Lovaniensia* 37 (1988): 211–243; Gareth Williams, *Pietro Bembo on Etna: The Ascent of a Venetian Humanist* (Oxford: Oxford University Press, 2017), 126.

4 On the richly empirical (or at least historical) character of Mabillon's method see Blandine Kriegel, *La querelle Mabillon-Rancé* (Paris: P.U.F., 1988; repr. Paris: Quai Voltaire, 1992), 79–95.

5 Jean Mabillon, *De re diplomatica libri vi, in quibus quidquid ad veterum instrumentorum antiquitatem, materiam, scripturam, et stilum, quidquid ad sigilla, monogrammata, subscriptiones, ac notas chronologicas; quidquid inde ad antiquariam, historicam, forensemque disciplinam pertinet, explicatur et illustratur* (Paris: Billaine, 1681), 1: "Novum antiquariae artis genus aggredior, in qua de veterum instrumentorum ratione, formulis et auctoritate agitur. Praecipuam eius fidem, si modo vera et genuina fuerint, tribuendam esse censent omnes, maxime quantum ad rei transactae circumstantias et ad res chronologicas attinet, quae nullo aliunde certiori testimonio, quam ejusmodi monumentis resciri et confirmari possunt."

6 Daniel van Papenbroeck, "Propylaeum antiquarium circa veri ac falsi discrimen in vetustis menbranis," in *Acta Sanctorum Aprilis*, 3 vols. (Antwerp: Cnobbaert, 1675). The fullest account of this story are now Jan Marco Sawilla, *Antiquarianismus, Hagiographie und Historie im 17. Jahrhundert: zum Werk der Bollandisten. Ein historiographischer Versuch* (Tübingen: Niemeyer, 2009), and Maciej Dorna, *Mabillon und andere: Die Anfänge der Diplomatik*, tr. Martin Faber, Wolfenbütteler Forschungen, 159 (Wiesbaden: Harrassowitz, 2019), 107–121. On the institution in which Mabillon spent so much of his working life, see Maarten Ultee, *The Abbey of St. Germain des Prés in the Seventeenth Century* (New Haven: Yale University Press, 1981).

7 For recent surveys of Mabillon's book and for bibliography about it see Jakob Zouhar, "'De re diplomatica libri sex' by Jean Mabillon in Outline," *Listy filologické / Folia philologica* 133, 3–4 (2010): 357–388; Dorna, *Mabillon und andere*, 128–142.

8 On Mabillon's work in diplomatics and its context the fullest treatment is Dorna, *Mabillon und andere*.

9 Alfred Hiatt, "Diplomatic Arts: Hickes against Mabillon in the Republic of Letters," *Journal of the History of Ideas* 70, no. 3 (2009), 351–373, at 358.

10 Both Hiatt, "Diplomatic Arts," and Sawilla, *Antiquarianismus, Hagiographie und Historie im 17. Jahrhundert*, make this point.

11 L. D. Reynolds and N. G. Wilson, *Scribes and Scholars: A Guide to the Transmission of Greek and Latin Literature,* 4th ed. (Oxford: Oxford University Press, 2013), 192–193.

12 Papenbroeck to Mabillon, July 10, 1683, quoted in Richard Rosenmund, *Die Fortschritte der Diplomatik seit Mabillon, vornehmlich in Deutschland-Österreich* (Munich and Leipzig: Oldenbourg, 1897), 17–18.

13 Bodleian Library OUA SEP / Y / 1. For text and discussion, see *The Cartulary of the Monastery of Saint Frideswide at Oxford,* ed. Spencer Robert Wigram, 2 vols. (Oxford: Oxford Historical Society and Clarendon Press, 1895), 1:44–45; H. E. Salter, *Mediaeval Archives of the University of Oxford,* 2 vols. (Oxford: Oxford Historical Society, 1917), 1:1–2.

14 Bodleian Library MS Twyne 3, 139. See Strickland Gibson, "Brian Twyne," *Oxoniensia* 5 (1940): 94–114, at 99.

15 Bodleian Library MS Twyne 3, 139.

16 Ibid., 140, 139.

17 *Orbis eruditi literaturam a charactere Samaritico hunc in modum favente Deo deduxit Eduardus Bernardus A.D. 1689* (Oxford, 1689; repr., 1700; repr. and expanded, 1759).

18 See the classic survey by Arno Borst, *Der Turmbau von Babel,* 4 vols. in 6 (Stuttgart: Hiersemann, 1957–1963).

19 In addition to a basic Latin alphabet, Bernard offers additional alphabets for AD 306, AD 400, and AD 500.

20 British Library MS Harley 6030, fols. 15^r-18^r, quotation from fol. 17^r, where he goes on to summarize Agrippa's treatment of the oldest alphabets (after August 6, 1687).

21 BL MS Harley 7505, fol. 1^v.

22 BL Harley MS 6466, fol. 87^r (January 17, 1696 / 1697).

23 See the classic treatment by Simon Keynes, "The Reconstruction of a Burnt Cottonian Manuscript: The Case of Cotton MS Otho A.1," *British Library Journal* 22, no. 2 (1996): 113–160. The progress of what Edmund Gibson described as Wanley's "Res Diplomatica, for England particularly" can be traced in *Letters of Humfrey Wanley: Palaeographer, Anglo-Saxonist, Librarian, 1672–1726,* ed. P. L. Heyworth (Oxford: Clarendon Press, 1989) (Gibson is quoted at xviii.11); and *A Chorus of Grammars,* ed. Richard Harris (Toronto: Pontifical Institute of Mediaeval Studies, 1992). He cites Mabillon in *Letters,* 63–64, 66, 68, 126–127, 158, 188, and 223, and describes himself, not quite sincerely, in a letter to Bernard de Montfaucon, as Mabillon's and Montfaucon's "aemulatorem" (427).

24 *Letters of Humfrey Wanley,* 15 (to Sir Thomas Smith, April 19, 1695).

25 Ibid., 68 (to Arthur Charlett, August 11, 1697).

26 Kenneth Sisam, *Studies in the History of Old English Literature* (Oxford: Clarendon Press, 1953; repr. with corrections, 1962), 263. On the growth of systematic collections of original materials and reference books, created to teach diplomatics and paleography, see Mark Mersiowsky, "Barocker Sammlerstolz, Raritätenkabinette, Strandgut der Säkularisation oder Multimedia der Aufklärung? Diplomatisch-paläographische Apparate im 18. und frühen 19. Jahrhundert," in *Arbeiten aus dem Marburger hilfswissen-*

schaftlichen Institut, ed. Erika Eisenlohr and Peter Worm (Marburg an der Lahn: Universitätsbibliothek Marburg, 2000), 229–241.

27 Carmela Vircillo Franklin, "Reading the Popes: The *Liber Pontificalis* and Its Editors," *Speculum* 92, no. 3 (2017), 607–629, at 620–624.

28 Ibid.; see also *Anastasii Bibliothecarii De vitis Romanorum pontificum,* ed. Francesco Bianchini, 4 vols. (Rome: Salvioni, 1718–1735), 2:xxii.

29 Silvia Rizzo, *Il lessico filologico degli umanisti* (Rome: Storia e Letteratura, 1973).

30 Annius of Viterbo, "De marmoreis volturrhenis tabulis," edited in Roberto Weiss, "An Unknown Epigraphic Tract by Annius of Viterbo," in *Italian Studies Presented to E. R. Vincent,* ed. Charles P. Brand, Kenelm Foster and Uberto Limentani (Cambridge: Heffer, 1962), 101–120, at 113: "literis longobardis excisa vetustissimis et ferme corrosis."

31 Daniele Rando, *Dai margini la memoria: Johannes Hinderbach (1418–1486)* (Bologna: Il Mulino, 2003), e.g., 376n.354. See also Mariano Weber, "Iohannes Hinderbach rerum vetustarum studiosus: Vita e cultura del vescovo di Trento Giovanni IV Hinderbach (1418–86)" (PhD Dissertation, Università Cattolica del Sacro Cuore, 1969–70), 295–296, and cf. 125–126, 178–179, 208, 209, 259, 280–281.

32 Anthony Grafton, *Joseph Scaliger: A Study in the History of Classical Scholarship,* 2 vols. (Oxford: Clarendon Press, 1983–1993), 1:66.

33 Ibid., chaps. 4, 6.

34 See Asaph Ben-Tov, "*Turco-Graecia.* German Humanists and the End of Greek Antiquity," in *The Renaissance and the Ottoman World,* ed. Anna Contadini and Claire Norton (London: Routledge, 2013), 181–195.

35 Martin Crusius, *Turcograeciae libri octo* (Basel: Henricpetri, [1584]), e.g., 191, 230. See Richard Calis, "Reconstructing the Ottoman Greek World: Early Modern Ethnography in the Household of Martin Crusius," *Renaissance Quarterly* 72 (2019): 148–193.

36 Bernardo José de Aldrete, *Del origen y principio de la lengua castellan o românce que oi si usa en España* (Rome: Carlo Willietto, 1606), 252–253.

37 Mabillon, *De re diplomatica,* plate XLV, 434–435, and esp. 432: "Cur tam diu ejusmodi thesauros in scrinijs suis residere patiuntur Hispani, dum quidam ex illis, male feriati, adulterinis chronicis orbem literarium ad suum dedecus infarciunt?" For Higuera and his forgeries, see Katrina Olds, *Forging the Past: Invented Histories in Counter-Reformation Spain* (New Haven: Yale University Press, 2015).

38 On Agustín, see *Antonio Agustín between Renaissance and Counter-Reformation,* ed. Michael Crawford (London: Warburg Institute, 1993); and William Stenhouse, *Reading Inscriptions and Writing Ancient History: Historical Scholarship in the Late Renaissance* (London: Institute of Classical Studies, 2005).

39 Juan Baptista Cardona, *De regia S. Laurentii bibliotheca. De pontificia Vaticana. De expungendis haereticor. propriis nominibus. De diptychis* (Tarragona: Mey, 1587), 5–6: "Ad codicum autem quod attinet vetustatem certius deprehendendam ratio haec poterit iniri: mandabitur provincia studioso cuipiam et antiquario, qui assidua membranarum, codicum, lapidum, et

nummorum veterum lectione et inspectione notatas habeat varias litterarum formas, pro temporum varietate, et usu earum dissimili: quique possit aetatem coniicere prudenter. is librum conficiet ejusmodi characterum in aetates distinctum diligenter, et cuique aetati suos tribuet characteres: ut horum comparatione facta facilius in bibliotheca de cuiusque codicis aetate certius possit iudicari. sed et significationes litterarum et singularum et complexarum eo in libro adscribentur: item notae ponderum et numerorum. Idque non Latine modo, verum etiam Graece, proque aliarum linguarum varietate. Qui etiam labor magnum afferet adiumentum legendis veter. monumentis. Quamquam hanc certe provinciam non uni, sed pluribus mandari velim." For the context and the original Spanish version of this plan, see Charles Graux, *Essai sur les origines du fonds grec de l'Escurial*, Bibliothèque de l'École des Hautes Études, 46 (Paris: Vieweg, 1880), 313–314.

40 See T. D. Kendrick, *St. James in Spain* (London: Methuen, 1960); J. Caro Baroja, *Las falsificaciones de la historia (en relación con la de España)* (Barcelona: Seix Barral, 1992); A. Katie Harris, "Forging History: the *Plomos* of Granada in Francisco Bermúdez de Pedraza's *Historia eclesiástica*," *Sixteenth Century Journal* 30, 4 (1999): 945–966; Harris, *From Muslim to Christian Granada: Inventing a City's Past in Early Modern Spain* (Baltimore: Johns Hopkins University Press, 2007); L. P. Harvey, *Muslims in Spain, 1500 to 1614* (Chicago: University of Chicago Press, 2005); Mercedes García-Arenal and Fernando Rodríguez Mediano, *The Orient in Spain: The Forged Lead Books of Granada and the Rise of Orientalism* (Leiden: Brill, 2013); and Olds, *Forging the Past.*

41 Gerold Meyer von Knonau, "Das *bellum diplomaticum lindaviense*," *Historische Zeitschrift* 26 (1871): 75–130; "Nachtrag zu Bd. XXVI S. 75–130: Das *bellum diplomaticum lindaviense*," ibid., 27 (1872): 208–210; Dorna, *Mabillon und andere*, 55–88. Dorna offers a very informative survey of ways in which charters were analyzed before Mabillon (ibid., 17–102).

42 Claude Saumaise to Claude Sarrau, October 15, 1648, in Claude Sarrau, *Epistolae* (Orange: n.p., 1654): 235–239, at 238: "Si quibus in libris MSS. diphthongus reperiatur Æ duabus literis non in unum coalitis sed separatis, expressa ad hunc modum A E, aut *a e*, scias codices illos & vetustos esse inprimis & fideli manu confectos. Si aliter efficta occurrat, aut per unam literam ex duabus conflatam, aut per unicum E, cui nota supposita sit hoc modo [cedillated *e*], qui primo modo scripti sunt, paulo maiorem vetustatem redolent: qui secundo ad infimum saeculum relegari debent."

43 Hermann Conring, *Censura diplomatis quod Ludovico Imperatori fert acceptum Coenobium Lindaviense* (Helmstedt: Muller, 1672), 317. Though Mabillon agreed with Conring, Meyer von Knonau condemns this argument (104 and n. 2).

44 See, e.g., Hans Erich Troje, *"Crisis Digestorum": Studien zur Historia pandectarum* (Frankfurt: Klostermann, 2011); Douglas Osler, "Humanist Philology and the Text of Justinian's Digest," in *Reassessing Legal Humanism and its Claims. Petere Fontes?*, ed. Paul de Plessis and John Cairns (Edinburgh: Edinburgh University Press, 2016), 41–51.

45 Mabillon, *De re diplomatica*, 356–367 and plate VII.3.

46 Dorna, *Mabillon und andere*, 128–129.

47 Emery Bigot to Nicolaas Heinsius, July 20, 1679, printed in Leonard Doucette, *Emery Bigot: Seventeenth-Century French Humanist* (Toronto and Buffalo, NY: University of Toronto Press, 1970), 94: "Le Pere Mabillon a dessein de faire imprimer en bref un livre pour faire connoistre toutes les anciennes écritures. Pour cet effet il a desja fait graver le commencement de plusieurs chartes de la premiere et seconde race de nos Rois. Il cherche presentement de tres anciens mss. ou soit marqué le temps que le mss. soit ecrit. Je luy ai indiqué le Virgile de Florence dans lequel il y a une epigramme qui designe le nom du consul qui estoit pour lors que ce Virgile fust ecrit. Si vous vou-liés m'ecrire ce que vous en avés autrefois remarqué, il le fairoit imprimer. Je luy ai indiqué de plus les Pandectes Florentines, qu'Antonius Augustinus croit estre escrites au temps de Justinian (je scai que Cujas et quelques au-tres en doutent, mais ils ne les avoient pas veues. Par l'inspection du carac-tere on en pourra porter son jugement)."

48 Curzio Inghirami, *Ethruscarum antiquitatum fragmenta* (Frankfurt: n.p., 1637).

49 Amos Funkenstein, *Perceptions of Jewish History* (Los Angeles: University of Chicago Press, 1993).

50 Ingrid Rowland, *The Scarith of Scornello: A Tale of Renaissance Forgery* (Chicago and London: University of Chicago Press, 2004); Luc Deitz, "Die Scarith von Scornello: Fälschung und Methode in Curzio Inghiramis 'Etrus-carum antiquitatum fragmenta' (1637)," *Neulateinisches Jahrbuch* 5 (2003): 103–133.

51 Leone Allacci, *Animadversiones in antiquitatum Etruscarum fragmenta ab Inghiramio edita* (Paris: Cramoisy, 1640), 51–60. He, in turn, relies on such evidence as a short and imprecise passage in Michael Thomasius's edition of the *Divinae institutiones* of Lactantius (Antwerp: Plantin, 1570), sig. A5^r: "Multis ab hinc annis, cum Bononiae iuri Pontificio ac civili operam darem, neque tamen aliarum rerum bonos scriptores, praesertim ecclesiasticos, negligerem; in bibliotheca Sancti Salvatoris vidi exemplar quoddam Lac-tantii literis maiusculis scriptum, quod, ut ex vetustate et literis ipsis ap-parebat, fuerat ante octingenos, aut etiam mille, annos exaratum. Illarum enim literarum, quas maiusculas vocamus, libri, sicut ex collatione mul-torum codicum comperimus, ante Gothorum in Italiam irruptione fuerunt scripti." He cites the expert testimony of Poliziano and Agustín and that of later compilers with apparently equal enthusiasm.

52 Allacci, *Animadversiones*, 57–59, esp. 58: "*Rotunda* autem erat . . . quae ob artis contemptum & celeriorem scriptionem, quasi in globulos, sed non eos perfectos, curvabatur"; Mabillon, *De re diplomatica*, 47: "Hinc minutae lit-erae apud veteres dictae, immo (ut quibusdam placet) *minutissimae & ro-tundae*, quae scilicet ob celeriorem scriptionem non tanta arte, nec tanta mole conformatae erant."

53 For examples of the new way in which scholars now discussed scripts, see *Correspondance inédite de Mabillon et de Montfaucon avec l'Italie*, ed. M. Valery, 3 vols. (Paris: Labitte, 1846), 2:24–25, 3:162–164.

54 The fullest study—and a sharp critique—of Mabillon's plates appears in Ludwig Traube, "Geschichte der Paläographie," in Traube, *Vorlesungen und Abhandlungen,* ed. Franz Boll, 3 vols. (Munich: Beck, 1909–1920), 1:27–30.

55 Francis Haskell, *History and Its Images: Art and the Interpretation of the Past* (New Haven: Yale University Press, 1993).

56 Simon Ditchfield, "Text before Trowel: Antonio Bosio's *Roma Sotterranea* Revisited," *Studies in Church History* 33 (1997): 343–360.

57 Biblioteca Apostolica Vaticana MS Vat. lat. 3750, fol. 2^{r-v}: "*De fundatore Basilicae sancti Petri Constantino Imperatore, & de modo et ratione scribendae historiae, et de admirabili visione sancte crucis, qua ad fidem Christi Constantinus ipse uocatus est.* Quam talem merito ac tantam sciendum est primum a Constantino Imperatore extructam fuisse: quod & si apud omnes iam percelebre sit, manifeste tamen id etiam demonstrat versus in arcu ipsius maiore ac triumphali scripti huiuscemodi:

Quod duce te mundus surrexit in astra triumphans,
Hanc Constantinus uictor tibi condidit aulam.

Quorum characteres longe uetusti peneque dixerim decrepiti, nullum etiam aliud, quam Constantini tempus, quo ibi conscripti sunt, manifeste arguere uidentur." On this work, see Fabio Della Schiava, "'Sicut traditum est a maioribus': Maffeo Vegio antiquario tra fonti classiche e medievali," *Aevum* 84, no. 3 (2010): 617–639, and Christine Smith and Joseph O'Connor, *Eyewitness to Old St. Peter's: A Study of Maffeo Vegio's "Remembering the Ancient History of St. Peter's Basilica in Rome" with Translation and a Digital Reconstruction of the Church* (Cambridge: Cambridge University Press, 2019) (for the passage in question, see 127).

58 Antonio Agustín, *Emendationum et opinionum libri quattuor* (Venice: Giunta, 1543), iiii: "Sed cum antiquissimum illud iuris civilis monumentum sine ullis aut raris verborum atque membrorum spatijs scriptum sit, ipsaque litterarum figura Romanae Graecaeque veteri scripturae proxime accedere videatur, nisi quod quaedam a Gothis accepta, qui iam inde a Theodosianis temporibus Latinis Graecisque hominibus coniuncti fuerunt, agnoscere videbamur."

59 Grafton, *Scaliger,* vol. 1, chap. 5, and Damiano Acciarino, "The Renaissance Editions of Festus: Fulvio Orsini's Version," *Acta Classica* 59 (2016), 1–22, 3 and fig. 1.

60 Peter J. Lucas, "Parker, Lambarde and the Provision of Special Sorts for Printing Anglo-Saxon in the Sixteenth Century," *Journal of the Printing Historical Society* 28 (1999): 41–69.

61 Anthony Grafton, "Matthew Parker: The Book as Archive," *History of the Humanities* 2 (2017): 15–50, at 42–44.

62 Asser, *Alfredi regis res gestae* (London: Day, 1574). See Suzanne Hagedorn, "Matthew Parker and Asser's *Alfredi regis res gestae,*" *Princeton University Library Chronicle* 51, no. 1 (1989–1990): 74–90.

63 Like Parker, Mabillon was taken in by the early section of the Chronicle ascribed to Ingulf (d. 1109), a fourteenth-century forgery that described the transformation of English documents brought about by the conquest: "Apud

Anglosaxones vero Saxonica scriptura viguit usque ad Guillelmi Conquaestoris principatum, quo tempore factum est, *ut modus scribendi Anglicus omitteretur, & modus Gallicus in chartis & in libris omnimodis admitteretur,* testante Ingulfo in historia Croylandensi"; see Mabillon, *De re diplomatica,* 52. On Ingulf, see Alfred Hiatt, *The Making of Medieval Forgeries: False Documents in Fifteenth-Century England* (London: British Library, 2004).

64 Henry Spelman, *Archaismus graphicus,* Corpus Christi College Cambridge MS 238, fol. 1ʳ: "Archaismus Graphicus ab Henrico Spelmanno conscriptus in vsum filiorum suorum, An: Dn: 1606." For similar efforts by other British scholars, see Michael Hunter, *John Aubrey and the Realm of Learning* (London: Duckworth, 1975), 156–157; William Poole, *John Aubrey and the Advancement of Learning* (Oxford: Bodleian Library, 2010), 88–90; Kelsey Jackson Williams, *The Antiquary: John Aubrey's Historical Scholarship* (Oxford: Oxford University Press, 2016), 17, 84–85.

65 See the interesting debate between John Millard and Sir Henry Ellis in *Report from the Select Committee on the Condition, Management and Affairs of the British Museum, Together with the Minutes of Evidence, Appendix and Index* (London: House of Commons, 1835), 138, 141, 169, 172, 173.

66 BL MS Stowe 1059, fol. 2ʳ: "Notae de libris manuscriptis." My thanks go to Aaron Shapiro, who provided me with a transcript of these notes and much further information on the copies of Spelman's work.

67 Ibid.: "Libri, ut antiquiores, ita caeteris paribus, meliores esse affirmantur."

68 Ibid.: "Libri Uncialibus, seu Capitalibus ut vocant, Literis integre conscripti, optimae sunt notae & fidei. Aubertus Miraeus ad calcem Chronici Hieronymi in margine, edit. Antu. Aº 1608."

69 *Rerum toto orbe gestarum chronica,* ed. Aubert le Mire (Antwerp: Verdussius, 1608), sig. [H4ʳ]: "Est enim uncialibus seu capitalibus, ut vocant, litteris integre conscriptus: cuius generis libri mss. optimae sunt notae ac fidei."

70 See Ann Blair, *Too Much to Know: Managing Scholarly Information before the Modern Age* (New Haven: Yale University Press, 2010); and Helmut Zedelmaier, *Werkstätten des Wissens zwischen Renaissance und Aufklärung* (Tübingen: Mohr Siebeck, 2015).

71 Jean Mabillon, *De re diplomatica,* 2d ed., 2 vols. (Naples: Orsini, 1789), 2:6: "Oculis tantum hic opus est. Sed oculos volo peritos, minime malignos, nullo affectos praejudicio, quales fuere eorum virorum, eruditione & auctoritate praestantium, quorum oculis ac censurae haec instrumenta ante annos viginti exposuimus."

72 Ibid., 2: "Inest veris et genuinis instrumentis antiquis nescio quae veritatis impressa species, quae non raro primo conspectu oculos peritorum rapit. Quemadmodum periti aurifices aurum sincerum a falso nonnumquam solo tactu discernunt: ut pictores prima tabellarum exemplaria a secundis; numismatum denique cognitores genuina a spuriis solo passim adspectu distinguunt."

73 Peter Rück, "Fünf Vorlesungen für Studenten der Ecole des Chartes (Paris, 24–28 April 1995)," in *Arbeiten aus dem Marburger hilfswissenschaflichen*

Institut, ed. Erika Eisenlohr and Peter Worm (Marburg an der Lahn: Universitätsbibliothek Marburg, 2000), 243–315, at 257 and 262.

74 Daniel van Papenbroeck, *Kunstdenkmäler zwischen Antwerpen und Trient: Beschreibungen und Bewertungen des Jesuiten Daniel Papebroch aus dem Jahre 1660,* ed. and tr. Udo Kindermann (Cologne: Böhlau, 2002).

75 Papenbroeck, "Propylaeum antiquarium," ix: "*Hac de re prænominatus ejus socius ad me scribens,* Conatus sum, *inquit,* singula perquam accurate primum ad fenestram vitream, ut litteræ per suprapositam membranæ chartam transparerent, dilineare singula: tum, separata a pergameno charta, unumquemque characterem sigillatim pressiore calamo sum remensus: quos si ære incidendos curare velis, secure id facere poteris."

76 For inscriptions see William Stenhouse, *Reading Inscriptions and Writing Ancient History: Historical Scholarship in the Late Renaissance,* Bulletin of the Institute of Classical Studies, Supplement 86 (London: Institute of Classical Studies, 2005); for coins see Martin Mulsow, "Hausenblasen. Kopierpraktiken und die Herstellung numismatischen Wissens um 1700," in *Objekte als Quellen der historischen Kulturwissenschaften: Stand und Perspektiven der Forschung,* ed. Annette Caroline Cremer and Martin Mulsow (Cologne, Weimar and Vienna: Böhlau, 2017), 261–344.

77 Emery Bigot to Antonio Magliabechi, July 1679, 95, printed in Doucette, *Bigot,* 95: "Io prego V.S. per l'amore ch'ella porta alle lettere di far mi copiare le due prime righe e linee dell'*Eneide.* Per ciò lei mando una carta transparente per metter sopra la scrittura, e doppo che la charta è mesa sopra la scrittura besogna con la penna e l'atramento disegnare la scrittura come si trova nel ms^to. M'è paruta l'inventione bellissima. Ella osserverà di estendere la charta ch'ella mettrà sopra la scrittura finchè quando si sarà per espandere la charta, la scrittura non si estendi e così non bene representi la scrittura del ms^to."

78 Ibid.: "Al meno della comparatione delle scritture si potrà conjetturare in quel tempo furono scritte."

79 BL MS Sloane 2052, fol. 53^v, printed in *Pictoria, Sculptoria, & quae subalternarum artium . . . 1620. Le manuscrit de Turquet de Mayerne,* ed. Marcel Faiutti and Camille Versini (Lyon: Audin, 1967), 72–73: "POUR CONTRE TIRER PIECES, CARTES, PARTERRES, OU QUOY QUE CE SOIT. Rien n'est si transparent que la membrane Allantoide d'une vache coupée en long, estendue et seichée: mais, pour la garder des vers, je la voudrais frottée de pétrole, ou la tenir avec l'absynthe. Trifol, odorat. fleur de houblon, Saule, ou aultres telles herbes, mises en poudre. [marginal note] J'en ay gardé dans un portefeuille et dans de l'urine sans que les vers y ayent touché. Le pericarde [interlinear note; ne vault rien] d'un boeuf sert à mesme usage. Le papier de Lion (papier à chassis venant de Lion, marqué au Serpent) ou de Venise, frotté ou oingt avec huile de lin et térébinthine chaudement. Ou bien avec de l'axunge de porc fraische, et estant bien transparent, le fault seicher et desgraisser avec du son autant que l'on pourra. Ces graisses soyent appliquées chaudes pour mieux pénétrer. Voyés de mesler avec l'axunge de l'huile blanche de thérèbinthine, pour la tenir liquide et faire qu'elle s'estende mieux avec la broisse, pinceau ou esponge fort molle. Le moyen

d'user de ces moyens transparents est de les appliquer sur la pièce de pour-
traitture, et tirer le trait avec crayon de plomb d'Angleterre, puis avoir un
papier noircy dudist plomb, lequel soit appliqué sur un papier blanc et sur
iceluy le papier huilé trace, puis les traicts seront tirés avec un poinçon ou
pooincte d'or ou d'ivoire, qui se marqueront sur le papier blanc. On pourra
aussi coller le papier huilé transparent sur un gros papier, piquer avec une
aiguille bien menue, et poncer. La peau d'un veau mort né, tiré hors du ventre
de la vache morte, ou abortif préparé en vélin est aussi fort transparente."

80 Franklin, "Reading the Popes," 621–624.

81 See the wonderful study by Eleonora Pistis, "'Farò con la copia.' Una rac-
colta inedita di disegni d'architettura nella Bibliothèque Carré d'Art de
Nîmes," *Pegasus: Berliner Beiträge zum Nachleben der Antike,* 11 (2009),
93–207, at 95; and Arnold Nesselrath, "Disegni di Francesco di Giorgio Martini," in *Francesco di Giorgio alla Corte di Federico da Montefeltro: Atti
del Convegno Internazionale di studi, Urbino, monastero di Santa Chiara,
11–13 ottobre 2001,* ed. Francesco Paolo Fiore, 2 vols. (Florence: Olschki,
2004), 2:337–367, esp. 350.

82 Daniel Papenbroeck, *Vita Bollandi,* chap. 18, in Susanne Daub, *Auf Heiliger
Jagd in Florenz: Aus dem Tagebuch des Jesuiten Daniel Papebroch* (Erlangen:
Palm & Enke, 2010), 169: "Nemo enim istic inveniebatur, qui operam mer-
cenariam aut vellet aut posset commodare, vetustorum characterum &
praecipue Graecorum peritus." In Rome, by contrast, they had worked with
amanuenses (ibid., 6 and n. 16).

83 Erasmus, *De recta pronuntiatione,* in his *Literary and Educational Writings,*
4, ed. J. Kelley Sowards, *Collected Works of Erasmus* (Toronto: University
of Toronto Press, 1985), 26:392.

84 Ibid., 397–398.

85 Mabillon, *De re diplomatica,* 1681, sigs. eij^r-v: "His omnibus subsidiis accesserunt specimina Petri Hamonis, quae opere iam promoto a Ludovico
Billanio accepi. Fuit is, Hamo inquam, Caroli IX Francorum Regis scriba et
regii cubiculi a secretis, cui in mentem venit omnigena scripturarum specimina in lucem proferre. Quod paullo ante Romae tentaverat Johannes Baptista Palatinus Paulo tertio Pontifice; atque Venetiis eodem tempore alius
quidam, cujus nomen memoriae meae modo non occurrit."

86 See, e.g., Rémi Jimenes, *Les caractères de civilité: Typographie et calligra-
phie sous l'Ancien Régime* (Reillanne: Atelier Perrousseaux, 2011).

87 See Lothar Müller, *White Magic: The Age of Paper,* tr. Jessica Spengler
(London and Malden, MA: Polity, 2014); and Arndt Brendecke, *The Empir-
ical Empire: Spanish Colonial Rule and the Politics of Knowledge* (Berlin:
De Gruyter Oldenbourg, 2016).

88 Stanley Morison, *Early Italian Writing Books: Renaissance to Baroque,* ed.
Nicholas Barker (Verona: Edizioni Valdonega; London: British Library, 1990);
Emanuele Casamassima, *Trattati di scrittura del Cinquecento italiano*
(Milan: Edizioni il Polifilo, 1966); Nicholas Barker, *The Glory of the Art of
Writing: The Calligraphic Work of Francesco Alunno of Ferrara,* 2 vols. (Los
Angeles: Cotsen Occasional Press, 2009); "Renaissance Writing Masters,"
online at http-//www.designhistory.org/Handwriting_pages/WritingMasters

.html, accessed March 23, 2017; Lee Hendrix and Thea Vignau-Wilberg, *The Art of the Pen: Calligraphy from the Court of the Emperor Rudolf II* (Los Angeles: J. Paul Getty Museum, 2003), 8: "In a curious turn of events, print further contributed to the development of writing as an art form, since it was principally through the publication of model books that scribes became widely recognized as distinctive personalities." The intellectual and scholarly foundations of scribal practice in the Italian Renaissance are investigated by Arielle Saiber, *Measured Words: Computation and Writing in Renaissance Italy* (Toronto; Buffalo, NY; and London: University of Toronto Press, 2017), esp. chaps. 1 and 2.

89 Ludovico Vicentino degli Arrighi, *Il modo & regola de scrivere littera corsiva over cancellerescha* (Rome: Vicentino, 1522), 8. For an English translation see John Howard Benson, trans., *The First Writing Book* (New Haven: Yale University Press, 1954).

90 New York, Pierpont Morgan Library MS MA 3230: Giovio, *Historiae sui Temporis*, Book VII (ca. 1520–1545), verso of last leaf.

91 Giovanni Antonio Tagliente, *Lo presente libro insegna la vera arte de lo excellente scrivere di diverse varie sorti de litere* (Venice: Giovanni Antonio and the Brothers Sabbio, 1530), in Oscar Ogg, *Three Classics of Italian Calligraphy* (New York: Dover, 1953), 112, 115.

92 Mabillon, *De re diplomatica*, 1681, sig. eij^r: "Verum isti non alia fere, quam recentium scripturarum exempla exhibuerunt."

93 Giovanni Antonio Palatino, *Libro . . . Nel quale s'insegna a scriver ogni sorte lettera, antica & moderna* (Rome: Antonio Blado, 1550), sigs. [Dv^v– Dvi^r]. See Casamassima, *Trattati di scrittura*, 14, 51 and 53.

94 Mabillon, *De re diplomatica*, 1681, sig. eij^r: "Fuit is, Hamo inquam, Caroli IX Francorum Regis scriba et regii cubiculi a secretis, cui in mentem venit omnigena scripturarum specimina in lucem proferre."

95 Ibid., sigs. eij^{r-v}: "sed Hamo de congerendis etiam antiquis sollicitus fuit, obtentis a Rege litteris et facultate mutuandi libros e regia Fontis-Blaudi Bibliotheca, et consulendi archiva coenobiorum S. Dionysii et S. Germani. Quod ipse aliquot speciminibus peritissime effictis, at inexcusis, exsecutus est annis M D L X V I ac sequente. Ex eo aliqua huc transtulimus, in primis specimen chartae plenariae (ut vocant) securitatis, in papyro Aegyptiaca scriptae, et in Fontis-Blaudi regio penu tum asservatae: cujus ille aliquot versus calamo expressit, et sub C. Julii Caesaris testamenti fallaci titulo in libellum sum cum aliis retulit."

96 Ibid.: "His omnibus subsidiis accesserunt specimina Petri Hamonis, quae opere iam promoto a Ludovico Billanio accepi."

97 Henri Omont, "Le recueil d'anciennes écritures de Pierre Hamon," *Bibliothèque de l'École des Chartes* 62 (1901): 57–73.

98 BNF, MS fr. 19116, fol. 73^{r-v}, edited in Omont, "Le recueil d'anciennes écritures de Pierre Hamon," 71–72.

99 BNF, MS fr. 19116, fol. 2^r, edited in Omont, "Le recueil d'anciennes écritures de Pierre Hamon," 60: "Nottes ciceroniennes. Ces Nottes ciceroniennes sont de plus de 1,200 ans. Par P. Hamon, escrivain du Roy et secretaire de sa Chambre, 1566."

100 Omont, "Le recueil d'anciennes écritures de Pierre Hamon," 57.

101 See Andrew Lintott, *Judicial Reform and Land Reform in the Roman Republic: A New Edition, with Translation and Commentary, of the Laws from Urbino* (Cambridge: Cambridge University Press, 1992; new ed., 2010), 66–70.

102 Barnabé Brisson, *De formulis et sollemnibus populi Romani verbis libri VIII* (Frankfurt: Wechel and Fischer, 1592), 156: "Atque ut suam cum Italia symbolam Gallia nostra conferat, proferam ex aenea Regiae bibliothecae tabula, excerptum priscae cuiusdam legis unum & item alterum fragmentum: illud his, quae quidem legi possunt, verbis constat: . . . MVLTAM SVPREMA DEI."

103 Isaac Casaubon, note in his copy of Brisson, 1592, Princeton University Library (Ex) 2014-0415N, 156.

104 BNF MS fr. 19116, fols. 17ʳ and 32ʳ.

105 BNF MS lat. 4608. See Léopold Delisle, "Cujas déchiffreur de papyrus," in *Mélanges offerts à M. Émile Chatelain*, ed. Émile Chatelain (Paris: A. Champion, 1910), 486–491.

106 BNF MS fr. 19116, fol. 15ʳ.

107 Ibid.

108 Mabillon, *De re diplomatica*, 1681, 37: "His adde Julii Caesaris testamentum in cortice scriptum, quod superiori saeculo in regia Fontis-Blaudi bibliotheca servabatur, teste Petro Hamone, ex quo ejus scripturae specimen alibi referemus."

109 Ibid., 344. The mistake is also corrected in the preface, sig. eijᵛ (written, as usual, after the main text was complete).

110 Henri Omont, "L'édition de la Palaeographia graeca de Montfaucon," *Revue des études grecques* 4 (1891): 63–67, at 66; Pierre Gasnault, "Traités des Mauristes avec leurs libraires et leurs graveurs," in his *L'Érudition Mauriste à Saint-Germain-des-Prés* (Paris: Institut d'Études Augustiniennes, 1999), 57–108, at 77.

111 Ibid.: "lesdites soixante planches seront en charactères anciens, excepté trois ou quatre au plus, qui seront en figures."

112 Jean LeClerc, *Ars critica*, 2 vols. (Amsterdam: Gallet, 1697), 2:336: "Exempli causa, ars est singularis dignoscendi aetatis MSS. Codicum, deque eorum characteribus judicandi; quae, si pro dignitate tractatur, justo volumini argumentum praebeat*, de qua tamen nemo seorsim sat studiose egit."

113 Ibid.: "* Nonnulla hac de re habet Joan.Mabillonius, de Re Diplomatica Lib. I. sed quae coposius excuti studiosorum interesset."

114 Traube, *Geschichte*, 29 (but clearly, as usual, Leclerc only criticized).

115 See Jean Boutier, "Étienne Baluze et 'Les règles générales pour discerner les anciens titres faux d'avec les véritables,'" in *Étienne Baluze, 1630–1718: Érudition et pouvoirs dans l'Europe classique*, ed. Jean Boutier (Limoges: Presses Universitaires de Limoges, 2008), 315–334.

116 Cf. Dorna, *Mabillon und andere*, 140,

117 Bernard de Montfaucon, *Palaeographia graeca* (Paris: Guerin, Boudot and Robustel, 1708), i: "Deinde anno 1693. periculum facere coepimus; videlicet si qui Codices in Bibliothecis Regia et Colbertina essent, anni et Calligraphi

notam ferentes, ex iis specimina excerpsimus: hinc ad alios notis vacuos nos contulimus, ac saepe facta cum prioribus notam habentibus comparatione, aliquam demum ea in re peritiam assequuti videbamur. Sub haec in Italiam profecti, solitam explorandi operam numquam intermisimus: sed in Bibliothecis variis Graeca exemplaria tractantes, aetatem eorum, qualem ad primum conspectum assignabamus, cum notis Calligraphorum annum indicantibus et ad calcem, sicubi exstarent, positis, apprime consentire passim experti sumus; idque persaepe in praesentia eruditorum. Cujus rei testes bene multi sunt, maxime Venetiis, ubi ad duos pene menses consedimus. In Italia vero, perinde atque in Gallia ex optimae notae Codicibus cujusvis aetatis specimina, quam accuratissime fieri potuit, excerpsimus."

118 Jean Leclerc, *Ars critica*, 3 vols. (Amsterdam: Jansson-Waesburg, 1712), 2:257: "qua de re, ut antea dixi, paucis, ad Latinos Codices quod adtinet, *Joan. Mabillonius*, in Diplomatica: sed pluribus de Graecis *Bernard. de Montfaucon*, in Palaeographiae Graecae egregio opere egit."

119 Sachiko Kusukawa, *Picturing the Book of Nature: Image, Text, and Argument in Sixteenth-Century Human Anatomy and Medical Botany* (Chicago and London: University of Chicago Press, 2011).

120 Lisa Jardine, *The Curious Life of Robert Hooke: The Man Who Measured London* (London: HarperCollins, 2003). For another case, see Catherine Abou-Nemeh, "The Natural Philosopher and the Microscope: Nicolas Hartsoeker Unravels Nature's 'Admirable Œconomy,'" *History of Science* 51 (2013): 1–32.

121 Stephanie Moser, "Making Expert Knowledge through the Image: Connections between Antiquarian and Early Modern Scientific Illustrations," *Isis* 105, no. 1 (2014): 58–99.

122 Steven Shapin, *A Social History of Truth: Civility and Science in Seventeenth-Century England* (Chicago and London: University of Chicago Press, 1994).

123 Ann Blair, "Early Modern Attitudes toward the Delegation of Copying and Note-Taking," in *Forgetting Machines: Knowledge Management Evolution in Early Modern Europe*, ed. Alberto Cevolini (Leiden: Brill, 2016), 265–285.

124 Hendrix and Vignau-Wilberg, *The Art of the Pen*, 5–9.

125 Still, active writing played a major role in training in palaeography and diplomatics until late in the nineteenth century and remains useful even now: see Rück, "Fünf Vorlesungen," 261–262.

126 Jean Mabillon, *Tractatus de studiis monasticis* (Venice: Poletus, 1705), 496: "Hoc ipsum quod dicto, quod relego, quod emendo, de vita mea tollitur. Quot puncta Notarii, tot meorum damna sunt temporum"; *Treatise on Monastic Studies*, tr. John Paul McDonald (Lanham, MD; Boulder, CO; New York; Toronto; and Oxford: University Press of America, 2004), 254. Mabillon quotes Jerome, *Ep.* 60.19.

CHAPTER 4 · POLYDORE VERGIL UNCOVERS THE JEWISH
ORIGINS OF CHRISTIANITY

An earlier draft of this paper was presented to a CRASSH workshop on comparison, on December 2014. My thanks to Simon Goldhill for inviting me to present and to him and the other participants—especially Giovanna Ceserani, Dmitri Levitin, Joan-Pau Rubiés, Richard Serjeantson and Jonathan Sheehan—for their comments.

1 J. C. Schöttgen, "Christus rabbinorum summus," in *Horae talmudicae et rabbinicae*, 2 vols. (Emden and Leipzig: Hekel, 1742), 2:884–885: "Unde vero, dicet aliquis, cognoverant Judaei, Jesum nostrum esse Rabbinum? Respondeo, vestitum ejus rei fuisse indicem. Credibile enim est Servatorem eo habitu indutum incessisse, qui temporibus istis a Judaeorum Doctoribus adhibitus est. Videor mihi tale quid exsculpere posse ex descriptione vestium Servatoris nostri, earundemque cum Rabbinorum Judaicorum habitu comparatione."

2 Ibid., 885–887, esp. 886: "Quicquid vero horum sit, hoc certum est, JEsum CHristum, Prophetam atque Doctorem nostrum, Rabbinos omnes in hoc multis post se parasangis relinquere, quod tantos brevi profectus ostenderit, qui a tota Rabbinorum Hierosolymitanorum cohorte non sine stupore auscultari potuerunt."

3 Ibid., 891: "Christus ergo et hac in parte se Rabbinorum summum exhibit, quod falsas veterum traditiones rejecit, illaque formula Judaeorum Doctoribus non inusitata, *v'ani omer lachem*, ἐγὼ δὲ λέγω ὑμῖν, meliores in earum locum substituit."

4 Ibid., 895–896, at 896: "Hi quidem viri docti non diffitebuntur, ut spero, majorem fuisse sapientiam et doctrinam Servatoris nostri, quam omnium, quotquot unquam fuerint, Rabbinorum, hinc facile quoque largientur, non opus habuisse Servatorem, ut de exemplari precum quarundam circumspiceret. Si ergo adest similitudo quaedam inter preces nostras et Judaicas: qualem quidem nemo negabit, qui orationem dominicam cum decem et octo capitum compendio apud Edzardum ad c. 1. Avoda Zara conferet, alia potius via incedendum est. Nimirum Servator docebat orationem dominicam inter Judaeos, hinc non poterat non iis expressionibus uti, quae Judaeis hominibus non essent incognitae."

5 Ibid., 893. For the formula, see, e.g., Babylonian Talmud (hereafter BT) Sanhedrin 37a.

6 Schöttgen, *Horae talmudicae et rabbinicae*, 2:887–900.

7 Ibid., 901: "Qua vero ratione Christus discipulos suos instituerit, et quantum hi ex ipsius doctrina profecerint, totus, quaqua patet, orbis novit. Neque Judaeis id est incognitum, quippe qui eorum, et miraculorum ab iisdem Magistri sui nomine patratorum, in Talmude mentionem faciunt. Adeoque et hi satis superque nos docent, JEsum, Magistrum ipsorum, Rabbinorum omnium esse supremum."

8 Nathanael Riemer, "'Der Rabbiner': Eine vergessene Zeitschrift eines christlichen Hebraisten," *PaRDeS. Zeitschrift der Vereinigung für Jüdische Studien* 11 (2005): 37–67.

9 Jonathan Smith, *Drudgery Divine* (Chicago: University of Chicago Press, 1990), esp. chaps. 2–3.

10 Aaron Katchen, *Christian Hebraists and Dutch Rabbis: Seventeenth Century Apologetics and the Study of Maimonides' Mishneh Torah* (Cambridge, MA: Harvard University Press, 1984); Carsten Wilke, "Splendeurs et infortunes du Talmudisme académique en Allemagne," in *Les textes*

judéophobes et judéophiles dans l'Europe chrétienne à l'époque moderne, XVIème-XVIIIième siècles, ed. Daniel Tollet (Paris: PUF, 2000), 97–134; Jason Rosenblatt, *Renaissance England's Chief Rabbi: John Selden* (Oxford and New York: Oxford University Press, 2006); Eric Nelson, *The Hebrew Republic: Jewish Sources and the Transformation of European Political Thought* (Cambridge, MA: Harvard University Press, 2010); Anthony Grafton and Joanna Weinberg, *"I have always loved the holy tongue": Isaac Casaubon, the Jews, and a Forgotten Chapter in Renaissance Scholarship* (Cambridge, MA: Harvard University Press, 2011).

11 G. J. Toomer, *John Selden: A Life in Scholarship,* 2 vols. (Oxford: Oxford University Press, 2010).

12 *Some Genuine Remains of the Late Pious and Learned John Lightfoot, D. D.,* ed. John Strype (London: Robinson and Wyat, 1700), viii. Lightfoot's practices matched his precepts; see ibid., xv–xvi: "But Lightfoot then stood up to confute the former Arguments, by shewing that the two Sanhedrins, and the two Consistories in every City, were not owned by the Jewish Authors. And for that he alledged Maimonides at large; and proved three Courts in Jerusalem; and yet no difference of one Ecclesiastical, and the other Civil. And by his skill in Jewish History made it out, that there was but one Court or Consistory in every City else." After much debate Lightfoot proposed a compromise, xvi: "[t]hat in the Church of the Jews there were Elders of the People joined to the Priests and Levites in the Government of the Church. Which middling way was very well liked"; xvi–xvii: "[a]nd Lightfoot by his Prudent and Learned Management of this Point pleased all, unless it were perhaps the Scotch Commissioners."

13 Eric Nelson, "From Selden to Mendelssohn: Hebraism and Religious Freedom," in *Freedom and the Construction of Europe,* ed. Quentin Skinner and Martin van Gelderen, 2 vols. (Cambridge: Cambridge University Press, 2013), 1:94–114.

14 Campegius Vitringa, *De synagoga vetere libri tres,* 2 vols. (Franeker: Gyzelaar, 1696); Benedetto Baccchini, *De ecclesiasticae hierarchiae originibus dissertatio* (Modena: Capponi, 1703). See Arnaldo Momigliano, s.v. Bacchini, Benedetto, in *Dizionario Biografico degli Italiani.*

15 Guillaume Du Choul, *Discours de la religion des anciens Romains* (Wesel: Hoogenhuyse, 1672). On Du Choul, see, in general, Margaret McGowan, *The Vision of Rome in Late Renaissance France* (New Haven and London: Yale University Press, 2000), esp. 71–81.

16 Fritz Saxl, "The Classical Inscription in Renaissance Art and Politics," *Journal of the Warburg and Courtauld Institutes* 4 (1940–1941): 19–46, at 26–27.

17 Andrew Hui, "The Birth of Ruins in Quattrocento Nativity and Adoration Paintings," *I Tatti Studies in the Italian Renaissance* 18, no. 2 (2015): 319–348.

18 Du Choul, *Discours de la religion des anciens Romains,* 220: "Quand les vierges venoyent à se rendre Vestales, j'ay observé qu'elles estoyent tondues, comme sont noz Nonnains d'auiourdhuy'; 280: 'Le prebstre tourné du costé d'Orient avecques meditations & solennelles prieres prioit les Dieux en grande devotion. . . . Par cecy nous congnoissons, que les Romains faisoyent leurs sacrifices et devotions droit à l'Orient, comme nous faisons encore aui-

ourdhuy. Ce que Porphyrius a monstré: qui veut que les entrées des temples & les statues soyent dresées à l'Orient. Et ce que je pense avoir leu dedans l'Architecture de Vitruve, quand il parle de la situation des temples des Dieux immortels"; 262: "La Coustume des Pontifes estoit de sacrer les imaiges des Dieux pour les adorer: non pour elles, comme dit Plaute, mais pour la representation de ceux, par le benefice desquels ils avoyent receu tant de biens. Et comme nous adorons la figure du petit aigneau de Dieu, pourcequ'elle represente IESUSCHRIST: & semblablement la figure de la Colombe, pource qu'elle denote le SAINCT ESPERIT: tout ainsi les Gentils avoyent en singuliere recommandation le fulgure de Jupiter: par lequel ils monstroyent la figure de leur grand Dieu, cuidants qu'il les gardoit de la tempeste, & qu'il eust une certaine vertu apres qu'il estoit sacré par le grand Pontife."

19 Margaret Hodgen, *Early Anthropology in the Sixteenth and Seventeenth Centuries* (Philadelphia: University of Pennsylvania Press, 1964).

20 Du Choul, *Discours de la religion des anciens Romains*, 312: "Et si nous regardons curieusement, nous cognoistrons que plusieurs institutions de nostre religion ont esté prises et translatées des cerimonies Aegyptiennes & des Gentils: comme sont les tuniques & surpelis, les coronnes que fout les prebstres, les inclinations de teste autour de l'autel, la pompe sacrificale, la musique des temples, adorations, prieres & supplications, processions & letanies: & plusieurs autres choses, que noz prebstres usurpent en noz mysteres, & referent à un seul Dieu JESUS-CHRIST ce que l'ignorance des Gentils, faulse religion & folle superstition representoit à leurs Dieux, & aux hommes mortels apres leurs consecrations." David Lupher, *Romans in a New World: Classical Models in Sixteenth-Century Spanish America* (Ann Arbor: University of Michigan Press, 2003), quotes this passage and describes it as "a much bolder and more extensive suggestion of Christian borrowing from pagan practices than the corresponding passages in the body of the text had implied" (284). For its source, see n. 37 below.

21 Du Choul, *Discours de la religion des anciens Romains*, 263–264, esp. 263: "Et ce que les Gentils faisoyent en leurs ridicules superstitions, nous avons transferé à nostre religion Chrestienne, en faisant consacrer et benistre noz petits Agnus Dei & noz cloches, qui prennent par ce moyen une vertu pour chasser la tempeste & le mauvais temps. Et tot ainsi le sel & l'eaue, par leurs benedictions & exorcismes, prennent une force & vertu pour dechasser les mauvais esperitz."

22 Cesare D'Onofrio, *Visitiamo Roma nel Quattrocento: La città degli umanisti* (Rome: Romana Società Editrice, 1989), 70: "Templi Pacis conspicui, quondam a Divo Vespasiano constructi, tres tamen arcus super ingentem reliquorum, qui sex erant, ruinam eminent ferme integri: ex pluribus vero mirae magnitudinis, unam tantum stare vides marmoream columnam, reliquis tum disiectis, tum inter templi ruinas sepultis."

23 Ibid.: "Huic proximum fuit divi Antonini divaeque Faustinae templum, nunc beato Laurentio dicatum; cuius porticus plurimae marmoreae columnae ruinam effugerunt."

24 Ibid., 70–72: "Castoris insuper et Pollucis aedes contiguae, loco edito in via sacra, altera occidentem, altera orientem versus (hodie *Mariam Novam*

appellant), inclytus quondam cogendi Senatus locus, majori ex parte col-
lapsae parvis vestigiis haerent, in quas me saepissime confero, revocans,
stupore quodam oppressus, animum ad ea tempora, quum ibi senatoriae
sententiae dicerentur, et aut L. Crassum mihi, aut Hortensium, aut Cice-
ronem orantem proponens."

25 Ibid., 172: "Extat et Vestae templum iuxta Tiberis ripam ad initium montis
Aventini, rotundum ac patens undique nullo muro, frequentibus tantum
suffultum columnis, id posteri martyri Stephano dedicarunt."

26 Flavio Biondo, *Rome in Triumph,* I: ed. Maria Agata Pincelli, trans. Frances
Muecke (Cambridge, MA: Harvard University Press, 2016), 12: "Itaque coepimus tentare si speculum, exemplar, imaginem, doctrinam omnis virtutis
et bene, sancte ac feliciter vivendi rationis, urbem Romam florentem ac
qualem beatus Aurelius Augustinus triumphantem videre desideravit, nostrorum hominum ingenio et doctrina valentium oculis et menti subiicere
ac proponere poterimus."

27 Ibid., 13; original on 12: "Praefari tamen hoc inicio libet nos de Romanorum
gentiliumque aliorum religione ea ratione ac intentione dicturos, ut deorum
appellationes cum templorum, aedium phanorumque vocabulis edocentes,
simul loca urbis Romae in quibus ea fuere ostendamus; inde rituum quos
dii gentium, sicut propheta inquit, daemonia suis sacrificiis adhiberi iusse-
runt spurcitia, impietate atque etiam maxima levitate ostensa Christianae
religionis sanctimoniam bonae voluntatis hominibus gratiorem faciamus
esse."

28 Ibid., 35; original on 34: "Quam admiratus insaniam beatus Ecclesiae doctor
Ambrosius, ut sacratissimam Dei nostri Iesu Christi religionem Christianis
hominibus redderet gratiorem, hunc Ophionem, qui et Latine serpens dicitur, qualis a gentilibus Italicis Phoenices imitatis colebatur, in sua Medio-
lanensi ecclesia conservari voluit, qui etiam nunc integer conspicitur."

29 Ibid., 39; original on 38: "Romanos . . . in deorum susceptione multas Aegyptiorum Phoenicumque et Graecorum ineptias impietatesque omisisse."

30 Ibid., 53; original on 52: "Inter multa vero quae Romana superstitio nobis
dicenda exhibit, nihil non respuendum ac omnino abhominabile est praeter
unum, quod viro Christiano in meliorem partem amplectendum converten-
dumque existimo, sacris scilicet ut appellarunt ac religioni Romanam
gentem accuratissime intentam fuisse."

31 See esp. Frances Muecke, *"Gentiles nostri:* Roman Religion and Roman
Identity in Biondo Flavio's *Roma Triumphans," Journal of the Warburg and
Courtauld Institutes* 75 (2012): 93–110, repr. in *The Invention of Rome: Bi-
ondo Flavio's* Roma Triumphans *and Its Worlds,* ed. Frances Muecke and
Maurizio Campanelli (Geneva: Droz, 2017), 77–99; and William Stenhouse,
"Panvinio and *descriptio:* Renditions of History and Antiquity in the Late
Renaissance," *Papers of the British School at Rome* 80 (2012): 233–256.

32 Flavio Biondo, *De roma triumphante libri X* (Basel: Froben, 1559), 14–18, 28,
30–31, 37, 44, 52, 102–104, and Muecke's precise analysis of these passages
in *"Gentiles nostri."*

33 *Commentarii a Philippo Beroaldo conditi in Asinum Aureum Lucii Apulei*
(Bologna: Benedictus Hector, 1500). See Konrad Krautter, *Philologische*

Methode und humanistische Existenz: Filippo Beroaldo und sein Kommentar zum Goldenen Esel des Apuleius (Munich: Fink, 1971); and Julia Gaisser, *The Fortunes of Apuleius and the Golden Ass: A Study in Transmission and Reception* (Princeton and Oxford: Princeton University Press, 2008).

34 Beroaldo, *Commentarii*, fol. 271ʳ, on Apuleius, *Golden Ass* 11.20: "Primam horam: Sic et nostri sacerdotes primam, tertiam, sextam, nonam horas habent sacrificiis legitimas et deputatas. Si curiose introspexeris novissimum hoc volumen Apuleianum, haud dubie cognosces pleraque omnia instituta nostrae religionis sumpta esse translataque: ex cerimonia ethnicorum."

35 Beroaldo, *Commentarii*, fol. 263ʳ, on Apuleius, *Golden Ass* 11.10: "Capillum derasi. Sacerdotes Egyptiaci erant capitibus derasis, quod Plinius noster indicat: et ante Plinium Herodotus sic scripsit: deorum sacerdotes alibi comati sunt. In Egypto derasi: idem refert solitos eos totum corpus alternis diebus deradere, ne inter deorum cultum quicquam pediculorum aut alterius excrementitiae sordis illos pollueret. . . . Ex hoc Isiacorum ritu videtur id quoque translatum esse, ut nostri sacerdotes comam alere prohibeantur. Capite deraso: quamvis ecclesiastici scriptores hoc veluti mystice et tropologice interpretantur. Nam Divus Hieronymus tradit quod rasio capitis est temporalium omnium depositio: et quod corona in capite designat regni coelestis coronam."

36 Beroaldo, *Commentarii*, fol. 262ᵛ, on Apuleius, *Golden Ass* 11.9: "Quod dii despicerentur: id est deorsum ex superiori cenaculi parte aspicerentur: quod nefas est, et ad pollutionem sacrorum pertinet. Vnde et nostri hodieque in pompa sacrificali pueros et puellas ex fenestris vetant despicere, hoc est superne in locum inferiorem despectare."

37 Beroaldo, *Commentarii*, fol. 264ᵛ, on Apuleius, *Golden Ass* 11.11: "Mecum ego subinde recollens haec instituta sacrorum ethnicorum venio in eam sententiam: ut credam pleraque omnia ad cerimoniarum nostrarum celebrationem pertinentia illinc esse translata transpositaque. Nimirum ex gentilium religione: sunt lineae vestes, derasa sacerdotum capita, vertigines in altari, pompa sacrificalis, musica modulamina, adorationes, preces aliaque id genus compluria, quae nostri sacerdotes in nostris mysteriis solenniter usurpant: haud dubia sumpta de cerimonia priscorum. Sic et apud nos homines incedunt in pompa sacrorum sub effigie sanctorum et prophetarum, qui dici possent dei humanis pedibus incedentes." This key passage has been quoted by Krautter in *Philologische Methode und humanistische Existenz* and by Catherine Atkinson, *Inventing Inventors in Renaissance Europe: Polydore Vergil's De inventoribus rerum* (Tübingen: Mohr Siebeck, 2007), 299, and she connects it with Du Choul, *Discours de la religion des anciens Romains*, at 240n.174.

38 Joannes Boemus, *The Fardle of Facions*, tr. William Waterman, 3 vols. (London: Kingstroke and Sutton, 1555; repr., Edinburgh: Goldsmid, 1888), I, 47–48; *De omnium gentium ritibus* (Augsburg: Grimm and Virsung, 1520), fol. Xᵛ: "Nam ut Philippus Beroaldus super Apuleianum Asinum scribit, pleraque etiam ex Aegyptiorum religione translata in religionem nostram sunt, ut lineae vestes, derasa sacerdotum capita, vertigines in altari, pompa

sacrificalis, musica modulamina, adorationes, preces, aliaque id genus plurima."

39 See the recent work by Carina Johnson, "Idolatrous Cultures and the Practice of Religion," *Journal of the History of Ideas* 67 (2006): 597–621, 598–599; and Guy Stroumsa, *A New Science: The Discovery of Religion in the Age of Reason* (Cambridge: Harvard University Press, 2010), 1–2. On the rise of travel writing in this period and its intellectual foundations see now Joan-Pau Rubiés and Manel Ollé, "The Comparative History of a Genre: The Production and Circulation of Books on Travel and Ethnographies in Early Modern Europe and China," *Modern Asian Studies* 50, no. 1 (2016): 259–309.

40 John Howland Rowe, "The Renaissance Foundations of Anthropology," *American Anthropologist* 67 (1965): 1–20, at 12; see also his comment on Biondo at 11: "There were also frequent comparisons with customs and institutions of the author's own time which represent the beginnings of an anthropological point of view."

41 Beroaldo, *Commentarii*, fol. 275ᵛ, quoted and translated by Gaisser in *The Fortunes of Apuleius*, 210: "Est videre in Lucio nostro orationes divinas tam sancte tam graviter tam sententialiter compositas absolvi, ut nihil religiosius quicquam possit, ut Apuleianae precationes possint commodissime aptari ad divam Christianorum, ut quicquid hoc in loco dicitur de Luna sive Iside, idem religiose et condecenter de beata virgine dici possit."

42 Beroaldo, *Commentarii*, fol. 270ᵛ, on 11.19, quoted by Gaisser in *The Fortunes of Apuleius*, 211n.60: "Divus Augustinus libro viii Confessionum hoc idem de se ipso scribens ait . . . modo ecce modo, sine paululum, sed modo et modo non habet modum, et sine paululum in longum ibat."

43 Beroaldo, *Commentarii*, fol. 274ᵛ, quoted and translated by Gaisser in *The Fortunes of Apuleius*, 212: "Ex hoc colligimus hominem qui vere consecratur fitque sacerdos integer et sanctus per quandam quasi mortem exuere vitam hanc irreligiosam, rapique numinis instinctu per superna et inferna, ut ea videat et agnoscat quae vidit et agnovit apostolus Paulus: quae ineffabilia sunt, nec licet homini eloqui, quae etiam audita non intelligantur, cum sint supra captum intellectumque mortalium."

44 Niccolò Machiavelli, *Discorsi sopra la prima deca di Tito Livio*, 3:2.

45 See *The Invention of Rome: Biondo Flavio's* Roma Triumphans *and Its Worlds*, ed. Muecke and Campanelli, esp. Frances Muecke, "The Genre(s) and the Making of *Roma Triumphans*," 33–53 at 35.

46 Du Choul, *Discours de la religion des anciens Romains*, 310: "Et quand premierement les sacerdotes des Aegyptiens venoyent à prendre leurs ordres des choses sacrées, la coustume estoit de leur donner des presents, & ils faisoyent un festin à ceux, qui avoyent assisté à leur recession. Puis le premier prebstre (que nous pourrions nommer en nostre religion l'Euesque) les enseignoit, & leur bailloit un liure qui estoit en role, comme sont ceux des Hebreux encores aviourdhuy."

47 Ibid.: "Les Romains eurent autre façon de faire leurs dignitez sacerdotales, comme le grand Pontife, les petits Pontifes, Flamines, Archiflamines, & Protoflamines: tout ainsi que nous avons le Pape, les Cardinaulx, Evesques, Archevesques & Patriarches: collieges, comme sont chanoines, & satellites,

comme sont les Chevaliers de Sainct Jean de Jerusalem. Et à tous ceux-là obeissoyent les Anciens par grande reverence & honneur, observants par grande cure leur religion."

48 Frances Muecke, "*Gentiles Nostri*"; Ann Blair, *Too Much to Know: Managing Scholarly Information before the Information Age* (New Haven: Yale University Press, 2010).

49 Guillaume Durand, *Rationale divinorum officiorum* (Antwerp: Heirs of Stelsius, 1570), 3:1, fol. 45^r: "secundum Isidorum in ritu templorum erant apud Gentiles Archiflamines, Protoflamines, Flamines & Sacerdotes."

50 Ibid.: "Apud Hebraeos quoque eadem erat diversitas personarum. . . . In templo erant summus Sacerdos, ut Melchisedech, minores Sacerdotes, Levitae, Nathinaei, luminum extinctores."

51 Boemus, *Fardle of Facions*, 2:71–72; *Mores*, 132: "Pari ordine apud Hebraeos in sacris summum Pontificem esse, minores sacerdotes, leuitas, nazaraeos, luminum extinctores, exorcistas, ianitores sive aedituos, & cantores."

52 Ibid.

53 Ibid.: "Romam deinde sede primaria translata, pro maximo ipse & successores sui semper habuere negotio, rudem & incultam adhuc Christi sui sectam eamque professos aliquo bono & ordine ex Mosaica lege, quam Christus non solvere, sed adimplere venisset . . . cultiores facere."

54 Ibid., 135.

55 Ibid., 137.

56 Polydore Vergil, *On Discovery*, ed. and tr. Brian Copenhaver (Cambridge, MA: Harvard University Press, 2002).

57 See, in general, Denis Hay, *Polydore Vergil: Renaissance Historian and Man of Letters* (Oxford: Oxford University Press, 1952). For Polydore's work on the history of Christianity, see the detailed account by Atkinson in *Inventing Inventors*.

58 See e.g. R. R. Bolgar, *The Classical Heritage and Its Beneficiaries* (Cambridge: Cambridge University Press, 1954; repr. with corrections, 1958); Anthony Grafton and Lisa Jardine, *From Humanism to the Humanities: Education and the Liberal Arts in Fifteenth- and Sixteenth-Century Europe* (London: Duckworth; Cambridge: Harvard University Press, 1986); Francis Goyet, *Le sublime du 'lieu commun': l'invention rhétorique dans l'Antiquité et à la Renaissance* (Paris: Champion, 1996); William Sherman, *Used Books: Marking Readers in Renaissance England* (Philadelphia: University of Pennsylvania Press, 2008); Ann Blair, *The Theater of Nature: Jean Bodin and Renaissance Science* (Princeton: Princeton University Press, 1997) and *Too Much To Know*; Martin Mulsow, *Prekäres Wissen: eine andere Ideengeschichte der Frühen Neuzeit* (Berlin: Suhrkamp, 2012); Richard Yeo, *Notebooks, English Virtuosi, and Early Modern Science* (Chicago and London: University of Chicago Press, 2014); *Lire, copier, écrire: les bibliothèques manuscrites et leurs usages au XVIIIe siècle*, ed. Elisabeth Decultot (Paris, 2003); *Note-Taking in Early Modern Europe*, ed. Ann Blair and Richard Yeo, special issue of *Modern Intellectual History* 20, 3 (2010).

59 Original in Boemus, *Mores*, IIII^r: "Memorabiliores gentium mores, ritus, leges, locorumque ubi degunt situs, quos historiae pater Herodotus, Diodorus

Siculus, Berosus, Strabo, Solinus, Trogus Pompeius, Ptolemaeus, Plinius, Cornelius Tacitus, Dionysius Apher, Pomponius Mela, Caesar, Iosephus: & ex recentioribus nonnulli, Vincentius, Aeneas Sylvius, qui postea Pij secondi pontificis maximi nomen tulit: Antonius Sabellicus, Ioannes Nauclerus, Ambrosius Calepinus, Nicolaus Perottus in Cornucopijs: alijque permulti clarissimi rerum scriptores in Commentarijs suis diffuse & ceu per partes celebravere: ut in uno libro conscriptos haberes, facileque quando usus deposceret invenires, historiarum lector cultorque studiosissime, per ocium succisivis horis undique conquaesivi, collegi, & in diarium hunc conscripsi, digessi."

60 British Library Add MS 41,068A; see Nella Giannetto, *Bernardo Bembo: umanista e politico veneziano* (Florence: Olschki, 1985), 359–393. For the evoluation of humanist zibaldoni into encyclopedic compendia that reached print in the years around 1500, see Silvia Rizzo and Sebastiano Gentile, "Per una tipologia delle miscellanee umanistiche," *Segno e testo* 2 (2004): 379–407 at 406–407.

61 Atkinson, *Inventing Inventors*, esp. 281.

62 Polydore Vergil, *De rerum inventoribus libri octo* (Paris: Estienne, 1529), fol. 89^r-v: "Post Evangelicum dogma inter gentes publicatum, ubi loci prima aedes Servatori nostro dicata fuerit, pro certo ponere non ausim, ne divinare potius quam veritati inhaerere dicar: sed in re parum nota conjectare licet."

63 Hay, *Polydore Vergil*, 71.

64 Polydore Vergil, *De rerum inventoribus libri octo* (Lyons: Gryphius, 1546), 224: "Verum ut non parum multa a Judaeis, ita non modica ab aliis gentibus instituta, aut casu rationeve accepta, tam in frequentem usum et consuetudinem venere, ut pro nostris habeantur. Quod equidem fecit, ut putarim me operae precium facturum, si origines ejusmodi rerum omnium quae ad religionem pertinerent, proderem, quo luculentius constaret, quas Servator, quas Apostoli, quas deinde Episcopi, quasve alii introduxissent."

65 Polydore Vergil, *De rerum inventoribus libri octo* (Strasbourg: Zetzner, 1606), 4:5, 234: "Haec suo ordine quo apud Hebraeos instituta sunt, exposuimus, ut initium cujusque rei, quod nostri in primis proposuti est, perapposite proderetur. Quae omnia cum umbra duntaxat futurorum fuerint, jam quae inde consecuta sint, explicemus."

66 Ibid., 4:7, 243: "Vestes vero sacras quibus nostri amiciuntur sacerdotes, ab Hebraeis, uti supra capite quinto dictum est, habent: cujus nempe rei argumentum est, quod nostri tum pontifices, tum sacerdotes, partim eadem induunt vestimenta, utputa Zonam seu Cingulum, Tunicam Talarem, quam vocamus Albam, tunicam hyacinthinam, ac Mitram, partim non longe forma aut colore differentia, cujusmodi sunt amictus capitis tegmen, qui loco cidaris usurpatur, planeta sive Casula, quam vocant, fabrefacta instar rationalis, hoc est, Logii pallium haud dissimile superhumerali, et caligae vice foeminalium. Unde denique liquido apparet, pleraque omnia ab ipsis Hebraeis uno vel altero modo sacerdotes nostros esse mutuatos."

67 Durand, *Rationale divinorum officiorum*, III.x, fol. 73^v: "In vet. test. erant duae tunicae: videlicet byssima & iacinthina Exo.39.c. & hodie etiam quidam Pontifices duabus vtuntur, ad notandum, quod proprium est eorum, habere scientiam duorum testamentorum, vt sciant de thesauro domini pro-

ferre noua & vetera. siue vt se ostendant diaconos & sacerdotes. . . . Secunda
tunica, quae iacinthina esse debet, sicut & olim erat coloris lapidis iacinthi,
qui aetheris serenitatem imitatur, sancto significant coelestia cogitantes, &
imitantes, siue coelestem cogitationem & conuersationem."

68 Polydore Vergil, *De rerum inventoribus*, 1529, fol. 69ʳ; 1606, 242: "Christiana
postmodum ecclesia Hebraeorum in hac parte secuta institutum ostiarios,
sive ianitores, lectores, seu psalmistas, exorcistas, acolytos, subdiaconos, diaconos, hoc est, levitas: quos numero septem ipsi Apostoli delegerunt, pres-
byteros et episcopos creavit, quo sic per gradus ad sacerdotium unusquisque
promoveretur."

69 Polydore Vergil, *De rerum inventoribus*, 1606, V.10, 356 (a passage censored
in some editions): "Quod vero sacerdos dicendo, Dominus vobiscum, saepius ad populum in altari se vertit, hoc de Hebraeorum quoque caeremonia
sumptum constat, quorum sacerdos inter sacra sese circumagebat, asper-
gendo sanguinem animalis immolati."

70 Polydore Vergil, *De rerum inventoribus*, 1529, fol. 69ᵛ: "Vnde denique liquido
apparet, pleraque omnia ab ipsis Hebraeis uno vel alio modo esse mutuo accepta: sicut illos ab Aegyptiis primitus sumpsisse verisimile est. Porro Ae-
gyptii sacerdotes ex Pythagorae placitis, lineum tantum vestimentum ut
purissimum mundissimumque in rebus divinis usurpabant. Laneum vero
ceu prophanum vituperabant: quia ab animato decerpitur, conficiturque ex
moricina materia. Contra linea ideo pura videbantur et sacrificantibus ac-
commodata: quoniam lineum ex terra oritur. Quaecunque autem ex terra
nascuntur, munda & pura existimarunt. Haec et id genus alia apud Philostratum memorat Tyaneus Apollonius. Atqui pari etiam ratione Hebraei Aegyptiorum institutum imitati videntur. Iosephus enim lib. VI. belli Iudaici
scribit sacerdotes ad altare templumque accedere solitos omni vitio carentes,
veste byssina id est linea amictos. Et Hiero." This is developed further in
1546, 261–262, and 1606, 243. His account of Egyptian vestments follows
Beroaldo, *Commentarii*, fol. 263ʳ, on Apuleius, *Golden Ass* 11.10: "Linteae
vestis candore. Orphei et pythagorae placita laneum vestimentum in rebus
divinis ut prophanum impurumque vituperant: cum linteum velamentum
ut purissimum mundissimumque maxime probent: unde non modo indutui
et amictui sanctissimis egyptiorum sacerdotibus sed opertui quoque in
rebus sacris usurpabatur. . . . haec et id genus alia apud Philostratum memorat Apollonius. Vnde sidonio data est occasio appellandi Apollonium inter
purpuratos linteatum. quid multa? nonne hodie quoque nostri sacedotes
linteati linigerique in sacrorum pompa incedere conspiciuntur? ritu opinor
translato ab Egyptiis sacerdotibus: de quibus haec Herodotus." Beroaldo in
turn draws on Herodotus, 2.37.3, and his own edition of Philostratus's life of
Apollonius of Tyana.

71 See Dmitri Levitin, "John Spencer's *De legibus Hebraeorum* (1683–85) and
Enlightened Sacred History: A New Interpretation," *Journal of the Warburg
and Courtauld Institutes* 76 (2013): 49–92; and Dmitri Levitin, *Ancient
Wisdom in the Age of the New Science: Histories of Philosophy in England,
c. 1640–1700* (Cambridge: Cambridge University Press, 2015).

72 Polydore Vergil, *De rerum inventoribus* (Basel: Froben, 1521), sig. Aᵛ: "Nos
proinde hunc desudavimus laborem, & instituta omnia nostrae religionis

aliarumque gentium complexi ac eorum primordia undecunque quaesita diligenter perscrutati, superioris aeditionis summae adglutinavimus, sic ut pars haec pro gravitate rei multo maior accesserit. Vnde iam omnes quibus religio, quae nos deo conciliat indissolubilique nodo connectit, cordi est tuo rogatu facilius haurire queunt, a quo fonte & eius deinde rivulis (nam semper scitu gratum iucundumque fuit, cuiusque rei nosse originem) manaverit tot ceremoniarum totve rituum flumen, quo demum cuncti mortales abluti hic placidam ac gaudialem agunt vitam, & alibi coelestem spe certa expectant. Cuius nos sospitator noster Christus participes facere dignetur."

73 Polydore Vergil, *De rerum inventoribus*, 1546, 224: "Christus Servator noster, qui, quemadmodum ipse testatur, ad nos mortales venerat, haud legis rescindendae, sed atque adeo confirmandae causa, jam inde a principio omnia pura, nuda, apertaque reddidit, quae antea Judaei umbram ipsius legis secuti suffecerant, colorarant, fucosaque fecerant, et denique quicquid isti laxarant, ac quo minus pietatis plusque ceremoniarum introduxerant, ille astrinxit, atque plus pietatis, minusque caeremoniarum esse voluit."

74 Ibid., 225: "demonstravique Patres olim in bona illorum parte recipienda, pie ac cum causa fecisse, quippe qui gentes etiam barbaras ad verae pietatis cultum ducere aventes, arbitrati sunt humanitatis condimentis tractandas, cum earum instituta haud prorsus horruerint, nec sustulerint, sed meliora fecerint, quo ne ullum religionis periculum crearetur, si vel minus admisissent, minusve mutassent, quemadmodum locis praepositis commodum demonstravimus. Atque isto ipso labore quem religionis causa non invitus suscepi, Deum Opt. Max. nobis propitium reddidisse confido."

75 Ibid., 224: "Caeterum deinceps sylva haec Judaicarum caeremoniarum sic paulatim agrum Dominicum occupavit, ut periculum sit, ne aliquando ipse Dominus illud agricolis crimini det, ab eisque petat, Quis enim quaesivit haec de manibus vestris?"

76 Flacius Illyricus, *Zwey Capitel vom Namen und Stiften der Mess* (Magdeburg: Rödinger, 1550), sig. [A iiiiʳ]. Elsewhere he prints part of Polydore's book 8, chap. 1: Flacius Illyricus, *Contra novos Detzelios Bullarum Iubilaei Antichristi praecones* (Magdeburg: Rödinger, 1550), sigs. [A7ᵛ–A8ʳ], using material on indulgences first added to the 1532 Basel edition of Polydore's work (see Atkinson, *Inventing Inventors*, 192–193).

77 Note on the title page of Flacius's copy of *Opus toti christianae Reipublicae maxime utile, de arcanis catholicae veritatis, contra obstinatissimam Iudaeorum nostrae tempestatis perfidiam ex Talmud, aliisque hebraicis libris nuper exceptum, et quadruplici linguarum genere eleganter congestum* (Ortona: Soncino, 1518), Herzog August Bibliothek E 390.2° Helmst.: "Godescalcus praetorius: Galatinus multa sumit ex Porcheto, adeo ut nonnunquam integrae pagellae monstrari queant sed nominis minimam facit mentionem."

78 See, in general, *Paul Eber (1511–1569): Humanist und Theologe der zweiter Generation der Wittenberger Reformation*, ed. Daniel Gehrt and Volker Leppin (Leipzig: Evangelische Verlagsanstalt, 2014).

79 Paul Eber, *Contexta populi iudaici historia a reditu ex Babylonico exilio, usque ad ultimum excidium Hierosolymae* (Wittenberg: Creutzer, 1548);

Herzog August Bibliothek, C 33.8° Helmst. (2). On the bottom of the title page, Eber dedicated this copy to Flacius: "Eruditissimo viro Domino M. Matthiae Illyrico Ebraicae linguae professo[ri] Paulus Eberus d.d."

80 Eber, *Historia*, fols. 22ʳ–41ᵛ.

81 Ibid., fols. 38ᵛ–39ʳ: "Et nominarunt se quidem Esseos, id est, operarios, quo titulo significabant et quid in aliis reprehenderent, et qua in re antecellere aliis vellent, videlicet, et fugere se prophanam licentiam Sadduceorum, et non probare histrionicam simulationem Phariseorum, sed se opera utilia aliis, praecepta divinitus facturos esse, et illam usitatam sententiam in ore habebant, ἅπας λόγος ἂν ἀπῇ τὰ ἔργα, μάταιον τι φαίνεται καὶ κενὸν [Demosthenes, Ol. 2.12]."

82 Ibid., fol. 39ʳ⁻ᵛ.

83 Ibid., fol. 40ᵛ: "sed collegii severitas haec erat, ut cum quispiam vel defraudasset alios, vel mentitus esset, vel libidine pollutus fuisset, statim eum communi sententia a toto coetu excluderent. Estque inter hos observata consuetudo vetustissima Synagogae, de qua contio loquitur in capite Matthei decimo octavo [18:15–18]. Non enim nova forma ibi institutitur, sed vetus mos recitatur, traditus a primis Patribus, cuius vestigia semper in Ecclesia manserant."

84 Ibid., 41ʳ: "Laudanda est disciplina, sed accedat vera agnitio filii Dei."

85 Flacius Illyricus et al., *Centuriae*, 7 vols. (Basel: Oporinus, 1561–1574), vol. 1, col. 237. On the origins and creation of this work see now Harald Bollbuck's monumental *Wahrheitszeugnis, Gottes Auftrag und Zeitkritik: Die Kirchengeschichte der Magdeburger Zenturien und ihre Arbeitstechniken* (Wiesbaden: Harrassowitz, 2014). Also essential is the digital archive that Bollbuck has created, hosted by the Herzog August Bibliothek, Wolfenbüttel: "Historische Methode und Arbeitstechnik der Magdeburger Zenturien: Edition ausgewählter Dokumente," online at http://diglib.hab.de/edoc /edo00086/start.htm, accessed August 25, 2018).

86 Flacius Illyricus et al., *Centuriae*, vol. 1, col. 232: "Orta est haec factio inde, quod in Pharisaeis hypocrisin, fucosamque pietatem, ambitionem, livorem, dominandi libidinem, et alia quaedam a vera pietate aliena cernerent. Deinde etiam a crasso ac prophano Sadducaeorum Epicureismo abhorrebant"; Eber, *Historia*, fol. 38ᵛ: "quo titulo significabant et quid in aliis reprehenderent, et qua in re antecellere aliis vellent, videlicet, et fugere se prophanam licentiam Sadduceorum, et non probare Histrionicam simulationem Phariseorum"; *Centuriae*, vol. 1, col. 233: "in extremam Iudeae oram, ad lacum Asphaltiten, haud procul a Iericho, ubi erant fragrantes balsami horti, se contulerunt": Eber, *Historia*, fol. 39ʳ "quia in extrema ora Iudeae ad lacum Asphaltiten, tanquam in secessu habitabant."

87 Flacius Illyricus et al., *Centuriae*, vol. 1, col. 234: "Deprehensos vero in peccatis, a sua congregatione depellunt: et qui taliter fuerit condemnatus, miserabili plerunque morte consumitur. Illis quidem sacramentis ac ritibus obligatus, neque carpere ab aliis oblatum cibum potest: herbas vero pecudum more decerpens, et fame exesus per membra corrumpitur."

88 Ibid., vol. 1, col. 232: "Tertia in Iudaico populo secta erat Essaeorum, seu ut alias vocantur Essenorum: quasi dicas, operatorum."

89 Lucas Osiander, *Epitomes historiae ecclesiasticae centuria I. II. III. [-XVI.]*, 9 vols. (Tübingen: Gruppenbach, 1592–1599), I.i.2.2, I, 2–4.

90 See the classic study of Joan-Pau Rubiés, "Hugo Grotius's Dissertation on the Origins of the American Peoples and the Use of Comparative Methods," *Journal of the History of Ideas* 52 (1991): 221–244, revised in his *Travellers and Cosmographers: Studies in the History of Early Modern Travel and Ethnology* (Aldershot and Birmingham: Ashgate, 2007), with references to further literature.

CHAPTER 5 · MATTHEW PARKER MAKES AN ARCHIVE

An earlier version of this essay was presented as one of my Sandars Lectures at Cambridge University on January 27, 2016. Heartfelt thanks go to Ann Jarvis, my host during my time as Sandars Lecturer; to Madeline McMahon, Paul Nelles, and Nicholas Popper, for invaluable comments on the earliest draft; to Markus Friedrich, for the invitation to present my findings to a wonderfully informed and critical audience in Berlin; and to the anonymous referees for *History of Humanities*, whose detailed comments prevented errors and prompted further thoughts.

1 Kevin Sharpe, *Sir Robert Cotton, 1586–1631: History and Politics in Early Modern England* (Oxford: Oxford University Press, 1979); Colin Tite, *The Manuscript Library of Sir Robert Cotton* (London: British Library, 1994); Tite, *The Early Records of Sir Robert Cotton's Library: Formation, Cataloguing, Use* (London: British Library, 2003); Julia Crick, "The Art of the Unprinted: Transcription and English Antiquity in the Age of Print," in *The Uses of Script and Print, 1300–1700*, ed. Julia Crick and Alexandra Walsham (Cambridge: Cambridge University Press, 2004), 116–134.

2 Anthony Grafton and Joanna Weinberg, *'I have always loved the holy tongue': Isaac Casaubon, the Jews, and a Forgotten Chapter in Renaissance Scholarship* (Cambridge, MA: Harvard University Press, 2011), 254–255.

3 William Lambarde, *A Perambulation of Kent*, British Library (hereafter BL) MS Sloane 3168, fol. 91^r.

4 Maidstone, Kent History and Archive Center, MS U47/48/Z1, fol. 94^r. On this manuscript and the composition of Lambarde's work see Ethan Shagan, "Print, Orality and Communications in the Maid of Kent Affair," *Journal of Ecclesiastical History* 52, no. 1 (2001): 21–33.

5 Lambarde, *A Perambulation of Kent* (London: Ralphe Newberie, 1576), 233. The text also appears in corrected form in BL MS Add 20033, fol. 124^{r-v}. For a full account, see Madeline McMahon, "Licking the 'bear whelpe': William Lambarde and Matthew Parker Revise the Perambulation of Kent," *Journal of the Warburg and Courtauld Institutes* 81 (2018): 154–171.

6 The manuscript in question is Corpus Christi College Cambridge (hereafter CCCC) MS 81.

7 Thomas James, *Ecloga Oxonio Cantabrigiensis*, 2 vols. (London: Bishop and Norton, 1600), I, 70: "*Homeri* opera Graece, cum duabus picturis, & quibusdam epitaphiis . . . hic liber est chartaceus, & fuit quondam *Theodori*

Archiep. sed fides sit penes lectorem." James clearly found the story of the discovery unconvincing, as will become clear below, but he may also have inferred that a paper manuscript must be recent. Compare his accurate comment on CCCC MS 250, ibid., 80: "Liber chartaceus nec valde antiquus." On James's work see Richard Clement, "Thomas James' *Ecloga Oxonio-Cantabrigiensis:* An Early Printed Union Catalog," *Journal of Library History* 22 (1987): 1–22. He himself may have been the prisoner of optimism when he described a Lambeth Palace Library MS of Gregory's *Register* as "MS Vetustissimum . . . quod creditur scriptum esse tempore Theodori Archiep. Cantu.": Neil Ker, "Thomas James's Collation of Gregory, Cyprian and Ambrose," *Bodleian Library Record* 4, 1 (1952): 16–29, at 21.

8 *Letters of Humfrey Wanley: Palaeographer, Anglo-Saxonist, Librarian,* ed. P. L. Heyworth (Oxford: Clarendon Press, 1989), 132–133; see also Helmut Gneuss, "Humfrey Wanley Borrows Books in Cambridge," *Transactions of the Cambridge Bibliographical Society* 12 (2001): 148. Most of Wanley's contemporaries, by contrast, still accepted Parker's ascriptions. See Stephanie West, "Before Palaeograpy: Notes on Early Descriptions and Datings of Greek Manuscripts," in *Studia codicologica,* ed. Kurt Treu (Berlin: Akademie-Verlag, 1977), 179–187 at 185–186.

9 *Oxford Dictionary of National Biography,* s.v. Walter, Hubert, by Robert Stacey.

10 Lambeth Palace Library MS 1212, fol. 26^r (fol. 13^r, 47), s. xiii ex.; fol. 116$^{r–v}$ (fol. 86$^{r–v}$, 224–225), s.xiii med. See the discussion at the *Magna Carta Project,* http://magnacarta.cmp.uea.ac.uk/read/newly_discovered_charters /Notification_of_the_King_s_grant_to_Hubert_Walter_of_the_right_to _convert_gavilkind_holdings_into_knights__fees.

11 *A Formula Book of English Official Historical Documents,* Vol. 1: *Diplomatic Documents,* ed. Hubert Hall (Cambridge: Cambridge University Press, 1908), 57.

12 Lambeth Palace Library MS 1212, fol. 26^r (fol. 13^r, 47).

13 On ecclesiastical and state archives in early modern England, see Nicholas Popper, "From Abbey to Archive: Managing Texts and Records in Early Modern England," *Archival Science* 10, no. 3 (2010): 249–266. For the larger story of the rise of archives in early modern Europe, see Markus Friedrich, *Die Geburt des Archivs: Eine Wissensgeschichte* (Munich: Oldenbourg, 2013), now available in English as *The Birth of the Archive: A History of Knowledge,* tr. John Noël Dillon (Ann Arbor: University of Michigan Press, 2018); *The Social History of the Archive: Record-Keeping in Early Modern Europe,* ed. Liesbeth Corens, Kate Peters, and Alexandra Walsham (Oxford: Oxford University Press, 2016); *Archives and Information in the Early Modern World,* ed. Liesbeth Corens, Kate Peters, and Alexandra Walsham (Oxford: Oxford University Press, 2018); and Randolph Head, *Making Archives in Early Modern Europe: Proof, Information and Political Record-Keeping* (Cambridge: Cambridge University Press, 2019).

14 R. I. Page, *Matthew Parker and His Books* (Kalamazoo, MI: Medieval Institute Publications, 1993); Mildred Budny, *Insular, Anglo-Saxon, and Early Anglo-Norman Manuscript Art at Corpus Christi College, Cambridge: An*

Illustrated Catalogue, 2 vols. (Kalamazoo, MI, and Cambridge: Medieval Institute Publications and the Parker Library, 1997); Timothy Graham, "Matthew Parker's Manuscripts: an Elizabethan Library and its Uses," in *The Cambridge History of Libraries in Britain and Ireland*, Vol. 1: *1640–1850*, ed. Giles Mandelbrote and Keith Manley (Cambridge: Cambridge University Press, 2006), 322–341; Jennifer Summit, *Memory's Library: Medieval Books in Early Modern England* (Chicago: University of Chicago Press, 2008), chap. 3.

15 For a survey of Parker's life and accomplishments, see *Oxford Dictionary of National Biography*, s.v. Parker, Matthew, by David Crankshaw and Alexandra Gillespie. John Strype, *The Life and Acts of Matthew Parker* (London: J. Wyat, 1711) and Victor Brook, *A Life of Archbishop Parker* (Oxford: Oxford University Press, 1962) remain essential.

16 For the growth and use of Parker's collection, see Bruce Dickins, "The Making of the Parker Library," *Transactions of the Cambridge Bibliographical Society* 6 (1977): 19–34; Timothy Graham and Andrew Watson, *The Recovery of the Past in Early Elizabethan England: Documents by John Bale and John Joscelyn from the Circle of Matthew Parker* (Cambridge: Cambridge Bibliographical Sociey, 1998); and Graham, "Matthew Parker's Manuscripts."

17 Stephen Batman, *The doome warning all men to the Judgemente* (London: Ralph Nubery, 1581), 399–400.

18 Graham, "Matthew Parker's Manuscripts."

19 See, in general, Ann Blair, *Too Much to Know: Managing Scholarly Information before the Modern Age* (New Haven and London: Yale University Press, 2010); and for a rich case study on the work of a master compiler, see Urs Leu, *Conrad Gessner (1516–1565): Universalgelehrter und Naturforscher der Renaissance* (Zurich: Verlag Neue Zürcher Zeitung, 2016).

20 Jeffrey Todd Knight, *Bound to Read: Compilations, Collections, and the Making of Renaissance Literature* (Philadelphia: University of Pennsylvania Press, 2013), 47–51.

21 Lambeth Palace Library MS 959, fol. 36^r: "This Historie was collected & penned by John Joscelyn one of ye sons of Sr. Tho. Joscelyn. knight by ye appointment & oversight of Matthwe Parker Archbp. of Cant. ye saide John being intertained in ye said Archb: howse, as one of his Antiquaries: to whom besides ye allowance afforded to hym in his howse. He gave to hym ye parsonage of Hollinborn in Kent, wherof he raised £300. for a lease by hym made out at house rent & reserved £30 rent John & his successors for ye years to cum."

22 See, e.g., BL MS Cotton Vitellius E XIV, and MS Cotton Vitellius D VII (the former is the earlier of the two).

23 CCCC MS 389, fol. 1^r: "Hic liber scriptus ante conquestum"; quoted by Graham, "Matthew Parker's Manuscripts," 333. In CCCC MS 1978, 245, a Parkerian dating appears: "fragmentum quatuor Euangeliorum. Hic Liber olim missus a Gregorio papa ad augustinum archiepiscopum: sed nuper sic mutilatus." This was an approximate but not unimpressive dating of a luxury copy of the Latin Gospels in insular half-uncial, written and illuminated in Northumbria in the beinning of the eighth century. See Bruce

Barker-Benfield, *St. Augustine's Abbey, Canterbury*, 3 vols. (London: British Library in association with the British Academy, 2008), 3:1733–1734.

24 Princeton University Library MS Scheide 159, 294 ("hic desunt quaedam"); 210 ("et hic quoque desunt nonnulla"); 365 ("hic deest nova historia ad robertum comitem glocestrie. W. Malmesbury").

25 CCCC MS 44, 235: "In orationibus, in admonitionibus, in benedictionibus nulla mentio cælibatus"; quoted with other examples in Graham, "Matthew Parker's Manuscripts," 334–335.

26 Alexander Neville, *De furoribus Norfolciensium, Ketto duce, liber unus* (London: Binneman, 1575), 4.

27 Michelle Brown, *The Book and the Transformation of Britain, c. 550–1050: A Study in Written and Visual Literacy and Orality* (London: British Library, 2011).

28 CCCC MS 44, 387; for Parker's other measures to make this manuscript neater, see Page, "Matthew Parker and His Books," 46–47.

29 Gervase of Tilbury, *Otia imperialia*, CCCC MS 14, 2: "In gratiam eorum qui huiusmodi abbreviationibus antiquorum non sunt exercitati" (example provided by Madeline McMahon).

30 Jean Mabillon, *De re diplomatica libri sex* (Paris: Billaine, 1681) (the 1709 edition is beautifully digitized at http://xob.de/mabillon/); for a modern handbook in a similar format, see, e.g., S. Harrison Thomson, *Latin Bookhands of the Later Middle Ages, 1100–1500* (London: Cambridge University Press, 1969).

31 Earlier accounts of this side of Parker's work are superseded by Madeline McMahon, "Matthew Parker and the Practice of Church History," in *Confessionalization and Erudition in Early Modern Europe: An Episode in the History of the Humanities*, ed. Nicholas Hardy and Dmitri Levitin (Oxford: Published for the British Academy by Oxford University Press, 2020), 116–153.

32 On Flacius's accomplishments and those of the team he assembled—which did most but not all of the actual writing—see Harald Bollbuck, *Wahrheitszeugnis, Gottes Auftrag und Zeitkritik: Die Kirchengeschichte der Magdeburger Zenturien und ihre Arbeitstechniken* (Wiesbaden: Harrassowitz, 2014), 664–666. This masterly treatment, which is dense with primary sources, now forms the basis of all work on the Centuries. Also important are Matthias Pöhlig, *Zwischen Gelehrsamkeit und konfessioneller Identitätsstiftung: Lutherische Kirchen- und Universalgeschichtsschreibung, 1546–1617* (Tübingen: Mohr Siebeck, 2007); and *Catalogus und Centurien: Interdisziplinäre Studien zu Matthias Flacius und den Magdeburger Centurien*, ed. Arno Mentzel-Reuters und Martina Hartmann (Tübingen: Mohr Siebeck, 2008). The fullest study of Flacius's practices as a collector and user of manuscripts is Martina Hartmann, *Humanismus und Kirchenkritik: Matthias Flacius Illyricus als Erforscher des Mittelalters* (Stuttgart: Thorbecke, 2001).

33 One form of this list appears in BL MS Egerton. 3790; see Nicholas Popper, *Walter Ralegh's History of the World and the Historical Culture of the Late Renaissance* (Chicago: University of Chicago Press, 2012), 59–60.

34 Norman Jones, "Matthew Parker, John Bale and the Magdeburg Centuriators," *Sixteenth Century Journal* 12 (1981): 35–49, at 38–39.

35 John Bale, *Scriptorum Illustrium maioris Brytanniae, quam nunc Angliam & Scotiam uocant, Catalogus* (Basel: Oporinus, 1557), sigs. α3ʳ⁻ᵛ: "Quod ut in aliis regionibus alii pii librorum et antiquitatis indagatores magno cum dolore senserunt, ita mihi quoque bibliothecas nostras in Anglia optimis scriptis aliquando instructissimas, perlustranti usu venit: ubi licet pauci integri invenirentur, plerique vel sine capite et fronte mutilati, vel prorsus detriti atque corrupti supinitate et ignorantia hominum male de literis meritorum reperiebantur." For Bale's form of bibliographical scholarship, which he adapted from precedents set by fellow monks as well as the antiquary John Leland, see Frederic Clark, "Dividing Time: The Making of Historical Periodization in Early Modern Europe" (PhD dissertation, Princeton University, 2014).

36 Quoted in Strype, *Life and Acts of Matthew Parker*, 528.

37 *The Recovery of the Past*, ed. Graham and Watson; McMahon, "Parker and the Practice of Church History."

38 See, esp., Graham, "Matthew Parker's Manuscripts" for a full account.

39 CCCC MS 81, fol. 1ʳ: "Hic liber Theodori repertus in monasterio divi Augustini Cantuariensis post dissolucionem et quasi proiectus inter laceras chartas illius cenobii. quem cumulum chartarum scrutatus quidam pistor quondam eiusdem coenobii invenit et domum portavit monachis et aliis idem coenobium inhabitantibus aut fugatis aut inde recedentibus. Sed tandem foeliciter in manus Matthaei Cantuariensis Archiepiscopi hic liber devenit. quem ut ingentem Thesaurum apud se asservat. Et reponendum vult vel in communi Bibliotheca Academiae Cantabrigiae, vel in fideli custodia magistri collegii (qui pro tempore fuerit corporis Christi et beatae Mariae) ibidem." Compare Thomas James's sharp comment on this note, in *Ecloga*, 1:70: "Miraculosam inventionem huius libri in pariete quodam, vide adnotatam in fine libri."

40 On the quality of Parker's collection see Alexander Nowell's letter to Parker (ca. 1565), in Matthew Parker, *Correspondence*, ed. John Bruce and Thomas Thomason Perowne (Cambridge: Cambridge University Press for the Parker Society, 1853), 251.

41 CCCC MS 418, edited by Pierre Fraenkel as Martin Bucer and Matthew Parker, *Florilegium patristicum* (Leiden: Brill, 1988). For the dating of Bucer's and Parker's work on this text see ibid., "Introduction," xiv–xvi.

42 CCCC MS 418, 1.

43 Ibid., 41, 83.

44 Ibid., 70, 74–75, 172, 175.

45 See Chapter 4. See also Catherine Atkinson, *Inventing Inventors in Renaissance Europe: Polydore Vergil's De inventoribus rerum* (Tübingen: Mohr Siebeck, 2007).

46 Polydore Vergil, *De rerum inventoribus libri octo* (Lyons: Gryphius, 1546), 224: "Verum ut non parum multa a Judaeis, ita non modica ab aliis gentibus instituta, aut casu rationeve accepta, tam in frequentem usum et consuetudinem venere, ut pro nostris habeantur. Quod equidem fecit, ut putarim me operae precium facturum, si origines ejusmodi rerum omnium quae ad religionem pertinerent, proderem, quo luculentius constaret, quas Servator, quas Apostoli, quas deinde Episcopi, quasve alii introduxissent."

47 Constantin Hopf, "Bishop Hooper's Notes to the King's Council, 3 October 1550," *Journal of Theological Studies* 44 (1943): 194–199, at 198–199. On this controversy see Hopf, *Martin Bucer and the English Reformation* (Oxford: Blackwell, 1946), 131–170; and Judith Anderson, *Translating Investments: Metaphor and the Dynamics of Cultural Change in Tudor-Stuart England* (New York: Fordham University Press, 2005), 78–111, 243–251.

48 *The Writings of John Bradford, M.A.*, ed. Aubrey Townsend (Cambridge: Cambridge University Press for the Parker Society, 1853), 381–383.

49 Robert Crowley, *Brief Discourse* (London: n.p., 1566), sig. Bviii^r.

50 Matthew Parker, *Brief Examination* (London: n.p., 1566), sig. ***** 3^v.

51 Ibid., sig. ***^v.

52 Bede, *Historia ecclesiastica gentis Anglorum* I.30.

53 Sir John Harington, quoted by Nancy Basler Bjorklund, "'A Godly Wyfe is an Helper': Matthew Parker and the Defense of Clerical Marriage," *Sixteenth Century Journal* 34 (2003): 347–365, at 364.

54 The MS is Gonville and Caius College Library 427/427. See Erwin Frauenknecht, *Die Verteidigung der Priesterehe in der Reformzeit* (Hannover: Hahn, 1997); Elizabeth Evenden and Thomas Freeman, *Religion and the Book in Early Modern England: The Making of John Foxe's 'Book of Martyrs'* (Cambridge: Cambridge University Press, 2011), 150–152; Catherine Hall, "The One-Way Trail: Some Observations on CCC MS 101 and G&CC MS 427," *Transactions of the Cambridge Bibliographical Society* 11, no. 3 (1998): 272–285.

55 Michael Murphy, "Anglo-Saxon at Tavistock Abbey," *Duquesne Review* 11 (1966): 119–124.

56 John Foxe, *The first volume of the ecclesiasticall history contaynyng the actes and monuments of thyngs passed in every kynges tyme in this realme, especially in the Church of England* (London: John Day, 1670), 1321; quoted in Evenden and Freeman, *Religion and the Book*, 152.

57 *The Works of John Jewel, D.D., Bishop of Salisbury*, ed. Richard William Jelf, 8 vols. (Oxford: Oxford University Press, 1848), 6:255; 4:616: "Notwithstanding, I have seen the same epistle written in parchment, in old hand, of good record, under the name of Volusianus Carthaginensis."

58 Parker, *Correspondence*, 253–254. The manuscript in question is now BL MS Cotton Vespasian A 1.

59 CCCC MSS 419 and 452. On this and many similar acts of Parker's see the grumpy but invaluable study by Page, *Matthew Parker and His Books*, in this case at 51. Parker's artisans also removed four pictures from the same thirteenth-century Psalter and inserted them into the ninth-century MacDurnan Gospels, now Lambeth Palace Library MS 1370, one before each gospel. See ibid.; see also Timothy Graham, "Changing the Context of Medieval Manuscript Art: The Case of Matthew Parker," in *Medieval Art: Recent Perspectives*, ed. Gale R. Owen-Crocker and Timothy Graham (Manchester: Manchester University Press, 1998), 189–193. My thanks go to one of the journal's anonymous referees for calling my attention to this point.

60 Asser, *Alfredi regis res gestae* (London: John Day, 1574), sig. Aij^r: "Latina autem cum sint, Saxonicis literis excudi curavimus, maxime ob venerandam

ipsius archetypi antiquitatem, ipso adhuc (ut opinio fert mea) Ælfredo superstite, ijsdem literarum formulis descriptam." The copy of this edition in
the Morgan Library, 62096, belonged to Robert Sidney, Earl of Leicester.

61　Asser, *Alfredi regis res gestae*, sig. Aij^v: "Augent coniecturam Pastoralia
quae ab ipso prudentissimo rege ex sermone Romano in Saxonicum conversa
fuerunt, atque illius imperio per quasdam Britanniae Ecclesias sparsa.
Quorum vetusta quaedam exemplaria, eodem etiam tempora descripta,
hodie extant similibus depicta characteribus." Parker had in mind such MSS
as Trinity College, Cambridge MS R 5.22, a note in which identifies it as a
presentation copy (fol. 1^r): "Hic ipsus [sic] liber est quem Aluredus Rex misit
ad Ecclesiam Syreburnensem, quem et transtulit è pastorali Gregorij Latine
in Anglicum."

62　See Suzanne Hagedorn, "Matthew Parker and Asser's *Ælfredi regis res
gestæ*," *Princeton University Library Chronicle* 51, no. 1 (1989–1990): 74–90.

63　*A Testimonie of Antiquitie* (London: John Day, 1566).

64　BL MS Add. 18160. See John Bromwich, "The First Book Printed in Anglo-
Saxon Types," *Transactions of the Cambridge Bibliographical Society* 3,
no. 4 (1962): 265–291; Erick Kelemen, "More Evidence for the Date of *A Testimonie of Antiquitie*," *The Library* 7, no. 4 (2006): 361–376.

65　Thomas James, "An Appendix to the Reader," in *A Treatise of the Corruption of Scripture, Councels, and Fathers, by the Prelates, Pastors, and Pillars of the Church of Rome, for Maintenance of Popery and Irreligion*
(London: Lownes, 1612), sig. A4^r–v, at A4^r.

66　See Francis Junius, ed., *Indices expurgatorii duo, testes fraudum ac falsa-
tionum pontificiarum* (Hanau: n.p., 1611), 10–11.

67　*Flores historiarum* (London: Marsh, 1570), sig. a2^r: "Tanta enim fuit olim
temporum nequitia, tam effrenata veritatis supprimendae cuiusque libido,
ut nihil dubitarint ad occecandas hominum mentes, veterum scriptorum,
vel universas periodos, multo minus verbula intrudere, extinguere, commu-
tare, prout cuique libitum fuerat, quae quidem mens mala et animus malus
non in istiusmodi solum Authorum veterum monumentis reperientur, sed
in hiis etiam authoribus qui de rebus divinis maxime seriis et sacris
scripsere."

68　CCCC MS 11, fol. 45^v, col. 1: "hic desunt. ex industria ut videtur, Scriptoris."

69　*Flores historiarum*, sig. a2^r–v: "Quid queso hisce maioribus propositum erat,
qui Rabani Magnentii Mauri, natione Scoti, abbatis Fuldensis, opera, adhuc
fere ante septingentos annos scripta, in publicum exponi decernentes, quam
tenebris perstringere hominum mentes, in illius, quem edidit, libri de uni-
verso sive de rerum naturis (adhuc ni fallor inexcusi) cap. xi. lib. 5. De ecclesiasticis officiis? Qui nequiter, et iniuriose ab hisce verbis (Sacramentum
ore percipitur, virtute sacramenti interior homo satiatur) hanc subsequentem
sententiam (Sacramentum enim in alimentum corporis redigitur, virtute
autem sacramenti aeternae vitae dignitas adipiscitur) etc. quasi spuriam et
illegitimam penitus abrasere. Cum tamen haec sententia, priori coniuncta,
in quolibet veteri exemplari (ante Guliclmi conquestoris tempora edito)
passim reperiatur."

70 Matthew Parker, *De antiquitate Britannicae ecclesiae* (London: John Day, 1572), sig. ¶iij^r: "Ac verbis praeterea illis plerumque usi sumus, quibus veteres illi scriptores suorum temporum mores actionesque expresserunt. Quae a nobis consulto quidem ideo facta sunt, ne cum Pontificiorum flagitia tam insigniter saepe ab ipsis Monachis & antiquis scriptoribus notata & deprehensa sunt, eadem a nobis ficta seu depravata quisquam comminiscatur, tum ne quacunque in re ab illorum mente & sententia videri possimus recessisse."

71 John Joscelyn, *Historiola Collegii Corporis Christi*, ed. John Willis Clark (Cambridge: Cambridge Antiquarian Society, 1880), 39–40; Robert Masters, *The History of the College of Corpus Christi and the B. Virgin Mary (commonly called Benet)*, 2 parts (Cambridge: Cambridge University Press, 1753), 78–80; Timothy Graham, "A Parkerian Transcript of the List of Bishop Leofric's Procurements for Exeter Cathedral: Matthew Parker, the Exeter Book and Cambridge University Library MS Ii. 2.11," *Transactions of the Cambridge Bibliographical Society* 10, no. 4 (1994): 421–459, at 452–453.

72 CCCC MS 582, fol. 1^v: "Hic liber complectens statuta Collegij, una cum alijs rebus in sequentibus memoratu dignis scriptus et absolutus fuit opera et industria Matthaei Cantuar: Archiepiscopi. Haec statuta sic renovata sunt in visitatione Domini EDWARDI regis sexti per assignationem et praeceptum Visitatorum Regiorum et demandatum est hoc opus Wilhelmo Mayr legum doctori et Matthaeo Parker sacre theologie professori, qui partim ex veteri libro statutorum istas constitutiones sic ordinarunt et postea cum visitatores dominae Elizabeth Reginae eas rursus approbaverunt et (in tribus tantum statutis) auxerunt et manuum suarum subscriptione testificarunt"; fol. 12^r: "Haec statuta subscripta sunt manibus visitatorum dominae Elizabethae Reginae Angliae &c. xxx° et xxxi° diebus Januarij Anno Domini 1573. Ceteri nominati Visitatores obierunt, qui antea etiam ea approbaverunt et subscripserunt."

73 Evenden and Freeman, *Religion and the Book*, esp. chaps. 4–5.

74 E.g., CCCC MS 340, 281–284.

75 *A Booke of Certaine Canons, Concernyng Some Parte of the Discipline of the Church of England In the Yeare of our Lord 1571* (London: John Day, 1571), 6.

76 Pamela M. Black, "Matthew Parker's Search for Cranmer's 'great notable written books,'" *The Library*, 5th ser., 29, no. 3 (1974): 301–322.

77 See Graham, "A Parkerian Transcript," 451–455.

78 CCCC MS 581, fol. 1^{r-v}; a facsimile was printed in J. Goodwin, "An Account of the Rites and Ceremonies which took place at the Consecration of Archbishop Parker," *Publications of the Cambridge Antiquarian Society* 1 (1841–1846): part 3, 17–27.

79 Gilbert Burnet, *The Reformation of the Church of England*, 6 vols. (London: Baynes, 1825), 2:2, 432–35.

80 *Registrum Matthaei Parker*, 10 parts in 3 vols. (London: Canterbury and York Society, 1928), 1:31–33.

81 Masters, "The History of the College of Corpus Christi," 84. See also Brook, *Parker*, 85–86. For archival documentation as performance, see Brigittte

Bedos-Rezak, "Civic Liturgy and Urban Records in Northern France, 1100–1400," in *City and Spectacle in Medieval Europe*, ed. Barbara Hanawalt and Kathryn Ryerson (Minneapolis: University of Minnesota Press, 1994), 34–55; Eamon Duffy, *The Voices of Morebath: Reformation and Rebellion in an English Village* (New Haven and London: Yale University Press, 2001); Eric Ketelaar, "Records Out and Archives In: Early Modern Cities as Creators of Records and Communities of Archives," *Archival Science* 10 (2010): 201–210.

82 CCCC MS 106, 11: "Concordat. Matthaeus Cantuar."

83 Asser, *Alfredi regis res gestae*, sig. Aiiij^v: "Quinetiam quoniam diplomata multa et vetustioris aetatis monumenta, tum regiae quae in archivis custodiuntur chartae, tam ante quam post Normannorum in Angliam adventum, adhuc extant."

84 This version of the printed *De antiquitate* appears in BL C.24.b.6, where the Accord is printed at 94–95.

85 In the standard text of the *De antiquitate*, the list of signatures after the Accord ends with the following statement (e.g., BL C.24.b.7. and C.24.b.8, 95): "Ego Gulielmus London. Episcopus consensi, cum multis alijs Episcopis et Abbatibus, ut in Archivis patet."

86 See, e.g., Friedrich, *Die Geburt des Archiv*; Randolph Head, "Documents, Archives, and Proof around 1700," *The Historical Journal* 56, no. 4 (2013): 909–930; *Archivi e archivisti in Italia tra Medioevo ed età moderna*, ed. Filippo de Vivo, Andrea Guidi and Alessandro Silvestri (Rome: Viella, 2015); and the other studies cited in note 13. For recent surveys of this burgeoning literature, see Elizabeth Yale, "The History of Archives: The State of the Discipline," *Book History* 18 (2005): 332–359; Markus Friedrich, "Introduction: New Perspectives for the History of Archives," in *Praktiken der Frühen Neuzeit: Akteure-Handlungen-Artefakte*, ed. Arndt Brendecke (Cologne: Böhlau, 2015), 468–472; and Nicholas Popper, "Archives and the Boundaries of Early Modern Science," *Isis* 107, no. 1 (2016), 86–94.

87 There is a translation (which is not wholly reliable) in Lester Born, "Baldassare Bonifacio and his Essay *De Archivis*," *American Archivist* 4 (1941): 221–237; for the original, see *De archivis liber singularis* (Venice: Pinelli, 1632).

88 See, esp., Elizabeth Yale, "With Slips and Scraps: How Early Modern Scientists Invented the Archive," *Book History* 12 (2009): 1–36; which is now incorporated in her *Sociable Knowledge: Natural History and the Nation in Early Modern Britain* (Philadelphia: University of Pennsylvania Press, 2016).

89 Parker, *De antiquitate*, sig. ¶iij^r: "Quam ex variis antiquis sumptam & delibatam scriptoribus tam apte atque concinne hic compositam & cohaerentem vides, ut unius potius scriptoris series, quam ex multis decerptae authoritates & sententiae videri possint."

90 Note also Joscelyn's description of Parker's commission to him to compose his *Historiola* of Corpus Christi College: "Praeterea commentarium hoc conscribi curavit et ex diversis collegii scriptis ac monumentis compingi"; *Historiola*, ed. Clark, 40.

91 See, in general, Andrew Carriker, *The Library of Eusebius of Caesarea* (Leiden and Boston: Brill, 2003); and Anthony Grafton and Megan Williams, *Christianity and the Transformation of the Book: Origen, Eusebius and the*

Library of Caesarea (Cambridge, MA, and London: Harvard University Press, 2006), chaps. 3–4.

92 Bede, *Historia ecclesiastica gentis Anglorum*, praefatio.

93 For a splendid case in point, see Katrina Olds, *Forging the Past: Invented Histories in Counter-Reformation Spain* (New Haven and London: Yale University Press, 2015).

94 Eusebius, *Life of Constantine* 2.23, quoted in Clifford Ando, *Imperial Ideology and Provincial Loyalty in the Roman Empire* (Berkeley, Los Angeles and London: University of California Press, 2000), 130, which notes Eusebius's inspiration by Roman archival practices.

95 Cited in *John Foxe's The Acts and Monuments Online*, at http://www.johnfoxe.org/index.php?realm=text&gototype=modern&edition=1563&pageid=5, accessed December 14, 2019.

96 Raffaele Maffei, "Anthropologia," in *Commentariorum urbanorum . . . octo & triginta libri* (Paris: Petit, 1511), bk. 15, fol. CLXIIʳ: "Hic teste Hieronymo in epistola xlvii. Constantino magno cum ille Caesaream venisset & si quid ei opus diceret respondit minime cum mihi tua liberalitate fit satis: verum quod magis opto: iube per orbem terrarum gesta martyrum & quicquid inter Christianos actum sit apud omnia loca ex publicis ac privati monumentis exquiri ac mihi adferri. Ex quo ille postea tam universae historiae scriptor apparuit." Gessner identified Maffei as one of his sources in *Bibliotheca universalis* (Zurich, 1545), sig. *6ʳ. He cited, but did not quote, the passage Maffei ascribed to Jerome on fol. 235ᵛ: "Quomodo hanc historiam conscripserit, & alia plura, vide in Anthropologia Raph. Volaterrani prope finem libri 16." Jerome's letter is not otherwise attested.

97 E.g., in one of Parker's copies, Princeton University Library MS Scheide 159, fols. 266ᵛ–267ᵛ.

98 CCCC MS 43, fol. 9ʳ.

99 *Rerum Anglicarum Scriptores*, 2 vols. in 3 (Oxford: Sheldonian Theatre, 1684–1691), 1:98: "chirographa nostra pulcherrima, litera publica conscripta, & Crucibus aureis & venustissimis picturis ac elementis pretiosissimis adornata."

100 Alfred Hiatt, *The Making of Medieval Forgeries* (London: British Library, 2004).

101 Matthew Parker, ed., *Matthaei Paris, Monachi Albanensis, Angli, Historia Maior, a Guilielmo Conquaestore, ad ultimum annum Henrici tertii. Cum indice locupletissimo* (London: Reginald Wolf, 1570–71), sigs. †iiiiᵛ–†iiiiʳ: "Sane studiosius eum hanc provinciam in se suscepisse credibile est, quod lege et communi decreto cautum erat apud nos, Monasteria et Collegia ecclesiastica, in primis vero et prae caeteris Albanense Coenobium, quasi communem thesaurum et receptaculum debere esse, ubi reponerentur ac fidelissime reservarentur omnia historica gesta huius Regni, et quaecunque memoria ac fama digna essent."

102 On Da Ponte see Roberto Ricciardi, "Da Ponte, Ludovico (Ponticus Virunius)," in *Dizionario biografico degli italiani* 32 (1986), online at http://www.treccani.it/enciclopedia/ludovico-da-ponte_%28Dizionario-Biografico%29/, accessed May 19, 2014.

103 Parker, ed., *Matthaei Paris Historia Maior*, sig. †iiii^r: "quod et notavit PONTICVS VIRVNIVS. in historia sua Britannica, in qua hoc testatum relinquitur, morem et consuetudinem Occidentalium Principum fuisse, semper apud se domi habere tales eruditos et doctos viros, qui sua et suorum dicta et facta egregia, vere possent et memoriter statim expedire: nolebant tamen haec sua magnifica et heroica gesta in publicum prodire et evulgari, quamdiu aut ipsi aut ipsorum filii viverent."

104 Ludovico Da Ponte, *Britannicae historiae libri sex* (Augsburg: Alexander Weyssenhorn, 1534), sig. C1^r: "Ad manus meas historiae regum Britannorum nobilissimae supra cladem Trioianorum pervenere, quas esse verissimas arguebat regum Occidentalium consuetudo semper secum habere, qui eorum gesta notarent veritate praecipua, sed nec viventibus ipsis, nec filijs aperire, obprobrium vero fore, scilicet attribuere, quae ipsi in tanto Imperio facere non potuissent, eas deinde in regalibus archivis in posteros custodire."

105 John Caius, *De antiquitate Cantebrigiensis Academiæ libri duo* (London: Binneman, 1568), 239: "imperavit coenobio Roffensi, ut in commentarios referrent res gestas sui temporis ut acciderint, idque coenobium cum multis alijs monast. & praecipue S. Albani, in hoc delegit, tanquam in Thesaurum et custodiam rerum memorabilium, uti Matth. Westm. & is qui Roffensem historiam aedidit, scribunt."

106 Ibid., 239-240: "Etenim Regibus occidentis mundi partis consuetum fuit olim, apud se habere eos, qui res eorum ut erant gesta, annis singulis bona fide scriberent. Sic tamen ut neque regis aetate, nec filiorum eius facerent publicas, sed ita concinnatas historias, in archiva referrent regia, ubi ad posteros reservarentur: uti Virumnus Ponticus in historia Britannorum refert."

107 For Caius's interest in Italianate forms of symbolism and sculpture, see Paul Fox, "On the Symbolism of the Arms of John Caius and of the College Caduceus," *The Caian*, November 1986, 46-56; and Anthony Radcliffe, "John Caius and Paduan Humanist Symbolism," *The Caian*, 1987, 121-126.

108 CCCC MS 114a, 49.

109 Ibid.

110 BL C.123.g.2., verso of flyleaf: "Roffensis praefat."

111 John Caius, *De libris propriis*, in *The Works of John Caius*, ed. Edwin S. Roberts (Cambridge: Cambridge University Press, 1912), 75-83, at 75.

112 For a parallel from a very different world, see Anna More, *Baroque Sovereignty: Carlos de Sigüenza y Góngora and the Creole Archive of Colonial Mexico* (Philadelphia: University of Pennsylvania Press, 2013).

CHAPTER 6 · FRANCIS DANIEL PASTORIUS

MAKES A NOTEBOOK

Heartfelt thanks go to Peter Stallybrass, who introduced me to Pastorius and encouraged my interest in him with great generosity; to Brooke Palmieri and Andrew Thomas for sharing their unpublished work and for their expert advice; to Ann Blair, Christian Flow, Nancy Siraisi, and Jacob Soll, for comments and criticism; and to the staffs of the Rare Book and Manuscript

Library of the University of Pennsylvania (hereafter UPL), the Library Company of Philadelphia (hereafter LCP), the library of the Pennsylvania Historical Society (hereafter PHS), the Bodleian Library, Oxford, the British Library, the Department of Special Collections, Princeton University Library, and the Herzog August Bibliothek, Wolfenbüttel. An earlier version of this chapter was presented at "The Industrious Bee: Francis Daniel Pastorius, His Manuscripts, and His World," a conference sponsored by the McNeil Center for Early American Studies and the University of Pennsylvania Libraries, on October 23–24, 2009.

1 On Pastorius (1651–1719), the standard study is still Marion Dexter Learned, *The Life of Francis Daniel Pastorius, The Founder of Germantown* (Philadelphia: Campbell, 1908). See also Marianne Wokeck, "Pastorius, Francis Daniel," American National Biography Online, at https://libserv7.princeton .edu:82/pul/nph-pul2.cgi/000000A/http/www.anb.org/articles/01/01-00703 .html=3fa=3d1&f=3dpastorius=252C=252ofrancis=252odaniel&ia=3d-at&ib =3d-bib&d=3d10&ss=3d0&q=3d1, accessed August 22, 2011; Christoph Schweitzer, "Introduction," in Pastorius, *Deliciae Hortenses or Garden-Recreations and Voluptates Apianae,* ed. Schweitzer (Camden, SC: Camden House, 1982), 1–6; and Margo Lambert, "Francis Daniel Pastorius: An American in Early Pennsylvania, 1683–1719/20" (PhD dissertation, Georgetown University, 2007).

2 Georg Horn, *De originibus americanis libri quatuor* (The Hague: Adrian Vlacq, 1652); *Dissertatio de vera aetate mundi* (Leiden: Elzevir and Leffen, 1659); *Arca Noæ* (Leiden and Rotterdam: Hack, 1666); *Orbis politicus* (Zwickau: Samuel Ebel and Michael Giebner, 1667); *Orbis imperans* (Leiden: Felix Lopes de Haro, 1668).

3 Georg Horn, *Arca Mosis* (Leiden and Rotterdam: Hack, 1669); LCP Rare | Am 1668 Hor Log 798.D. It seems likely that Pastorius meant to write "in illa."

4 Virgil, *Eclogues* 3.33–34.

5 Robert Darnton, *The Great Cat Massacre and Other Episodes in French Cultural History* (New York: Basic Books, 1984).

6 Rüdiger Mack, "Francis Daniel Pastorius: sein Einsatz für die Quäker," *Pietismus und Neuzeit* 15 (1989): 132–171, at 140. Pastorius also inscribed similar sentiments in Latin and English above his table, on the chest that held his manuscripts, and on doors and windows. See Learned's extracts from the *Bee-Hive* in Marion Dexter Learned, "From Pastorius' Bee-Hive or Bee-Stock," *Americana Germanica* 1, no. 4 (1897): 67–110, at 104–106.

7 Mack, "Pastorius," 140. However, according to Beatrice Pastorius Turner, "William Penn and Pastorius," *Pennsylvania Magazine of History and Biography* 57 (1933): 66–90, Penn laughed only once.

8 Alfred L. Brophy, "'Ingenium est Fateri per quos profeceris'": Francis Daniel Pastorius' Young Country Clerk's Collection and Anglo-American Legal Literature, 1682–1716," *University of Chicago Law School Roundtable* 3 (1996): 637–742. See more generally *Acta Germanopolis: Records of the Corporation of Germantown, Pennsylvania, 1691–1707,* ed. J. M. Duffin (Philadelphia: Colonial Society of Pennsylvania, 2008).

9   Alfred L. Brophy, "The Quaker Bibliographic World of Francis Daniel Pas-
    torius's *Bee Hive*," *Pennsylvania Magazine of History and Biography* 122
    (1998): 241–291.

10 Walter Woodward, *Prospero's America: John Winthrop, Jr., Alchemy, and the
    Creation of New England Culture, 1606–1676* (Chapel Hill: University of
    North Carolina Press for the Omohundro Institute of Early American His-
    tory and Culture, 2010); Richard Calis, Frederic Clark, Christian Flow, An-
    thony Grafton, Madeline McMahon, and Jennifer M. Rampling, "Passing
    the Book: Cultures of Reading in the Winthrop Family, 1580–1730," *Past and
    Present* 241 (2018): 69–141.

11 UPL, MS Codex 726, "The Bee-Hive" (2 vols. in 3). See also UPL, MS Codex
    89, "The Young Country Clerk's Collection"; and PHS, Pastorius Collection
    #475, "Alvearalia," "Res Propriae," and "Talia Qualia." Excerpts from the
    Bee-Hive have been printed in Marion Dexter Learned, "From Pastorius'
    Bee-Hive or Bee-Stock," *Americana Germanica,* 1, no. 4 (1897): 67–110; 2,
    no. 1 (1898): 33–42; 2, no. 2 (1898): 59–70; 2–4 (1899): 65–79; in *The Multilin-
    gual Anthology of American Literature: A Reader of Original Texts with
    English Translations,* ed. Marc Shell and Werner Sollors (New York: New
    York University Press, 2000); and in *The Francis Daniel Pastorius Reader,*
    ed. Patrick Erben with Alfred Brophy and Margo Lambert (State College:
    Pennsylvania State University Press, 2018).

12 Brophy, "'Ingenium est Fateri,'" and "The Quaker Bibliogrpahic World." See
    Patrick Erben, "Promoting Pennsylvania: Penn, Pastorius, and the Creation
    of a Transnational Community," *Resources for American Literary Study* 29
    (2003–2004; published 2005): 25–65; "'Honey-Combs' and 'Paper-Hives': Po-
    sitioning Francis Daniel Pastorius's Manuscript Writings in Early Pennsyl-
    vania," *Early American Literature* 37 (2002): 157–194; and Lambert, "Francis
    Daniel Pastorius."

13 Edwin Wolf II, *The Book Culture of a Colonial American City: Philadel-
    phia Books, Bookmen, and Booksellers* (Oxford: Clarendon Press, 1988). On
    Pastorius's library, see also Lyman Riley, "Books from the 'Beehive' Manu-
    script of Francis Daniel Pastorius," *Quaker History* 83 (1994): 116–129.

14 Brooke Palmieri, "'What the Bees Have Taken Pains For': Francis Daniel Pas-
    torius, The Beehive, and Commonplacing in Colonial Pennsylvania" (BA
    thesis, University of Pennsylvania, 2009); available via the University of
    Pennsylvania Scholarly Commons at http://www.google.com/search?q
    =pastorius%20bee-hive%20digitization&ie=utf-8&oe=utf-8.

15 For the digitized *Bee-Hive,* see http://dla.library.upenn.edu/dla/medren
    /pageturn.html?id=MEDREN_2487547, accessed December 5, 2011.

16 Bodleian Library, Oxford, MS Casaubon 19. For Casaubon's work on Poly-
    bius, see Isaac Casaubon, *Polibio,* ed. Guerrino Brussich (Palermo: Sellerio
    editore, 1991).

17 Bodleian Library, Oxford, MS Casaubon 19, title page: "In hoc auctore non
    placet nobis quod toties suum institutum, scopum et finem repetit et ob
    oculos ponit. Nam quorsum idem toties? nisi putaret solum se a mili-
    tibus Graecanicis lectum iri, aut hircosis centurionibus. Tale omnino vi-
    tium licet notare in Varronis lib. De L. L. Perlege principia et fines singu-

lorum librorum, eadem ubique reperies non sine aliquo taedio, meo certe, repetita." On the smelly centurions, see a text Casaubon edited, Persius, *Satirae* 3.77.

18 See Lisa Jardine and Anthony Grafton, "'Studied for Action': How Gabriel Harvey Read his Livy," *Past & Present* 129 (1990): 30–78; and William Sherman, *John Dee: The Politics of Reading and Writing in the English Renaissance* (Amherst: University of Massachusetts Press, 1995).

19 For Petrarch, see the classic work of Pierre de Nolhac, *Pétrarque et l'humanisme,* new ed., 2 vols. (Paris: H. Champion, 1907); and Carol Quillen, *Rereading the Renaissance: Petrarch, Augustine, and the Language of Humanism* (Ann Arbor: University of Michigan Press, 1998); for Poliziano, see the materials gathered in *Pico, Poliziano e l'Umanesimo di fine Quattrocento: Biblioteca medicea laurenziana, 4 novembre-31 dicembre 1994. Catalogo,* ed. Paolo Viti (Florence: L. S. Olschki, 1994); for Machiavelli, see Alison Brown, *The Return of Lucretius to Renaissance Florence* (Cambridge, MA: Harvard University Press, 2010); and Ada Palmer, *Reading Lucretius in the Renaissance* (Cambridge, MA: Harvard University Press, 2014).

20 Readers often entered lists of topics on fly-leaves and title pages. These, though helpful, were rarely systematic and usually followed the order of the text rather than that of the alphabet, which made them less useful than more formal indexes.

21 Ann Moss, *Printed Commonplace-Books and the Structuring of Renaissance Thought* (Oxford: Clarendon Press, 1996); Francis Goyet, *Le sublime du "lieu commun": L'invention rhétorique dans l'Antiquité et à la Renaissance* (Paris: Honoré Champion, 1996); Earle Havens, *Commonplace Books: A History of Manuscripts and Printed Books from Antiquity to the Twentieth Century, in conjunction with an exhibition at the Beinecke Rare Book & Manuscript Library, Yale University, 23 July through 29 September 2001* (New Haven: Beinecke Rare Book and Manuscript Library; Hanover, NH: Distributed by University Press of New England, 2001); Ann Blair, "Reading Strategies for Coping with Information Overload, ca. 1550–1700," *Journal of the History of Ideas* 64 (2003): 11–28; Blair, "Note-Taking as an Art of Transmission," *Critical Inquiry* 31 (2004): 85–107; Blair, "Scientific Reading: An Early Modernist's Perspective," *Isis* 95 (2004): 64–74; Blair, *Too Much to Know: Managing Scholarly Information before the Modern Age* (New Haven: Yale University Press, 2010). Valuable material is also available at the "Commonplace Books" page of Harvard's Open Collections Program, at http://ocp.hul.harvard.edu/reading/commonplace .html, accessed August 26, 2011.

22 British Library MS Add. 6038.

23 William Sherman, *Used Books: Marking Readers in Renaissance England* (Philadelphia: University of Pennsylvania Press, 2008).

24 Anthony Grafton and Joanna Weinberg, *"I have always loved the holy tongue": Isaac Casaubon, the Jews, and a Forgotten Chapter in Renaissance Scholarship* (Cambridge, MA: Harvard University Press, 2011), 21; Rita Calderini de-Marchi, *Jacopo Corbinelli et les érudits français* (Milan: Hoepli, 1914), 176.

25 Jeremias Drexel, *Aurifodina artium et scientiarum omnium, excerpendi sollertia, omnibus litterarum amantibus monstrata* (Antwerp: Widow of Jean Cnobbart, 1641).

26 Georg Horn, *Orbis imperans* (Frankfurt and Leipzig: Johannes Birckner Bibl: Erffurt, 1688); LCP Rare | Am 1668 Hor Log 798.D.

27 Georg Horn, *Arca Mosis* (Leiden and Rotterdam: Hack, 1669), LCP Rare | Am 1668 Hor Log 798.D, blank leaf before p. 1:

> Deus creavit varias Species, pag. 1.
> his Benedixit. p. 100.
> Et Maledixit. p. 109.
> Maledictionem sustulit. p. 128.
> Tandemque mundum Instaurabit. p. 219.

(God created the various species, p. 1; he blessed them, p. 100; and cursed them, p. 109; he removed the curse, p. 128; and at last he will restore the world, p. 219).

28 Georg Horn, *Orbis politicus* (Leipzig: Arnstius, 1668), LCP Rare | Am 1667 Hor Log 777 D, 11.

29 Ibid., 96.

30 See Petrarch, *Letters to Classical Authors*, tr. and ed. Mario Cosenza (Chicago: University of Chicago Press, 1910).

31 Horn, *Arca Mosis*, 47: "Aethiopia cutis mollis & porosa, quia sol absumsit particulas rigidas."

32 See Palmieri, "Bees," 18–19 and figure 4.

33 Michael Pexenfelder, *Apparatus eruditionis tam rerum quam verborum per omnes artes et scientias* (Nuremberg: Michael & Joh. Friedrich Endter, 1670); LCP Rare | Sev Pexe Log 626.O, title-page: [Top:] "Mundus non alio debebat nomine dici: / Nomen ab ornatu convenienter habet"; [Right margin:] "Quisquis amas mundum, tibi prospice, quo sit eundum / Est via qua vadis, via pessima, plenaque cladis"; [Bottom:] "Inservio studiis Francisci Danielis Pastorij"; "Rebus in humanis omnia sunt dubia, incerta, suspensa; magisque veritati similia, quam vera. Minuc. Felix."

34 Johann Valentin Andreae, *Menippus* (Cologne: Volckers, 1673); LCP Rare | Sev Andr Log 359.D, 194. Here, between cap. 79, *Nova reperta*, and cap. 80, *Perspicilia*, Pastorius has written: "Multiplicata fides numero decrescit ab ipso, / Nunquam plus Fidei, Perfidieque fuit."

35 Georg Horn, *Arca Mosis*, LCP Rare | Am 1668 Hor Log 798.D, sig. **3ʳ. Horn writes: "Nec dubium est, omnes istos famam novitate aliqua aucupantes animas statim nostras negotiari. Hinc illae circa aegros miserae sententiarum concertationes, nullo idem censente, ne videatur accessio alterius. Hinc illa infelicis monumenti inscriptio turba se medicorum perisse." Pastorius marked the passage throughout and commented on the bottom of the same page: "Quod morbus non potuit, fecerunt Medici, / Illorum turba me peremit: / Multorum Auxilio oppressus sum." The first phrase alludes to a famous Pasquinade from seventeenth-century Rome, directed against the harm supposedly done to the city by the Barberini family: "Quod non fecerunt barbari, fecerunt Barberini" (what the barbarians have not done, the Barberini have done).

36 Compare Pastorius's remark about borrowing books: "Grata mutuo datorum librorum recordatio," quoted in DeElla Victoria Toms, "The Intellectual and Literary Background of Francis Daniel Pastorius" (PhD dissertation, Northwestern University, 1953), 151.

37 See Frederick Tolles, *James Logan and the Culture of Provincial America* (Boston: Little, Brown, 1957).

38 Edwin Wolf II, *The Library of James Logan of Philadelphia, 1674–1751* (Philadelphia: Library Company of Philadelphia, 1974).

39 James Logan, note on the fly-leaf of Michael Pexenfelder, *Apparatus eruditionis tam rerum quam verborum per omnes artes et scientias* (Nuremberg: Michael & Joh. Friedrich Endter, 1670); LCP Rare | Sev Pexe Log 626.O: "Emptus hic Liber a Phillipo Munckton cui vendidit eum filius mihi Amicissimi ffr. D. Pastorij Germanopolitani. 15.9bris. 1720." See also the inscription John Winthrop entered in a book that had been a favorite possession of the inventor Cornelis Drebbel, which was given to Winthrop by Drebbel's son-in-law: Woodward, *Prospero's America*, 32.

40 Quoted by Toms, "The Background of Pastorius," 154.

41 Pastorius to Richard and Hannah Hill, 23 January 1716 / 1717; PHS, Pastorius Collection #475: "Of the old Romans we read that they had their 1st, 2d and 3d rate friends, admitting some only into the Court-yard or hall, others into the Antichamber of parlour, but their privados into their Closets, and bed-rooms. So me thinks we may do the same with a blameless partiality."

42 April Shelford, *Transforming the Republic of Letters: Pierre-Daniel Huet and European Intellectual Life, 1650–1720* (Rochester, NY: University of Rochester Press, 2007); Sarah Ross, *The Birth of Feminism: Woman as Intellect in Renaissance Italy and England* (Cambridge, MA: Harvard University Press, 2009); Carol Pal, *Republic of Women: Rethinking the Republic of Letters in the Sevententh Century* (Cambridge: Cambridge University Press, 2012).

43 Pastorius to Lloyd Zachary, Germantown, 19 December 1719; PHS, Pastorius Collection #475: "PS Remitto denique tomum IVum Spectatoris sive contemplatoris skeptici Magnae Britanniae, qui me nescio diutius inter seclusos meos libellulos in Conclavi hac hyeme parum frequentato delituit, quam illi concessissem, si non jam pridem remeasse putassem. Veniam igitur juste irascentis Proprietariae humiliter deprecor, et ne propter Peccatum hoc Ignorantiae Volumen V deneget Tua, quod spero, Intercessio procurabit." For Pastorius's correspondence with Zachary in French and Latin see Toms, "The Background of Pastorius," 155–161.

44 Pastorius to Lydia Norton, Germantown, June 14, 1710; PHS, Pastorius Collection #475.

45 Pastorius to Isaac Norris, n.d.; PHS, Pastorius Collection #475.

46 UPL, MS Codex 726, fol. 1ʳ.

47 Kate Peters, *Print Culture and the Early Quakers* (Cambridge: Cambridge University Press, 2005).

48 UPL, MS Codex 89, 1.

49 For the impact of Pliny's work in later eras, see Charles Nauert, "Humanists, Scientists, and Pliny: Changing Approaches to a Classical Author," *American Historical Review* 84 (1979): 72–85; Arno Borst, *Das Buch der*

Naturgeschichte: Plinius und seine Leser im Zeitalter des Pergaments (Heidelberg: Winter, 1994); Mary Beagon, in *The Classical Tradition*, ed. Anthony Grafton, Glenn Most, and Salvatore Settis (Cambridge, MA: Harvard University Press, 2010); and Peter Fane-Saunders, *Pliny the Elder and the Emergence of Renaissance Architecture* (Cambridge: Cambridge University Press, 2016).

50 Pliny the Younger, *Epistolae* 3.5.7: "opus diffusum eruditum, nec minus varium quam ipsa natura."

51 Ibid., 3.5.10: "Nihil enim legit quod non excerperet; dicere etiam solebat nullum esse librum tam malum ut non aliqua parte prodesset."

52 Ibid., 3.5.17: "Hac intentione tot ista volumina peregit electorumque commentarios centum sexaginta mihi reliquit, opisthographos quidem et minutissimis scriptos; qua ratione multiplicatur hic numerus. Referebat ipse potuisse se, cum procuraret in Hispania, vendere hos commentarios Larcio Licino quadringentis milibus nummum; et tunc aliquanto pauciores erant." On the portrait that this letter paints of the elder Pliny, see John Henderson, *Pliny's Statue: The Letters, Self-Portraiture & Classical Art* (Exeter: Exeter University Press, 2002), 69–103; and Aude Doody, *Pliny's Encyclopedia: The Reception of the Natural History* (Cambridge: Cambridge University Press, 2010), 14–23. For the details of his method of reading, annotating and excerpting, see Tiziano Dorandi, "Den Autoren über die Schulter geschaut: Arbeitsweise und Autographie bei den Antiken Schriftstellern," *Zeitschrift für Papyrologie und Epigraphik* 87 (1991): 11–33, at 13–15; Valérie Nass, *Le projet encyclopédique de Pline l'Ancien* (Rome: École Française der Rome, 2002), 108–136.

53 UPL, MS Codex 726, fol. 1^v.

54 For a classic and influential critique of Pliny's bookishness, see G. E. R. Lloyd, *Science, Folklore and Ideology: Studies in the Life Sciences in Ancient Greece* (Cambridge: Cambridge University Press, 1983), 135–149.

55 On the nature of Pliny's scholarship, see Sorcha Carey, *Pliny's Catalogue of Culture: Art and Empire in the Natural History* (Oxford: Oxford University Press, 2003); Trevor Murphy, *Pliny the Elder's Natural History: The Empire in the Encyclopedia* (Oxford: Oxford University Press, 2004), 52–73; and Mary Beagon, *The Elder Pliny on the Human Animal: Natural History Book 7* (Oxford: Clarendon Press, 2005), 20–38.

56 Pliny the Elder, *Naturalis Historia*, praefatio 21–22: "Argumentum huius stomachi mei habebis quod in his voluminibus auctorum nomina praetexui. est enim benignum, ut arbitror, et plenum ingenui pudoris fateri per quos profeceris, non ut plerique ex iis, quos attigi, fecerunt. Scito enim conferentem auctores me deprehendisse a iuratissimis ex proximis veteres transcriptos ad verbum neque nominatos, non illa Vergiliana virtute, ut certarent, non Tulliana simplicitate, qui de re publica Platonis se comitem profitetur, in consolatione filiae Crantorem, inquit, sequor, item Panaetium de officiis, quae volumina ediscenda, non modo in manibus cotidie habenda, nosti." For Pliny's understanding of intellectual property and scholarly integrity, see Eugenia Lao, "Luxury and the Creation of a Good Consumer," in *Pliny the Elder: Themes and Contexts*, ed. Roy Gibson and Ruth Morello (Leiden: Brill, 2011), 35–56.

57 UPL, MS Codex 89, 301: "Ingenuum est fateri per quos profeceris. Plin. ex quibus scripseris."

58 John Whitaker, "The Value of Indirect Tradition in the Establishment of Greek Philosophical Texts or the Art of Misquotation," in *Editing Greek and Latin Texts*, ed. John Grant (New York: AMS, 1989), 63–95.

59 UPL, MS Codex 726, fol. 1ᵛ.

60 Robert Burton, *The Anatomy of Melancholy*, ed. Thomas Faulkner, Nicolas Kiessling and Rhonda Blair, 3 vols. (Oxford: Clarendon Press, 1989–94), 1:11, 8. The words "omne meum, nihil meum" were Burton's own invention. See Angus Gowland's letter in the *London Review of Books*, July 15, 2021.

61 *Spectator* 316.

62 John Locke, *A New Method of Making Common-Place-Books* (London: Greenwood, 1706); see *A Little Common Place Book* (Brooklyn, NY: Cabinet Books & Proteotypes, 2010), for a commonplace book constructed on Locke's principles. For Locke's method for indexing notebooks and its influence, see Blair, *Too Much to Know*; on the larger history of commonplace books and associated practices in early modern England, see Richard Yeo, *Notebooks, English Virtuosi, and Early Modern Science* (Chicago and London: University of Chicago Press, 2014).

63 Jonathan Swift, *A Tale of a Tub, and Other Work*, ed. Angus Ross and David Woolley (Oxford: Oxford University Press, 1986).

64 Pastorius, *Deliciae hortenses*, ed. Schweitzer, 74.

65 *Multilingual Anthology of American Literature*, ed. Shell and Sollors.

66 See the classic study of Erich Trunz, "Der deutsche Späthumanismus um 1600 als Standeskultur," in *Deutsche Barockforschung: Dokumentation einer Epoche*, ed. Richard Alewyn (Cologne: Kiepenheuer & Witsch, 1965), 147–181; for more recent perspectives, see Anton Schindling, *Humanistische Hochschule und freie Reichsstadt: Gymnasium und Akademie in Strassburg, 1538–1621* (Wiesbaden: Steiner, 1977); Wilhelm Kühlmann, *Gelehrtenrepublik und Fürstenstaat: Entwicklung und Kritik des deutschen Späthumanismus in der Literatur des Barockzeitalters* (Tübingen: Niemeyer, 1982); Gunter Grimm, *Literatur und Gelehrtentum in Deutschland: Untersuchungen zum Wandel ihres Verhältnisses von Humanismus bis zur Frühaufklärung* (Tübingen: Niemeyer, 1983); Manfred Fleischer, *Späthumanismus in Schlesien. Ausgewählte Aufsätze* (Munich: Delp, 1984); *Späthumanismus: Studien über das Ende einer kulturhistorischen Epoche*, ed. Notker Hammerstein und Gerrit Walther (Göttingen: Wallstein, 2000); and Axel Walter, *Späthumanismus und Konfessionspolitik: Die europäische Gelehrtenrepublik um 1600 im Spiegel der Korrespondenzen Georg Michael Lingelsheims* (Tübingen: Niemeyer, 2004).

67 UPL, MS Codex 726, 222. On Schumberg and his relationship with Pastorius, see Toms, "The Background of Pastorius," 28, 117–118.

68 Terence Cave, *The Cornucopian Text: Problems of Writing in the French Renaissance* (Oxford: Clarendon Press, 1979); Moss, *Printed Commonplace-Books*; Kathy Eden, *Friends Hold All Things in Common: Tradition, Intellectual Property, and the Adages of Erasmus* (New Haven: Yale University Press, 2001).

69 Anthony Grafton and Lisa Jardine, *From Humanism to the Humanities: Education and the Liberal Arts in Fifteenth- and Sixteenth-Century Europe* (London: Duckworth, 1986).

70 Cotton Mather, *The Christian Philosopher*, ed. Winton Solberg (Urbana: University of Illinois Press, 1994), 10; William Darlington, *Memorials of John Bartram and Humphry Marshall* (Philadelphia: Lindsay and Blakiston, 1849), 352.

71 See Leonard Forster, *The Icy Fire: Five Studies in European Petrarchism* (London: Cambridge University Press, 1969); and Forster, *The Poet's Tongues: Multilingualism in Literature* (London: Cambridge University Press, 1970).

72 UPL, MS Codex 726, fol. 1ᵛ.

73 See, in general, R. J. W. Evans, *The Making of the Habsburg Monarchy, 1550–1700: An Interpretation* (Oxford: Clarendon Press, 1979); and Anthony Grafton, "The World of the Polyhistors: Humanism and Encyclopedism," *Central European History* 18 (1985): 31–47. On Kircher, see *The Great Art of Knowing: The Baroque Encyclopedia of Athanasius Kircher*, ed. Daniel Stolzenberg (Stanford, CA: Stanford University Libraries, 2001); *Athanasius Kircher: The Last Man Who Knew Everything*, ed. Paula Findlen (New York and London: Routledge, 2004); Angela Mayer-Deutsch, *Das Musaeum Kircherianum. Kontemplative Momente, historische Rekonstruktion, Bildrhetorik* (Berlin: Diaphanes Verlag 2010); and Daniel Stolzenberg, *Egyptian Oedipus: Athanasius Kircher and the Secrets of Antiquity* (Chicago and London: University of Chicago Press, 2013).

74 Peter Lambeck, *Prodromus historiae literariae, et Tabula duplex chronographica universalis*, ed. Johann Albert Fabricius (Leipzig and Frankfurt: Christian Liebezeit, 1710).

75 Martin Gierl, *Pietismus und Aufklärung: Theologische Polemik und die Kommunikationsreform der Wissenschaft am Ende des 17. Jahrhunderts* (Göttingen: Vandenhoeck & Ruprecht, 1997).

76 Blair, *Too Much to Know*. See also Markus Krajewski, *Paper Machines: About Cards & Catalogs, 1548–1929*, trans. Peter Krapp (Cambridge, MA, and London: MIT Press, 2011), 17–21. Placcius's account of the *scrinium litteratum* appears in his *De arte excerpendi* (Stockholm and Hamburg: Liebezeit, 1689), 124–159. For Harrison and the Hartlib circle, see the magnificent article by Noel Malcolm, "Thomas Harrison and His 'Ark of Studies': An Episode in the History of the Organization of Knowledge," *The Seventeenth Century* 19 (2004): 196–232.

77 Conrad Samuel Schurzfleisch, *Schurzfleischiana, sive varia de scriptoribus librisque iudicia*, ed. Godofredus Wagener (Wittenberg: Schlomach, 1741), 108: "Sunt, qui coniicere ausint, Iosephum a patre Iulio Caesare castratum esse, ne matrimonium iniret, neque splendorem familiae illustris detereret."

78 The richest study of these methods, their sources, and their afterlife is Blair, *Too Much to Know*.

79 I used Christoph August Heumann, *Conspectus reipublicae literariae: sive Via ad historiam literariam iuuentuti studiosae aperta a Christophoro Augusto Heumanno*, 5th ed. (Hanover: Heirs of Nicolaus Förster and Son, 1746).

80 Melchior Adam Pastorius, *Römischer Adler, oder Theatrum electionis et coronationis Romano-Caesareae* (Frankfurt am Main: Fickwirdt, 1657).

81 Melchior Adam Pastorius, *Franconia rediviva. Das ist: Des hochlöblichen Fränkischen Kraises so wohl genealogische als historische Beschreibung* (Nuremberg: Author, 1702).

82 Melchior Adam Pastorius, "Liber intimissimus omnium semper mecum continens thesaurum thesaurorum Iesum, quem diligo solum. in quo vivo et in quo moriar ego"; PHS, Pastorius collection #475; UPL, MS Codex 1150, for which see below.

83 UPL, MS Codex 726, 223.

84 Johann Heinrich Boecler, *Bibliographia historico-politico-philologica curiosa: quid in quovis scriptore laudem censuramve mereatur, exhibens, cui praefixa celeberrimi cuiusdam viri de studio politico bene instituendo dissertatio epistolica posthuma* (Germanopolis [Frankfurt am Main: Schrey und Hamm], 1677). For another form of compilation—entitled "excerpts," but actually consisting of discussions of such great events as the condemnation of the Templars, reduced to outline form and lists of references to the sources—see his *Excerpta controversiarum illustrium* (Strasbourg: Schmuck, 1680).

85 Johann Heinrich Boecler, *Bibliographia critica scriptores omnium artium atque scientiarum ordine percensens, nunc demum integra* (Leipizg: Heirs of Gross, 1715).

86 Johann Gottlieb Krause, "Praefatio," ibid., sig. b^r.

87 Boecler, *Bibliographia historico-politico-philologica curiosa*, sigs. F^v–Fa^r.

88 Boecler, *Bibliographia critica*, 232–233.

89 Christophorus Schrader, *Tabulae Chronologicae a Prima Rerum Origine ad Natum Christum* (Helmstedt: Heinrich David Mueller, 1673); LCP Rare | *Sev Tabu 1405.F.10.

90 Heinrich Schaevius, *Sceleton Geographicum*, 4th ed. (Braunschweig: Duncker/Hauenstein, 1671), LCP *Sev Tabu (b.w.) 1405.F.12., sig. A^r, where the text mentions "Cosmographia, quae totum mundum visibilem depingit: id quod intendit Plinius," Pastorius adds "& Munsterus."

91 Ibid., sig. A2^r; where the text discusses "Divisio Terrae quintuplex," Pastorius writes: "Totus terrarum Orbis etiam dividitur in 3. partes, sive Insulas magnas, quas Oceanus circumfluit, quarum 1a continet Europam, Asiam et Africam, 2a Americam, et 3a Megallanicam, quae et Australis et Incognita vocatur."

92 Carlo Sigonio, Marquard Freher, and David Chytraeus, *Romanorum Germanorumque Caesarum nominum, successionum et seculaorum a nato Christo distincta notatio* (Helmstedt: Muller, 1666), LCP *Sev Tabu 1405 F.11. At the end of Chytraeus's list of historians, sig. [H2^r], is a note: "Gottfrid Arnolds unparteyische kirchen und ketzer histori, von Christi geburt an biss auffs Jahr 1688. in folio, gedruckt zu Franckfurt." On the other side of the page, sig. [H2^v], appears a manuscript "Index scriptorum ecclesiasticorum."

93 On the study of cryptography and steganography and their relation to other forms of scholarship in this period, see Gerhard Strasser, *Lingua universalis:*

Kryptologie und Theorie der Universalsprachen im 16. und 17. Jahrhundert (Wiesbaden: In Kommission bei O. Harrassowitz, 1988).

94 Pexenfelder, *Apparatus*, 309: "Steganographia est clandestina seu clancularia scribendi ratio, occultis utens signis, ex compacto paucorum, intelligibilibus, dum vel trajiciuntur & transponuntur, ut B pro A; C pro B. Vel numeri adhibentur pro literis, ut 1 pro a. 2. pro b. 3. pro c. Vel pro arbitrio transmutatur alphabetum. Vel novi characteres efformantur: vel inaspecti quopiam illiti succo exarantur in panno, non nisi frigida madefacti legendi, aut in charta ad lucernam transparente colligendi, &c."

95 Ibid.: "Vide pag. seq. sub finem."

96 Ibid., 310–311. Pastorius has wreathed the margins with leaf prints and where Pexenfelder writes "Characteres seu literae sunt metallicae," Pastorius has added a note in the bottom margin: "vel Naturales, hortorum Camporumque propago, ut quaedam apparent in Margine: vel Artificiales. Ex prioribus Absinthium denotat A. Beta B. Crocus C. Filix F. &c. hasque Botanici optime intelligunt."

97 See also Shirley Hershey Showalter, "'The Herbal Signs of Nature's Page': A Study of Francis Daniel Pastorius's View of Nature," *Quaker History* 71 (1982): 89–99; Christoph Schweitzer, "Francis Daniel Pastorius, the German-American Poet," *Yearbook of German-American Studies* 18 (1983): 21–28; and above all, Andrew Thomas, "Gardening in the New World: Francis Daniel Pastorius's Conception of Community in the Settlement of Germantown," *William & Mary Quarterly*, forthcoming.

98 UPL, MS Codex 726, 65.

99 Michael Aitzinger, *De leone Belgico, eiusque topographica atque historica descriptione liber* (Cologne: Hogenberg, 1583). See G. N. Clark, *War and Society in the Seventeenth Century* (Cambridge: Cambridge University Press, 1958).

100 For the rise of journals in the German world, see Hubert Laeven, *The "Acta eruditorum" under the Editorship of Otto Mencke (1644–1707): The History of an International Learned Journal between 1682 and 1707*, tr. Lynne Richards (Amsterdam: APA–Holland University Press, 1990); Gierl, *Pietismus und Aufklärung*, 395–417; and, more generally, Anne Goldgar, *Impolite Learning: Conduct and Community in the Republic of Letters, 1680–1750* (New Haven: Yale University Press, 1995).

101 *Monatliche Unterredungen* 3 (1691): 278–288.

102 On Penn and the long peace, see James Merrell, *Into the American Woods: Negotiations on the Frontier* (New York: W. W. Norton, 1999). For the later history of relations between white settlers and native Americans in the Middle Colonies, see Peter Silver, *Our Savage Neighbors: How Indian War Transformed Early America* (New York: W. W. Norton, 2008).

103 *Monatliche Unterredungen* 3 (1691), 287–288: "Ex his elementis, sive etiam, quod matrem *ana*, uxorem *squáa*, vetulam *hexis*, diabolum *menitto*, domum *wicco*, praedium *hockihócken*, vaccam *muss*, suem *Kuschkusch*, appellitent, si tu Indorum horum incunabula divinaveris, bonus mihi eris Philologus &c." For early modern scholars' theories about the origins of the Indians, see Lee Eldridge Huddleston, *Origins of the American Indians: Eu-*

ropean Concepts, 1492–1729 (Austin: University of Texas Press for the Institute of Latin American Studies, 1967); Giuliano Gliozzi, *Adamo e il nuovo mondo: la nascita dell'antropologia come ideologia coloniale: dalle genealogie bibliche alle teorie razziali (1500–1700)* (Florence: La nuova Italia, 1977); and David Livingstone, *Adam's Ancestors: Race, Religion, and the Politics of Human Origins* (Baltimore: Johns Hopkins University Press, 2008).

104 Nigel Leask, *Curiosity and the Aesthetics of Travel Writing, 1770–1840: "From an Antique Land"* (Oxford: Oxford University Press, 2002).

105 *Monatliche Unterredungen* 3 (1691), 283: "pergamus, et ne silentio viam transigamus veluti pecora, sermocinemur aliquid de Nili, vel quae aeque obscura est, Indorum nostrorum origine. Nam licet non desint, qui eos Ebraeorum arbitrentur prosapiam, non sine signis verosimillimis: quosdam tamen longius hinc habitantium ex Cambria emersisse, nativa illorum loquutio innuit. Quibus autem temporibus atque navigiis Atlanticum hoc mare exantlaverint, Polyhistor tuus Altdorfinus distinctius explicet: ego nec ullo pene libro instructus tam dubiam litem meam non facio."

106 On Horn, see Adalbert Klempt, *Die Säkularisierung der universalhistorischen Auffassung* (Göttingen: Musterschmidt, 1960), which emphasizes his originality; and Erich Hassinger, *Empirisch-Rationaler Historismus* (Bern and Munich: Francke, 1978), which stresses his limitations.

107 Sanjay Subrahmanyam, *Three Ways to Be Alien: Travails and Encounters in the Early Modern World* (Waltham, MA: Brandeis University Press, 2011); Daniel Smail, *On Deep History and the Brain* (Berkeley: University of California Press, 2008).

108 UPL, MS Codex 726, fol. 1ᵛ: "For as much as our Memory is not capable to retain all remarkable words, Phrases, Sentences or Matters of moment, which we do hear and read, It beseems every good Scholar to haue a Common Place-Book, and therein to treasure up what euer deserues his Notice, &c."

109 See Justin Stagl, *Apodemiken: Eine räsonnierte Bibliographie der reisetheoretischen Literatur des 16., 17. und 18. Jahrhunderts* (Paderborn: Schöningk, 1983); Stagl, *A History of Curiosity: The Theory of Travel, 1550–1800* (Chur: Harwood, 1995)

110 UPL, MS Codex 726, 223.

111 UPL, MS Codex 1150: Melchior Adam Pastorius, Erffurtensis, *Itinerarium et vitae curriculus, das ist, Seine voellige Reis-Beschbunge und gantzer Lebenslauff, sampt einigen Merckwuerdigen Begebenheiten und anzaigungen derer iedes Orth befindlichen Raritäten,* partly edited, with other materials, in *Des Melchior Adam Pastorius . . . Leben und Reisebeschreibungen von ihm selbst erzählt,* ed. Albert Schmitt (Munich: Delp, 1968).

112 UPL, MS Codex 726, 166.

113 Toms, "The Background of Pastorius," 154.

114 Franciscus Schottus, *Itinerarium Italiae* (Amsterdam: Jansson, 1655); LCP Rare | Sev Scho Log 654.D. On this book and its evolution, see Ludwig Schudt, "Das 'Itinerarium Italiae' des Franciscus Schottus," in *Adolf Goldschmidt zu seinem siebzigsten Geburtstag am 15. Januar 1933 dargebracht* (Berlin: Würfel Verlag, 1935), 144–152; and E. S. de Beer, "François Schott's *Itinerario d'Italia*," *The Library,* 4th ser., 23 (1942): 57–83.

115 Schottus, *Itinerarium Italiae*, sigs. A3^v–A4^r, at A4^r: "Vulgi mores: quo pertinent ratio victus et vestitus; item opificia."

116 Johann Burkhard Mencke, *The Charlatanry of the Learned*, trans. Francis Litz, ed. H. L. Mencken (New York: Knopf, 1937), 61–62, 69, 64 (slightly altered); *De charlataneria eruditorum declamationes duae* (Leipzig: Gleditsch, 1715), 13, 20, 15–16. See, in general, Conrad Wiedemann, "Polyhistors Glück und Ende: Von D. G. Morhof zum jungen Lessing," in *Festschrift Gottfried Weber*, ed. Heinz Otto Burger and Klaus von See (Bod Homburg, Berlin and Zurich: Verlag Gehlen, 1967), 215–235; Leonard Forster, "'Charlataneria eruditorum' zwischen Barock und Aufklärung in Deutschland," in *Res publica litteraria: die Institutionen der Gelehrsamkeit in der frühen Neuzeit*, ed. Sebastian Neumeister und Conrad Wiedemann (Wiesbaden: Harrassowitz, 1987), 1:203–220; Pascale Hummel, *Moeurs érudites: étude sur la micrologie littéraire (Allemagne, XVIe–XVIIIe siècles)* (Geneva: Droz, 2002); Alexander Košenina, *Der gelehrte Narr: Gelehrtensatire seit der Aufklärung* (Göttingen: Wallstein, 2003); Kasper Risbjerg Eskildsen, "How Germany Left the Republic of Letters," *Journal of the History of Ideas* 65, no. 3 (July 2004): 421–432; Marian Füssel, "'The Charlatanry of the Learned': On the Moral Economy of the Republic of Letters in Eighteenth-Century Germany," *Cultural and Social History* 3 (2006): 287–300; *Diskurse der Gelehrtenkultur in der frühen Neuzeit: ein Handbuch*, ed. Herbert Jaumann (Berlin: De Gruyter, 2011). On the rituals and mores of the Republic of Letters, and especially for the forms of conduct and publication that could lead to expulsion from it, see Martin Mulsow, *Die unanständige Gelehrtenrepublik: Wissen, Libertinage und Kommunikation in der Frühen Neuzeit* (Stuttgart: Metzler, 2007)

117 UPL, MS Codex 726, 222: "Anno 1668. the 31th of July I went with some others to the University of Altdorf, there to be initiated among Students which they call Deponisten, giving to those Novices with abundance of impertinent Ceremonies the Salt of Wisdom, Sal Sapientiae."

118 Note esp. his copy of Andreae's *Menippus*; LCP Rare | Sev Andr Log 359.D.

119 Daniel Franciscus Pastorius, "Circumstantial Geographical Description of Pennsylvania," in *Narratives of Early Pennsylvania, West New Jersey and Delaware, 1630–1707*, ed. Albert Cook Myers (New York: Charles Scribner's Sons, 1912), 362–363, 446–447. For a detailed discussion of this work, see Lambert, "Pastorius."

120 See, e.g., UPL, MS Codex 726, fol. 59^v, 113: "Augustus Hermannus Francke his Pietas Hallensis, or historical Narration of the Orphan-house & other Charitable Institutions at Glaucha near Hall in Saxony. London in 80 1675. Vide infra Num. 119"; 116: "Pietas Hallensis, or an Abstract of the Marvellous Footsteps of Divine Providence attending the Managemt of the Orphan house at Glaucha near Hall. London 80. 1710."

121 Ian Hunter, "Christian Thomasius and the Desacralization of Philosophy," *Journal of the History of Ideas* 61, no. 4 (2000): 595–616.

122 On Thomasius see generally Notker Hammerstein, *Jus und Historie: Ein Beitrag zur Geschichte des historischen Denkens an deutschen Universitäten im späten 17. und im 18. Jahrhundert* (Göttingen: Vandenhoeck und Ruprecht, 1972), 43–147.

123 Gierl, *Pietismus und Aufklärung*, 21–324.

124 On early modern eclecticism, see, in general, Michael Albrecht, *Eklektik: eine Begriffsgeschichte mit Hinweisen auf die Philosophie- und Wissenschaftsgeschichte* (Stuttgart-Bad Cannstatt: Frommann-Holzboog, 1994). On Thomasius's own position, see F. M. Barnard, "The 'Practical Philosophy' of Christian Thomasius," *Journal of the History of Ideas* 32, no. 2 (1971): 221–246; Horst Dreitzel, "Zur Entwicklung und Eigenart der 'Eklektischen Philosophie,'" *Zeitschrift fur Historische Forschung* 18 (1991): 281–343, at 324–330; and Martin Mulsow, "Eclecticism or Skepticism? A Problem of the Early Enlightenment," *Journal of the History of Ideas* 58, no. 3 (1997): 465–477.

125 Christian Thomasius, *Introductio ad philosophiam aulicam* (Leipzig: Thomasius, 1688), 46: "Ita praestat, navem habere ad navigandum aptam, etsi saepius in partibus renovatam, quae renovatio tamen identitatem non tollit, quam retinere perpetuo eandem non bene cohaerentem et rimarum plenam. Ita praestat aedificium a variis artificibus adornatum quam tuguriolum a rustico etsi uno extructum."

126 Hammerstein, *Jus und Historie*, 43–147, 205–265. For the Renaissance foundations of "historia literaria," see Wilhelm Schmidt-Biggemann, *Topica universalis: Eine Modellgeschichte humanistischer und barocker Wissenschaft* (Hamburg: Meiner, 1983), 1–66; and Michael Carhart, "*Historia Literaria* and Cultural History from Mylaeus to Eichhorn," in *Momigliano and Antiquarianism: Foundations of the Modern Cultural Sciences*, ed. Peter Miller (Toronto: University of Toronto Press, 2007), 184–206.

127 See Schmidt-Biggemann, *Topica universalis*, 212–225.

128 Gierl, *Pietismus und Aufklärung*, 487–574. For the role of religion in Thomasius's thought see Thomas Ahnert, *Religion and the Origins of the German Enlightenment: Faith and the Reform of Learning in the Thought of Christian Thomasius* (Rochester, NY: University of Rochester Press, 2006).

129 Grafton and Weinberg, *"I have always loved the holy tongue,"* 15.

130 Ibid., 267–280.

131 UPL, MS Codex 726.

132 Thomasius, *Introductio*, sig.)o()o(2ᵛ: "Putavi igitur, convenientius esse si de ejusmodi aberrationibus in tempore admonerer ab aliis veritatis amatoribus, ut in fusiore deductione hujus doctrinae ea, quae clarius et distinctius forte cogniturus essem, emendatius etiam ponerentur. Quare obligabunt me omnes atque singuli sapientiae studiosi, sive Cartesiani sive Peripatetici, sive alii cuidam sectae addicti sint, aut Philosophiam Eclecticam sequantur, si me forte incautum in devia incidentem ad genuinam veritatis semitam reducere haud gravatim velint."

133 For Thomasius on witchcraft, see Christian Thomasius, *Über die Hexenprozesse*, ed. and tr. Rolf Lieberwirth (Weimar: Böhlau, 1967); on torture, see Thomasius, *Über die Folter*, ed. Lieberwirth (Weimar: Böhlau, 1986), excerpted in translation in *The Witchcraft Sourcebook*, ed. Brian Levack (London: Routledge, 2005), 168–170.

134 The original text of the 1688 petition is held in the Quaker and Special Collections, Haverford College. A digitized text is available at http://en

.wikipedia.org/wiki/File:The_1688_germantown_quaker_petition_against
_slavery.jpg, accessed December 5, 2011. For Pastorius's part in the 1688 Germantown Protest, see Hildegard Binder-Johnson, "The Germantown Protest of 1688 against Negro Slavery," *Pennsylvania Magazine of History and Biography* 65 (1941): 145–156; and Katharine Gerbner, "Antislavery in Print: The Germantown Protest, the 'Exhortation,' and the Seventeenth-Century Quaker Debate on Slavery," *Early American Studies: An Interdisciplinary Journal* 9 (2011): 552–575, which warns against hagiographical interpretations.

135 Ulrich Huber, "Oratio de pedantismo," in Thomasius, *Introductio,* 243: "Ostentatores sunt . . . 3. qui versiculos, sententias, verba Latina, Graeca, Hebraea, terminos scholasticos, leges, praecepta medica, aliaque *eruditionis argumenta* proferunt, ubi nihil usui veniunt."

136 Ulrich Huber, "Oratio de pedantismo," ibid., 292–293: "Prorsus opera danda est. ne eruditio nostra cuidam gravis aut molesta sit; nec scio, an non huc, ipsum Latini sermonis commercium redigere nos oporteat, ut nec illud pedantismi sit expers, si absque necessitate frequentetur apud homines, quibus in promptu non est facultas hujus linguae, vel qui promiscuo ejus usu non delectantur. Dolendum equidem est, hoc commune gentium Christianarum vinculum ita resolvi in desuetudinem, ut etiam inter homines doctrinam professos Latine loqui, de rebus a studiorum disceptatione alienis, paedagogicum habeatur"; 295: "Demus hoc socordiae seculi et tralatitiae humanitati, ut eorum, qui Latina reformidant pudori ignoscamus; sed nunquam inter nos invicem illam gentis gentium dominae linguam cessemus reddere nobis familiarem; sine cujus exprompta facultate omnis eruditio nostra tanquam situ squalida sordescit et sapientia balbutire videatur."

137 Erben, "'Honey-Combs' and 'Paper-Hives.'"

138 Palmieri, "Bees."

139 For recent research of various forms on these themes see, e.g., J. G. A. Pocock, *Barbarism and Religion,* 6 vols. (Cambridge: Cambridge University Press, 1999–2015); Peter Miller, *Peiresc's Europe: Learning and Virtue in the Seventeenth Century* (New Haven: Yale University Press, 2000); Jonathan Sheehan, *The Enlightenment Bible: Translation, Scholarship, Culture* (Princeton: Princeton University Press, 2005); Jacob Soll, *Publishing The Prince: History, Reading, & the Birth of Political Criticism* (Ann Arbor: University of Michigan Press, 2005); Dan Edelstein, "Humanism, l'Esprit Philosophique, and the Encyclopédie," *Republics of Letters* 1 (2009), online at http://arcade.stanford.edu/journals/rofl/issues/volume-1/issue-1; Edelstein, *The Enlightenment: A Genealogy* (Chicago: University of Chicago Press, 2010); David Sorkin, *The Religious Enlightenment: Protestants, Jews, and Catholics from London to Vienna* (Princeton: Princeton University Press, 2008); and Guy Stroumsa, *A New Science: The Discovery of Religion in the Age of Reason* (Cambridge, MA: Harvard University Press, 2010).

140 See now *Confessionalization and Erudition in Early Modern Europe: An Episode in the History of the Humanities,* ed. Nicholas Hardy and Dmitri Levitin (Oxford: Published for the British Academy by Oxford University Press, 2020).

CHAPTER 7 · ANNIUS OF VITERBO STUDIES THE JEWS

Earle Havens, Walter Stephens and Joanna Weinberg commented on an earlier version of this article, greatly to my profit.

1 See Cesare Vasoli, "Profezia e astrologia in uno scritto di Annio da Viterbo," in his *I miti e gli astri* (Naples: Guida, 1977), 17–49; and Monica Azzolini, *The Duke and the Stars: Astrology and Politics in Renaissance Milan* (Cambridge, MA: Harvard University Press, 2012).

2 Basic works on Annius and his world include Roberto Weiss, "Traccia per una biografia di Annio da Viterbo," *Italia medioevale e umanistica* 5 (1962): 425–441; Walter Stephens, "Berosus Chaldaeus: Counterfeit and Fictive Authors of the Early Sixteenth Century" (PhD dissertation, Cornell University, 1979); Walter Stephens, *Giants in Those Days: Folklore, Ancient History, and Nationalism* (Lincoln: University of Nebraska Press, 1989); *Annio da Viterbo: documenti e ricerche* (Rome: Consiglio nazionale delle ricerche, 1981); Ingrid Rowland, *The Culture of the High Renaissance: Ancients and Moderns in Sixteenth-Century Rome* (Cambridge: Cambridge University Press, 1998); and Brian Curran, *The Egyptian Renaissance: The Afterlife of Ancient Egypt in Early Modern Italy* (Chicago: University of Chicago Press, 2007). For an up-to-date synthetic account, see Walter Stephens, "Annius of Viterbo," in *The Classical Tradition*, ed. Anthony Grafton, Glenn Most, and Salvatore Settis (Cambridge, MA: Harvard University Press, 2011), 46–47.

3 For the long scholarly afterlife of this notarial vision of how to authenticate documents, see Randolph Head, "Documents, Archives, and Proof around 1700," *Historical Journal* 56, no. 4 (2013): 909–930.

4 Annius, *Antiquitates* (Paris: Jean Petit and Josse Bade, 1512), fol. LXXXIIII^v. I cite this edition because it is well organized, clearly printed, and easily accessible in digital form at http://books.google.com/books?id=A4lNAAA AcAAJ&printsec=frontcover&dq=antiquitatum+variarum&hl=en&sa=X&ei =W96rUeWbCJG34APBx4CQCQ&ved=0CCUQ6AewAQ, accessed June 2, 2013.

5 E. N. Tigerstedt, "Ioannes Annius and *Graecia Mendax*," in *Classical, Mediaeval and Renaissance Studies in Honor of Berthold Louis Ullman*, ed. Charles Henderson Jr., 2 vols. (Rome: Edizioni di Storia e Letteratura, 1964), 2:293–310.

6 Beatus Rhenanus, *Rerum Germanicarum libri tres*, 2nd ed. (Basel: Froben and Episcopius, 1551), 39, citing Erasmus's adage "Mulgere hircum," *Adagia* 1.3.51 (from Lucian). See Karl Joachim Weintraub, review of *Defenders of the Text* by Anthony Grafton, *Classical Philology* 88 (1993): 269–273, at 271.

7 Christopher Krebs, *A Most Dangerous Book: Tacitus's Germania from the Roman Empire to the Third Reich* (New York: Norton, 2011).

8 On the impact of Annius's forgeries, see, e.g., T. D. Kendrick, *British Antiquity* (London: Methuen, 1950); Frank Borchardt, *German Antiquity in Renaissance Myth* (Baltimore: Johns Hopkins Press, 1971); Anthony Grafton, *Forgers and Critics: Creativity and Duplicity in Western Scholarship* (Princeton: Princeton University Press, 1990; repr. with additions, Princeton: Princeton University Press, 2019); Marianne Wifstrand Schiebe, *Annius von Viterbo und die schwedische Historiographie des 16. und 17.*

Jahrhunderts (Uppsala: K. Humanistiska vetenkaps-samfundet i Uppsala, 1992); R. E. Asher, *National Myths in Renaissance France: Francus, Samothes and the Druids* (Edinburgh: Edinburgh University Press, 1993); and Thomas Lehr, *Was nach der Sintflut wirklich geschah: die "Antiquitates" des Annius von Viterbo und ihre Rezeption in Deutschland im 16. Jahrhundert* (Frankfurt am Main: Peter Lang, 2012).

9 Leo Wiener, *Contributions toward a History of Arabo-Visigothic Culture,* Vol. 3: *Tacitus' Germania & Other Forgeries* (Philadelphia: Innes and Sons, 1920), 203–204.

10 Norbert Wiener, *Ex-Prodigy: My Childhood and Youth* (New York: Simon and Shuster, 1953).

11 Wiener, *Contributions,* 3:203–204.

12 Quoted in ibid., 203. For the original text (and much more), see Joanna Weinberg, "Azariah de' Rossi and the Forgeries of Annius of Viterbo," in *Essential Papers on Jewish Culture in Renaissance and Baroque Italy,* ed. David Ruderman (New York and London, 1992), 252–279, at 259 and 274n.46.

13 *Scaligerana* (Cologne [Amsterdam], n.p. 1695), 184: "Il y a deux cens ans que qui eust enseigné l'Hebreu, ou en eust sceu, on l'eust estimé heretique."

14 See, in general, *Crossing Borders: Hebrew Manuscripts as a Meeting-Place of Cultures,* ed. Piet van Boxel and Sabine Arndt (Oxford: Bodleian Library, 2009); and, for the medieval origins of Robert Wakefield's Hebrew scholarship, see Judith Olszowy-Schlanger, "Robert Wakefield and the Medieval Background of Hebrew Scholarship in Renaissance England," in *Hebrew to Latin, Latin to Hebrew: The Mirroring of Two Cultures in the Age of Humanism,* ed. Giulio Busi, Berlin Studies in Judaism, vol. 1 (Berlin: Freie Universität, Institut für Judaistik; Turin: Nino Aragno, 2006), 61–87.

15 Christopher Ligota, "Annius of Viterbo and Historical Method," *Journal of the Warburg and Courtauld Institutes* 50 (1987): 44–56.

16 Stephens, "Berosus Chaldeus," 186–194.

17 Annius, *Antiquitates,* fol. LIII^r: "Invenimus autem in Itinerario Antonini Caesaris: iter a Roma thyberinum: in Gallias hoc modo. Thyberinum iter est Gallera: Larthenianum sive Veiens: Rosulum: Sutrium: Ocilianum: Cyrminia iuga: Volturrena: cuius praeclaris gestis invidit Livius. Saleumbrona.: Larthis: et reliqua: ut in commentariis eius dicemus. Sale autem Aramea lingua est: origo et exitus alicuius: ut Rabi Samuel interpretatur. Similiter divus Hieronymus: Sale dicit dignificare egressum: libro de interpretationibus nominum. Quare Saleumbrona est locus ab Herodoto et aliis dictus ubi fuit prisca Vmbris habitatio: ubi orti: et a qua egressi diffusi sunt per eius tractum in thuscia usque ad mare et transthyberim ad montes Umbriae."

18 See Adam Kamesar, *Jerome, Greek Scholarship and the Hebrew Bible* (Oxford: Clarendon Press, 1993), 104; and Jerome, *Hebrew Questions on Genesis,* tr. C. T. R. Hayward (Oxford: Clarendon Press, 1995), 18–19.

19 Jerome, *Liber interpretationis hebraicorum nominum,* ed. Paul de Lagarde et al. (Turnhout: Brepols, 1959), 40,8: "Salec egrediens."

20 Annius, *Antiquitates,* fol. LX^v: "Phese autem transcensus est: et ulai palus: ut Samuel noster exposuit: et divus Hieronymus lib. de interpretationibus

consentit. Hinc Phesulai prolatione Aramea et Phesulae prolatione Romana est transcensus a paludibus. Subiacens enim planities paludosa erat."

21 Jerome, *Liber interpretationis hebraicorum nominum* 64,21–22: "Fase transitus sive transgressio, pro quo nostri psacha legunt"; 56,21–22: "Ulai palus, a palude, non a palo, sive dolor femoris vel umbraculi."

22 This text is preserved in Hartmann Schedel's sylloge in Munich, Bayerische Staatsbibliothek, clm 716, and was published in O. A. Danielsson, *Etruskische Inschriften in handschriftlicher Überlieferung* (Uppsala: Almqvist & Wiksell; Leipzig: Harrassowitz, 1928).

23 Danielsson, *Etruskische Inschriften*, xv.

24 See, most recently, David Price, *Johannes Reuchlin and the Campaign to Destroy Jewish Books* (Oxford and New York: Oxford University Press, 2011); and Hans-Peter Willi, *Reuchlin im Streit um die Bücher der Juden: zum 500jährigen Jubiläum des "Augenspiegel"* (Tübingen: Buchhandlung H. P. Willi, 2011).

25 Roberto Weiss, "An Unknown Epigraphic Tract by Annius of Viterbo," in *Italian Studies Presented to E.R. Vincent*, ed. C.P. Brand et al. (Cambridge: W. Heffer, 1962), 101–120, at 102–103 and 111; Amanda Collins, "Renaissance Epigraphy and Its Legitimizing Potential: Annius of Viterbo, Etruscan Inscriptions, and the Origins of Civilization," in *The Afterlife of Inscriptions*, ed. Alison Cooley (London: Institute of Classical Studies, School of Advanced Study, University of London, 2000), 57–76.

26 See respectively Annius, *Antiquitates*, fols. CII^v, CXXIX^r, IX^v, XII^r, LXIV^v, CXIII^v, CXV^v, CXXIV^v, CXXV^r, CXXXI^r, CXXXII^v, LXIV^v.

27 See respectively ibid., fols. XIX^v, CLVIII^v, CLVIII^v; XV^v, XL^v, LXXIX^v (idem Talmudista); LIII^r, CLXX^r, XL^v, LXXIII^r, LXXX^r, CLVIII^r.

28 Ibid., fols. C^r, C^v.

29 Ibid., fols. LIX^v, LXV^r, CXXVI^v, CXXX^v, CXXXIX^r, CXXXIX^v, CXLIV^v, CLXIII^r.

30 Ibid., fol. CLVIII^v.

31 Ibid., fols. XLVIII^v, CXVI^r, CXXXIII^r, CXXVII^v, CXXXIII^v.

32 Ibid., fols. CX^r, CII^v.

33 Ibid., fols. CXXVII^v, LXXXIV^v.

34 This point was well made by Micaela Procaccia, "*Talmudistae Caballarii* e Annio," in *Cultura umanistica a Viterbo. Atti della giornata di studio per il V centenario della stampa a Viterbo, 12 nov. 1988* (Viterbo: Associazione Roma nel Rinascimento, 1991), 111–121, at 112–114.

35 Annius, *Antiquitates*, fol. CXXVII^v.

36 Ibid., fol. CLXIX^v: "Quaeris quae et quot sint illa nomina quae in octavis pascae ferme quinque jam annis superioribus cum rabi Samuele et duobus aliis Talmudistis conferebam."

37 David Nirenberg, *Communities of Violence: Persecution of Minorities in the Middle Ages* (Princeton: Princeton University Press, 1996).

38 R. Po-chia Hsia, *Trent 1475: Stories of a Ritual Murder Trial* (New Haven: Yale University Press in cooperation with Yeshiva University Library, 1992).

39 Annius, *Antiquitates*, fol. CLVIII$^{r–v}$.

40 Walter Stephens, "Complex Pseudonymity: Annius of Viterbo's Multiple Persona Disorder," *MLN* 126 (2011): 689–708.

41 Annius, *Antiquitates*, fol. C^v: "Duobus annis minus regnasse Asmonai Iosephus tradit, id est, viginti septem supra centum. Talmudistae vero in libro Aaboda Zara, in distinctione quae incipit Lipfne Idiem, aiunt: Rabi Iocep tradere Asmonai regnum durasse annis tribus et centum, videlicet vigintisex minus quam ponat Philo. Sed dicendum quod Iocep dicit regnum, scilicet pacificum."

42 Ibid., fol. CI^r: "ubi glosa Rabi Selamo dicit."

43 Ibid, fol. CI^v: "De Zanedrin vero deletione Hebraei scribunt in Talmud in libro Baba Bathra, in distinctione Assutafin. Herodes, inquit, Ascalonita servus fuit Asmonam, qui suscepto per vim regno, interfecit universos Zanedrin septuaginta iudices, uno reservato Bab filio Bota, cui eruit oculos."

44 See, in general, *Printing the Talmud: From Bomberg to Schottenstein*, ed. Sharon Liberman Mintz and Gabriel Goldstein (New York: Yeshiva University Museum, 2006).

45 Reuchlin remarked that he obtained it "diligenter": Badische Landesbibliothek Karlsruhe, MS Reuchlin 2, fol. 96^v.

46 Johann Reuchlin, *Recommendation Whether to Confiscate, Destroy and Burn All Jewish Books*, tr. Peter Wortsman (New York and Mahwah, NJ: Paulist Press, 2000), 39–40.

47 Postel to Pellikan, July 5, 1553, in *Museum Helveticum* 28 (1753), 655.

48 For Riccius's translations, see *Artis Cabalisticae, hoc est, reconditae theologiae et philosophiae scriptorum tomus I*, ed. Joannes Pistorius (Basel: Henrich Petri, 1587), 258–287.

49 Paulus de Heredia, *Illustrissimo ac sapientissimo Domino D. Enigo de Mendocza . . . salutem perpetuamque foelicitatem* (Rome: n.p., ca. 1487); *The Epistle of Secrets*, ed. J. F. Coakley, tr. Rodney Dennis (Oxford: Jericho Press, 1998). See François Secret, "L'*Ensis Pauli* de Paulus de Heredia," *Sefarad* 26 (1966): 79–102, 253–272.

50 Flavius Mithridates, *Sermo de passione Domini*, ed. Chaim Wirszubski (Jerusalem: Israel Academy of Sciences and Humanities, 1963). For Christian interest in Hebrew traditions in fifteenth-century Italy, see further David Marsh, *Giannozzo Manetti: The Life of a Florentine Humanist* (Cambridge and London: Harvard University Press, 2019), ch. 5; Guido Bartolucci, *Vera religio: Marsilio Ficino e la tradizione ebraica* (Turin: Paideia, 2017); and Brian Copenhaver, *Magic and the Dignity of Man: Pico della Mirandola and His Oration in Modern Memory* (Cambridge and London: Belknap Press of Harvard University Press, 2019), pt.1.

51 See the articles collected in *Guglielmo Raimondo Moncada alias Flavio Mitridate: un ebreo converso siciliano. Atti del convegno internazionale, Caltabellotta (Agrigento), 23–24 ottobre 2004*, ed. Mauro Perani (Palermo: Officina di studi medievali, 2008).

52 Mithridates, *Sermo*, 35–36, 96, 117; Chaim Wirszubski, *Pico della Mirandola's Encounter with Jewish Mysticism* (Cambridge, MA, and London: Harvard University Press, 1989), 241–242.

53 Annius, *Antiquitates*, fol. CXLIII^r.

54 Weiss, "Unknown Tract," 110; see also Collins, "Renaissance Epigraphy," 61.

55 This passage was first discussed in Procaccia, *"Talmudistae Caballarii."*

56 Annius, *Antiquitates*, fol. LXXXII^r: "Quod vero Romam derivari ab altero occulto nomine satis mihi fuit antea occultum. Nunc vero quid sentiam explicabo relinquendo iudicium doctiori. Plinius tradit in disciplina Etrusca contineri quo pacto possint evocari dii: fulgura: ignes: et eiuscemodi. Quare etiam quia oppositorum est eadem disciplina: rituales continebat: quo pacto non possent evocari. Hoc autem nullo modo fieri melius poterat: quam occultando nomen ipsius dei: in cuius tutela urbs ipsa erat. Eius occultandi modus erat Etruscis: mysterio quodam: et litteris quibusdam ab ipso dei nomine alterum extrahere: cuius ritu et mysterio: nunc soli Talmudistae et Cabballarii utuntur: i. disciplina quam vocant Caballa."

57 Danielsson, *Etruskische Inschriften*, xv: "Etsi rudissimus sim in vocabulis arameis et hebreis: quippe quam paucis mensibus cum viterbiensibus hebreis in eorum scolis puer commoratus fui."

58 See Stephens, "Berosus Chaldaeus"; Stephens, "When Pope Noah Ruled the Etruscans: Annius of Viterbo and His Forged *Antiquities*," *MLN* 119 (2004): S201–S223; and A. C. Dionisotti, "On Fragments in Classical Scholarship," in *Collecting Fragments = Fragmente Sammeln*, ed. Glenn Most (Göttingen: Vandenhoeck & Ruprecht, 1997), 1–33.

59 Jeremy Cohen, *The Friars and the Jews: The Evolution of Medieval Anti-Semitism* (Ithaca, NY: Cornell University Press, 1982), chap. 6.

60 Annius found his quotation from Avodah Zarah—with Rashi's gloss, which he also quoted—in Ramon Martí, *Pugio fidei*, ed. Joseph de Voisin (Paris: Henault and Henault, 1651), 2:vii, 283, and his quotation from Bava Batra at ibid., 2:iv, 255.

61 Annius, *Antiquitates*, fol. CIII^r: "Quia interfectis legis doctoribus et zanedrin Herodes posuit zanedrin ex neophitis et proselitis: qui dicti sunt pharissaei et scribae. Vnde et Mayr auctor totius doctrinae Talmudicae fuit Idumeus conversus ad iudaismum: ut sparsim in Talmud traditur: et Rabi Moyses aegyptius narrat in prologo summae de auctoritate Talmudica. Et ita haec quaestio de genealogia doctoratus nunquam fuit definita."

62 According to Babylonian Talmud Gittin 56a, Nero became a Jewish proselyte and Meir was one of his descendants.

63 Moses Maimonides, *Mishneh Torah*, prologue, 9–10, ed. and trans. by the Mechon Mamre project, at http://www.mechon-mamre.org/p/index.htm, accessed June 2, 2013.

64 Jacob Dienstag, "Christian Translators of Maimonides' *Mishneh Torah* into Latin," in *Salo Wittmayer Baron Jubilee Volume*, ed. Saul Lieberman and Arthur Hyman (Jerusalem: American Academy for Jewish Research, distributed by Columbia University Press, 1974), 287–309; Aaron Katchen, *Christian Hebraists and Dutch Rabbis: Seventeenth Century Apologetics and the Study of Maimonides' Mishneh Torah* (Cambridge, MA: Harvard University Center for Jewish Studies, distributed by Harvard University Press, 1984).

65 Paul of Burgos, Additio on Isaiah 34:1, quoted in Görge Hasselhoff, *Dicit Rabbi Moyses: Studien zum Bild von Moses Maimonides im lateinischen Westen vom 13. bis zum 15. Jahrhundert* (Würzburg: Königshausen & Neumann, 2004), 274–275n.217. I owe this essential point to Joanna Weinberg.

66 Annius, *Antiquitates*, fol. C^r: "Vocabulum vero Zanedrim, quia saepe occurrit, interpretatur a Talmudistis, collegium sceptri et publicae potestatis totius regni, quae erat penes septuaginta seniores ex principalioribus de tribu Iuda et aliarum tribuum, quibus unus rex praeerat, et loco sui Salomon ex decreto David et dei, posuit Matathim ut exposuimus. Dicunt autem Talmudistae in lib. Zanedrim, quod hoc erat publicum sceptrum institutum a deo in deserto Num. 11." For the Jewish sources that Annius had in mind here, see Martí, *Pugio fidei*, ed. De Voisin, 2:4, 251–252.

67 Annius, *Antiquitates*, fol. C^{r-v}: "Vnde Zanedrim erat collegium publici regiminis et potestatis quibus unus praeerat. Et hi dicuntur usitato veteri vocabulo senes sive veteres. Romana vero lingua Senatores, Aramea et Etrusca Lucij, ultima syllaba habente accentum, et Graece Palei. Porro etiam est opus ut sint magistri i. verbistae, cuius verbo pareatur, quos Romani a verbo et dicto imperioso Dictatores vocant, et communi vocabulo unico Magistratus. Ergo collegium publicae potestatis etiam apud Hebraeos vetustissimos dicebatur Senatorium magistrale, apud Romanos senatorium dictionale, apud Etruscos Lucumonium: apud graecos Paleologum. Vnde nomina importantia publicam potestatem apud veteres composita invenimus ex duabus dictionibus: quarum altera vetustatem et senium, altera verbum et rationem imperiosam importet: ut apud Ebreos zanedrim: apud Romanos senatum decretum, apud Graecos Paleologum, a paleos vetus, et logos ratio et verbum, apud Etruscos Lucumonium a lucu vetus et moni ratio et verbum. Et tandem Viterbum veterum verbum sive dictatura. Quare a loco et argumentatione non modo a vetustissimo more, verumetiam ab inexpugnabili et semper invicta interpretatione, eadem sunt apud Romanos Senatus decretum et verbum quae apud Talmudistas et zanedrim, et apud Graecos paleologum, et apud Desyderium regem Viterbum, et apud Etruscos Lucumonium. De his hactenus."

68 The most recent detailed study is Marie-Dominique Couzinet, *Histoire et méthode à la Renaissance: Une lecture de la* Methodus ad facilem historiarum cognitionem *de Jean Bodin* (Paris: Vrin, 1996).

69 Jean Bodin, *Methodus ad facilem historiarum cognitionem*, in *Artis historicae penus* (Basel: Perna, 1579), 42.

70 Ibid., sig.):():(4^r: "Quam quidem ad rem, Iurisconsultorum simul et Historicorum ponderibus utimur, ut Persarum, Graecorum, Aegyptiorum, non minus quam Romanorum legibus tribuatur. Ex Hebraeorum quoque Pandectis, potissimum ex libris Senadrim optima quaeque haurire proposuimus: in quo mihi suam operam Ioan. Quinquarborerus ac Mercerus Hebraicae linguae regii doctores mihi non defuturam spoponderunt."

71 Jacob Guttmann, *Jean Bodin in seinen Beziehungen zum Judentum* (Breslau: Marcus, 1906). Gutmann used the 1650 edition of Bodin's book. Comparison of the Paris 1566 and 1570 editions of the *Methodus* established that Bodin's substantive discussions of the Talmud appeared for the first time in the latter.

72 Eric Nelson, *The Hebrew Republic: Jewish Sources and the Transformation of European Political Thought* (Cambridge, MA: Harvard University Press, 2010).

73 On Annius and later Christian interpreters of the Talmud, see Anthony Grafton, "'Pandects of the Jews': A French, Swiss and Italian Prelude to John Selden," in *Jewish Books and Their Readers: Aspects of the Intellectual Life of Christians and Jews in Early Modern Europe*, ed. Scott Mandelbrote and Joanna Weinberg (Leiden: Brill, 2016), 169–188.

74 Christopher Krebs of Stanford University is preparing an edition and translation of Annius's *Antiquitates* for the I Tatti Renaissance Library.

CHAPTER 8 · JOHN CAIUS ARGUES ABOUT HISTORY

An earlier version of this chapter was presented as one of my Sandars Lectures at Cambridge University on January 26, 2016. Heartfelt thanks go to Ann Jarvis, my host during my time as Sandars Lecturer, and to David Abulafia, James Carley, Nicholas Hardy, Madeline McMahon, Nicholas Popper, Nancy Siraisi, and Francis Young for comments, criticism, and information. My debt to the work of Vivian Nutton is evident throughout.

1 See, in general, *Oxford Dictionary of National Biography*, s.v. Caius, John, by Vivian Nutton.

2 For this program, which was completed only after Caius died, see Tom Nickson, "Moral Edification at Gonville and Caius College, Cambridge," *Architectural History* 48 (2005): 49–68; and Paul Binski, "Humfrey Lovell and the Gates of Gonville and Caius College: A Note on the Sources," *Journal of the British Archaeological Association* 166 (2013): 179–188.

3 Christopher Brooke, *A History of Gonville and Caius College* (Woodbridge, Suffolk; Dover, NH: Boydell Press, 1985), 75.

4 John Caius, *De antiquitate Cantebrigiensis academiæ libri duo* (London: Bynneman, 1568).

5 Anthony Grafton, "Conrad Gessner and John Caius: The Meanings of Learned Friendship in Renaissance Europe," in *Conrad Gessner (1516–1565): Die Renaissance der Wissenschaften / The Renaissance of Learning*, ed. Urs Leu and Peter Opitz (Berlin: De Gruyter, 2019), 353–374.

6 William Bulleine, *Hereafter Ensueth a Little Dialogue Betweene Two Men, the one called Soreness and the other Chirurgi, Concerning Apostumations, & Woundes, their Causes and also their Cures* (London: Kyngston, 1579), fol. 4ʳ.

7 Vivian Nutton, "John Caius and the Linacre Tradition," *Medical History* 23 (1979): 373–391.

8 Caius, *De libris propriis*, in *Works*, ed. E. S. Roberts (Cambridge: Cambridge University Press, 1912), 82: "Admonuimus etiam lectorem in eis commentariis seu annotationibus quorundam Galeni locorum in Anatomicis, quos Vesalius corruperat, cum illi eorum castigandi provinciam Antonius Iunta typographus Venetus commiserat. Inter quos unus est libro anatomicωn 9. pagina 335. de intercepto cerebri. Addidimus & veram effigiem ginglymi

ad Galeni sensum pag. 299 quem Vesalius ante expressit in prima editione libri sui anno Domini 1543. pagina 14. longe aliena, & plane dissimili, quod in ea mutuus ferri ingressus non sit, ut est in ginglymo ossium humani corporis."

9   See John Venn, "John Caius," ibid., 1–78; Nutton, "Caius, John."

10 Thomas Muffett, *Health's Improvement: or, Rules Comprizing and Discovering the Nature, Method, and Manner of Preparing all sorts of Food used in this Nation*, corrected and enlarged by Christopher Bennett (London: Thomson, 1655), 123. On Muffett, see *Dictionary of National Biography*, s.v. Moffett, MOUFET, or MUFFET, Thomas (1553–1604), by Sidney Lee.

11 Anthony Grafton, *Cardano's Cosmos* (Cambridge, MA: Harvard University Press, 1999), 184–185, 254n.26.

12 Alfred Hiatt, "Forgery at the University of Cambridge," *New Medieval Literatures* 3 (1999): 95–118; Alfred Hiatt, *The Making of Medieval Forgeries: False Documents in Fifteenth-Century England* (London: British Library, 2004); Ad Putter, "King Arthur at Oxbridge: Nicholas Cantelupe, Geoffrey of Monmouth, and Cambridge's Foundation Myth," *Medium Aevum* 72, no. 1 (2003): 63–81; and James Carley, "'Many Good Autours': Two of John Leland's Manuscripts and the Cambridge Connection," *Transactions of the Cambridge Bibliographical Society* 15, no. 3 (2014): 27–53.

13 Matthew Parker, *De antiquitate Britannicae ecclesiae* (London: John Day, 1572), 292–293 at 293.

14 John Caius, *De antiquitate Cantebrigiensis academiæ libri duo* (London: Bynneman, 1568).

15 John Strype, *The Life and Acts of Matthew Parker* (London: John Wyat, 1711), book 3, chap. 18, 257.

16 Corpus Christi College Cambridge (hereafter CCCC) 340.

17 Nancy Siraisi, *History, Medicine and the Tradiions of Renaissance Learning* (Ann Arbor: University of Michigan Press, 2008).

18 William Lambarde, *A Perambulation of Kent* (London: Newberie, 1576), 233.

19 D. M. Owen, *Cambridge University Archives: A Classified List* (Cambridge: Cambridge University Press, 2011), 66–67. The documents in question appear in Collect. Admin. 9, 28–39.

20 Caius, *De antiquitate*, 1568, 37.

21 CCCC MS 106, 43.

22 John Leland, *Cygnea Cantio* (London: Wolfe, 1545), quoted and tr. in Carley, "'Many Good Authors,'" 32–33.

23 Robin Darwall-Smith, *A History of University College, Oxford* (Oxford: Oxford Universiy Press, 2008), 106–107.

24 Thomas Caius, *Assertio antiquitatis Oxoniensis Academiae*, in Caius, *De antiquitate*, 1568, 389.

25 Caius, *De antiquitate*, 1568, 38.

26 Cambridge University Library (hereafter CUL) MS Hare A 1.

27 See *Oxford Dictionary of National Biography*, s.v. Hare, Robert, by Elisabeth Leedham-Green.

28 Willison to Caius, March 31, 1571, ibid., 42.

29 Bodleian Library 8° Rawl. 470.

30 Caius, *De Antiquitate*, 1568, 37.

31 Thomas Hearne printed Thomas Caius's marginalia, with the text of John Caius's 1568 *De antiquitate*, in his edition of the former's *Vindiciae antiquitatis academiae Oxoniensis*, 2 vols. (Oxford, 1730), in this case 1:27, from the original, which he owned: Bodleian 8° Rawl. 470, 37: "Haec admodum antiqua non est, quae Cantelupum authorem habet. Vixit enim Cantilepus tempore Henrici 6^i, & annis abhinc plus minus 70. vita functus est. Neque multum refert quam nova sit aut vetus historia: sed quam vera sit, et veterum scriptis consentanea."

32 John Caius, *De antiquitate academiae Cantebrigiensis*, 1568, Beinecke Library 2011 534, 15: "Unde dicatur Niger codex? An ob colorem atrum? An ad terrorem oxoniensium? An ob nigros authoris mores? An quia non plus habeat candoris, quam virtutis [MS virtus] iste Caius? An quod affinis sit vanitati mendacij? An quod diabolum inprimis referat, qui fuit mendax ab initio?"

33 Felicity Heal, "'What Can King Lucius Do for You?' The Reformation and the Early British Church," *English Historical Review* 120, no. 487 (2005): 593–614.

34 Caius, *De antiquitate*, 1568, 78: "Atque ita constat Vniversitatem fuisse Cantabrigiae & Honorij primi aetate, & longe ante, Eleutherij quoque tempore."

35 Note in Caius, *De antiquitate*, Beinecke 2011 534, 78: "commentum ioculare, & impudens."

36 Caius, *De antiquitate*, 1568, 79: "ut nulli Archiepiscopo seu Episcopo, alijve ecclesiasticae personae vel seculari liceat . . ."; note in Caius, *De antiquitate*, Beinecke 2011 534, 79: "hic non erat stylus, pontificum illius seculi."

37 Caius, *De antiquitate*, 1568, 83: "Transcripta praeterea diplomata . . . propter vetustatem consumpta"; note in Caius, *De antiquitate*, Beinecke 2011 534, 83: "blattis & tineis debet cantabrigia."

38 John Caius, *Works*, [223]–227: "Catalogus scriptorum, quibus usus est duobus hisce libris Londinensis. Historici nostri antiqui & scripti."

39 Ibid., viii–x, after the preface, where a note by M. R. James appears, identifying as many of the sources Caius used as possible. He points out Caius's use "of Parker's collection before it was bequeathed to Corpus Christi College" and of "many of the MSS, which Sir Robert Cotton (who seems to have begun to collect books about 1588) afterwards secured" (x). He does not note that the Cotton MSS, or many of them, would have been at Lambeth Palace. See also Philip Grierson, "Appendix IV: John Caius's Library," in *Biographical History of Gonville and Caius College, 1349–1897*, ed. John Venn et al. (Cambridge: Cambridge University Press, 1897–1998), 7:509–535, at 523. For the growth and use of Parker's collection, see Timothy Graham and Andrew Watson, *The Recovery of the Past in Early Elizabethan England: Documents by John Bale and John Joscelyn from the Circle of Matthew Parker* (Cambridge: Cambridge Bibliographical Society, 1998); and Graham, "Matthew Parker's Manuscripts: An Elizabethan Library and its Uses," in *The Cambridge History of Libraries in Britain and Ireland*, 3 vols. (Cambridge: Cambridge University Press, 2006), 2:322–341. The portion of it that Parker left

to Corpus Christi College has been digitized and made available as the Parker Library on the Web, https://parker.stanford.edu/parker/, accessed September 8, 2018. See also Mildred Budny, *Insular, Anglo-Saxon, and Early Anglo-Norman Manuscript Art at Corpus Christi College, Cambridge: An Illustrated Catalogue*, 2 vols. (Kalamazoo: Medieval Institute Publications, 1997); and Chapter 5.

40 Strype, *Parker*, 257.

41 Henry Plomer, "The 1574 Edition of Dr. John Caius's *De antiquitate Cantebrigiensis academiae libri duo*," *The Library*, 7th ser., 3 (December 1926): 252–268. London, British Library C.32.h.15. (1.) is the Arundel/Lumley copy. A note on the title page reads: "Ex dono Mathei Cantuariensis Archiepiscopi."

42 London, British Library C.24.a.27. (1.) is a presentation copy from John Parker to King James VI and I, with a bespoke colored title page. On the verso of the first fly-leaf appears the following: "Excellentissimo Principi Iacobo Angliae Scotiae/Franciae et Hiberniae Regi dignissimo./(Matthei dudum Archiepiscopi filius.)/Subditus humilimus/Johannes Parker/hunc." James's response is quoted in Brooke, *A History of Gonville and Caius College*, 75.

43 Lambeth Palace Library MS 959, fol. 359^r: "Johannes Lydgatus, Galfridi Chauceri discipulus author est tempore Gurguntij Regis Britanni qui regnavit anno mundi 4317. Cantabrum Regis Hispaniae, filium Bartholum regis Hiberniae fratrem Cantabrigiam super Cantam fluvium condidisse, nomenque Cantabrigiae dedisse: anno mundi 4346. A transmigratione babylonica anno 538. eumque Athenis edoctum inde Philosophos advocasse et Cantabr. docendi gratia collocasse & ab alijs initijs ad suam Bedae et Alfredi memoriam primae scholae et universitatis nomine Cantabr. claruisse. Johannes Caius"; fol. 374^v: "Singulares patronos et restitutores habuit Cantabrigia: et habet hodie quoque multos. Habet enim tot ex multis paucos referam.) lucens ille et pulcherrimus orbis literarum et virtutum Cantabrigia prae caeteros, tres summos et primarios viros, tanquam tres stellas radiantes, de quibus multum sane gloriatur. Reverendissimum Matthaeum Parker Cantuar. Archiepm. et totius Angliae primatem: D. Nicolaum Bacon equestris ordinis virum, summi Cancellarij locum tenentem et Magni Sigilli custodem. Et Guliel. Cecilium equitem auratum, summum Angliae Thesaurarium, regiae maiestati a Consiliis, atque Cantabrigiensis Academiae Cancellarium summum. Qui ut eodem tempore Cantabrigiae omnes studuerunt etc. ut Caius de antiquitate Canteb. Academiae. p^a. 129 et 130."

44 "Non tam solicitus fuit Caius noster cum adversario suo de utriusque Academiae antiquitate in hoc opere contendere, quam quae ex varijs antiquis monumentis de statu, privilegijs, dignitate, ac praerogativa Cantebrigiae ipse collegisset, edere ac in lucem proferre. In quo eum maxime elaborasse facile erit sano ac prudenti lectori deprehendere." See Nicholas Popper, "An Information State for Elizabethan England," *Journal of Modern History* 90, no. 3 (2018): 503–535.

45 CCCC 110, 225: "Memorandum quod Collegium Gunwelli et Caii habet unum volumen sive rotulam in pergameno scriptum datum a Roberto Hare Armigero illi Collegio. A° domini 1568. Et hec rotula precipue tractat de ecclesia wintoniensi quomodo incepta, aucta, et variis temporibus a diversis

habitatoribus, quandoque monachis, quandoque secularibus canonicis et refert etiam numerum annorum quo tempore quisque rex tam Britorum quam Saxonixorum et Normannorum usque ad henricum quintum caepit. Refert etiam originem Academiae Cantabrigiensis videlicet tradens a Cantabro etc. et est illud volumen de quo doctor Caius scribit in libro suo de Antiquitate Cantabrigiae quem tertium testem citat. He continentur in illo volumine omnes gratiae expediendae in Curia Romana. Et dispensationes a sede Apostolica: tam pro matrimonio illicito, contractis, quam pro religiosis."

46 John Caius, note in Gonville and Caius College MS 717/717: "Hoccleue in epitome chronicon transtulisse videtur hoc scriptum ad verbum, nisi quod contigit melius exemplar et ad suam aetatem accommodavit, qui floruit a° Domini 1454, septem annis postquam scriptum hoc est."

47 Gonville and Caius College MS 717/717: "Universitas Cantebriggie edificata est a Cantebro duce, a mundi creacione anno iiij°.lxxxxv. et frequentata a philosophis ante christi incarnacionem per annos ccc.lxxx.iiij. Ab adventu Bruti in hanc terram a° ii.cccc.xxv°. Ab edificacione London. Civitatis ii.cccc.xxx annis."

48 Ibid.: "Cantebriggia constat esse universitas millenis octingentis xxv annis."

49 Caius, De antiquitate, 1568, 53: "Is inquam author incerti quidem nominis, authoritatis tamen grandis, anno a Christo nato 1447. minio & atramento in charta pergamena scriptus."

50 Ibid., 53–54: "universitatem Cantabrigiensem (sic enim vocat) a Cantabro duce aedificatam asserit . . . addit praeterea constare (hoc enim verbo utitur) Cantabrigiam fuisse universitatem ante tempus quo haec scripserat annis 1825."

51 Ibid., 286.

52 Asser, Alfredi regis res gestae (London: Day, 1574), sig. Aij^v: "vetusta quaedam exemplaria, eodem etiam tempore descripta."

53 Trinity College Cambridge MS R 5 22, fol. 1^r: "Hic ipsus [sic] liber est quem Aluredus Rex misit ad Ecclesiam Syreburnensem, quem et transtulit è pastorali Gregorii Latine in Anglicum."

54 See May McKisack, Medieval History in the Tudor Age (Oxford: Clarendon Press, 1971); Frederic Clark, Anthony Grafton, Madeline McMahon, and Neil Weijer, "The Life Cycle of the First County History: William Lambarde's Perambulation of Kent from Conception to Reception," Journal of the Warburg and Courtauld Institutes 81 (2018): 129–212.

55 CCCC MS 281, fol. 81^r: "hic baptizati sunt novem ex doctoribus et scolaribus cantebrigie."

56 Caius, De antiquitate, 1568, 95; 1574, 73: "Praeter hos omnes, in pervetustis Annalibus Burtonensibus sic lego, Anno domini, 141. Hic baptisati sunt novem ex doctoribus & scholaribus Cantebrigiae. Vnde scire licet fuisse Gymnasium Cantebrigiae ante Lucij tempora & receptum Evangelium ante Lucij regnum, etsi non publice, fuisseque per ea tempora doctores."

57 CCCC MS 281, 1ro: "Iste liber est de communitate Burtoniae, qui eum alienaverit anathema sit."

58 When working on Galen, by contrast, Caius took care to treat marginal notes and other additions as potential sources of textual corruption.

59 See Chapter 5.

60 Caius, *De rariorum animalium historia, Works,* ed. Roberts, 53.

61 See Anthony Grafton, "Philological and Artisanal Knowledge Making in Renaissance Natural History: A Study in Cultures of Knowledge," *History of Humanities* 3, no. 1 (2018): 39–55.

62 Vivian Nutton, *John Caius and the Manuscripts of Galen* (Cambridge: Cambridge Bibliographical Society, 1987).

63 CUL Adv.d.3.1.

64 Florence, Biblioteca Medicea Laurenziana, Laur. 75, 8, fol. 398ʳ: "Angeli Politiani Liber emptus de Paulli physici Florentini heredibus: pellegeram ego Ang. Politianus in rusculo meo Faesulano XVII. Kal. Quintilis anno sal. 1487." Paolo Viti, *Pico, Poliziano e l'Umanesimo del fine Quattrocento* (Florence: Olschki, 1994),

65 Caius, *De libris propriis* (1570), in *Works,* 101: "duobus libris comprehensam ab Angelo Politiano (Leonis Pontificis Romani praeceptore) in rusculo suo Faesulano septimo Calend. quintiles anno salutis 1497. emptis, ut si quis transcribere eos atque aedere cupiat, aut Galeni libros Graecos ad eos emendare studeat, inde petat."

66 Ibid., 100.

67 For a brief account, see Anthony Grafton, *Joseph Scaliger: A Study in the History of Classical Scholarship,* 2 vols. (Oxford: Clarendon Press, 1983–1993), vol. 1, chaps. 1–2.

68 Gonville and Caius College Library MS 625 / 404, with the note: "Joannes Caius collegio Gonevilli & Caij suo dedit, aᵒ 1557."

69 Gonville and Caius College Library MS 625 / 404, fol. 2ʳ: "Nunc vero acceptus est in usum ecclesiasticum sapientiae liber, quem quidam suspicantur esse philonis iudei."

70 *PL* 28, col. 1241.

71 Gonville and Caius College Library MS 625 / 404, fol. 2ʳ: "licet de machabeis quos ipsi חשמוני vocant nonnihil in historijs habent. sunt [sicut?] munsterus superioribus annis edito libello ex Josippo os [line over this last] edit."

72 Ibid.: "Caius iuvenis adhuc, & Hebraicae linguae studiosus, cantabrigie scripsit."

73 Nicholas Popper, "The English Polydaedali: How Gabriel Harvey Read Late Tudor London," *Journal of the History of Ideas* 66 (2005): 351–381.

74 John Caius, *De libris propriis* (1570), in *Works,* 86–87, contrasting "Bibliotheca publica illustrissimi principis Cosmi Medices, quae omnibus literarum studiosis principis humanitate atque gratia patet" (86) with the library at Urbino ("usque adeo difficilis accessus est in Bibliothecam ejus viri") (87).

75 Ibid., 100–102.

76 Nutton, *Caius and the Manuscripts of Galen;* Stéphane Berlier, "John Caius et les manuscrits de Galien," *Revue d'Histoire des Textes,* new ser., 6 (2011): 1–14 (which argues that Caius probably stole at least portions of one of the manuscripts that he saw in Italy).

77 Caius, *Historia,* in *Works,* 68: "Ita utraque Oxoniensium Bibliotheca cum alijs perquisitis in illas scholas Theologicas translata, a nobilibus viris ornata quondam fuit. Quae iam vereor ne una cum Patronorum memoria

deleta pene atque consumpta sit. Tam paucis annis gratitudinem extinguit negligentia, & benemeritorum oblivionem parit. Proinde admonendi sunt utriusque universitatis studentes, ut diligenter conservandis his quibus affecti sunt beneficijs, colendaque fraequenter Patronorum memoria a supina illa negligentia se prorsus vendicent atque seiungant. Eo enim modo Patronos novos indies conciliabunt, & quae profutura sibi sunt, acquirent."

78 Ibid., 68–71: "Hi autem veteres libri in Cantebrigiensi Bibliotheca iam supersunt." At [115–116] there is a "Note on pp. 68–71 by Dr. M. R. James, Provost of King's College," which identifies many of the books and manuscripts listed by Caius. For its special status see David McKitterick, "Libraries and the Organization of Knowledge," in *Libraries in Britain and Ireland,* 1:592–593.

79 Caius, *De antiquitate,* 184: "Etenim si quis volet superiorum temporum omnia comprehendere, ex ipso fonte petat, unde ad alios rivus dimanavit. Quapropter neque ego certe usus essem recentium authoritate, nisi tibi in hac controversia hos placere ex usu animadvertam, sic ut non alij aeque. Usus autem sum paucissimis, ut & impressis paucis, coeteris omnibus scriptis, quibus delector maxime, ut incorruptae & venerandae vetustatis exemplaribus." Note also his description of the value of Asser as a contemporary witness to Alfred's doings, ibid., 174: "Quid multis? Fidem & authoritatem maiorem semper affert vetustas in omnibus controversijs, ut quae, res ut erant viderat, aut illis quam proxime accesserat. Posteriores igitur examinabo ad primos illos incorruptae vetustatis scriptores, qui fide supereminent omnes, quod aut illis diebus vixerant quibus haec gesta sunt, aut his non longe aberant, aut quam proxime (ut dixi) accesserant, ut ex illis haurire possent. Inter quos primus primaeque fidei Asser seu Asserus est, oculatus & auritus testis, qui ex intimis Aluredi familiaribus fuit, qui in eius Aula vixit, res eius & domesticas & forenses novit, atque etiam cum doctis regiae familiae viris consuetudinem habuit, omniaque in vita & in morte diligenter observavit, ut solent qui historias veras scribere decreverunt." It was of course Parker who arranged for the publication of Asser's work on Alfred.

80 Though Caius's bibliography contains substantive comments on some of the works it lists, it says nothing about their provenance or location. See, e.g., *Works,* 226: "Antonini Augusti itinerarium, in quod vir magnae diligentiae, & praestabilis nostri temporis Antiquarius Robertus Talbotus scripsit commentarios, satis certe luculentos atque elaboratos." For Talbot's comments on the Antonine itinerary, see his copybook, CCCC MS 379, fols. 24^r-66^v, and CCCC MS 101, 145–168.

81 Caius, *De libris propriis* (1570), in *Works,* 100: "De antiquis urbibus librum item unum, ubi docemus quae illae olim erant, quibus nominibus consebantur [censebantur?] & olim & nunc quoque quae nunquam interciderunt, facta etiam mentione earum quae esse desierunt."

82 Caius, *De rariorum animalium historia libellus* (1570), in *Works,* 39: "Damam Plinii ex caprarum genere esse indicat pilus, aruncus, figura corporis, atque cornua; nisi quod his in adversum adunca, cum caeteris in aversum acta sint. Caprae magnitudine est, & colore Dorcadis. Plinii &

Romanorum esse, indicio est, quod Romae in columna quadam marmorea & triumphali superstite adhuc, cum anno domini 1543. essemus Romae, insculpatur, & cum Pliniana descriptione conveniat."

83 John Caius to Matthew Parker, April 8, 1567: Matthew Parker, *Correspondence*, ed. John Bruce and Thomas Thomason Perowne (Cambridge: At the University Press, 1853), 299.

84 John Caius, *Historiae Cantebrigiensis Academiae ab urbe condita liber primus [-secundus]*, in *Works*, 76–77: "Quas ob res eos tum temporis omnes fovebant, omnes amplexabantur, ut quos virtus, & eruditio commendabant populo, non ut hodie insolentia alienabat, non luxurians mensa, non vestis, non cubiculum, non intumescentia crocotillis crusculis faemoralia, non inter disputandum galeri, non ambiguae vestes, non crispatae camisiae, non rotundi pilei, non capiti pressi, non tonsa levitas, non barbata vanitas, non lascivia, non arma, non alea, non choreae, universitatis legibus iam olim prohibitae, non fastus denique vestis atque vitae, in quo multi ita splendent luce aliena, ut solet luna."

85 Caius, *De antiquitate*, in *Works*, 26: "Nam postquam ab uno atque altero recentiori auspicatus fueris, ut Polydoro, Baleo, atque Lilio (quorum oscitante uno oscitat & alter, nam unum Polydorum authorem sequuntur omnes) cum locus sit introducendi veteres scriptores, nullum prorsus introducis, sed in alium locum differs . . . quasi trium istorum testimonia unum non essent, sed plura, uno Polydoro authore, pluribus qui eum authorem sequuti sunt, referentibus."

86 Ibid., 133: "Sed ad rhetoricam tuam, quae etsi dicat, nude & ieiune proferenda adversarij verba, non tamen dicit decerpenda duo aut tria vocabula testimonij ut causam adiuves: (incivile enim est arripere historiae particulam, & totam ex ea causam iudicare) nec ita implicanda scriptorum testimonia ut imponas."

87 Petra Schulte, *Scripturae publicae creditur: Das Vertrauen in Notariatsurkunden im kommunalen Italien des 12. und 13. Jahrhunderts* (Tübingen: Niemeyer, 2003).

88 CCCC MS 106, p. 111: "Concordat Matthaeus Cantuar."

89 Caius, *De antiquitate* (1574), 68–71.

90 Caius, *Annals of the College of Physicians*, in *Works*, 38: "Ante hunc annum, Collegium nullo fuit ornatum tapete, pulvinari nullo, cistella suffragatoria nulla, nulla arcula, nulla campanella vocali, rationali libro nullo, nullo annalium, nec ullo a candidatis aut admissis exceptum conuiuio, quo recreetur honestum studium, & aletur mutuus amor. Actorum liber erat, ut et statutorum, sed ille sine nomine, hic sine ordine, sine perfectione, sine concordia. Quare illi pandectarum nomen dedi, quod omnia reciperet tumultuarie, hunc perfeci, excogitatis atque additis quae ad perfectionem deerant, & per collegium approbatis, in eoque omnia digessi, in ordinem & concordiam redegi, & mea manu rescripsi, ut & hunc Annalium"; Caius, *The Annals of Gonville and Caius College*, ed. John Venn (Cambridge: Deighton Bell, 1904), v–vi: "Volumus etiam et statuimus ut ex sociis aliquis qui quam scitissime scribat, et optimi stili sit, eligatur per custodem et majorem sociorum partem, qui pro tempore fuerint, in Collegii secretarium, seu

registrum, in annum, biennium aut triennium, prout spes melioris aut metus deterioris fuerit: ut sine foedatione librorum & varietate literarum omnia referantur in libros quaeque suos quam pulcherrime, videlicet in rationalem rationes accepti et expensi: in annales res gestae singulo quoque anno: in evidentiarum volumen evidentiae: et in commentarium rerum gestarum sive pandectas omnia promiscue usque ad tempus computorum. Quo tempore omnia memorabilia secernantur, et in suos cujusque argumenti libros, ordinis et circumstantiarum habita ratione, digerantur."

91 Ibid., 79: "Cogebamur insuper evidentias multas hinc inde per seniorum sociorum cubicula distractas conquirere, suis locis ordine reponere, quae laceris chartis citra ordinem commissa sunt pergameno ordine rescribere, ad notanda acta seu res gestas libros instituere, de acceptis et expensis, concreditis atque debitis, rationum libros componere."

92 Richard Serjeantson, "Testimony and Proof in Early-Modern England," *Studies in History and Philosophy of Science* 30, no. 2 (1999): 195–236.

93 Annius of Viterbo described Berosus the Chaldean, one of his forged historians of the ancient world, as "notarius & scriba publicus" and described his procedures as notarial: "Quamobrem omnem Chaldaicam defloravit historiam & tanquam publicae fidei notarius transumpsit omnia tempora & antiquitates" (*Antiquitatum variarum volumina xvii* [Paris: Ascensius, 1512], fol. ciiii^r). See also Chapter 5.

94 CCCC MS 340, 189.

95 Caius, *Vindiciae*, ed. Hearne, I, 227, 276.

96 BL MS Cotton Vitellius C.IX, fol. 117^r–v, published in Warren Boutcher, "Polybius Speaks British: A Case Study in Mid-Tudor Humanism and Historiography," in *Tudor Translation*, ed. Fred Schurink (Basingstoke: Palgrave Macmillan, 2011), 101–120, at 115. It seems likely that Watson knew John Joscelyn, Parker's chief secretary (ibid., 113).

97 Brooke, *A History of Gonville and Caius College*, 72–73; Margaret Aston, "English Ruins and English History: The Dissolution and the Sense of the Past," *Journal of the Warburg and Courtauld Institutes* 36 (1973): 231–255; Alexandra Walsham, *The Reformation of the Landscape: Religion, Identity, and Memory in Early Modern Britain and Ireland* (Oxford: Oxford University Press, 2011).

98 Lambeth College Library MS 720, quoted in Venn, "John Caius," 26. Caius was also accused of papism in a memorandum of 1572 or later, written by a critical member or members of the Royal College of Physicians, of which he was elected president nine times: G. N. Clark and A. M. Cooke, *A History of the Royal College of Physicians of London*, 3 vols. (Oxford: Clarendon Press, 1964–1972), 1:127–130.

99 Brooke, *A History of Gonville and Caius College*, 76–77.

100 Caius, *Annals of Gonville and Caius College*, 185.

101 See Francis Young, "Sandars Lecture 2016: 'John Caius: History as Argument,'" at https://drfrancisyoung.com/2016/01/27/sandars-lecture-2016-john-caius-history-as-argument/, accessed October 12, 2019.

102 See the rich materials, both printed and manuscript, collected in Lambeth Palace Library MS 720.

103 John Caius, *De pronunciatione Graecae et Latinae linguae cum scriptione nova libellus (1574)*, ed. and tr. John Butler Gabel (Leeds: Leeds University School of English, 1968), 16–17: "Non est tamen tam stupidus quisquam aut impudens et insulsus rei alicuius novae author, qui non sit habiturus suae stultitiae fautores et sectatores, vel homines adolescentes, vel stultam plebeculam: at gravem virum cui sit iudicium, ne unum quidem. Nisi si forte ingenii sui ostendandi causa hoc fecerint, ut Isocrates laudando Busyrim, Libanius Thersitem, Lucianus Muscam, Quartanam Favorinus, Calviciem Synesius Cyrenensis, Comam Dion Chrysostomus, et nostri saeculi . . . Copernicus de motu terrae et statione coeli volumen: et Erasmus Roterodamus de febre et Phalarismo libellos. Nam rhetores subinde animi causa solent tractare materias ἀδόξους et exercendi gratia argumentum infame declarant."

104 Ibid., 6–7: "Nova enim Romanis, viris certe in omni re sapientibus, quae praeter consuetudinem et morem maiorum suorum illata sunt, neque placuerunt neque recta videbantur."

105 Ibid., 7–8: "Hinc factum existimem, ut scholae iuris nostri publici nullo modo adduci possunt [possint?], ut relinquant suum octabis: nec scholae quaedam Academicae, ut deficiant a suis sotulis, cum artium magisterio invitandi sunt: aut ocreis, cum S. S. Theologiae Doctoratus gradu insigniendi sunt: aut ovis vario modo praeparatis cum in determinationibus Bacchalaurei novitii seniores sui gradus conviviis excipiant: nec in disputationibus, sedentibus disputatoribus, ut auditores humi non procumbant, fusi per densum substratum iuncum: nec ut caputium patientiamque quam vocant stamineam (peculiare gestamen collegis Hispanorum Collegii apud Bononienses) deponant Hispani Bononiensis Academiae. Quos omnes laudo equidem, quod levibus momentis non impellantur huc atque illuc inconstanter, nec a veteri sua consuetudine avellantur desciscantque facile: ut nonnullae solent Academiae in quibus levitas iuvenilis magna parvis, quadrata rotundis, et formas formis mutat imprudenter admodum, nullo servato ordine, nulla consuetudine aut gravitate."

106 Ibid., 10: "Licet tamen hic contemplari iudicium iuventutis, quae vitia pro virtutibus amplectitur, ut solet vulgus Aulicorum, qui camisias crispatas et cothurnos coraceos inducunt ornamenti causa, qui principio causa contegendi crura et colla morbida ad quotidianum usum sunt inventa [read: inventi]. Nam olim et nostra memoria, cum sana essent omnia, nec cothurnis utebantur, et denudata corporum colla erant ad pectus, et pectora expapillata (ut Plauti verbo utar) atque ad papillia denudata, etiam brumali tempore."

107 "Decree against Excess in Apparel," in *Cambridge University Transactions during the Puritan Controversies of the 16th and 17th Centuries*, ed. James Heywood and Thomas Wright, 2 vols. (London: Bohn, 1854), 1:216–219, at 217.

108 Ibid., 218.

109 Ulinka Rublack, *Dressing Up: Cultural Identity in Renaissance Europe* (Oxford: Oxford University Press, 2010).

110 Angelo Poliziano, quoted in Grafton, *Scaliger*, 1:26.

111 See Madeline McMahon, "Matthew Parker and the Practice of Church History," in *Confessionalization and Erudition in Early Modern Europe: An Episode in the History of the Humanities*, ed. Nicholas Hardy and Dmitri Levitin (Oxford: Published for the British Academy by Oxford University Press, 2020), 116–153.

112 Randolph Head, "Documents, Archives, and Proof around 1700," *Historical Journal* 56, no. 4 (2013): 909–930.

113 New York Academy of Medicine RB (1).

CHAPTER 9 · BARUCH SPINOZA READS THE BIBLE

This chapter, which was originally presented as a lecture and retains that form, presents a highly provisional map of an immense territory. Warm thanks go to Henk Nellen, Dirk van Miert, and their colleagues for inviting me to speak about Spinoza and for their editorial corrections to the published version; to Jerry Seigel for inviting me to present a revised version to the New York Area Seminar in Intellectual and Cultural History; and to Charly Coleman, Jeffrey Freedman, Dan Garber, Michah Gottlieb, Nicholas Hardy, Russ Leo, Scott Mandelbrote, and Jerry Seigel, for valuable suggestions. I owe a special debt to Henk Nellen, for supplying new evidence about Leibniz's response to the *Tractatus*, which is discussed at the end of this chapter.

1 Lodewijk Meijer, *Philosophy as the Interpreter of Holy Scripture (1666)*, tr. Samuel Shirley, ed. Lee C. Rice and Francis Pastijn (Milwaukee: Marquette University Press, 2005); Adriaan Koerbagh, *A Light Shining in Dark Places, to Illuminate the Main Questions of Theology and Religion*, ed. and tr. Michiel Wielema, introduction by Wiep van Bunge (Leiden and Boston: Brill, 2011).

2 J. Samuel Preus, "A Hidden Opponent in Spinoza's Tractatus," *Harvard Theological Review*, 88 (1995): 361–388; Preus, *Spinoza and the Irrelevance of Biblical Authority* (Cambridge: Cambridge University Press, 2001); Noel Malcolm, *Aspects of Hobbes* (Oxford: Oxford University Press, 2002); Susan James, *Spinoza on Philosophy, Religion and Politics: The Theologico-Political Treatise* (Oxford: Oxford University Press, 2012); some other exceptions are cited in the following notes.

3 Stanislaus, Graf von Dunin-Borkowski, *Spinoza*, 4 vols. (Münster i. W.: Aschendorff, 1933–1936), 3:161–308.

4 Henri de Valois, *Emendationum libri quinque et de critica libri duo* (Amsterdam: Pieter Burman, 1740), 152: "cavendumque praecipue est, ne animo praeoccupato atque addicto, ac prae verecundia submisso, ad legendum accedamus: neve auctoritatem ac vetustatem scriptoris nobis imponere atque illudere patiamur." This passage was first discussed in the classical article by Benedetto Bravo, "*Critice* in the Sixteenth and Seventeenth Centuries and the Rise of the Notion of Historical Criticism," in *History of Scholarship*, ed. Christopher Ligota and Jean-Louis Quantin (Oxford: Oxford University Press, 2006), 135–195, at 180–183.

5 Valois, *Emendationum libri quinque*, 152: "Solis Divinis libris hic honos habeatur, ut animo quasi in servitutem redacto, et judicii nostri libertate abjecta eos perlegamus. De caeteris vero omnibus assuescamus inter legendum judicium ferre: quoniam hic praecipuus lectionis fructus est, animadvertere quid commode, quid perperam dictum sit, ut hoc fugere, illud vero imitari possimus."

6 Pieter Burman, ibid., 152 n. (a): "Nescio an his in verbis plane ex animi sententia loquatur Valesius. Nam quod ad sensum et res ipsas, quae sacris continentur paginis, adtinet, iis honorem et reverentiam ab omnibus, qui bonae menti litant, deberi nemo sanus, ut opinor, in controversiam vocare sustinebit. Sed quoniam de Critica ejusque praestantia hic agitur, nemo etiam usum illius modestum et opportunum a divinis libris procul arcendum esse contendet, quos qui describendo ad posteritatem transmiserunt, manus habuerunt aeque ut ceteris aliorum Auctorum librariis contigit, erroribus et scripturae vitiis obnoxias, quibus eximendis Viri doctissimi sincerae Critices subsidio feliciter usi sunt."

7 Paul Hazard, *The European Mind, 1680–1715*, tr. J. Lewis May (London: Hollis & Carter, 1953; repr. Cleveland: World Pub. Co., 1963; New York: New York Review Books, 2013); Jonathan Israel, *Radical Enlightenment: Philosophy and the Making of Modernity, 1650–1750* (Oxford: Oxford University Press, 2001); Israel, *Enlightenment Contested: Philosophy, Modernity, and the Emancipation of Man, 1670–1752* (Oxford: Oxford University Press, 2006).

8 For a fine introduction to the *Tractatus*, see Steven Nadler, *A Book Forged in Hell: Spinoza's Scandalous Treatise and the Birth of the Secular Age* (Princeton: Princeton University Press, 2011). For a contemporary approach to the issues that Spinoza hoped to solve from biblical evidence, see Karel van der Toorn, *Scribal Culture and the Making of the Hebrew Bible* (Cambridge, MA, and London: Harvard University Press, 2007). And for an erudite (if sometimes contentious) history of research on the notion that someone compiled or edited the Bible, see John Van Seters, *The Edited Bible: The Curious History of the "Editor" in Biblical Criticism* (Winona Lake, IN: Eisenbrauns, 2006).

9 Benedict Spinoza, *Theologico-Political Treatise*, tr. Michael Silverthorne and Jonathan Israel, ed. Jonathan Israel (Cambridge: Cambridge University Press, 2007), viii, 119; Spinoza, *Tractatus theologico-politicus* (Amsterdam: Jan Rieuwertsz, 1669), 104.

10 Warren Zev Harvey, "Spinoza on Ibn Ezra's 'Secret of the Twelve,'" in Yitzhak Melamed and Michael Rosenthal, eds., *Spinoza's Theologico-Political Treatise: A Critical Guide* (Cambridge: Cambridge University Press, 2010), 41–55.

11 Ibid., 48–55. On earlier Jewish discussion of the authorship of biblical books see Louis Jacobs, "Rabbinic Views on the Order and Authority of the Biblical Books," in his *Structure and Form in the Babylonian Talmud* (Cambridge: Cambridge University Press, 1991), 31–41.

12 *Catullus et in eum Isaaci Vossii Observationes* (London: Littlebury, 1684), 241, quoted by Burman, *Emendationum libri quinque*, 152 n (a): "Verum hoc

esse norunt illi, qui tractant libros et antiqua cum antiquis committunt exemplaria. Passim et in omnibus etiam sacris id observare licet scriptoribus,
ut ubi similia aut eadem occurrant vocabula, omittantur a librariis ea quae
in medio ponuntur. Nemo doctus haec nescit aut negat, futiles tantum et
inepti aliquot homines, qui tamen Theologi videri cupiunt, haec non admit-
tunt, libenterque sacros libros ab hac labe immunes velint, ac propterea
sanctos et ἀναμαρτήτους quosdam fingunt sibi librarios, quales tamen nemo
hactenus aut vidit, aut unquam videbit. Sed ut ad institutum redeamus."
On the scholarship of Isaac Vossius, see esp. David Katz, "Isaac Vossius and
the English Biblical Critics," in *Scepticism and Irreligion in the Seventeenth
and Eighteenth Centuries*, ed. Richard Popkin and Arjo Vanderjagt (Leiden:
Brill, 1993), 142–184, and the articles collected in *Isaac Vossius (1618–1689),
Between Science and Scholarship*, ed. Eric Jorink and Dirk van Miert
(Leiden: Brill, 2012).

13 *Casauboniana*, ed. J. C. Wolf (Hamburg: Libezeit, 1710), 67, quoted by
    Burman, *Emendationum libri quinque*, 152 n (a): "Ad quaestionem de cor-
    rupt. Sacri codicis ita respondet Casaubonus: Literae quidem sacrae h.e. ὁ
    νοῦς utriusque testamenti ἄφθαρτα sunt, et nulli depravationi obnoxia: at
    lingua, quae literarum illarum veluti φόρημα est, quin aliquam labem aut
    labeculam sed sine detrimento τοῦ νοῦ acceperit longi temporis tractu, non
    est, ut puto, dubitandum. In Graeco res manifesta: multa leviter immutata,
    quaedam gravius tentata, sed sic, ut veritas inconcussa maneret. In Hebr.
    cur dubitemus? nonne tota Masora certissimum ejus rei testimonium
    praebet?" On Casaubon's approach to the study of ancient texts of different
    kinds, see Hélène Parenty, *Isaac Casaubon, helléniste: des studia humani-
    tatis à la philologie* (Geneva: Droz, 2009); and Anthony Grafton and Joanna
    Weinberg, with Alastair Hamilton, *"I have always loved the holy tongue":
    Isaac Casaubon, the Jews, and a Forgotten Chapter in Renaissance Schol-
    arship* (Cambridge, MA: Harvard University Press, 2011).

14 Grafton and Weinberg, *"I have always loved the holy tongue,"* "Appendix
    2: Casaubon and the Masoretic Text."

15 For this and other documents, see Jacob Freudenthal, *Die Lebensgeschichte
    Spinozas*, 2d ed., ed. Manfred Walther and Michael Czelinksi, 2 vols. (Stutt-
    gart-Bad Cannstatt: Frommann-Holzboog, 2006).

16 On Pignoria, see Erik Iversen, *The Myth of Egypt and Its Hieroglyphs in Eu-
    ropean Tradition* (Copenhagen: Gad, 1961; repr., Princeton: Princeton Uni-
    versity Press, 1991).

17 Lorenzo Pignoria, *Mensa Isiaca* (Amsterdam: Frisius, 1669), 1–2, addressing
    Welser: "rem igitur aggrediar optimis auspicijs tuis; ejusdem Tabulae sim-
    ulacra non ἀλληγορικῶς, sed ad veterum narrationum fidem pro viribus ex-
    positurus, odi enim ego si quis alius nimias illas, et a proposito plerumque
    alienas hujusmodi rerum interpretationes, quas in confirmationem laban-
    tium Fabularum Platonici, Praeceptoris dogmatum parum memores, invex-
    erunt: satiusque duxi ignorationem fateri, quam erudite Lectori fastidio
    esse"; see also ibid., 9–10: "Mihi neque Notas (paucis exceptis) agnoscere,
    nec sensus abditos depromere datum fuit. Potuissem quidem ex ingenio,
    multo cum labore, pauco cum fructu aliquid comminisci: sed quis postea

recepisset illum, qui notas duxerat ita sensisse? At Horapollo, dicet aliquis libello peculiari, Clemens Alexandrinus et alij praeiverunt. Utatur per me qui volet: sentiet enim, quod et vidit magnus vir ANT. AVGVSTINVS, non magis eos huic rei quam tractamus conducere, quam versus aliquot Plauti ad vetustam Poenorum linguam expediendam."

18 Lodewijk Meijer, *Philosophia S. Scripturae interpres*, 2d ed., published as Daniel Heinsius, *Operum historicorum collectio secunda* (Leiden: Herculis, 1673), Epilogus, 189. Here Meyer attributes to "Viro Clarissimo, istarumque rerum peritissimo" the following thoughts: "quod faciat ad variantes S. Scripturae lectiones explorandas, et quaenam spuriae, quaenam genuinae sint dignoscendas, quarum uberrima est in utriusque Foederis libris seges, adeo ut in Veteri *tantam esse earum copiam et confusionem, ut difficile sit veras a falsis dignoscere, ipsos Rabbinos fateri; et siquis omnes inter se committeret, et excuteret scriptos N. Testamenti codices, quot verba totidem pene esse inventurum discrepantias,* apertis verbis dicere non vereatur idem ille Vir in omni istius Doctrinae et literarum genere longe versatissimus."

19 See Anthony Grafton, "Isaac Vossius, Chronologer," and Scott Mandelbrote, "Isaac Vossius and the Septuagint," in *Isaac Vossius,* ed. Jorink and van Miert, 43–117.

20 Isaac Vossius, *Dissertatio de vera aetate mundi, qua ostenditur, natale mundi tempus annis minimum 1440 vulgarem Aeram anticipare* (The Hague: Adrian Vlacq, 1659), V: "Bene sane si Mosis haberemus autographum. Adeone vero quis inops judicii, ut existimet adfuisse Deum semper Judaeis librariis, ac direxisse illorum manus calamumque?"

21 Ibid., VI: "Certum quippe est, teste beato Hieronymo, Esdram post captivitatem Babylonicam, Chaldaicas invexisse literas, iisque libros sacros descripsisse, neglectis veteribus Hebraicis, quae eaedem erant, atque nunc sunt Samaritanae. Si itaque revivisceret Moses, ne unum quidem apicem in Judaeorum libris adsequeretur, cum literas habeant a Chaldaeis, puncta vero et apices a Massoretis." Vossius's argument here comes from Joseph Scaliger; see Anthony Grafton, *Joseph Scaliger: A Study in the History of Classical Scholarship,* 2 vols. (Oxford: Oxford University Press, 1983 and 1993). For Jerome's views, see Reinhard Pummer, *Early Christian Authors on Samaritans and Samaritanism* (Tübingen: Mohr Siebeck, 2002), 189–190.

22 Adam Sutcliffe, *Judaism and Enlightenment* (Cambridge: Cambridge University Press, 2002).

23 See Vossius, *Dissertatio,* V, where he argues that those who claim that God guided the hand of the Jewish scribes who copied and preserved the Old Testament maintained, in effect, that he showed no concern for "eorum qui descripsere novi foederis libros, in quibus tanta est lectionum varietas, ut si quis omnes inter se committeret codices, quot verba totidem pene sit inventurus discrepantias."

24 Ibid., ep. ded.: "Proculdubio recordaris GODOFREDE SLINGELANDI, vir amplissime, non semel nobis sermones fuisse de diversitate opinionum circa mundi natalem."

25 Joseph Scaliger, *Correspondence,* ed. Paul Botley and Dirk van Miert, 8 vols. (Geneva: Droz, 2012), 7:174–175, at 175.

26 Malcolm, *Aspects of Hobbes*, 383–431.

27 For the history of the *Scaligerana*, see Jérôme Delatour, "Pour une édition critique des *Scaligerana*," *Bibliothèque de l'École des Chartes* 156 (1998): 407–450; and for the larger context, see Erich Haase, *Einführung in die Literatur des Refuge: der Beitrag der französischen Protestaten zur Entwicklung analytischer Denkformen am Ende des 17. Jahrhunderts* (Berlin, 1959); and Francine Wild, *Naissance du genre des ana (1574–1712)* (Paris, 2001).

28 *Secunda Scaligerana*, in *Scaligerana, Thuana, Perroniana, Pithoeana, et Colomesiana*, ed. Pierre des Maizeaux, 2 vols. (Amsterdam, 1740), 2:398–399 (s.v. "Josephe"): "Cela d'Herodias femme d'Herode, qui est autrement dans Josephe, est une chose terrible . . . car qui l'auroit induit à mentir? . . . Josephe est un Auteur tres veritable en son histoire, & plus veritable que pas un Auteur, et tres fidelle; il dit l'avoir ex actis Herodis." For Herod's diaries, see Josephus, *Jewish Antiquities* 15.14.

29 *Secunda Scaligerana*, 2:398–399: "les Chrestiens anciens ont beaucoup adjousté au Nouveau Testament. Ils peuvent aussi avoir changé celui-là."

30 Ibid., 2:313 (s.v. "Error in litteris sacris"): "poterunt corrumpi ut nunc exemplaria: semper scriptum super chartam potuit corrumpi."

31 Ibid., 2:312: "Quod apud Evangelistam aliquem mulieres dicuntur summo mane Sole exoriente ad sepulchrum venisse, error est et corruptio librarii: nescio quid dicam, torserunt se frustra Ambrosius, Augustinus, Chrysostomus."

32 Ibid., 2:399 (s.v. "Josephe"): "Il y a plus de 50 additions ou mutations au Nouveau Testament et aux Evangiles: c'est chose estrange, je n'ose la dire; si c'estoit un Auteur profane, j'en parlerois autrement." For Scaliger's views on the New Testament, see the classic studies of Henk Jan de Jonge, "The Study of the New Testament," in *Leiden University in the Seventeenth Century: An Exchange of Learning*, ed. Th. H. Lunsingh Scheurleer et al. (Leiden: Leiden University Press and Brill, 1975), 65–109; de Jonge, *De bestudering van het Nieuwe Testament aan de Noordnederlandse universiteiten en het Remonstrants Seminarie van 1575 tot 1700* (Amsterdam: Noord-Hollandse Uitgevers Maatschappij, 1980); and Philipp Nothaft, *Dating the Passion: The Life of Jesus and the Emergence of Scientific Chronology (200–1600)* (Leiden: Brill, 2012). De Jonge stoutly maintains that there was no connection between the philological work of Scaliger and other humanists and the development of radical criticism of the Bible. As will be clear, I disagree on this point. For Scaliger's Old Testament criticism, see Grafton, *Scaliger*, vol. 2; and Nothaft, "The Calendar of Noah: The Chronology of the Flood Narrative and the History of Astronomy in Sixteenth- and Seventeenth-Century Europe," *Journal of the Warburg and Courtauld Institutes* 74 (2011): 191–211. For a valuable, if sometimes overstated, analysis of the learned tradition of criticism, as it took shape at Scaliger's university, see Mark Somos, *Secularisation and the Leiden Circle* (Leiden: Brill, 2011).

33 Malcolm, *Aspects of Hobbes*, 383–431.

34 Yosef Kaplan, "Spanish Readings of Amsterdam's Seventeenth-Century Sephardim," in *Jewish Books and Their Readers: Aspects of the Intellectual Life of Christians and Jews in Early Modern Europe*, ed. Scott Mandelbrote

and Joanna Weinberg (Leiden: Brill, 2016), 312–341. See also the remarkable work of Preus, "A Hidden Opponent in Spinoza's Tractatus" and *Spinoza and the Irrelevance of Biblical Authority*, which revealed the extent to which Spinoza responded to Lodewijk Meijer's effort to found exegesis on philosophy and the works of his critics, the Utrecht theologians Ludwig Wolzogen and Lambert van Velthuysen, who emphasized the need to ground the study of the Bible in history.

35 Spinoza, ix, 141; 125 (all future references include chapter numbers in lowercase numerals; then reference to the 2007 translation by Silverthorne and Israel; and finally to the 1669 edition of the *Tractatus Theologico-Politicus*). The quoted passage comes from Jacob ben Chajim ibn Adonijah, *Introduction to the Hebrew Bible*, ed. and tr. Christian Ginsburg (London, 1867), 64.

36 Spinoza, ix, 141; 125 (translation altered).

37 Cf. the suggestive remark of Manuel Joël, a rabbi who had taught in Zecharias Frankel's Breslau Seminary, in his *Spinoza's Theologisch-Politischer Traktat auf seine Quellen geprüft* (Breslau: Schletter'sche Buchhandlung [H. Skutsch], 1870), 15: "Er hat sich aber auch die Lektüre der Vorrede des Correktors nicht entgehen lassen, und, während er blos die superstitiose Haltung dieses Correktors hervorhebt, unterlässt er es zu sagen, wie viele freisinnige Ansichten der Rabbinen über die Verbesserungen der Sopherim, über Keri und Chethib und ähnliche Fragen in der Vorrede selbst citirt und allerdings von diesem Correktor nicht acceptirt werden."

38 On this work, see Abraham Wasserstein and David Wasserstein, *The Legend of the Septuagint from Antiquity to Today* (Cambridge: Cambridge University Press, 2006), 71.

39 Spinoza, ix, 142; 126.

40 Ibid.

41 Ginsburg, *Introduction to the Hebrew Bible*, 52–54.

42 See Paul Hirst, "Foucault and Architecture," *AA Files* 26 (Autumn 1993): 52–60.

43 Alan Kors, *Atheism in France, 1650–1729: The Orthodox Sources of Unbelief* (Princeton: Princeton University Press, 1990; new ed., 2014); Kors, *Naturalism and Unbelief in France, 1650–1729* (Cambridge: Cambridge University Press, 2016); Kors, *Epicureans and Atheists in France, 1650–1729* (Cambridge: Cambridge University Press, 2016); Dmitri Levitin, "From Sacred History to the History of Religion: Pagans, Jews and Christians in European Historiography," *Historical Journal* 55 (2012): 117–160; Levitin, "What Was the Comparative History of Religions in 17th-Century Europe (and Beyond)? Pagan Monotheism / Pagan Animism, from T'ien to Tylor," in *Regimes of Comparatism: Frameworks of Comparison in History, Religion and Anthropology*, ed. Renaud Gagné, Simon Goldhill and Geoffrey E. R. Lloyd (Leiden and Boston: Brill, 2018), 49–115; and Levitin, *Ancient Wisdom in the Age of the New Science: Histories of Philosophy in England c. 1640–1700* (Cambridge: Cambridge University Press, 2015; repr., 2017).

44 Preus, *Spinoza and the Irrelevance of Biblical Authority*, chaps. 2 and 4. For the detective work that was necessary to establish the relation between the *Tractatus* and these texts, see ibid., xi and n. 4.

45 Spinoza, vii, 100; 85.

46 Ibid., 98; 84.

47 Ibid., 99; 85: "Tota itaque Scripturae cognitio ab ipsa sola peti debet." On inconsistency in Spinoza's method of interpretation, see also Michah Gottlieb, *Faith, Reason, Politics: Essays on the History of Jewish Thought* (Boston: Academic Studies Press, 2013), 81–85.

48 Spinoza, vii, 100–101; 85–87.

49 Le Clerc, *Sentimens de quelques theologiens de Hollande* (Amsterdam: Henri Desbordes, 1685), 6–7, quoted by Maria Cristina Pitassi, *Entre croire et savoir: Le problème de la méthode critique chez Jean Le Clerc* (Leiden: Brill, 1987), 13. See Spinoza, vii, 101; 87: "Denique enarrare debet haec historia casus omnium librorum Prophetarum, quorum memoria apud nos est: videlicet vitam, mores, ac studia authoris uniuscujuscunque libri, quisnam fuerit, qua occasione, quo tempore, cui, et denique qua lingua scripserit. Deinde uniuscujusque libri fortunam: nempe quomodo prius acceptus fuerit, et in quorum manus inciderit, deinde quot ejus variae lectiones fuerint, et quorum concilio inter sacros acceptus fuerit, et denique quomodo omnes libri, quos omnes jam sacros esse fatentur, in unum corpus coaluerint. Haec omnia inquam historia Scripturae continere debet."

50 See, in general, Nadler, *A Book Forged in Hell*, 131–132; James, *Spinoza on Philosophy, Religion and Politics*, 141–144; Israel, "Introduction," in Spinoza, *Theologico-Political Treatise*, tr. Silverthorne and Israel, xiv–xv. The case for a Baconian, inductive reading is well made by Alan Donagan, *Spinoza* (Chicago: University of Chicago Press, 1989), 16–17; and Preus, *Spinoza and the Irrelevance of Biblical Authority*, 160–164, which discusses Spinoza's "bottoms-up, inductive approach—more British-looking than Continental" (160) and dismisses the objections made by Sylvain Zac, *Spinoza et l'interprétation de l'Écriture* (Paris: Presses Universitaires de France, 1965), 29–33. See also Gottlieb, *Faith, Reason, Politics*, 71–79.

51 Johann Buxtorf, *Tiberias, sive commentarius Masorethicus, quo primum explicatur, quid Masora sit: Tum Historia Masoretharum ex Hebraeorum Annalibus excutitur* (Basel: Ludovicus König, 1620).

52 Ibid., 5: "Caput II: Quid Masora"; 8: "Caput III. De causa efficiente, sive authoribus Masorae"; 202: "Caput XX. De fine Masorae"; 212: "Atque haec in genere de Masorae causis, Efficiente, Materia, Forma et Fine, dicta sufficiant."

53 Ibid., preface, sig.):(|:(3ʳ: "Historiam itaque, ut potui, pertexui: rem totam pro viribus explicavi"; sig.):(|:(3ᵛ: "At tu, Lector, in omnibus sis benevolus interpres: Historiam cape, ut ex suis authoribus refertur: si quid displicet, culpa sit authorum, qui majori diligentia in iis annotandis non sunt usi; aut potius injuriae temporum ascribe, quorum acerbitas certiori istorum notitia posteros privavit."

54 Spinoza, ix, 130; 115: "Hezras (eum pro Scriptore praedictorum librorum habebo, donec aliquis alium certiorem ostendat)."

55 Grafton and Weinberg, *"I have always loved the holy tongue,"* 321–328.

56 Buxtorf, *Tiberias*, 130–131, esp. 131: "Atque haec sunt, quae de Masorae origine et authoribus, in tanto historiae antiquae defectu tantaque Scriptorum raritate in medium proferre licuit. Qui potest, meliora et certiora

afferat, ut veritas pleniori luce e tenebris affulgeat." Buxtorf's profession of uncertainty was not empty. In the *Tiberias,* he wrote, picking his words carefully, that the antiquity of the vowel points was confirmed by the references to them "in zohar, libro iuxta Hebraeos ipso Talmude antiquiore" (174). Jewish tradition did consider the Zohar older than the Talmud. But erudite and critical Christian scholars like Scaliger and Drusius disagreed with the Jews, as they had pointed out to Buxtorf a decade and a half before (Grafton and Weinberg, *"I have always loved the holy tongue,"* 321–322). That is why he gave only the Jews' opinion in this case.

57 James, *Spinoza on Philosophy, Religion and Politics,* 170.

58 Alastair Minnis, *Medieval Theory of Authorship: Scholastic Literary Attitudes in the Later Middle Ages* (London: Scolar, 1984; rev. ed., Philadelphia: University of Pennsylvania Press, 1988).

59 Spinoza, viii, 126–127; 112: "Nam cum Historicus (quem jam scimus unum tantum fuisse) historiam producat usque ad Jojachini libertatem, et insuper addat, ipsum Regis mensae accubuisse tota ejus vita (hoc est vel Jojachini vel filii Nebucadnesoris, nam sensus est plane ambiguus) hinc sequitur eum nullum ante Hesdram fuisse."

60 Ibid., viii, 127; 113: "At Scriptura de nullo, qui tum floruit, nisi de solo Hesdra testatur (vide Hesdrae Cap. 7. vers. 10) quod ipse suum studium applicuerit ad quaerendam legem Dei, et adornandam, et quod erat Scriptor (ejusdem Cap. vers. 6) promptus in Lege Mosis" (translation altered).

61 Ibid., viii, 127; 113: "Quare nullum praeter Hesdram suspicari possum fuisse, qui hos libros scripserit" (translation altered).

62 Azariah de' Rossi, *The Light of the Eyes,* ed. and trans. Joanna Weinberg (New Haven and London: Yale University Press, 2001), 451.

63 See Anthony Grafton, *Joseph Scaliger,* 2:298–324.

64 Spinoza, x, 149; 132.

65 Ibid., 148; 131.

66 Ibid., 149; 132: "atque neminem existimare credo, quod Hezras aut Nehemias adeo longaevi fuerint, ut quatuordecim Reges Persarum supervixerint."

67 Ibid., 144; 127–128: "Psalmi collecti etiam fuerunt et in quinque libros dispartiti in secundo templo; nam Ps. 88 ex Philonis Judaei testimonio editus fuit, dum Rex Jehojachin Babiloniae in carcere detentus adhuc erat, et Ps. 89. Cum idem Rex libertatem adeptus est" (translation altered).

68 Ibid., 144–145; 128: "nec credo, quod Philo hoc unquam dixisset, nisi vel sui temporis recepta opinio fuisset, vel ab aliis fide dignis accepisset."

69 Spinoza, *Opera,* ed. Carl Gebhardt, 5 vols. (Heidelberg: Carl Winter, [1925]–1987), 5:68–69.

70 Basic works on Annius and his world include Roberto Weiss, "Traccia per una biografia di Annio da Viterbo," *Italia medioevale e umanistica* 5 (1962): 425–441: Walter Stephens, "Berosus Chaldaeus: Counterfeit and Fictive Authors of the Early Sixteenth Century" (PhD dissertation, Cornell University, 1979); Stephens, *Giants in Those Days: Folklore, Ancient History, and Nationalism* (Lincoln: University of Nebraska Press, 1989); *Annio da Viterbo: documenti e ricerche* (Roma: Consiglio nazionale delle ricerche, 1981); Ingrid Rowland, *The Culture of the High Renaissance: Ancients and Mod-*

erns in Sixteenth-Century Rome (Cambridge: Cambridge University Press, 1998); and Brian Curran, *The Egyptian Renaissance: The Afterlife of Ancient Egypt in Early Modern Italy* (Chicago: University of Chicago Press, 2007). For an up-to-date synthetic account, see Walter Stephens, "Annius of Viterbo," in *The Classical Tradition*, ed. Anthony Grafton, Glenn Most, and Salvatore Settis (Cambridge, MA: Harvard University Press, 2011), 46–47. On the impact of Annius's forgeries, see, e.g., T. D. Kendrick, *British Antiquity* (London: Methuen, 1950); Frank Borchardt, *German Antiquity in Renaissance Myth* (Baltimore: Johns Hopkins Press, 1971); Anthony Grafton, *Forgers and Critics: Creativity and Duplicity in Western Scholarship* (Princeton: Princeton University Press, 1990); Marianne Wifstrand Schiebe, *Annius von Viterbo und die schwedische Historiographie des 16. und 17. Jahrhunderts* (Uppsala: K. Humanistiska vetenkaps-samfundet i Uppsala, 1992); and R. E. Asher, *National Myths in Renaissance France: Francus, Samothes and the Druids* (Edinburgh: Edinburgh University Press, 1993). On his knowledge of Hebrew and Jewish texts, see Chapter 7.

71 The Annian material appears in chapter 32 of de Rossi's work: *The Light of the Eyes*, ed. and tr. Weinberg, 416. For the original Latin, see Annius, *Antiquitatum variarum volumina xvii* (Paris, 1512), fol. XCIX[r]. Annius gives the Psalms in question the numbers 87 and 88, which are indeed those found for them in the Vulgate and other Christian Bibles. De' Rossi, by contrast, gives both the Vulgate numbers and the different ones of the Hebrew Bible: "In the course of the next 6 years, Psalm 87 was published (it is 88 in our text) . . . Psalm 88 (89 in our text) was then published." As Spinoza simply gives the numbers 88 and 89, he seems clearly to be drawing on de' Rossi's translation of the text.

72 On Azariah's methods, see Weinberg's introduction in *The Light of the Eyes*, xv–xxxi.

73 Ibid., 423–424.

74 Ibid., 473.

75 See Weinberg's introduction, ibid., xlii–xliv.

76 Spinoza's debt to Azariah was first uncovered by Joël, *Spinoza's Theologisch-Politischer Traktat*, 62–63.

77 For the sixteenth-century rediscovery of Hellenistic Judaism, which revolutionized many scholars'—but not Spinoza's—way of thinking about Philo, see Joanna Weinberg, "The Quest for Philo in Sixteenth-Century Jewish Historiography," *Jewish History: Essays in Honour of Chimen Abramsky*, ed. Ada Rapoport-Albert and Steven Zipperstein (London: Halban, 1988), 163–187; and Charles Touati, "Judaïsme talmudique et rabbinique: La découverte par le judaïsme de la Renaissance de Flavius Josèphe et de Philon le Juif," *Annuaire École Pratique des Hautes Études*, Ve section: *Sciences Religieuses* 97 (1988–89): 214–217.

78 See also Nathan Wachtel, *The Vision of the Vanquished: The Spanish Conquest of Peru Through Indian Eyes, 1530–1570*, tr. Ben and Siân Reynolds (New York: Barnes and Noble, 1977); and Wachtel, *The Faith of Remembrance: Marrano Labyrinths*, tr. Nikki Halpern (Philadelphia: University of Philadelphia Press, 2013).

79 For the larger history of comparisons between the textual histories of Homer and the Bible, see Van Seters, *The Edited Bible*. On Scaliger's views, see Grafton, *Scaliger*, vol. 2. For Casaubon's (largely unfinished) comparative analysis of ancient textual scholarship, Greek and Hebrew, see Grafton and Weinberg, *"I have always loved the holy tongue,"* esp. 313–316.

80 The book in question is preserved in the Universitätsbiblioothek Erfurt. It was discovered by Ursula Goldenbaum, who published Leibniz's marginalia and another, longer text in his hand. The marginal note quoted in the text reads: "is unus compilator mihi non magis autor videtur, quam Aristarchus librorum Homeri, et Tucca Variusque versuum Virgilii, et Calliopius Dramatum Terentii." See Ursula Goldenbaum, "Die 'Commentatiuncula de judice' als Leibnizens' erste philosophische Auseinandersetzung mit Spinoza nebst der Mitteilung über ein neu aufgefundenes Leibnizstück," in *Labora diligenter: Potsdamer Arbeitstagung zur Leibnizforschung vom 4. Bis 6. Juli 1996*, ed. Martin Fontius, Hartmut Rudolph, and Gary Smith, Studia Leibnitiana, Sonderheft 29 (Stuttgart: Franz Steiner Verlag, 1999), 61–107, at 107.

81 Ibid., 106–107: "Haec explicationes possunt esse glossemata recentiorum, nihil antiquitati operis detractura"; "at dictio reliquorum quae tu adjectitia clamas, cum his quae genuina agnoscis eadem est, ut adeo minime tot seculis posterior esse videatur"; "imo potius: reliquit ut invenit, non composuit ut volebat, sed connexuit ut habebat"; "a quo potius quam ipso Mose."

82 "Epistola D. B. a Boineburg ad Ephorum filii, cum Argentorati studiorum causa versaretur, de Spinoza. Ex Msto," in *Unschuldige Nachrichten von alten und neuen Theologischen Sachen* (1710), 386–387: "Contra hunc Spinozam, qui canonem SS. Veteris Test. ab Esdra demum repetit, forte hoc argumentum videtur: Certum est, Ebraeos omnes ex captivitate Babylonica non rediisse Hierosolymas, sed magnam eorum partem toto oriente, Babylone inprimis, inque Perside, Media, Mesopotamia, & Aegypto, ac ceteris Imperii Babylonici ac Persici partibus, dispersam remansisse. Quare etsi Esdras libros suos, quos non pro suis utique sed veterum libris venditabat, obtrudere potuisset iis, apud quos cum summa auctoritate morabatur (quanquam ne inter eos quidem *ullum fuisse* (f. defuisse) credibile sit, qui traditionum veterum memoriam & MSStorum reliquias servasset) totam tamen gentem in tam dissitis locis terrarum, in confingendam novam legem, imo & novam scribendi legendique rationem, si & puncta Esdrae debentur, conspirasse, nec dissensiones inde aut schismata in natione tam superstitiosa & minutiarum, praesertim quo tempore misera, captiva, dispersa erat, uti nonc quoque est, observatrice orta esse, nondum mihi persuaderi potest. Interpolari quaedam, & in recensendo insensibiliter immutari quaedam ferunt homines, nova condi non perinde ferunt."

83 Ibid., 387–388: "Certe jam temporibus Esdrae, & seculis ad Christi Salvatoris nostri apparitionem usque secutis non multis, toti genti per Asiam universam (quam ubique Judaeis etiam ante alteram destructionem Templi refertam fuisse ex Actis Apostolorum constat) firmissime impressam persuasamque fuisse Genuitatem seu Germanitatem & Divinitatem horumce librorum, e Nehemia, Esdra, Zacharia, Haggaeo, Maccabaicis, Evangeliis & Actis, ex Thalmude denique constat. Coaetaneos autem ac prope coaetaneos

non sensisse tam manifestam novitatem, non contradixisse, ne suspicatos quidem de incohaerente sutura artificii tam palpabilis, tam crassi, credat quisquis volet, ego mihi nec tum persuadere sustinebo."

84 Ursula Goldenbaum published Leibniz's version of the text in "Die 'Commentatiuncula de judice'" and provided a revised version in "Leibniz's Marginalia on the Back of the Title of Spinoza's *Tractatus Theologico-Politicus*," *The Leibniz Review* 18 (2008): 269–272, at 270–271 (text); 271–272 (translation). I have adapted her translation to fit the text of Boineburg's letter.

85 See esp. Gerald J. Toomer, *John Selden: A Life in Scholarship*, 2 vols. (Oxford: Oxford University Press, 2009); and Grafton and Weinberg, *"I have always loved the holy tongue."*

86 For a specimen of Scaliger's views, see his *Elenchus utriusque orationis D. Davidis Parei* (Leiden: Elzevir, 1607); Casaubon adorned his presentation copy of this work (British Library C.79.b.16.) with largely approving notes (e.g., on the title page, where he regularly recorded his estimate of the value of the books, he annotated: "Doctrinam et facundiam viri magni hic liber eximie ostendit").

87 See, e.g., Lionel Rothkrug, *Opposition to Louis XIV: The Political and Social Origins of the French Enlightenment* (Princeton: Princeton University Press, 1965); Lionel Gossman, *Medievalism and the Ideologies of the Enlightenment: The World and Work of LaCurne de Sainte-Palaye* (Baltimore: Johns Hopkins Press, 1968); Carlo Borghero, *La certezza e la storia: Cartesianesimo, pirronismo e conoscenza storica* (Milan: Franco Angeli, 1983); J. G. A. Pocock, *Barbarism and Religion*, 6 vols. (Cambridge: Cambridge University Press, 1999–2015); Jonathan Sheehan, *The Enlightenment Bible: Translation, Scholarship, Culture* (Princeton: Princeton University Press, 2005); Dan Edelstein, *The Enlightenment: A Genealogy* (Chicago: University of Chicago Press, 2010); Martin Mulsow, *Prekäres Wissen: eine andere Ideengeschichte der Frühen Neuzeit* (Berlin: Suhrkamp, 2012); Anthony Ossa-Richardson, *The Devil's Tabernacle: The Pagan Oracles in Early Modern Thought* (Princeton: Princeton University Press, 2013); and, for a recent (and polemical) review of much of this literature, Levitin, "From Sacred History to the History of Religion."

ACKNOWLEDGMENTS

WHILE AT WORK on the chapters collected in this book, I acquired many debts. The American Academy in Rome, the Scaliger Institute at Leiden, Christ's and Trinity Colleges in Cambridge, Merton College Oxford, the Andrew W. Mellon Foundation, the Cullman Center at the New York Public Library, the Humanities Council of Princeton University and the Department of History at Princeton provided generous financial and institutional support. Many libraries in both Europe and the United States granted me access to manuscripts and rare books: the Biblioteca Apostolica Vaticana, the Biblioteca Casanatense, the Biblioteca Corsiniana, the Bibliothèque Nationale de France, the Bodleian Library, the British Library, the Cambridge University Library, the Herzog August Bibliothek in Wolfenbüttel, the Historical Society of Pennsylvania, the Kent Archive and History Centre, the Leiden University Library, the Library Company of Philadelphia, the Library of Gonville and Caius College in Cambridge, Marsh's Library in Dublin, and the Parker Library of Corpus Christi College and Wren Library of Trinity College, both in Cambridge. Equally large are my debts to the digital collections that have enabled me to explore an ocean of primary sources from central New Jersey at all hours of the day and night: DigiVatLib, e-rara.ch, Gallica, Google Books, Munich Digital and the Parker Library on the Web. For their wealth of modern as well as rare books, finally, a tip of the old fedora to the Firestone Library of Princeton University and the Warburg Institute, where my research has so often begun and reached completion.

I have revised some chapters in this book that were originally published in the following:

CHAPTER 1   *Humanists with Inky Fingers: The Culture of Correction in Renaissance Europe,* The Annual Balzan Lecture 2 (Florence: Olschki, 2011).

CHAPTER 2   "Divination: Towards the History of a Philological Term," in *The Marriage of Philology and Scepticism. Uncertainty and Conjecture in Early Modern Scholarship and Thought,* ed. Gian Mario Cao, Anthony Grafton, and Jill Kraye (London: Warburg Institute, 2019), 47–69.

CHAPTER 4   "Christianity's Jewish Origins Rediscovered: The Roles of Comparison in Early Modern Ecclesiastical Scholarship," *Erudition and the Republic of Letters* 1 (2016): 13–42.

CHAPTER 5   "Matthew Parker: The Book as Archive," *History of Humanities* 2, no. 1 (2017): 15–50.

CHAPTER 6   "The Republic of Letters in the American Colonies: Francis Daniel Pastorius Makes a Notebook," *American Historical Review* 117, no. 1 (February 2012): 1–39.

CHAPTER 7   "Annius of Viterbo as a Student of the Jews," in *Literary Forgery in Early Modern Europe, 1450–1800,* ed. Walter Stephens and Earle Havens, assisted by Janet E. Gomez (Baltimore: Johns Hopkins University Press, 2019), ch. 7.

CHAPTER 9   "Spinoza's Hermeneutics: Some Heretical Thoughts," in *Scriptural Authority in the Dutch Golden Age: God's Word Questioned,* ed. Dirk van Miert, Henk Nellen, Piet Steenbakkers, and Jetze Touber (Oxford: Oxford University Press, 2017), 177–196.

Endnotes to the individual articles record my debts to the many friends who provided essential information and indispensable criticism. Here it is my pleasant duty to thank those who have helped me to remake the articles into a book. Both the referees consulted by Harvard University Press provided precise, constructive suggestions. One of them, Ada Palmer, did much more. Her extraordinarily detailed comments mapped out a set of connected revisions that I have put into effect, and that have changed the original text in many ways. During the hot June weeks of 2019, William Theiss went over the entire manuscript, detecting and correcting errors small and large with unflagging energy, patience, and good humor. He and Ann Blair, Madeline McMahon, and Jacob Soll read the introduction, which I researched and wrote in summer 2019. I am indebted to them for many corrections and suggestions. Brooke Fitzgerald provided essential help in the preparation of the final manuscript. Lindsay Waters first suggested that I assemble this collection, and then helped me shape it. The dedication of this book records both that debt and the many others that I have run up in thirty years of happy collaboration. Through all this time, Lindsay has kept my fingers inky.

INDEX